LAND, POPULAR POLITICS AND AGRARIAN
VIOLENCE IN IRELAND

To my wife, Leanne,
who I love so much

LAND, POPULAR POLITICS & AGRARIAN VIOLENCE IN IRELAND

THE CASE OF COUNTY KERRY, 1872–86

Donnacha Seán Lucey

UNIVERSITY COLLEGE DUBLIN PRESS

PREAS CHOLÁISTE OLLSCOILE BHAILE ÁTHA CLIATH

First published 2011
by University College Dublin Press
Newman House
86 St Stephen's Green
Dublin 2
Ireland
www.ucdpress.ie

© Donnacha Seán Lucey 2011

ISBN 978-1-906359-66-9 pb

CIP data available from the British Library

The right of Donnacha Seán Lucey to be identified as the
author of this work has been asserted by him

Typeset in Scotland in Adobe Caslon and
Bodoni Oldstyle by Ryan Shiels
Printed in England on acid-free paper by
CPI Antony Rowe, Chippenham, Wilts.

Contents

—

Acknowledgements

—

I would like to take this opportunity to thank a number of people for their assistance in the completion of this work. I would in particular like to thank my supervisor Professor R.V. Comerford for his invaluable encouragement and assistance throughout the course of this study. I would also like to thank Professor Virginia Crossman for her never-ending advice, assistance and support since my time in Oxford Brookes. Professor Eunan O'Halpin has also been a source of great help and advice.

I would also like to thank a number of colleagues whom I have met in my time in NUI Maynooth, Oxford Brookes University and Trinity College Dublin and who have provided me with friendship and intellectual stimulation. These include: Dr Juliana Adelmain, Dr Fergus Campbell, Dr Brian Casey, Dr Frank Cullen, Dr Anne Dolan, Dr Terence Dooley, Dr Raymond Gillespie, Dr Brian Hanley, Professor Jackie Hill, Dr John Johnson-Kehoe, Dr Georgina Laragy, Professor Maria Luddy, Dr Conor McCabe, Dr Kevin McKenna, Dr Feichin McDermott, Dr Dympna McLoughlin, Dr Eoin McLaughlin, Dr Gerry Moran, Dr Stephen O'Connor and Dr John Walsh. In particular, I would like to thank Dr Paul Dillon whose knowledge of late nineteenth and early twentieth-century Kerry has provided me with a sounding board for much debate concerning the intricacies of the land war and popular politics. Dr Dillon also kindly read a draft of this book and provided me with many suggestions and ideas. I would also like to think UCD Press and in particular Barbara Mennell.

My sincere thanks to the directors and staff of the following libraries and archives who have helped me during the course of my work: the National Library of Ireland, John Paul II and Russell libraries at Maynooth, the library of Trinity College Dublin, the National Archives of Ireland, Dublin City Archive, the Valuation Office and University College Dublin Library. I would also like to thank the staff of the Kerry County Library Service. I would like to thank a number of individuals whose knowledge of Kerry history has greatly added to my own understandings. These include Bernie Goggin, Gerry Lyne and Gerry O'Leary.

I would like to thank my family without whom I would never have undertaken this work. My two sisters, Sinéad and Eileen, my aunt Eileen and uncle Seán have been a great source of encouragement and support for me. I especially want to thank my parents, my mother Joan and my late father

Robert, whose belief in me and my abilities has been of immeasurable importance. I would also like to thank my wife's parents, Paul and Renée, who have always been very supportive of me.

DONNACHA SEÁN LUCEY
Dublin, June 2011

List of Maps, Graphs, Tables

—

Maps

Graphs

Tables

Abbreviations

—

CI	County Inspector
CO	Colonial Office
CSO	Chief Secretary's Office
CSO ICR	Chief Secretary's Office Irish Crime Records
CSO RP	Chief Secretary's Office Registered Papers
DCA	Dublin City Archive
DI	District Inspector
ED	Electoral Division
GAA	Gaelic Athletic Association
HC	House of Commons
IAAA	Irish Amateur Athletic Association
IPP	Irish Parliamentary Party
IHS	Irish Historical Studies
ILLNLP	Irish Land League and National League Papers
IRB	Irish Republican Brotherhood
JCHAS	*Journal of the Cork Historical and Archaeological Society*
JKAHS	*Journal of the Kerry Archaeological and Historical Society*
JP	Justice of the Peace
KDRK	Kerry Diocesan Records, Killarney
KI	*Kerry Independent*
KS	*Kerry Sentinel*
KTDA	Kerry Tenants Defence Association
LGB	Local Government Board
MP	Member of Parliament
NAI	National Archives of Ireland
INL	Irish National League
NLI	National Library of Ireland
NUI	National University of Ireland
PDA	Property Defence Association
PLU	Poor Law Union
PPP Act	Protection of Person and Property Act
RM	Resident Magistrate
RIC	Royal Irish Constabulary
SRM	Special Resident Magistrate

TC	*Tralee Chronicle*
TCD	Trinity College Dublin
TNA	The National Archives, Kew
UCC	University College Cork
UCD	University College Dublin
UI	United Ireland

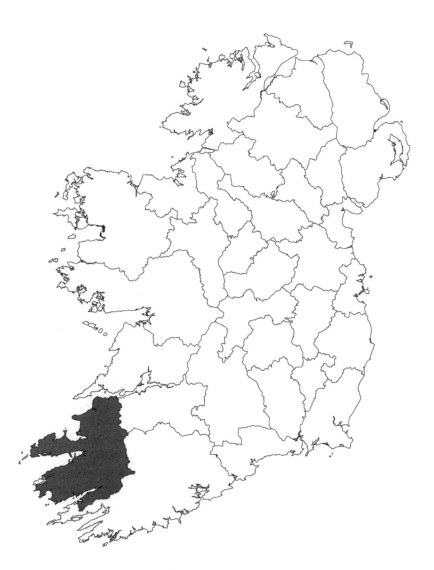

Map 1: Kerry and Ireland

Map 2: Towns and Villages in Kerry

Introduction

—

This book concentrates on agrarian and political developments in County Kerry in the period 1872–86. These years witnessed some of the most dramatic events in modern Irish history including the emergence of home rule politics, the economic depression of the late 1870s, the land war (1879–82), and the establishment and development of the Irish National League in the mid 1880s. These events were marked by much political and agrarian violence as 'outrages' reached record levels. Although this era is often seen through the lens of landlord–tenant society, it is apparent that a range of political, social and economic dynamics underpinned popular agrarian and political activity. Within the broad nationalist community tenant farmers, urban home rulers, Fenian-inspired activists and radical agrarians all participated in various movements, which challenged the power of landlordism and the state. During critical stages these groups existed in a complex juxtaposition creating powerful social and political mobilisations. However, these sections of society often had conflicting aims and objectives leading to dissension and disunion. This examination of such political and agrarian activities provides an analysis of the development of nationalist politics during one of its most critical and formative periods.

Late nineteenth and early twentieth-century Irish politics have been the centre of much historical research which has greatly enhanced modern comprehension on the period. Despite the many insights achieved by this extensive body of scholarly work, certain aspects of the era remain under researched. Much of this work inevitably concentrates on issues either from the perspective of 'high politics' or providing general countrywide and national studies. Internationally, trends in the discipline of history have witnessed a move away from the focus on 'national' histories. Topics such as gender studies, race, and ethnic groups have all emerged as lucrative fields of research, which have 'challenged the traditional historiography, which had concentrated on political and social elites'.[1] This international historiographical movement has also affected the modern writing of Ireland's history. Extensive research into the history of medicine, gender, welfare and landed estates has provided fresh and innovative approaches to Irish historiography.[2] Scholarly local and regional studies are another vital element in this process of broadening the scope of Irish history.[3] Importantly, national histories provide 'only partial answers to the problems presented and other perspectives are badly needed to correct and deepen our understanding of the evolution of Irish society. Local history is the groundwork fundamental to our understanding of the country as a whole.'[4] Furthermore, it is essential that local studies are located in the wider context of national developments and highlight the interrelationship between local and national history.

The post-Famine and land war period has received a large amount of analysis from a generation of historians during the past thirty to forty years. This body of research has illuminated the background, origins and socio-economic implications of the land war in a clinical and dispassionate manner, which in turn debunked the quasi-mythical aura that distorted past comprehension of the period. Important aspects of this research concentrated on the economic relationship between landlords and tenants in the post-Famine period. Initiated by Barbara Solow's *The Land Question and the Irish Economy*, and examined in its greatest detail to date by William Vaughan in *Landlords and Tenants in Mid-Victorian Ireland*, this body of work has highlighted that post-Famine agricultural rents did not rise at the same rate as agricultural prices.[5] This ensured that some tenant farmers received a significant slice of the rural prosperity. Some of these findings have been challenged by new research, which has revised estimates concerning changes in the values of agricultural output, rent, and labour costs to illustrate that farmers' profits fell behind these rising costs.[6] While current debate concentrates on the degree to which tenants benefited in the post-Famine prosperity, notions of landlordism as a predatory, rack-renting class have largely been discarded.

Unsurprisingly, the understanding that tenant farmers were a stronger socio-economic force than previously supposed provided the basis for extensive questioning of the background and emergence of the land war. J. S. Donnelly Jr has posited that 'the land war was a product not merely of agricultural crisis, but also of a revolution of rising expectations'.[7] By the beginning of the depression in the agricultural economy in the late 1870s, tenants' 'relative elevation in the world was hard won and had to be defended at all costs'.[8] Samuel Clark offered another perspective by concentrating on the class structure of post-Famine Ireland. He drew attention to the significance of a 'challenging collectivity', which was composed of tenant farmers, shopkeepers and publicans who were socially and economically interdependent. This group, along with support from the Catholic clergy and agricultural labourers, mobilised under the Land League and effectively opposed and challenged the power of landlordism.[9] In contrast to these viewpoints, Paul Bew has offered a Marxist perspective, which highlighted the socio-economic divisions between agricultural labourers and small farmers and large holders and graziers. These divisions led to the ultimate fragmentation of the Land League movement.[10] David Fitzpatrick diluted the importance of class in understanding the land war and concentrated on the existence of intra-tenant disputes and the role of familial inheritance practices as a source of agrarian unrest.[11]

This impressive panoply of opinions has provided a rich source of debate and greatly lengthened the basis of potential inquiry. However, as William Vaughan and latterly Fergus Campbell have noted, these new interpretations on the land question do not constitute a new orthodoxy but 'are tinged with scepticism and purged of faith ... they open rather than conceal the subject'.[12] As Donald Jordan has observed, these interpretations are based 'upon analyses of social and economic changes on provincial or national levels. This approach . . . can illuminate major economic trends but necessarily distorts economic and social organisation at the local level, where the battle between landlords and their tenants was waged.'[13] A limited number of studies have concentrated on the period from a regional perspective, including the work of Jordan on County Mayo, J. W. H. Carter's study of the land war in Queen's County, J. S. Donnelly Jr's *The Land and the People of Nineteenth-Century Cork*, and Frank Thompson's *The End of Liberal Ulster: Land Agitation and Land Reform, 1868–88*.[14] This book provides an insight into the period from another regional perspective, that of County Kerry.

While some attempt has been made to analyse the post-Famine and early land war period at a regional level, for the remainder of the 1880s the historiography has invariably concentrated largely on politics at a high level. This period is widely acknowledged as vital to the development of nationalist identity, leading to the political mobilisation of large sections of the population in the Parnellite election success of 1885. Significantly, current understandings on the period offer little insight into how, at a local level, the semi-revolutionary, divided and often violent anti-landlord agitation of the land war was transformed into a constitutionalist mass movement, which had home rule as its central objective. Pivotal to this development was the emergence of the Irish National League as the largest countrywide political organisation witnessed in nineteenth-century Irish nationalism. Intellectual perceptions on this movement are largely currently limited to Conor Cruise O'Brien's assessment of the National League, which highlights its autocratic nature and primary role as an 'electioneering machine' of the Irish parliamentary party.[15] Joseph Lee has also concentrated on the National League's function as an electioneering body, believing that the 1885 general election success made it 'among the most remarkable political movements established in a primarily rural society'.[16] The

National League undoubtedly played a vital role in the 1885 election, but little is known of the realities of the movement at a local level. Some limited research has suggested that the nationalism promulgated by the National League was neither popular nor in tune with mass beliefs during various stages of its existence.[17] Salient issues such as the social composition of its membership and the motivations for joining the movement have received little attention. In contrast to historical research on Ulster Unionism, little or no attempt has been made to explore the formation of nationalist identities during this period.[18] By incorporating the period between 1882 and 1886, this work provides an analysis of the under-researched political body, the Irish National League, and the development of nationalist politics at a regional and local level during these critical years.

Furthermore, understandings of the agrarian violence of the period and its relationship with the Land League and National League remain ambiguous. Agrarian violence in the pre-Famine period has received much more historical analysis, and has been the centre of various debates.[19] The agrarian violence of the 1880s has not been comparatively analysed even though, as R. F. Foster has noted, the Land League's power partially relied on 'a substratum of intimidation and real violence, though it was hard to quantify or apprehend'.[20] Central questions remain concerning the extent to which local violence was orchestrated by wider political influences. This becomes particularly pertinent in relation to the ostensible constitutionalism of the National League. Although Margaret O'Callaghan has explored agrarian violence in Kerry to some extent, this is undertaken in an attempt 'to consider the nature of the connection between high and low politics as manifested in administration and law' and her 'focus is on government'.[21] There remains no in-depth analysis of agrarian violence during the 1880s at a local or regional level. Other studies of localised violence in agrarian and political campaigns during the late nineteenth and early twentieth centuries have demonstrated the importance of such an approach to understanding the development of Irish politics.[22] This monograph concentrates on agrarian violence in County Kerry during the 1880s and explores the relationship between such agrarian secret society activity with the Land League and National League movements and the role played by Fenianism and the republican underground organisation, the Irish Republican Brotherhood (IRB). This exploration of IRB involvement at a local and grassroots level throughout the 1880s addresses the current lack of understanding on the relationship between agrarian radicalism and Fenianism. Despite extensive recent scholarship on the IRB in the work of Matthew Kelly and Owen McGee, there has been very little local research on Fenianism in general and during the 1880s in particular.[23] The book highlights the tensions within the wider nationalist movement in Kerry between the constitutionalism of the home rule campaign and the radicalism associated with violent agrarianism and Fenianism. It also explores the basis of agrarian and political violence in the 1880s vis-à-vis the wider historiography on the understanding of violence in later years and particularly during the war of independence period which has been the focus of much exploration through the work of amongst others Peter Hart and Joost Augusteijn.[24]

A large amount of research on various aspects of the history of County Kerry has been published in the *Journal of the Kerry Archaeological and Historical Society*.[25] Of particular significance here are three articles published by J. S. Donnelly Jr, concentrating on the Kenmare estates during the nineteenth century. Based primarily on the Kenmare Estate papers, his work provides an excellent insight into landlord–tenant relations in the region.[26] Landlord–tenant relations are also systematically examined by G. J. Lyne on the Lansdowne estate.[27] Another highly important work is William Feingold's analysis of voting patterns during the 1881 poor law election for the Tralee Board of Guardians.[28] While these studies provide salient investigations into various aspects of agrarian and political developments within County Kerry during the latter half of the nineteenth century, they do not offer a full analysis of popular political activity at a local level.

WHY LOCAL STUDIES AND WHY KERRY IN THE 1870S AND 1880S?

Local studies and local history have emerged as a significant aspect of recent Irish historiography. This growth in local history and the associated methodology of adopting such an approach to historical research has greatly added to the pursuit of understanding of Ireland's past. The validity and necessity for such a localist perspective lies with the truism that national narratives rarely reflect the reality of events that occurred at an everyday level. Equally important is the placing of events at a local level within a wider national or even international level. As Maura Cronin argues, while local history is about 'people and place' it also 'provides a lens through which one can view the evolution of both the micro world of the locality and the wider world composed of many such localities'.[29] The relevance of local history on not just the immediate area of study but also to the wider picture has been developed upon by Moran and Gillespie, who have argued that 'the reality is that history written at national level provides only partial answers to the problems presented and other perspectives are badly needed to correct and deepen our understanding of the evolution of Irish society. Local history is the groundwork fundamental to our understanding of the country as a whole.'[30] However, such an approach, which has a tendency to 'nationalise' local history, needs to be aware of the danger of using a well-tried structure for national history when exploring local problems.[31]

The implication of such a proposition is that a range of works examining various regions is necessary to further understanding of any particular period of national history while such local studies must also be fully attuned to the complexities and divergences of each region of study. Such an approach has been particularly fruitful for the war of independence period where Peter Hart's *The I.R.A and Its Enemies* acted as a catalyst for a range of works on the revolutionary period (1916–23) which explored the period through the prism of a specific locality, usually the county.[32]

However, unlike the 1916–23 period, the land war and particularly the 1880s, also a major era in the development of modern Ireland, have not received a similar amount of historical attention at a regional and/or local level although the wider national narrative is well traversed. While the local and regional variety of the nature of the political and agrarian agitations of the 1880s has been well established, limited systematic and empirical study on a region-by-region basis has emerged.[33] By providing one of the few local studies of the land war and the 1880s this work offers an important addition to our understanding on this critical juncture in the development of modern Irish history. Furthermore, the county of Kerry emerged as the most politically active and agitated region in the country by the mid-1880s. It had the highest levels of evictions, agrarian outrages and levels of politicisation of any Irish county for much of the period in question and was the focus of wider attention as events in Kerry were politicised in the home rule dramas of the 1880s. For supporters of home rule the high level of evictions and police activity in Kerry ensured that the county was upheld as an example of capricious landlordism and unjust government; for opponents to home rule the persistent and uncontrollable nature of agrarian violence in Kerry acted as a portentous warning against the advisability of granting home rule. The central place of the county in the rhetoric and propaganda on the national stage became evident during the 1888 Special Commission which focused extensively on agrarian violence in Kerry and attempted to connect such acts with the Home Rule Party.[34] In many ways Kerry was one of the most important regions during the land war and the 1880s which makes such an historical examination of the period within the county important.

This book is divided into seven chapters. The first chapter highlights the major developments in the decade leading up the land war. It describes the social and economic circumstances of society and landlord–tenant relations. It also highlights the development of home rule and agrarian politics. Chapter two explores the outbreak of economic distress and describes the initial reaction to it. Chapter three explores the emergence of 'radical' agrarianism and the Land League, and examines the course of the anti-landlord agitation. Chapter four concentrates on the role of agrarian violence during the Land League period and the violent conclusion to the agitation with the No Rent Manifesto. The attempt by Parnell to transform the agrarianism of the Land League into a constitutional movement, with home rule as its central objective through the Irish National League, is examined in chapter five. Chapter six provides a systematic analysis of the development of the National League as a mass movement in 1885. This chapter concentrates on the objectives and social composition of the movement at a local level while also exploring the effect it had on the development of nationalism. Chapter seven deals with the nature of agrarian violence throughout the period of the National League and examines the divisions amongst moderate constitutionalists and Fenian-inspired agitators that orchestrated agrarian violence.

ONE

BACKGROUND TO THE LAND WAR IN COUNTY KERRY

—

ECONOMY IN POST-FAMINE KERRY

The post-Famine years provided the economic, social and political background to the land war of the 1880s. The period was largely one of economic prosperity due to a prolonged era of high prices for agricultural produces. A Catholic middle class of middle to large tenant farmers and urban traders were the primary benefactors of this prosperity. This middle-class grouping became increasingly politicised and was central to the development of the home rule movement and the moderate agrarian politics of the decade. However, the existence of high agricultural prices ensured that these potential causes of agitation failed to mobilise large sections of the population, and through-out the decade tenants became increasingly incorporated into an agrarian capitalist economy. This led to the expansion of a consumer society and the development of extensive systems of lending and credit and of a vibrant trade in tenant-right. This chapter focuses on these transformations.

Post-Famine changes in the Irish economy have long been viewed as bringing about widespread structural changes in Irish society which in turn greatly altered the nature of local political life. Along with the rest of Ireland these changes were apparent in Kerry as the agricultural economy underwent a transformation from a crop and arable economy to one in which animals and livestock became the mainstay of Irish farmers.[1] The period from the Famine to the outbreak of the land war also witnessed the commercialisation of farming and the development of an agrarian capitalism in the Irish and particularly in the Kerry countryside. In Kerry, an agricultural economy developed which was based on livestock and connected to the export not just of cattle but also of butter. The total area under crops in the county grew from 128,795 acres in 1847 to 160,165 acres by 1880. The most significant increase in this land usage was the number of acres under meadow which increased from 47,091 to 85,699 during the same period.[2] This increase in grasslands was matched by a rise in the total number of cattle in the county which rose from 131,680 in 1847 to 211,986 in 1870.[3] This change in land usage towards a livestock economy suited to the export of cattle and the production of butter was facilitated by the depopulation brought about by the emigration and clearances of the Famine. In 1848, 22,710 agricultural holdings existed in Kerry of which 43.8 per cent were over 30 acres. By 1860 the number of holdings had decreased to 18,117, leading to an increase in farm sizes with 53.6 per cent of all farms over thirty acres.[4] This consolidation of agricultural holdings was linked largely to the near-disappearance of the cottiers and labourers who suffered the most from Famine depopulation.[5] This increase in farm size brought about a larger tenant farmer class who were to benefit from the post-Famine resurgence in the agricultural economy.

Although much debate has centred on the extent to which tenant farmers benefited from the post-Famine economy, and the level that rents rose in accordance, agricultural prices undoubtedly grew to a large extent.[6] The key to the success of the agrarian economy was the region's high capability for dairy farming and butter production in particular. The climate of the southwest of Ireland was ideal for the process of making butter during the nineteenth century. The coolness of the peak-producing summer months enabled farmers to turn out firm butter, capable of holding its original quality longer without the artificial cooling required in hotter climates.[7] As industrialisation in Britain developed rapidly in the post-Famine years, the demand for Irish agricultural produce such as butter, beef and mutton grew in accordance. In a period spanning from the 1850s to the middle of the 1870s the demand for butter in British cities created a 'seller's paradise'.[8] Kerry farmers took full advantage of this growth in the butter trade. In the immediate post-Famine period butter prices increased. In 1864 the landlord, Sir John Benn-Walsh, was informed by his land agent that in Kerry 'butter is [at] an extraordinary price and altogether the prospects of landlords and tenants [are] better than they have been for several years'.[9] Prices continued to rise and by 1871 the price farmers were getting for their butter per cwt had increased from 56s in 1851 to 93s.[10] The level of income that farmers derived from this product was high. In February 1876 tenant farmers received between £4 5s and £4 15s for every firkin of butter in Tralee.[11] On average a cow was expected to produce two firkins of butter every year.[12] Considering that there were over 100,000 milch cattle in the county, the return Kerry farmers received from butter was at the very least above £800,000 per annum. Unsurprisingly the parish priest for Listowel commented in 1881: 'all north Kerry is principally butter producing. The cow is the standard of produce.'[13] The widespread commercialisation of Kerry agriculture was further facilitated by the proximity of the Cork Butter Market which by the post-Famine period had emerged as one the world's largest centres for the exportation of butter.[14]

The large differences in terrain and quality of land within the county led to geographically varying regions of prosperity. The most prosperous tenant farmers were largely situated in an interconnected low-lying region that comprised parts of the Tralee, Listowel and Killarney poor law unions. This region was roughly centred between Listowel town in the north, Castleisland in the east, Killarney in the south and Tralee in the west and contained land of medium to high value. The area, which provided the longest continuous stretch of low land in the southwest, was 'at best a rich, well drained pasture and meadow'.[15] The high quality land in this region was signified in the fact that seventy seven per cent of the county's holdings valued above £10 were located in these unions.[16] This area contrasted with the southern and western unions of Caherciveen, Dingle and Kenmare, which were regions of extremely poor, barren and mountainous land. These differences are demonstrated in the government valuation (Griffith's) of agricultural holdings in each union. The poor law unions of Caherciveen, Dingle and Kenmare had 84, 76, and 75 per cent respectively of the holdings below the valuation of £10. The northern and central unions of Tralee, Listowel and Killarney were better off with 63, 60 and 59 per cent respectively of holdings valued at less than £10.[17]

Table 1.1 Number and valuation of agricultural holdings in each poor law union in County Kerry, Ulster, Munster, Leinster, Connaught and Ireland

Poor law union	under £10	£10<£40	£40<	Total number of holdings
	%	%	%	
Caherciveen	83.6	15.8	0.5	2,874
Dingle	76.3	22.4	1.2	2,900
Kenmare	74.3	24.3	0.8	2,117
Killarney	58.8	34.9	6.2	4,618
Listowel	60.3	34.3	5.4	3,905
Tralee	63.2	30.1	6.7	5,747
Ulster	63.3	32.2	4.4	243,977
Munster	53.6	34.8	11.5	143,159
Leinster	52.7	33.2	14.1	134,794
Connaught	81.4	15.3	3.3	138,255
Ireland	60.6	30.7	8.7	660,185

Source: *Return of agricultural holdings, compiled by the local government board in Ireland from the returns furnished by the clerks of the poor law unions in Ireland 1881,* pp. 4–7 [C 2934], HC 1881, xcii, 793.

Many farmers in the northern and central lowlands achieved a relatively prosperous standard of living. At the highest level within tenant society were the large farmers who held valuable lands. This group of large farmers were predominately located in the three northern unions. In these areas 888 farms had a valuation above £50, compared to the southern and western unions, which had a mere 70 with such valuations.[18] A tenant farmer named Florence O'Sullivan, who resided in Ardfert, one of the highest valued Poor Law Union Electoral Divisions in the county, exemplified these large farmers.[19] He held 150 acres on a holding that had a government valuation of £160. On his farm he employed a number of male and female farm servants at a cost of between £12 and £16 a year. Additional seasonal labour was hired during harvest time. O'Sullivan clearly derived a large income form as he paid £400 in rent to his landlord, Colonel Talbot-Crosbie, in 1876. Although this rent was almost two and half times the government valuation (Griffith's) he commented in 1881: 'I have no complaint to make against Mr Crosbie. I have every right to be thankful to him.'[20] Evidently, the farm produced enough income to satisfy all demands of landlord, labourer and himself.

Although O'Sullivan's circumstances were exceptionally good, medium-sized farmers also experienced a relatively high standard of living. The farming community was increasingly concerned with education. In the Catholic parishes of Ardfert and Kilmoyley, the number of children attending National School grew from under 200 in the pre-Famine period to over 1,100 in 1880.[21] With increased participation in education, illiteracy rates in the county dropped from 75 per cent in 1841 to 35 per cent in 1881.[22] Illiteracy rates were lowest in the areas with highly valued land. In some areas of good land, such as Kilnanare, the illiteracy rate was as low as 17 per cent.[23] The northern and central lowland corridor demonstrated low illiteracy rates. The northern region experienced a growth in church building, as did much of the rest of the country. In the 25 years after the Famine, £7,000 had been laid out for the construction of two Catholic churches in Ardfert, half of which was paid by the local congregation.[24] The tenant population's dietary and dress habits had also developed since the Famine. According to Father Denis O'Donoghue in 1880, the parish priest of Ardfert, tenants no longer depended on potatoes or home manufactured clothing. Instead, food and ready-made dress were largely bought by much of the tenantry.[25] The increased participation in education, the outlay of large sums to the church and the emergence of a consumer society demonstrated the region's relative prosperity. These transformations also highlighted the emergence of an affluent Catholic middle class who aspired to new models of respectability.[26] These developments were in line with social changes common to much of Ireland in the post-Famine period.

Although the richer northern unions experienced a more extensive growth in the standard of living, the poorer southern part of the county also benefited. By 1891 a farmer with a farm valued at £12 was considered at the higher end of the agrarian social scale in the Dingle region. From this holding he could expect an annual return of £68.[27] Of this income, he spent £20 on groceries and a further £10 on clothing. The average dwelling of such a farmer consisted of a thatched house with a living room, kitchen and a loft. Nearly always, livestock occupied the kitchen.[28] While the standard of living of farmers increased to some degree in the poorer unions, much of the population still relied on migratory labour. In Castlegregory, many farmers' sons and daughters went as labourers and farm servants to areas around Tralee and north Kerry. Similarly, young men and women from Killorglin left for the dairying regions of the county and also for Limerick and Cork.[29] The flux of people to the areas of higher valued land in search of employment illustrated the contrasting economies of the two regions.

While the post-Famine prosperity brought significant changes to the social life of tenant farmers in the county, it also significantly altered the nature of land tenure. As a result of this prosperity in the agricultural economy, the value of land greatly increased. As demonstrated, landlords attempted to take advantage of this with rent increases that were particularly common in the 1870s. Although the issue of rent increases was met with a degree of criticism and outcry from tenants and their representatives, landlord–tenant relations were largely calm and stable. There was little serious agrarian disorder. Between 1871 and 1878 only 59 agrarian outrages were committed in the county.[30] Landlords did carry out evictions during the 1870s and, between 1872 and 1875, 201 tenants were evicted from their holdings, of which only 48 were readmitted.[31] However, in the three years between 1876 and 1878, only 52 evictions were carried out in the county. Compared to periods of economic and social upheaval, such as the Great Famine, these were low figures. The low level of agrarian outrage and eviction, coupled with the failure of the tenant-right organisations including the Kerry Tenants Defence Association (KTDA) to mobilise widespread tenant support indicated a level of stability within the rural economy. The increased rents did little to turn tenants away from land. In fact, competition for land greatly increased during the period. Although the low level of eviction restricted a traditional form of access to extra land for tenants and graziers, the selling of tenant-right and farmers' interest in their holdings created vibrancy in the land market. This provided open access to land for prospective speculators who were willing to outlay large sums of cash to obtain agricultural holdings.

Although the 1870 Land Act granted evicted tenants the right to compensation, it did not amount to the right of 'free sale' or 'tenant-right'. The meaning of tenant-right is somewhat ambiguous, but it essentially refers to the right of the departing tenant to sell his 'right' in the holding to the highest bidder with the approval of the landlord. 'Right' amounted to what was commonly thought to include not only the value of any improvements made by the tenant but also the difference between the competitive market rent and the lower rent actually paid. The extent of tenant-right outside Ulster has been a topic dealt with by historians. Donnelly has highlighted the restrictions and interference by landlords and land agents on the sale of tenants' interest, such as preventing public sales and insisting on certain incoming tenants. These limitations made 'the privilege of restricted sale much less attractive than the full-blown right of free sale'.[32] Vaughan has argued that some form of tenant-right existed in the southern counties but was limited with small sums paid for holdings. He contends that 'before 1881 southern tenants had a potentially valuable interest that was only partially realisable through *sub rosa* payments and small donations from landlords.'[33] In contrast, David Steele has described a large trade in tenant-right right across Ireland during the post-Famine period.[34]

For various reasons it would appear that tenant-right was extensive on a number of Kerry estates. Landlords' ability to prohibit the sale of a lease by a tenant was limited. With the agricultural depression of the late 1870s tenants started to sell their interest to defraud creditors on the Kenmare estate. The estate's agent, Hussey, responded by warning tenants that they must obtain permission from him to sell. When a number of tenants sold without his consent he moved to evict the yearly tenants but admitted that 'with regard to the leaseholders, nothing can be done'.[35] The number of tenants who held their farms under lease had increased greatly in the county. Landlords such as Drummond (30,870 acres situated largely in the Castleisland region) attempted to induce all his tenants into leases and by 1873 the majority were under such agreements.[36] The north Kerry landlord, Colonel Talbot-Crosbie, believed that all tenants should have leases, and by the early 1880s the 'great majority' of his tenants were under contract with him.[37] Increasingly, landlords forced leases on their tenants and often threatened unwilling tenants with eviction.[38] In the neighbouring county of Cork, leaseholders had become 'the solid majority of Cork tenants'.[39] This large body of the tenantry, who were leaseholders, could sell their tenant interest with little interference from landlords. In one instance a tenant of Pierce Chute, named Maurice Kearney residing at Ballyroe outside Tralee, bought a lease after his landlord refused to give him the consent to do so. After signing for it, he merely persuaded a friend to go and inform the landlord of his action.[40] On the Trinity College estates in south Kerry, the tenants' interest was saleable 'subject only to a not easily maintained right of approval of the incoming tenant by the college'.[41] It was also reported that on some estates a clandestine trade in tenant's goodwill existed. When a tenant wished to surrender a farm, the interested party paid him secretly and bribed the bailiff to supposedly carry out an eviction, who would in turn use his

influence to secure the holding for the secret buyer.[42] Such underhand techniques did not prevent the open sale of tenant-right, which landlords largely
failed to restrict in the county.

The sale of tenant-right was particularly prevalent on the Lansdowne
estate in south Kerry. Although the estate was strictly controlled by the agent
William Stuart Trench, 30 farms were sold by tenants between 1867 and 1880.
The value of the interest varied from 20 years' rent to three years', with the
average amounting to ten years' purchase.[43] The sale of tenants' interest in
farms was regularly advertised in the county's newspapers. The details commonly published included the acreage, annual rent and net profit.[44] 'Fines'
were paid to buy the interest in a farm. At public auctions high 'fines' were
regularly paid to outgoing tenants. In one particular sale in 1876 a tenant
received £1,020 for a farm with a government valuation of only £21 10s. The high
price was induced by the long lease of 31 years on the farm.[45] The prices that
tenants obtained often varied. On another occasion, a tenant received £450 for
a 36-acre farm that had an annual rent of £48 5s.[46] When *The Times* of London
journalist, Finlay Dun, visited the Kenmare estates in the winter of 1880–1, he
found evidence of extensive sale of tenant-right by tenants. One tenant, with a
lease of 41 years and a rent of £82, received £1,000 for his goodwill. Another
tenant with a similar lease and a rent of £35 achieved £850 for his interest.[47]
Other evidence from the period further suggests that the sale of leases by tenants was common. In February 1876, the Knight of Kerry (5,372 acres, Valentia)
provided an example of a sale of a lease of 31 years in which two years had
elapsed. The lease of the farm, which had an annual rent of £70, was sold for
£1,400. The Knight believed that he could 'multiply these examples'.[48] The high
prices paid for the interest in farms was not restricted to the larger holdings.
The parish priest for Molahiffe believed that rents for smaller holdings were
higher because competition was more intense.[49] Correspondingly, the interest
in a holding with a government valuation of £7 and a lease of one life was
reportedly sold for £454.[50] This was undoubtedly an extremely high price for
such a holding. A more common price paid for small farms valued at £4 or £5
was £37, which was the average for such holdings on the Lansdowne estates.[51]
Although tenants with leases were in the most advantageous position to
achieve high prices for their interest, yearly tenants also profited. According
to Dun, a yearly tenancy on a farm in the Kenmare estate with a government
valuation of £23 was sold for £120.[52] The sale of tenant-right was a common
feature within agrarian society and the land market throughout the 1870s.

The high prices for which tenants sold the interest in their holdings
indicated that despite the rent increases of the post-Famine period land was
rented lower than its market value. Landlords did also benefit from sales of
holdings and leases. During one auction in 1875 for a 31-year lease, the outgoing

tenant whose agreement had expired was outbid by another tenant for the holding. A £525 'fine' was paid to the landlord for a 33-acre farm.[53] Leases were also sold by landlords with tenants still in possession. Jonathan Walpole, a large farmer and member of the KTDA, had his lease sold by his landlord, Henry Herbert, for a £400 'fine' to another tenant with two years remaining on it.[54] 'Fines' were also paid by sitting tenants to landlords. When a large farmer near Listowel named Flaherty had his 21-year lease expire, he paid the landlord a £200 'fine' for a new tenancy agreement.[55] 'Fines' were also reported as being paid when a lease was inherited on the death of a father or marriage of a son.[56] These instances demonstrate that landlords sold leases and received 'fines' from sitting tenants and thus benefited from the demand for land.

The high prices paid were laden with potential dangers. In the economically depressed 1880s, landlords were accused of 'living in fearful temptation from insane competition for land' during the previous decade.[57] Undoubtedly competition for holdings did inflate prices. Merchants and shopkeepers who benefited from the increased consumer society of the post-Famine period invested their profits in holdings for grazing purposes. When the tenant organisation, the KTDA, was originally established in 1875, it highlighted the emergence of this grazing influence in agriculture when it stated:

> [high agricultural prices] brings parties forward who know nothing of the soil or of farming – such as merchants and cattle dealers – who have money to bid recklessly. These, and some of the landlords, are the parties who are sending the labourers to America, by turning their land into grazing, selling the meadows, and letting the aftergrass to dairymen.[58]

In 1879, Thomas O'Rourke, the secretary of the KTDA, informed the leading and national tenant-right organiser, John Sweetman, that 'a class of well to do nothings . . . act as vampires on the life blood of the nation and whose sole ambition is to turn this old and fertile land into a huge bullock walk'.[59] While the emergence of graziers is largely associated with the period after the land war, it is apparent that the system had already emerged prior to 1880.[60] For example, when Talbot-Crosbie of Ardfert evicted a tenant for giving his holding to his daughter's husband without his permission, he re-let it for nine months of the year as a grazing farm (commonly known as the eleven-month system). The economic incentive for this was clear, as the rent for the holding increased from £26 to £42.[61] Also, the letting of land on the eleven-month principle became more popular amongst landowners as it freed them for the legal obligations of the 1870 Land Act and subsequent land legislation.[62] In the years preceding the outbreak of the land war, a significant amount of land was available on the land market. Tenants regularly sold their interest in their holdings for large sums and landlords began letting untenanted land on the eleven-month system. Other rentable land included landlord untenanted property, the small number of evicted holdings, and holdings which tenants voluntarily surrendered.[63] These avenues provided access to land for ambitious tenants and opportunities for the rural and urban middle class to invest in land and benefit from the high agricultural prices. The availability of rentable land demonstrated the existence of an exuberant market which was often free of landlord control. By the 1870s significant alterations had occurred in the nature of land tenure in the county. The post-Famine prosperity brought about by a rise in prices for agricultural products led to greater competition amongst the tenantry for access to land in a market which was increasingly open.

Another result of the post-Famine rise of agricultural prices was the emergence of a credit-based economy. The nature of agricultural production, which left the farmer with one or two pay days in the year, created a culture of constant lending. Money and credit were lent by various sources, including mortgage brokers, banks, merchants and traders. Mortgages from banks and brokers were a common method of raising capital for tenants. Mortgage brokers advertised mortgages at low rates of interest with easy terms of repayment.[64] The practice of mortgaging holdings was even more prevalent in banks. One tenant who bought a new lease described the scene in a bank manager's office in Killarney town:

> I suppose hundreds of persons in the county have done that [mortgaged their farm], for the time Mrs O'Connor gave me the lease the manager went into a private room, which was all shelves, with papers on them, and pulled out the lease. I thought they were all leases then.[65]

Lending from banks increased in the post-Famine period. The rise in agriculture prices and the benefits of the 1870 Land Act gave tenants more security to borrow against. These factors facilitated an increase in the number of banks operating in the county. In 1863 there were five banks in the county.[66] By 1871 this had increased to eleven while in 1881 sixteen banks had set up business. In 1881 Tralee had four different branches, Listowel three, and Killarney and Caherciveen two each. Castleisland, Killorglin and Kenmare all had a financial institution, while Ballylongford had a sub branch which opened on fair and market days.[67] Competition between banks was intense, particularly after the establishment of the Munster Bank in 1864 which threatened the National Bank's hegemony. In 1880 the controversial land agent, Samuel Hussey, stated to the Richmond Commission:

within the last few years in the county of Kerry, there were two banks [that] set up branches in all the small towns. They competed with each other, and gave out a great deal of money that had not previously been given to the country people, and thus they encouraged the smallest farmers to buy things that otherwise they might have done without . . . [leading to an increase in lending due to] the competition between the Munster and National Banks.[68]

Farmers had widespread access to loans from banks during this period. Farmers with holdings with an annual rental as low as £5 were freely given loans of £5.[69] By the latter half of the 1870s lending from banks had become a common feature of the rural economy. The increased value of agricultural holdings coupled with the capital created by the high prices for agricultural produce led to much competition for land.

Others borrowed money from private individuals who in turn often charged high interest. A hotel owner from Castleisland, named Maurice Murphy, believed that private moneylenders charged up to 30 and 40 per cent interest.[70] Also, tenant farmers in Kerry often relied on cash advances from butter merchants, and particularly those in the Cork Butter Market. The largest market of its kind in the world, it averaged over 400,000 firkins a year, the majority of which was drawn from farmers in Cork, Limerick and Kerry. By 1880 between 20 and 24 per cent of the total value of the market supplies was on credit to farmers.[71] In turn, these merchants charged high rates of interest ranging from ten per cent, if paid within six months, and 20 per cent after that. As a result of these loans 'the farmers [were] completely in the power of the butter merchant as to the price of the butter'.[72]

The most common form of credit received by tenant farmers was from local shopkeepers. Professor Baldwin, who was an agricultural inspector for the government, described the emergence of shopkeepers as usurers to the Richmond Commission:

the growth of wealth led to the establishment of a great many banks; the banks gave money on easy terms to shopkeepers, and then the shopkeepers as it were, forced a system of credit upon the small farmers.[73]

In turn, shops emerged as a central form of credit for farmers. Food, provisions, seed and clothing were all purchased from shops on credit. Shopkeepers freely gave out this credit, along with cash loans to create a dependent clientele who were in constant debt to them.[74] The system was described by a congested district board inspector in the 1890s as:

[credit] nearly if not fully paid for towards the end of each year, when a new account is started runs on to the end of the next year. Interest is seldom charged, but the price of goods is usually somewhat higher than they would be if sold to a cash customer.[75]

The post-Famine economic changes in the Irish and Kerry economies were widely apparent by the late 1870s. The steadying rise in prices of agricultural products from the 1850s to 1876 created large sums of money for Irish and Kerry farmers. Many were willing to speculate further on agriculture and the price of land greatly increased. Landlords in general failed to intervene or prevent high prices or 'fines' being offered for farmer's interest in holdings, while on other occasions they took advantage by demanding high 'fines' themselves. Much of the money obtained to pay for these holdings was raised on loan on the back of the high return available from agriculture. Landlords also put 'fines' on farmers in an attempt to achieve a higher return from their property and a larger share of money from the agriculture economy. Tenants were regularly indebted to merchants and shopkeepers and dependent on credit. Central to this economy based on loans and credit was the high prices of agricultural produce.

The level of lending and credit was exceptionally high and provided an extremely unstable base for the agricultural economy. Even during good agricultural years, large numbers were unable to meet the demands of their creditors. During years of poor agricultural output or lower prices, the payment of non-landlord debts often created extra pressure on tenant farmers. The high level of litigation in the county courts reflected the excessive amount of unpaid debts in the county. Shopkeeper, bank, butter merchant and landlord debts were all heard and dealt with by the county judge during the quarter sessions.

The number of processes of civil bills applied for in the county court was exceptionally high. As early as 1869 1,179 civil bills were applied for in the county.[76] In 1876, a year of high prices for agricultural products, 2,398 were lodged.[77] The majority of these were for small sums of money. During this year the total amount decreed for was £4,978. Of this sum, £3,656 was for bills of under £5.[78] The proceedings of these small claims courts demonstrate the myriad number of complicated financial transactions within the credit economy. At a quarter sessions case in Listowel, it was heard how a shopkeeper from Listowel town gained a decree for £30 against a farmer who owed him three years' credit. He got a bailiff to seize a number of the farmer's cows and sold them to redeem the money owed. In another case at the same sessions, a shopkeeper from Ballybunion was sued. He had previously seized a heavily indebted tenant's hay for payment of money owed. A number of decrees prior to the shopkeeper's had already been issued against the tenant. In this case, the original creditors were suing the shopkeeper for the price of the hay, claiming they had first right to the tenant's assets.[79] At another quarter sessions in Tralee, the multi-layered credit economy was further demonstrated. One case saw a farmer sue a shopkeeper for £10 for damage done to his cattle. He claimed the cattle were underfed in the county pound after they had been seized for payment of a debt to the shopkeeper. In another case, a farmer sought a decree against another farmer for a £30 loan.[80] Evidently tenant farmers were operating under large-scale debt. The weakness and vulnerability of the credit system were demonstrated in 1873 when the heavy rains of the previous year led to poor returns in tillage and potatoes. The number of civil bills swelled to 3,716. Yet the maintenance of high prices smoothed over any impending collapse in the economy.[81]

POLITICS: HOME RULE AND FENIANISM

The post-Famine changes greatly altered Kerry society. Along with the commercialisation of the agrarian economy, towns and in particular a class of shopkeepers and publicans grew in tandem with the agricultural prosperity. With an emerging and more prosperous middling class of tenant farmers and townsmen, political activity began to be transformed as such figures became active at a local level in various ways. [82]

In Kerry this class was slow to emerge within the local political landscape during the immediate post-Famine years. For the first two decades after the Famine, electoral politics in the county had been dominated by the landed gentry. Under an agreement in operation since the 1850s, two gentry families shared the two seats of the constituency of the county. The Kenmare family held one seat while the Herberts of Muckross controlled the other.[83] The Kenmares, who owned a large estate of over 130,000 acres mostly in the vicinity of Killarney, as Catholics were co-religionists with their tenants and were generally regarded as 'good' and 'popular' landlords. They were also politically aligned with the hierarchy of the Catholic Church in the county and in many ways represented the classic Whiggish politics of the Catholic landed and religious hierarchy of mid-Victorian Ireland that supported the English Liberal Party.[84] Both the Kenmares and Herberts, who were also in the Liberal interest, dominated the Kerry County constituency and by 1872 neither of the House of Commons seats had been contested since 1841.[85] Electoral politics in the post-Famine years is largely seen as a time of little activity due to the period of increased economic growth which undermined any potential for the emergence of a mass political challenge to the power of landlordism similar to the tenant-right of the 1840s or even O'Connell's

Repeal movement, while the Independent Irish Party's role in Irish politics was limited to a brief period in the 1850s.[86] Although occasional tenant-right meetings were held after the collapse of the Independent Party preceding the 1852 election, no real effort was made to resurrect the movement and increased prosperity made discussion of the land question less urgent.[87] Notwithstanding the general lack of elections at a national level in the 20 years after the Famine, the total inactivity in the Kerry constituency was exceptional and was far lower than the national average of elections contested which rested at 38 per cent of all Irish county elections between the years 1852 and 1868.[88]

The inactive nature of parliamentary politics in the county contrasted with specific counties such as King's which witnessed contests in every election between 1852 and 1874 bar one in 1868. [89] Other western seaboard counties such as Mayo also witnessed a level of political activity and the elections of 1846, 1847, 1852 and 1857 were 'spirited affairs' which marked a struggle for power between conservative landlords and a 'popular' coalition of priests, tenant farmers and townsmen.[90] The lack of electoral politics in Kerry during this period demonstrates the prevalence of localism within mid-Victorian politics. With little if any national movement in existence to galvanise a wider campaign under a nationalist banner, electoral politics were often dominated by the particular circumstances in each county.[91] Within Kerry the support of the hierarchy of the Catholic Church of the Kenmare's control of one of the parliamentary seats and the lack of any form of Conservative threat ensured that parliamentary contests in the county were uncommon. In contrast to many constituencies, Kerry did not witness the reorganisation and electoral drive of the Conservative Party during the 1850s which resulted in increased political contests with Liberals and led to 59 Tory seats by 1859, 26 of which were outside Ulster.[92] In many ways, the maintenance of the political equilibrium achieved between the two Liberal landed families was a result of the calm nature of landlord–tenant relations in the county. Such stability in agrarian society was demonstrated in the low level of eviction which was a fraction of the rate during the Famine period. During the 1850s and early 1860s the rate of eviction fluctuated and at times was lower or higher than the Munster provincial and national levels (graph 1.1). By the mid-1860s eviction levels remained lower in the county than either Munster or Ireland rates, indicating the lack of tension within agrarian society in the county.

In Kerry, the tranquil nature of landlord–tenant relations along with the alignment of the two major political forces in mid-Victorian Ireland – the hierarchy of the Catholic Church with the Liberal landed families – ensured that little if any challenge emerged to the political status quo. The 1868 general election witnessed a wider Liberal alliance in many Irish constituencies by a middle class of priests, farmers and some of the urban shopkeeper/publican class. This middle-class grouping was galvanised around the issues of the disestablishment of the Irish church and land reform which were the cornerstone of the policies of William Gladstone, the Liberal Party's leader, which resulted in the party increasing its number of Irish Westminster seats from 50 in 1859 to 66 in 1868.[93] Within many constituencies this led to a heightened political awareness of matters that were of national importance and were beyond the local and parochial. The experience still varied greatly and in regions such as King's County no contest took place, while the election in Longford continued to be marked by local issues.[94] Notwithstanding these wider developments the political status quo in the County Kerry constituency was not challenged and no electoral contest emerged as the two seats remained within the Liberal interest.

Graph.1.1 Evictions per 1,000 of population in Kerry, Munster and Ireland, 1853–80

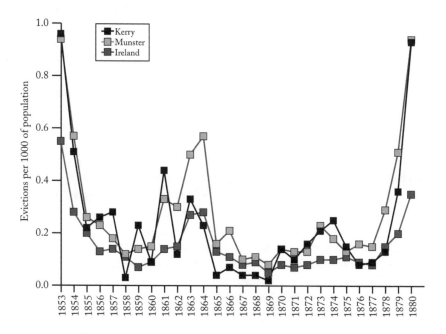

Sources: Population figures are taken from A. J. Fitzpatrick and W. E. Vaughan (eds), *Irish Historical Statistics Population, 1821–1971* (Dublin, 1978); *Return by provinces and counties (compiled from returns made to the Inspector General, RIC) of cases of evictions which have come to the knowledge of the constabulary in each of the years from 1849–1880 inclusive* HC 1881 (185), lxxvii, 725.

In 1870 Isaac Butt established the Home Government Association, which in effect created a new political movement behind the goal of home rule. Butt had previously associated himself with Fenianism through his legal defence of Fenian prisoners and his presidency of the Amnesty Association. He had also written on and championed the cause of moderate agrarian reform. In doing so, he managed to create a new 'coalition that embraced not only the artisans and labourers who had originally been attracted to Fenianism, but also priests and farmers who had remained aloof'.[95] From this point on, home rule became the catch cry of Irish Nationalists and led to an immediate wave of home rule successes at elections. In 1871–2 seven by-elections returned home rule candidates, and after the 1874 general election 54 MPs supported the home rule cause.[96] During this initial surge in home rule popularity, the 1872 by-election contests in Galway and Kerry illustrated 'the place achieved by home rule in the politics of the Catholic counties'.[97]

The 1872 by-election was precipitated by the death of the sitting earl of Kenmare. Signalling an end to the trend of uncontested elections during the mid-nineteenth century, a young Protestant landowner candidate, Rowland Ponsonby Blennerhassett, was nominated as a home rule candidate to challenge the traditional landlord and Catholic nominee, John A. Dease. Despite large-scale clerical and landlord opposition in one of the last elections to be held under open voting, the Protestant home ruler secured the seat. The electorate remained dominated by the better-off sections of the farming community, with county voters required to occupy property with a valuation of £12 or more.[98] This group utilised the election to assert their political power at an electoral level for the first time in the post-Famine period in the county. By the start of 1872 three farmers' clubs had been formed in the county. Located in Listowel, Tralee and Killarney, the clubs represented the areas with the highest valued land in the county. No farmers' clubs were reported active in the poorer southern and western tracts of the county.[99] At a countrywide level such clubs predominated in the province of Leinster, in eastern parts of Munster and in parts of Ulster.[100] This preponderance of farmers' clubs in the regions of the country with the most valuable land and largest farmers was mirrored in County Kerry. Farmers' clubs had a long history, but until the late 1860s had been little more than social organisations concerned with conviviality and improvements in agricultural techniques.[101] By the 1868 general election many of these clubs had begun to campaign on traditional tenant-right issues and within a few months meetings were held all over the country and steps were taken to establish a tenant league.[102]

The introduction of Gladstone's 1870 Land Act further galvanised tenant politics in Ireland and many meetings were held throughout the country in the run up to the legislation in 1869–70.[103] Although the terms of the act turned out to be a 'monumental irrelevance' to a large proportion of the tenantry, it did represent the abandonment of *laissez-faire* British policy to the Irish land question and a form of government intervention.[104] The act was conferred by parliament to tenants which in turn increased the expectation of other political relief among Irish political and tenant classes.[105] This was undoubtedly evident in Kerry by 1871 where the North Kerry Farmers' Club and Tenant League, which was located in Listowel town, continued to campaign on the land question through extensive criticism of the 1870 legislation.[106] Similarly, such tenant-righters began to adopt an increasingly political tone and to merge with the nascent home rule movement. This was demonstrated in the north Kerry tenant organisation, which resolved in August 1871 that 'we want to unite the electoral power of the club to return no member to parliament for the county. . . who will not pledge himself for home rule'.[107] The merging of tenant-right and home rule interests in the early 1870s in Kerry was part of a trend that developed in farmers' clubs in many areas in southern Ireland. The Tipperary Tenant League, Limerick and Clare Club and the Queen's County Independent Club all rejected the 1870 Land Act and supported the emerging home rule movement in the early 1870s.[108] In turn, constituency candidates were increasingly declared in the home rule interest and in 1871 three home rule candidates including Isaac Butt in Limerick city succeeded in gaining seats in uncontested elections.[109]

Within Kerry, the emergence of a nationalist home rule movement aligned with a renewed anti-landlord tenant-right campaign led to the first challenge to the Whiggish landed and clerical hierarchy domination of electoral politics in the county. The 1872 by-election in Kerry further galvanised organised popular politics and led to the deeper alignment of urban home rulers and tenant-righters. During the run up to the election, an extensive local organisation emerged which provided electoral support to the home rule candidate, Blennerhassett, and organised political demonstrations supporting his candidature.[110] Local associations were established in the towns of the county. Although the Catholic hierarchy vigorously supported Dease, the Catholic landlord nominee, much of the local clergy diverged from the bishop and supported the home rule candidate. In Ardfert, the local parish priest, Rev. Denis O'Donoghue, announced he was taking his politics from the bishop of Clonfert who supported home rule, and not from his own bishop.[111] In the north Kerry parish of Lixnaw, Rev. John O'Connor was removed as parish priest and replaced by a supporter of Dease, the Rev. Andrew Higgins. After O'Connor's removal a public letter from a number of his parishioners supporting him appeared in the press. It was signed by the largest farmers in the region. One of the signatories had a holding with a valuation of £146, another £160 while a third had a 124-acre farm.[112] These figures were representative of the large farmer class in the county. When the newly appointed Father Higgins attacked home rule during Sunday mass, the majority of the congregation walked out, illustrating the popularity of the movement.[113] While middling to larger farmers and the urban class of shopkeepers and publicans were central to the local leadership of the electoral campaign behind Blennerhassett, the appeal of home rule went lower down the social scale. In Killarney, Listowel and Castleisland, attempts by Dease to canvass were disrupted by hostile 'mobs'. In Castleisland, 'dead dogs, cats and empty firkins were thrown at the party', which was eventually forced out of the town.[114] Blennerhassett succeeded in attracting support from the Fenian core in Tralee by addressing a Fenian Amnesty meeting in the town, which was attended by representatives from the town's trades.[115]

Despite landlord and clerical pressure, popular opinion and sentiment were largely with the home rule candidate. Blennerhassett easily won the election with 2,237 votes to Dease's 1,398.[116] In the northern region of the county, spurned on by the North Kerry Farmers' Club and Tenant League, 83 per cent of the 1,100 votes cast in the area went to Blennerhassett. Only the Killarney region witnessed a majority vote for Dease, which was undoubtedly a result of the strength and popularity of the Kenmare landed family, most of whose lands were located in the region.[117] The election demonstrated the alignment of various classes and groups within Kerry society under the banner of home rule. While middling to larger tenant farmers along with townsmen provided much of the local leadership, it was clear that the Kerry election mobilised support lower down the social scale. The election also demonstrated the political divisions among Catholic clerics in the county between the hierarchy who supported the Liberal and landed candidate and the lower clergy who openly defied the bishop by supporting the Protestant home ruler. The divided nature of the clergy ensured that while they were an important force they were not as dominant as in other regions and constituencies. Aligned with the new home rule movement, which supported agrarian reform, large tenant farmers had the local power to compete with the traditional political patronage of both the Catholic hierarchy and the landlords. In successfully promoting Blennerhassett's candidature, the tenant farmers and the advocates of home rule demonstrated extensive organisational skills at a local level. This emergence of a newly politicised middle class represented a highly significant development in the county. Although such a middle class had grown as an important group in parliamentary electoral politics during the post-Famine years throughout the country, and had acted as the local leadership of many of the clubs and associations that came to the fore at election time, the 1872 election was the first occasion that they emerged as a vital group during an election in post-Famine Kerry. The 1872 by-election in Kerry was an expression of the power and status that the Catholic middle class had achieved as a result of the post-Famine prosperity. The emergence of this class into electoral politics in Kerry was facilitated by the wider nationalist home rule movement demonstrating that the localism of the earlier years had failed to provide the necessary platform to challenge the political status quo in the county.

The 1874 general election marked the widespread introduction of the home rule movement in Ireland and resulted in the return of a large number of MPs for the Home Rule Party. The electoral techniques and processes in Irish constituencies varied greatly, however, with little influence or control in the selection of candidates and campaigns from the central branch of the Home Rule Association.[118] In Longford, for example, the local clergy selected the candidates on the basis of the promotion of the church's interests, while in Louth the clergy were somewhat marginalised and the process was in the hands of the existing local independent club.[119] In Mayo, Fenians dominated proceedings. Notwithstanding the emergence of home rule on the political landscape, the political fervour in the county surrounding home rule had dissipated by 1874; much of the energy of the movement had faded after the famous 1872 by-election. The election for the two county seats went uncontested with only the two sitting MPs nominated: Blennerhassett representing the home rule interest and Herbert the traditional Liberal landed gentry. While the equilibrium established in the aftermath of the 1872 by-election was not threatened, the parliamentary borough of Tralee town became the focal point of the election. The long-standing politician and MP, The O'Donoghue, was the sitting member for the borough. Although he had aspired to lead a nationalist movement during the 1850s and 1860s, by the 1870s he had become a peripheral figure on the national stage and remained aloof from Buttite politics and a supporter of Gladstone and Liberalism.[120] In Kerry, he still derived much political support and was representative of the localism of mid-Victorian politics. A home rule candidate named John Daly was nominated against The O'Donoghue who remained within the Liberal ranks. With 366 electors within the borough, only a fraction of the borough's population, which reached over 10,000 in 1871, was entitled to vote.[121] Despite the socially exclusive nature of the electorate, the home rule candidate received much support within the town. In a public letter to the *Tralee Chronicle*, 134 signatories stressed their support for the home rule candidate and called for The O'Donoghue to resign. Out of a random sample of 63 of these signatories, only three had holdings valued at £4 or under. Twenty-nine of the number had holdings valued between £4 and £12 while the remaining 31 were valued above £12. Most of this group belonged to the urban middle class of merchant, grocer and vintner.

Table 1.2 Value and number of holdings in Tralee Parliamentary Borough in 1874

No of tenements valued at £4 and under	Valued over £4 and under £12	Valued at £12 and over
1009	319	308

Source: *Return for each parliamentary city, town, and borough in England and Wales, in Scotland, and in Ireland, of population and number of electors on registry 1866, 1869, and 1873*, p. 3, HC, 1874 (381), liii, 43.

Table 1.3 Valuation of holdings of 63 signatories of a pro-home rule address during the Tralee Parliamentary Borough election, 1874

Number of signatories with holdings £4 or under	Number of signatories with holdings over £4 and under £12	Number of signatories with holdings above £12
3	29	31
4.7%	46.1%	49.2%

Source: The sample was taken randomly from an address signed by 134 people in *TC*, 3 Feb. 1874. Valuation of holdings taken from; Valuation Books, Tralee E.D. (Valuation Office, Dublin).

As demonstrated in Tralee, home rule had gained the support of the rising middle class in the towns. Their political appetite had grown and the home rule movement provided them with a constitutional, legal and political agitation to acquire increased social and political power from the upper middle and gentry classes. The strong support for home rule during the election was overcome and the traditional Liberal network in the town marginally returned The O'Donoghue by a mere three votes (143 to 140) in the general election.[122] Although Liberal orientated politics remained an important strand within the elite electorate of the Tralee borough, the ability of the home rule candidate to push The O'Donoghue in such a tight contest demonstrated the increasing strength of home rule in the town. The O'Donoghue's success also demonstrated that the Whiggish and political localism of mid-Victorian Ireland remained powerful in Tralee politics. Whereas the Kerry 1872 by-election led the way by introducing home rule into regional politics, the 1874 general election witnessed no contest in the county constituency with the only contest taking place in Tralee town.

Unlike the farmers' clubs whose primary concern was agrarian reform, the primary aim of these urban nationalists was legislative independence. Yet a degree of common ground was evident between the townsmen and large farmers. The two groups shared a common religion, close kinship bonds and were interconnected through stable economic exchanges.[123] The elections of

1872 and 1874 highlighted the increasing politicisation of these two groups behind the home rule movement. In both the rural and urban political worlds it was the power of the gentry that townsmen and large farmers aspired to. Although the early home rule movement had 'considerable political potential' for uniting Protestant Conservative dissidents with Catholic Liberals in a popular platform, its most consequential effect on Irish politics was the political alliance of urban and rural middle-class socio-economic groupings.[124] The two elections in Kerry demonstrated that home rule had emerged as a major political movement at a local level. While there was a genuine appetite for a desire to take part in politics through nationalism amongst various groupings such as traditional tenant-righters, townsmen attracted to home rule, local Catholic parish priests and even trade unions and Fenians, much of the impetus for the local developments came from 'above'. Gladstone's land legislation provided a catalyst for the re-emergence of tenant-right throughout Ireland leading up to and after the 1870 Act, and the existing farmers' clubs in Kerry were influenced by this tide of activity. Similarly, the establishment of the home rule movement was highly important as it allowed Blennerhassett the political platform to challenge the status quo in the county. Politically, the local in Kerry and the centre in the form of Butt and the Home Rule Party in Dublin were interdependent. Wider developments at a national stage allowed for the necessary momentum for politicisation at a local level. In turn, the 1872 by-electoral success in Kerry and Galway demonstrated the degree to which Butt's home rule politics had developed beyond the confines of Dublin politics, thus giving it even more credence. In Kerry the 1872 election also represented a watershed in the development of the county's political culture. The lack of any contested election in the county since the 1840s highlighted that electoral politics in Kerry during the 1850s and 1860s were of a 'localism and particularism' variant, which was in line with much of the political landscape of Ireland during this period.[125] By the early 1870s, this parochial approach to politics in the county had been replaced by an increasingly nationalised form of activity derived from the social aspirations of various groups who were willing to challenge the power of 'landlordism' over politics and land. In Kerry it was evident from the 1872 by-election that the Catholic clergy remained highly divided, with the lower clerics willing to actively support the emerging nationalist politics while the higher clergy continued to support the Liberal landed families. The weakening of the previously unassailable position of the Catholic hierarchy was also demonstrated in other constituencies such as King's County.[126]

The most prominent political movement in the post-Famine period to emerge outside the nationalism of the Catholic bourgeoisie was that of Fenianism. The movement alienated support from middle to large tenant farmers as it promoted the idea that a successful political revolution would result in the redistribution of land.[127] During the 1860s Fenianism in the county appealed 'predominantly to respectable wage earners and some of the urban lower-middle class'.[128] The high proportion of this group who supported the movement can be seen in an analysis of the people suspected of supporting Fenianism in Kerry during the later half of the 1860s.[129] The vast majority of those suspected by the police were involved in the commercial and industrial sector. Within this group, almost 50 per cent were tradesmen and artisans signifying their lower middle-class status. The failure of Fenianism to take hold in the countryside is illustrated in the fact that less than ten per cent of the people suspected of involvement were in the agricultural sector. Within this group, no farm or agricultural labourers were identified with Fenianism. Those who did support Fenianism were largely farmers' sons, as opposed to farmers holding land. Of those arrested for involvement in the 1867 rising, it was reported by the local police that no farmer had been detained. The sole prisoner involved with agriculture in the county was a farmer's son who had returned from America.[130] The dominance of artisans, tradesmen and clerks was a common feature of Fenianism countrywide during the period. In Cork city it was apparent by the mid 1860s that Fenianism and artisans were intermeshing.[131]

Table 1.4 Occupations of suspected Fenians in County Kerry, 1861–9

Occupations	Percentage of suspects %	Number of suspects
Professional sector	1.8	1
Teachers	1.8	1
Clergy	0	0
Commercial and industrial sector	69.6	36
Tradesmen and artisans	47.1	24
Clerks and commercial assistants	20.7	11
Urban labourers	1.8	1
Agricultural sector	9.4	5
Farmers and farmers' sons	9.4	5
Farm Labourers	0	
Unknown/unemployed	20.7	11
Total suspects	100	53

Sources: Fenianism: index of names 1861–5, vol. 1 (NAI, CSO ICR); Fenianism: index of names 1867, vol.1 (NAI, CSO ICR).

Geographically, the support for the movement was confined to Tralee town and the southern half of the county. Killarney had the highest proportion of suspected Fenians with 30 per cent from the town. Twenty-eight per cent of suspects were located along the Iveragh and Caha peninsulas. The towns of Caherciveen and Kenmare had significant numbers while Fenian activity was also identified in the villages of Sneem and Waterville. The concentration of Fenianism in this region emerged out of a post-Famine 'commercialised economy [that] supported a small class of artisans and clerks in modest prosperity' in the south-west of Ireland from Clonakilty to Killarney.[132] Fundamental to the prominence of Fenianism in this region was the inspirational figure of Jeremiah O'Donovan Rossa, who emerged as a central Fenian leader in the 1860s and established a Phoenix Society in the south-western Cork town of Skibbereen in 1856. Influenced largely by Irish-American nationalism, the society merged with the Irish Republican Brotherhood after a visit by James Stephens to the area in May 1858. After this, the society spread rapidly throughout the vicinity.[133] Although the police were successful in arresting a number of the society's members in Kenmare and Killarney, the organisation formed the base for the emergence of Fenianism in the region.[134] In the more prosperous northern part of the county, Tralee town apart, Fenianism failed to develop with only a single suspect in the town of Castleisland and no evidence of Fenianism at all in Listowel town.[135] In Kerry, Fenianism in the 1860s developed along regional lines and the prominence of the movement in the southern half of the county was a direct result of O'Donovan Rossa's influence from West Cork. In this region, and in Tralee town, Fenianism developed as a predominately urban movement supported by the petit bourgeoisie.[136] The failure of Fenianism to attract support from the rural society was a common feature of the movement in the 1860s.

While Fenianism was geographically limited and with a narrow social base, it had received a degree of popular support by the 1870s. Much public sympathy emerged for the imprisoned Fenians after the 1867 rising. The trials that followed the rising 'left an impression in the minds of many people that it had been carried out by sincere and dedicated, if very foolish men'.[137] The nascent home rule movement of the early 1870s drew on this popular Fenian sentiment while also 'benefiting from the high level of national political awareness achieved by the Fenians and the Amnesty campaign'.[138] This fusion of Fenianism with home rule politics was very apparent in Kerry. Blennerhassett supported the Fenian amnesty movement as part of his election bid in a clear indication of the popularity of Fenians in the county during 1872. After his successful election he was the leading speaker at an amnesty meeting in which banners representing the various trades in the town depicted the movement's strong artisan and lower middle-class background.[139] In turn, known Fenians supported the electoral home rule movement in 1872 and 1874.[140] At least one former Fenian prisoner, John Kelly, publicly supported the home rule candidate in the contest for the Tralee borough in 1874.[141]

Table 1.5 Geographical breakdown of suspected Fenians in regions in County Kerry, 1861–9

Occupations	Percentage of suspects %	Number of suspects
Caherciveen	13.2	7
Castleisland	1.8	1
Kenmare	11.3	6
Killarney	30.2	16
Sneem/Waterville	3.8	2
Tralee	15.1	8
Tarbet	1.8	1
Beaufort	1.8	1
Brosna	1.8	1
Unknown	18.9	10
Total suspects	100%	53

Sources: Index of names 1861–5, Fenian Papers (NAI, Police and Crime Records). In this index names up until 1869 are included.

Although Fenianism had emerged as a popular political sentiment, the movement appeared to be largely on the wane in the early 1870s and it remained limited in rural regions. Fenianism in Kerry contrasted with that of Mayo where it had become influential amongst small farmers and Fenians had begun employing their organisational experience and political conscious-ness in support of an agrarian movement. According to the historian Donald Jordan, the rise in agrarian outrages in Mayo in the early 1870s was related to Fenian organisation in the county. The strength of Mayo Fenianism was fur-ther demonstrated in the 1874 general election when John O'Connor Power, a member of the Supreme Council of the IRB, was elected to one of Mayo's seats.[142] Fenianism had evidently succeeded in Mayo in merging with agrarian interests along with leading the nascent home rule movement. In Kerry, in contrast, outside its urban bases, Fenianism appeared to have been more of a political sentiment than a coherent movement and there is little evidence of the movement's alignment with agrarian activity in the county. Although Fenianism was of significant importance for Blennerhassett to offer support towards the amnesty movement, and a number of individuals arrested in the 1860s were evident in the home rule electoral campaigns, it did not emerge to a similar extent as it did in Mayo during this period. In many ways, Mayo appears to have been an exceptional case and the level of Fenian organisation and its integration with the agrarian motivations of small farmers evident in the county were not replicated beyond the 'west'. Kerry appeared more attuned to the wider developments on a countrywide level, where the support of a middling class of tenant farmers aligned with urban townsmen was mobilised behind the home rule movement which combined the objectives of tenant-right with a constitutional nationalism, resulting in the electoral successes of 1872 and 1874. These elections witnessed the involvement of farmers' clubs in home rule politics not just in Kerry but in Kildare, Wicklow, Limerick, Queens County, Armagh, Cork and 'almost certainly elsewhere as well'.[143]

AGRARIAN POLITICS AND THE KERRY TENANTS DEFENCE ASSOCIATION, 1875–8

After the 1874 general election the political impetus behind home rule began to wane. Although voters supported the idea of home rule, a broad movement composed of local clubs and associations similar to those of Daniel O'Connell's politics of repeal failed to emerge. The public were not impassioned on the topic and showed no great willingness to subscribe to its funds.[144] In turn, the Home Rule Association became a Dublin-based pressure group with little if any local organisation,[145] and failed to develop beyond the highly limited organisational structure it had reached in the 1874 general election.[146] The dissipation of home rule post-1874 allowed the land question to dominate the political agenda. A land conference was held in Dublin in early 1875 which was attended by representatives of tenant associations countrywide. The focus of the conference remained agrarian and centred on criticism of the 1870 Land Act and its failure to provide full fixity of tenure.[147] The conference remained apolitical and gained support from Ulster tenant-righters while avoiding any commitment to home rule.[148] With the lack of any parliamentary elections, home rule had limited relevance on a day-to-day basis and the focus of farmers' clubs easily returned to the land question.

In contrast to the politics of home rule, tenant-right criticism of the 1870 Land Act had an immediacy at a local level and could be adopted and applied to any aspect of contested landlord–tenant relations locally. Kerry was distinguished by a landlord body who were dedicated improvers and investors in their properties and, as J. S. Donnelly Jr has argued, rent increases were 'rarely excessive'.[149] Notwithstanding the good reputation of many of Kerry's landlords, the number of evictions in the county began to rise during the mid 1870s and was higher than either provincial or national levels (see graph 1.1).

Between the late 1860s and late 1870s, landlords, eager to gain an increased share of the profit derived from the rise in prices for agricultural products, began increasing rents. Historical research has indicated that these rises were generally moderate, increasing by or even below 30 per cent.[150] Within Kerry increases did occur during this period. Evidence submitted to the Bessborough Commission of the early 1880s, told that Wilson Gunn increased his rents on his Ballybunion property by 31 per cent. Similarly, a 24 per cent rent increase was enacted on the Lansdowne estate in south Kerry and Lord Ventry also raised rents during the period.[151] On the Talbot-Crosbie estate in north Kerry, there was a systematic campaign to raise rents. As can be seen from table 1.6, rents rose significantly in the 22-year period between 1855 and 1877.

Table 1.6 Annual rental of Talbot-Crosbie's estate, 1855–77

Year	Annual rent £
1855	5,051
1860	6,611
1870	7,339
1875	7,824
1877	8,362

Source: Talbot-Crosbie cash book: (NLI, MS. 5036).

In 1875 a number of ejectment notices were issued against tenants of Talbot-Crosbie. They had refused to agree to boundary changes and an increased rent on the estate, which had been initiated a number of years previously. Meetings of the tenantry were reported and the parish priest, Rev Denis O'Donoghue, declared that Crosbie 'drew the sword against my people'.[152] By 1877 Crosbie had fully evicted at least three tenants in the previous two years over the issue.[153] Although low in number, the eviction cases received much attention in the local newspapers. Tensions in the relationship between landlords and tenants in the county were further aggravated when Samuel Hussey, the earl of Kenmare's new land agent, began increasing rents on the large estate to pay for a new £100,000 mansion for the earl. Hussey attempted to increase the rents of six of the most prosperous tenants on the estate (all had farms ranging from 70 to 140 acres).[154] The tenants opposed the increase which led to a limited amount of agitation. In 1875 a threatening notice appeared in Killarney town, warning any farmer against bidding for a farm from which a tenant had been evicted.[155]

Publicly, relations between tenants and landlords were further soured when the north Kerry land agent, George Sandes brought libel proceedings against a large tenant named Thomas Bolton Silles of Lixnaw who held 133 acres. At a dinner given by an absentee landlord named Henry B. Harenc in north Kerry to his tenantry, Silles referred to Sandes as unjust, dishonest and oppressive during a speech. Sandes then sued for £3000.[156] Landlords and agents in the county set up a fund to support Sandes in what the *Cork Examiner* described as a 'sort of landlords' trade union'.[157] In turn, a fund was established to support Silles. The *Tralee Chronicle* supported the case and its editor, J. J. Long, emerged as the main organiser of the fund for Silles. Although the controversy centred on the north Kerry region, it came to be seen as a test of landlord–tenant relations in general. Meetings were held in the north Kerry areas of Causeway and Ardfert.[158] The movement spread to other regions of the county and meetings were reported in the town of Killorglin in the southern half of the county.[159] It was reported that subscriptions to the fund were made from Tralee town: 'as every merchant, shopkeeper, and artisan is clearly identified with the prosperity or depression of those citizens [tenants]'.[160] Other contributions were made by the Cork, Clare and Limerick Farmers' Clubs.[161] The case was heard in Dublin, came to national prominence and Isaac Butt defended Silles. The *Freeman's Journal*, the moderate nationalist and tenant-right newspaper, highlighted the case's significance when it stated that

> a number of landlords and land agents of Kerry have formed a sort of combination to support Mr Sandes . . . this is a matter in which all the tenant farmers of Ireland are directly interested . . . Those who have backed up Mr Sandes have made this a question of landlord against tenant.[162]

In the subsequent trial, a number of witnesses gave evidence to demonstrate Sandes's bad record as a land agent, including a tenant who claimed he had been evicted after his wife had refused Sandes's sexual approaches.[163] When the trial failed to deliver a verdict, a retrial was called, with the same result. While the episode heightened landlord–tenant tensions in the county, it also demonstrated that a network of tenant-right activists and organisations could easily be called upon throughout the county. The *Tralee Chronicle* and its editor, Long, acted as the mouthpiece for the movement to support Silles. The structure which had been so impressive in organising the election of Blennerhassett in 1872 could evidently still be called on in the mid 1870s. The case transcended the immediate and local and achieved support from farmers' clubs in the surrounding counties, the *Freeman's Journal* and Isaac Butt. Within the wider historiography of the land war period, the years 1872–8 are largely viewed as ones of landlord-tenant harmony with little indication of the subsequent upheaval.[164] However, in Kerry during this period, tenant-right politics was a constant feature of landlord–tenant relations. Organisationally, a similar network to that apparent in the home rule electoral successes was in place that promoted tenant interests as in the Silles case.

As landlord–tenant relations became increasingly strained a new tenants' organisation emerged in Kerry. Unlike the North Kerry Farmers' Club and Tenants Defence Association (largely defunct after the 1872 by-election), which had demonstrated its highly politicised tendencies during the 1872 by-election, other farmers' clubs in the county had not emerged as serious tenant-right organisations. As late as 1874, the Kerry Farmers' Club remained heavily influenced by landlords. During a meeting of the club in January 1874, H. A. Herbert MP (47,238 acres, Muckross, Killarney), a Killarney Catholic land-owner named Daniel C. Clotsman (10,316 acres, Gleflesk), and the land agent for the Lansdowne estate, Townsend Trench, were reported as attending a meeting of the club.[165] Tensions between these figures and tenant members arose when it was reported that Herbert was taking eviction proceedings against a tenant in April and May 1874, and attempts were made to expel him.[166] By June 1875 the club was disbanded and re-established as the Kerry Tenants Defence Association (KTDA).[167] The focus of the new organisation was clearly on tenant-right. It claimed that tenants had higher costs in relation to labour, standard of living and taxes which negated against rises in agricultural prices, thus countering landlords' demands for higher rents. Farmers who believed they were dealt with harshly by their landlords were called to come before the association.[168] The association also pledged to undertake the legal defence of tenants who faced eviction, to the return of MPs who advocated tenant-right and to make farmers more secure on their holdings.[169] After the home rule high point of 1874, local political activity throughout Ireland appeared to have returned to tenant-right politics in many regions. Even in Ballinasloe in County Galway, where the leader of the local tenant defence association was the known Fenian Matthew Harris, the movement in the town was based entirely on tenant-right and its rules and regulations placed the attainment of the 'three Fs' and grand jury reform as its main objectives with no mention of home rule.[170] Similarly in Ulster, where the 1874 election saw widespread successes for the Liberal Party over the conservatives, tenant-right dominated the movement from 1874 to 1880.[171]

Middle-class supporters in the towns of Kerry had been an important element of the home rule leadership in the 1872 and 1874 elections and re-emerged in the new tenant association. Its president, J. J. Long, was editor of the *Tralee Chronicle* while the association's secretary was one of the leading grocers in Tralee town, Thomas O'Rourke. These middle-class townsmen had become increasingly politicised during the home rule by-election of 1872 and the 1874 contest in Tralee parliamentary borough. As the home rule movement lost its initiative, and particularly the local organisation that

characterised its early election victories in the county, these townsmen channelled their energies into the emerging tenant-right movement. The rural
members were made up of the large farmer class. The vice-president of the
association, Jonathan Walpole, had a farm of over 200 acres.[172] In January
1876 a public subscription was established to support Long, the president.
Out of a group of 19 who had signed the subscription, 17 were designated as
'prominent farmers' in *Guy's Munster Directory* and at least three were Poor
Law Guardians, indicating that they were among the largest tenants in their
respective regions.[173] This group represented the elite within the tenant rural
society which were 'politically conscious and experienced men who were
influential among the tenantry'.[174] This agrarian tenant elite constituted 'a
new upper middle class [which] turned to politics as a means of fulfilling their
social and economic aspirations'.[175]

Geographically, the members of the KTDA were largely drawn from the
northern richer region of the county. Although the movement was largely a
local one, with little initiative from the central body, other regions in Ireland
were also active in such tenant-right politics. In 1877, associations and clubs
were meeting in Kilkenny, Limerick, Ballinasloe, Wexford and Queens County.
These regions, including north Kerry, made up the area containing the highest
and oldest concentration of livestock farms in the south of Ireland, demonstrating a connection between tenant wealth and tenant political organisation
in the 1870s.[176] The emergence of tenant-right as the leading issue in local
non-landlord politics in the county replicated the national trend. While the
Home Rule League dissipated with little engagement with the locales, the
tenant-right movement held a number of land conferences in 1875 and 1876
ensuring that it took centre stage in national politics during the mid-1870s.[177]

Although the KTDA was dominated by the elite of tenant society, it
attempted to induce all farmers to join. The association was acutely aware of
the potential political power of the lower orders of the farming class. In
August 1875 the association's secretary, O'Rourke, wished that tenant farmers
'could only be made conscious of the great power they could muster by uniting
together and becoming members of the association'.[178] The new movement
enjoyed a degree of success and within six months the association's membership
had grown to 100, despite reports of landlord harassment of those that joined.[179]
In 1876 the Dublin based Central Tenants Defence Association sent a circular
to all elected local government bodies, seeking a memorial of support for Isaac
Butt's Land Bill. On the Tralee Board of Guardians the memorial was defeated
on a vote of 33 to 14. The Killarney Board of Guardians voted similarly to
reject it 33 to 9. In both votes a large number of elected guardians voted
against the pro-tenant memorial.[180] The *ex-officio* landlord guardians demonstrated that their power remained intact at local government level and over

sections of the farming community, although a degree of politicisation, not evident before, had reached the poor law boards as a result of the actions of the KTDA. The attempts to bring the tenant-right movement into the workings of local government demonstrated the emergence of new forms of agitation. A central-local dynamic was at play and the members of the KTDA were willing to receive directions from the higher body.

The KTDA's largest success was achieved in early 1877 with a large public demonstration. With an estimated attendance of 10,000, the meeting highlighted the potential strength of a movement promoting the cause of tenant farmers. Those on the platform represented the various segments of popular opinion and politics other than the landlords and their allies. Twenty-six Catholic priests, 13 poor law guardians (all tenant farmers) and five members of Tralee's Town Commission were present. Significantly, a Fenian element was also represented with John Kelly, a former Fenian prisoner, and Michael Power (reportedly the leader of Feniansim in Tralee town) also on the platform.[181] Both MPs The O'Donoghue and Blennerhassett were also present.[182] This was an impressive panoply of public opinion apparently behind one movement. Three years previously The O'Donoghue had fought an election campaign against home rulers. The presence on the platform of Dean Mawe of the Tralee Deanery (this was one of the most important positions in the diocese) demonstrated some support from the Catholic hierarchy, a group which had bitterly opposed home rule in the 1872 election of Blennerhassett. The presence of radical Fenians further added to the political diversity of those that were prominent at the meeting; yet the meeting remained agrarian in tone with no reference to politics. The potential for disunion between the varying political stances was widely evident. In a meeting of the KTDA leading up to the demonstration Michael Power led a deputation 'of Nationalists [Fenians] from Tralee'. He stated that while they fully supported the tenant farmers if Isaac Butt, who was expected to attend, spoke about home rule, they 'would wish not to hear it'.[183] Other political divisions also existed in the movement, with certain tenant farmer elements refusing to support Fenianism. This was evident as early as December 1875 when a majority of members of the KTDA refused to pass a resolution supporting the amnesty of Fenian prisoners.[184]

Despite the apparent unity of the varying groups behind the land question during the 1877 demonstration, the KTDA soon became divided. These divisions were based on the emergence of The O'Donoghue in the tenant-right movement. Although The O'Donoghue continually failed to support home rule or the Irish Party, by 1876 he increasingly promoted tenant-right. In May 1876 he led the attempt to pass a resolution on the Killarney Board of Guardians supporting Butt's land bill.[185] In August he published a letter supporting the movement in the county's newspapers.[186] Sections of the leadership of the KTDA were apprehensive towards The O'Donoghue's involvement and resolved not to accept him as their representative in parliament.[187] However, The O'Donoghue's courtship of the association continued and in September 1876 he, along with Blennerhassett, addressed the association and spoke in favour of tenant-right, and by the time of the Tralee demonstration he had become a member.[188] The O'Donoghue's membership of the movement quickly led to dissension between home rulers and his supporters. In February 1877 a meeting of the association became divided over The O'Donoghue's failure to support home rule and the parliamentary party. Several members such as Jonathan Walpole, a gentleman tenant farmer and vice-president of the association, promoted The O'Donoghue's position on the grounds that he supported tenant-right and insisted that politics should not be introduced to the movement.[189] In turn, the president of the association, J. J. Long, resigned in protest over The O'Donoghue's 'present attitude in the Irish cause, which is, to say the least of it, questionable'.[190] The Fenian section of the association under the influence of Michael Power took a similar stance to Long. In Long's place, a tenant farmer named John O'Flaherty who supported The O'Donoghue faction was appointed president.[191]

Regardless of the political divisions within the association, it remained very active, met regularly and acted as watch dog for tenants in the county. Along with highlighting specific cases of landlord 'injustice', the association also became directly involved in landlord–tenant disputes such as one on the North Kerry Harenc estate where an increasingly complicated and embittered dispute had emerged between the tenants and the agent Samuel Hussey over the purchase of holdings.[192] In an appreciation of the association's potential role in the general election that was looming in 1880, the KTDA also began heavily criticising Herbert, the sitting MP for the county, who was a landlord. After Herbert's opposition to Butt's 1878 land bill the KTDA called for his immediate resignation.[193] In October 1878 the KTDA's secretary Thomas O'Rourke began a series of communications with the leading tenant-right organiser John Sweetman, where he outlined his own views on the direction of the movement.[194] While informing Sweetman that the association met weekly and was 'in permanent session', he complained that Irish MPs along with other 'clubs and associations are not doing their duty as they ought' and was of the opinion that the tenant-right movement was limited at a national level and dominated by 'lip patriots'.[195] In reference to the funds collected for the ongoing legal agitation on the north Kerry Harenc estate, O'Rourke stated that of all the tenant-right associations and home rule clubs in existence only a handful including the Mallow Club, the Edenderry Home Rule Club and the Wexford Independent Club gave subscriptions to the Kerry tenants.[196] O'Rourke continued to communicate with Sweetman and express his views on the disjointed nature of the tenant-right movement. Sweetman ensured that reports of meetings of the KTDA appeared in the *Freeman's Journal* along with advising O'Rourke on the development of tenant-right policy.[197] Indeed, O'Rourke and Sweetman appeared to have had similar opinions on the potential for the development of the tenant-right movement. By 1879 Sweetman had printed a prospectus proposing an Irish Farmers' Union, designed to amalgamate all the farmers clubs and tenant defence associations in the country and had begun communicating with groups countrywide.[198]

Between 1874 and 1878 politics in Kerry took a definite agrarian tone while the nationalism of Butt and home rule became diluted from the high points of 1872 and 1874. Tenant-right politics in Kerry centred on the activities of the newly established KTDA, which witnessed a large degree of politicking from the various influences in local politics including Fenians, home rulers, traditional tenant-righters and the attempt of The O'Donoghue to superimpose himself on the movement. It was evident that while the issue of tenant-right was easily ascribed to by the various diverging groups, the national question remained highly divisive. The KTDA was in many ways typical of those local, often county-based bodies which acted as a focal point of nationalist and agrarian activity outside the traditional forces of the Catholic clergy and landlords in many parts of Ireland during the 1870s.[199] Although many of these clubs and associations acted as the local electoral organisation for the home rule movement during the early 1870s, by the mid-1870s the lack of elections ensured that the activities of these bodies varied greatly within Ireland. Some organisations such as the Cavan Home Rule Club proved highly active during this period and the two Home Rule MPs for the constituency, Joseph Biggar and Charles Fay, were among the first parliamentarians to address their constituents on a yearly basis, while the Edenderry Home Rule Club was centrally concerned with securing home rule and monitoring the elected MPs for the county.[200] Although many of these clubs such as the Edenderry group were in some way divided along radical and moderate lines, they did not appear to be as fragmented as the KTDA, where there were constant tensions between the various political and agrarian factions. Despite these divisions the KTDA remained a constant presence in the county, met regularly and was centrally involved in promoting tenant-right and in particular the case of the tenants on the Harenc estate. While for much of this period the wider tenant-right movement clearly lacked any effective national leadership, by 1878 and 1879 attempts were made to unify the disparate clubs and associations under one homogeneous movement with the national tenant-right organiser, John Sweetman. In Kerry, the KTDA and its secretary, Thomas O'Rourke, advocated the development of a strong tenant-right movement and were closely connected to Sweetman during this period. In many ways the KTDA was a forerunner to the Land League in provincial tenant-right politics. Its involvement in landlord–tenant disputes, electoral politics and attempts to develop links with a nascent national leadership demonstrated that it was one of the most active groups in the country.

By the start of 1878 the KTDA remained largely divided along political lines. Although all the members supported tenant-right, home rule, and particularly the role of The O'Donoghue, continued to divide members. During 1878 the political situation in Kerry and Ireland countrywide changed significantly. The Home Rule Party was split as Parnell increasingly challenged Butt's leadership and throughout much of the year the 'New Departure' between Parnell and the IRB was in the making. The 'New Departure' was a compact reached between Parnell, Michael Davitt and the Fenian leader John Devoy in 1879. It essentially linked the Fenian ideal of the establishment of a republic with the land question and maximised Parnell's ability to engage with all shades of nationalist opinion. Significantly for the development of political activity in the county, Timothy Harrington, a school teacher originally from Castletownbere in south-west Cork, established the *Kerry Sentinel* newspaper in April 1878. Although the newspaper's initial editorial stance concentrated on promoting the Catholic education question, it quickly began supporting the emerging politics of Parnell.[201] By November 1878 the newspaper criticised the past failures of the Irish Party and promoted Parnell and his supporters as 'the party of action'.[202] Commenting on Kerry politics, the *Sentinel* condemned The O'Donoghue and stated that 'he is the worst enemy his country can have, so long as he holds aloof from the Irish Party'. The newspaper also criticised the KTDA for its support of The O'Donoghue and commented: 'when it becomes a question of glossing over his past political recreancy, or endeavouring to rehabilitate him in politics, we shall do everything in our power to oppose [the KTDA]'.[203] In a clear attempt to influence the policy of the association, Timothy Harrington, along with his brother Edward, had started attending its meetings by September 1878.[204]

With the increasing radicalisation of politics from 'above' by Parnell and the 'New Departure', and the emerging influence of Timothy Harrington and the *Kerry Sentinel* in Kerry, the KTDA invited Parnell to address it in November 1878. On 15 and 16 November Parnell spoke in Tralee just as details emerged in public of the 'New Departure' and Devoy's celebrated telegram offering IRB support to Parnell.[205] When Parnell arrived in Tralee he was met by a deputation that consisted of Timothy Harrington of the *Sentinel*, the secretary of the KTDA Thomas O'Rourke, the leading Tralee Fenian Michael Power, and a solicitor from the town named O'Connor Horgan.[206] Although the KTDA had invited Parnell, sections of its leadership remained apprehensive about the visit. The association's new president Thomas G. Pierse, a gentleman farmer from Causeway, continued to support The O'Donoghue who he believed was: 'no doubt an advocate of tenant-right and . . . a brother member of the association'.[207] Walpole, the vice-president, stated that while he welcomed Parnell to speak on the land question, he himself was 'no Home Ruler' and warned that if Parnell 'went into other matters of course they couldn't be prevented'.[208] Parnell did address the concerns of such traditional tenant-righters in the association, but also stated that whenever he 'heard some people say, oh I am not a Home Ruler, I am a tenant-righter . . . had to say to such a man [,] I don't care what you are whether you are for one or both provided you are determined to carry either.'[209] In his address, he outlined his views on the land question, which concentrated on Butt's moderate plan of settlement based on the 'three Fs' principle. He then spoke of what he thought 'was the most important issue . . . [That] we have to contend with some 400 men in the House of Commons, who are determined to do that which is wrong to this country.'[210] Parnell went on to speak of the necessity of electing MPs who would be united and work behind his efforts in the Commons. Although he did not directly mention any of the Kerry MPs, some members in attendance criticised The O'Donoghue and a resolution was passed calling on Herbert to resign.[211] Parnell concentrated on constitutional issues and advocated nothing more than the 'three Fs'. Although he was in favour of peasant proprietorship, he seemed to accept that as a practical strategy the moderate Buttite approach, which laid greatest emphasis on fair rents and fixity of tenure, was the way forward. This also placated the traditional tenant-righters who appeared somewhat apprehensive about the political direction of the movement. Although the meeting itself was marked by a tone of moderation, more militant influences were present. Shouts from the crowd included 'the land is ours', 'Butt to the devil' and 'total separation'.[212] William O'Brien, the later Parnell lieutenant who was attending the meeting as a journalist, noted in his diary that 'Parnell addressed a rough and tumble meeting, half farmers, half Fenians'.[213]

At the end of 1878 the KTDA remained divided. Gentleman farmer members who supported The O'Donoghue failed to substantially support either the Home Rule Party or the emerging politics of Parnell. Such divisions contrasted with other similar organisations such as the Ballinasloe Tenants' Defence Association, which under the direction of individuals such as Matthew Harris were more united in their support of home rule.[214] Many of the rural members of the KTDA were increasingly drawn to The O'Donoghue, who was continually making overtures towards tenant-right. This led to conflict with prominent urban-based home rulers and Fenians, resulting in the resignation of Long from the presidency of the association. However, the increasingly prominent Parnell successfully achieved the support of the town members and significantly the backing of Timothy Harrington and the *Kerry Sentinel*. In many ways the KTDA reflected the disparate nature of non-landlord politics in the mid to late 1870s which was a combination of Liberal tenant-righters, home rulers and Fenians.

CONCLUSION

The 1870s were characterised by a number of economic and political developments. The 1872 and 1874 parliamentary elections resulted in the emergence of home rule politics in the county. Supported by varying non-landlord groupings such as Fenians, urban traders and enfranchised tenant farmers, the movement offered a direct political challenge to the power of landlordism. Without the focus of elections, the early successes of the home rule movement quickly dissipated within the county, although the newly empowered socio-political group of a rural and urban middle class continued to contest the social and economic status of the landed elite. This invariably became focused on agrarian issues and particularly on a number of rent increases that were occurring on estates in the county. The mobilisation of this group led to the creation of the Kerry Tenants Defence Association in June 1875, which directly attempted to undermine the landlords' right to raise rents and evict and promoted a solution to the land question on the principles of the 'three Fs'. In 1877 the KTDA organised a mass demonstration in Tralee town when it appeared to have unified the Catholic clergy, home rulers and tenant farmers under the one movement. This success was to prove largely illusory as the movement became divided along political lines. The attempts of The O'Donoghue to gain the patronage of the association led to fragmentation between urban home rulers and more agrarian-minded tenant farmers. The increasing popularity of Parnellite politics, which at this stage attempted to concentrate politics on parliamentary issues, further divided the movement. The biggest obstacle to the principles promoted by the KTDA in the 1870s was the continued buoyancy in the agrarian economy. The high prices of agricultural produce ensured that landlord–tenant relations remained peaceful. Within the economy tenants demonstrated a large degree of independence from their landlords. This was particularly evident in relation to the vibrant market in tenant-right, where tenants frequently achieved large sums for their holdings. As the tenantry entered a consumer and capitalist economy, they became ever dependent on credit. This provided the economy with an unstable foundation, which would eventually act as an important factor in the subsequent economic depression and invigorate the agrarian principles formerly promoted by the failed KTDA to an unprecedented level of popularity.

TWO

AGRICULTURAL DEPRESSION AND THE EMERGENCE OF RADICAL AGITATION

—

AGRICULTURAL DEPRESSION, COLLAPSE OF CREDIT ECONOMY AND DESTITUTION, 1879–80

The frailties and dangers of the credit-based agrarian economy were high-lighted with the onset of the agricultural depression in 1877. The poor season of 1877 and the continued drop in agricultural prices, particularly for butter, led to the lodgement of 4,056 processes for civil bills in Kerry in 1878.[1] In January 1879 the *Kerry Sentinel* believed that not since the 'appalling misery of the Famine years . . . was the conditions of the Irish agricultural classes so precarious'.[2] Ominously, butter prices continued to drop in 1879. In February, a month traditionally associated with high prices due to stocks being at their annual lowest, prices for a firkin of butter in Tralee fell well below £3.[3] When agricultural prices had been at their height, firkins fetched close to £5.[4] Prices for store cattle also dropped and purchasing at fairs in the county was reported as poor. During the Ardfert fair in June, the selling of livestock was confined to local butchers and 'the buyers from the grazing districts who generally patronise the fair were conspicuously absent'.[5] In the same month at the Tralee fair: 'there was a good supply of cattle of all descriptions; but from the scarcity of grass in the country, buyers were very few'.[6] In an attempt to offset these trends, farmers in the county invested in rearing cattle of less than one year (yearlings) in 1879 to benefit from the high prices of the previous year leading to the number of yearling cattle in the county rising by over 5,000 from 48,626 to 53,901 in the 1878–9 period.[7] When the price of such livestock fell by as much as 50 per cent in 1879 farmers who speculated on yearlings were further distressed.[88] In late 1879, the RIC county inspector believed that the low prices of butter and 'for young cattle, have been the immediate causes of the crisis' in the economy.[9]

A number of factors within the local economy combined with wider inter-national trends to bring about the drop in the price of butter which greatly undermined Kerry tenant farmers. Continuous wet weather during 1879 further exacerbated the agricultural distress. During the six months ending in

September it was reported that on two out of every three days it rained.[10] These incessant rains seriously undermined the quality of grass, which further affected butter production and by September the number of butter firkins at markets was reportedly lower than previous years.[11] Anecdotal commentary suggested that the quality of land and grass in the county was damaged by over grazing. A correspondent for the *Freeman's Journal* described how in Kerry the 'soil has been drawn to a thread' by the dairy system. The newspaper complained that the once 'rich and luxuriant' land was worked to the 'utmost point' without any crop rotation and highlighted that 'the making of butter . . . seems to produce a speculative and unsettled disposition'.[12]

The butter industry was further hampered in the region by the failure to maintain production standards. In an attempt to break the monopoly the Cork Butter Market had over Kerry farmers, smaller markets were established in Tralee, Listowel and Killorglin. Of the 1,400 firkins that left Tralee during the height of the butter-producing season only 600 were bound for Cork.[13] These smaller markets failed to maintain the high standard of butter for which the Cork Market was famed, and the painstaking inspection of butter, on which that market's reputation was founded, was not as systematic in Kerry.[14] During late 1879, merchants who had attended the Killorglin butter market from Cork and Limerick reportedly left without buying anything when firkins were found to contain water.[15] The method of production in Kerry further undermined the price and quality of butter in the county. Owing to the slow and small-scale home production of butter, by the time firkins reached the market they were often sour. It was impossible to achieve a uniformity of colour, texture or taste when the butter was sold in large quantities.[16] All these factors undermined the quality of butter that farmers produced and therefore the price they achieved.

The prolonged agricultural depression began to have serious consequences for the agrarian economy by late 1879. During the final quarter of the year it was increasingly clear that widespread distress, particularly amongst agricultural labourers and small farmers, was inevitable in the winter and spring of 1879–80. The credit system which had sustained tenants in the first years of the depression had exceeded its limits. As one witness at the Bessborough Commission in 1880 stated:

> [during] the last three years the land produced nothing, the crops failed, and the farmer was buying all year round from first of November to the first of November again, and certainly he was not buying with his own money, he was buying from the shopkeepers on credit, and the result was that at the end of the three years the farmers owed a great deal to the shopkeepers, and they ruined the shopkeepers and they ruined everybody else.[17]

In October 1879, RIC officers in the county believed that rent collection there was going to be paid with difficulty 'owing to the sudden cessation of credit'. The police believed that the pressure on farmers was intensified by their creditors pressing for repayment. It was reported that tenants had to sell their stocks to meet civil bills and writs for eviction leaving them nearly bank-rupt.[18] By the end of September, tenant farmers in the county had £14,180 in judgments taken against them by their creditors during the previous nine months. In comparison, during the corresponding period in 1869, only £746 was decreed for against farmers in the county.[19] A Local Government Board official in the Kenmare region believed 'the small farmers . . . owe a large debt to farmers and others, who I will fear, look for their demands at the next October and January [quarter] sessions'.[20] Large numbers of civil bills were issued at the quarter sessions in October (Killarney 592, Listowel 500 and Tralee 1,150).[21] The combined effects of the drop in agricultural prices along with the paralysis in the credit system put the agrarian economy on the verge of collapse. This agri-cultural crisis was not unique to Kerry and occurred throughout the country.

The socio-economic groups initially most affected by the distress were the lower orders of agricultural labourers and small farmers.[22] By late autumn the impending distress amongst this class was increasingly apparent. These people relied heavily on turf and potatoes and the yields from these were drastically reduced by the wet weather. Local Government Board inspectors believed that the distress would hit 'certain localities [more] than in others, amongst the small farmers and labouring class, where the potatoes are mostly bad, the turf scarcely fit for fuel, and no credit to be had at the nearest town or village.' The inspectors surmised that the poorest parts of the county, 'Cahirciveen Union, parts of the sea-coast of Listowel and Tralee, parts of Dingle, Kenmare', would be affected the most.[23]

In January 1880 the full effects of the distress became evident as reports emerged that many small farmers were close to destitution and starvation. The LGB inspector in Dingle believed that 'tales of the people re-digging their tillage in order to find any potatoes left behind in the first instance come from reliable and authentic sources'.[24] One figure from Ballybunion, writing to the Mansion House Fund seeking relief, described the destitution in the region:

> The surging crowds of deserving and naked poor who throng the streets every day seeking relief show unmistakably that dire distress prevails in the locality and that unless immediate relief be given and held on for some time there can be no alternative but the blackest Famine . . . the state of our poor is hourly verging on absolute destitution and the condition of the poor children attending our schools deplorable.[25]

Despite the earlier opinion of the LGB inspectors that the distress would be confined to the poorer regions in the county, it spread into the areas that had larger farmers and higher valued land. Firies, lying in the central lowland between Tralee and Killarney, was characterised by good agricultural land and considered generally more prosperous than the costal poorer parts of the county which traditionally suffered from distress. However, by January 1880 it was reported that up to 50 families were in need of relief in the parish. The distress in the area was exacerbated after large farmers failed to provide seasonal employment to labourers.[26] Instead of providing employment, larger farmers deposited money as savings in light of the depression.[27] In the 12-month period between December 1878 and December 1879 the amount on deposit in post offices in the county grew from £18,969 to £21,299, indicating the tenant farmer's impulse to save as opposed to investing in their holdings.[28] During January 1880 the parish priest of Molahiffe, the Rev. Patrick O'Connor believed that the small farmers in the region were in dire distress. Interestingly, the priest believed that although this small landholding class were 'suffering hunger and want' they were 'ashamed to make their privation known' and believed that in many cases they were 'worse off than the labourers who make their wants known publicly'.[29] There were clearly differing attitudes towards distress and poverty between even the smallest landholders and landless labourers. Yet by the start of 1880 the prolonged depression in the agrarian economy had led to widespread distress which would have portentous consequences for social relations in the county. Similar outbreaks of distress occurred throughout the western seaboard and the effects were especially evident in evident in counties such as Galway, Mayo and Cork.[30] Beyond the poorest western seaboard counties, increased destitution was also recorded in areas such as Queen's County.[31]

REACTION TO THE DISTRESS

During 1879 the distress of the small farmers and labourers was partly relieved by the actions of the government and landlords and by the dispersion of private charity. A number of landlords readily reduced their rents. As early as July 1879 seven Kerry landlords were reported as giving abatements in rent.[32] After Wilson Gunn granted a 20 per cent abatement in rent his agent, Cussen, was deemed 'excellent and popular' by the *Kerry Sentinel*.[33] Lord Ventry also gave a 20 per cent abatement on the March and November gales.[34] The government were slow to respond to the distress with no relief initiatives until the start of 1880. In January, the government granted up to £500,000 in loans to landlords and local authorities to undertake improvement projects, and thus provide employment. The following month another grant of £250,000 was made for the same purpose.[35] Dispersed through the Board of Works, landlords in Kerry were attracted to this government money and between November 1879 and January 1880 they applied for £164,353. Similarly, the sanitary authorities which were a subsidiary to boards of guardians sought £12,280. With a limited amount available, the government sanctioned £74,393 to baronies in Kerry which was dispersed slowly and by late March only £13,565 was made available to Kerry landowners.[36] Relief works were established in some regions. Lord Listowel opened up works on various parts of his estate where it was reported that, as a result, 'his lordship is spoken of with great gratitude in the homes of these poor people'.[37] Notwithstanding the Board of Works' initial slowness to grant loans, larger sums were given after March. By October 1880, 277 loans totalling £203,733 had been granted in the county. Until the start of the harvest in September, 6,396 labourers and tenants were employed by their landlords in relief works.[38]

Despite the extent of the government relief works, a number of problems with the process were apparent. Some landlords attempted to offload much of the cost on to the tenants by including the interest charged on the loans in their rents.[39] Landlords offered the relief money directly to farmers on rates of interest that the increasingly insolvent tenants refused to take. For example, tenants of Lord Headley (12,769 acres, Aghadoe House, Killarney) declined an offer of £2,000 on loan at an interest of six and a half per cent.[40] While many landlords did offer relief work on their estates others failed to provide any. This was demonstrated in the Brosna region where only one of the twelve landlords in the area, an absentee named Richard Drummond (29,780 acres, London), provided relief work.[41] Landlords also tried to offer the relief works to tenants they were friendly with, as opposed to those that were most necessitous.[42] These factors undermined the relief effort to some extent.

The government also attempted to use the poor law system to relieve the distress. Entry to the workhouse remained highly unpopular and for many was to be avoided at all costs. Despite the large increase in distress between January and June in 1880 the numbers in the six workhouses in the county dropped from 1,932 to 1,802 (this was a normal seasonal pattern), indicating that those who were suffering from distress were not turning to the work-house.[43] The government relaxed the restrictions on granting outdoor relief to enable guardians to relieve the small landholders outside the workhouse (previously only those who occupied less than a quarter acre could gain outdoor relief).[44] Correspondingly, during the rest of the year the level of outdoor relief grew at a high rate on the county's six poor law boards from 1,650 cases in 1879 to 5,553 in 1880, while the figure rose countrywide from 86,426 recipients to 180,153.[45] The most effective and practical measure that was introduced through the poor law system was the supply of seeds to tenants for the growing of oats and potatoes. Under the Seed Supply Act, passed on 1 March 1880, guardians in distressed districts obtained interest free loans for the purchase of seed potatoes for distribution amongst tenants. This was an important measure as tenants had previously been forced to eat their seed from a lack of other food, thus using up the necessary stock for replanting.[46] To counter this, £26,584 worth of seed was distributed by boards of guardians in the county to tenants.[47] The distribution of seed was a countrywide endeavour with £598,795 expended nationally, the majority of which went to the provinces of Connaught (£220,805) and Munster (£162,097).[48]

Of greater significance to the emergence of tenant politics was the development of local relief committees. These bodies sought charity from sources such as the Marlborough Fund and the Irish National Land League, although the largest private body to dispense relief was the Mansion House Fund. By 1880 46 local relief committees in the county were in receipt of aid from this body.[49] These committees, which distributed £9,415 in relief, largely in the form of Indian meal, during the first nine months of 1880, provided the popular response from the local non-gentry community to the distress of the small farmers and labourers. These committees were composed of the leading figures in each locality. Each committee had to include clergymen of all denominations, local poor law guardians and the medical officer from the dispensary. The Dublin Mansion House Committee paid scrupulous attention to the composition of each committee, only granting aid when specific instructions were compiled with.[50] Despite this, the committees became influenced, and to a large extent controlled, by Catholic clergy, 'strong' farmers, merchants and shopkeepers.[51] Of the five hundred individuals that sat on the committees in the county, eighty-two were Catholic clergy, 21 clergy from other denominations, 29 medical officers, 72 poor law guardians while the remaining 296 were 'other lay members'.[52] Although the local gentry did at times lead the committees, such as in Ardfert where the chairman was the largest local landlord (Talbot-Crosbie), and the secretary his land agent (Trench), the bodies were largely in the hands of the Catholic middle classes.[53] In the Firies and Ballyhar committee, the local parish priest, Father O'Connor, was chairman and his curate was secretary. Large farmers such as John O'Connell Curtin, who held a 258-acre farm valued at £167, sat on the committee.[54] In Ballybunion, the Catholic parish priest was chairman, the local schoolteacher was secretary, while two merchants from Ballybunion village acted as the treasurers. The committee was composed of eight poor law guardians along with the local rector, doctor and one gentry figure.[55] Many of those who sat on these local relief committees went on to become leading local members of the Land League. The distribution of this relief placed the Catholic middle class of tenant farmers, traders and clerics at the centre of social relations within their local communities. The control of this relief allowed such figures to emerge as an effective tenant leadership as they were at the forefront of efforts to relieve the increased distress of labourers and small farmers. Middle-class nationalists distributed this relief throughout the western coastline, and this was central to meeting destitution in counties such as Mayo and Galway.[56] It was not just the poorer western seaboard regions which witnessed the emergence of these relief committees in more prosperous areas such as Queen's County similar efforts were made and a cross over was evident in the personnel of those that distributed relief and the leadership of the emerging Land League.[57]

POLITICAL REACTION TO THE DISTRESS OF 1879

Despite the extensive distress amongst the small farmers and agricultural labourers the situation failed to become politicised or radicalised in Kerry during the 1879–80 winter. In County Mayo this group, under similar economic strain, provided the impetus behind the emergence of a land agitation, which famously began with a mass meeting in Irishtown in April 1879. Small farmers and agricultural labourers, heavily influenced and organised by Fenians, set off the land war in Connaught.[58] No similar agitation developed in County Kerry in 1879, and not until the latter half of 1880 was the Land League established in the county.

The political reaction to the impending distress from the tenant population began with a meeting in Sneem in February 1879. It was called in response to the serving of an ejectment notice on a farmer on the estate of F. C. Bland (25,576 acres, Derryquinn Castle, Sneem).[59] The crowd was informed by the Rev. John O'Halloran, the local parish priest, that landlords had to be prevented from raising rents and carrying out evictions. Corresponding to contemporary moderate thought on the land question, support was offered to Butt's land bill.[60] More radical agrarian action was also promoted when O'Halloran proposed to ostracise socially those who attempted to gain posses-sion of another tenant's holding. The priest declared that 'a man who comes in and offers an excessive rent, thereby forcing its occupiers to surrender it, such a man is an enemy to the community, and he should be treated as an enemy'.[61] Opposition to evictions, rent increases and the promotion of moderate land reform were common demands of tenant organisations through-out the 1870s, including the KTDA. Such demands did not equal the emerging radicalism of the anti-landlord agitation in Connaught. As 1879 wore on, the popular response to the continual agrarian distress remained moderate. In June 1879 the Catholic clergy in the county took the lead. After a conference of the leading Catholic clergy in Tralee, the priests attributed the distress to 'excessive rents'. They claimed that rents had gradually increased over the previous twenty years which in light of the drop in agricultural prices were 'excessive'. The trebling of wages for farm labourers and servants further exacerbated the financial situation of tenant farmers. In turn, the clerical address demanded the reduction of rents.[62] Within a week, similar statements were issued by leading Catholic clergy in Dingle and Caherciveen.[63]

The middle and large farmer orientation of the clergy's addresses was easily visible. When giving the reasons for landlords to reduce rent, they cited the loss in agricultural revenue and the high expense of labourers and servants (small farmers did not hire labour and often acted as labourers themselves). The Caherciveen clergy provided a balance sheet of a farmer to demonstrate the loss they operated under. Indicating the large farmer bias of the higher clergy, the example was for a farmer who had an annual rent of £104 in a union where eight-three per cent of farms were valued at under £10.[64] Although rents were generally somewhat higher than the government (poor law) valuation, a tenant that paid £104 in rent was invariably a large farmer who was not reflective of small farmers who predominated in the Caherciveen region. The emphasis on the economic circumstances of larger farmers by the higher Catholic clergy contrasted with the agitation concurrently emerging in the western Connaught counties which, under the banner of the Land League, promoted a radical agrarianism that supported the call for land for smaller farmers and agricultural labourers. Such radicalism was not evident in 1879 in County Kerry's agrarian politics.

Despite the growing depression and the developing agrarian agitation in parts of the west of Ireland, no land meeting occurred in Kerry until September 1879. Held in Listowel, the meeting was headed by Rowland Ponsonby Blennerhassett MP and illustrated the continued influence of traditional tenant-right activists in the county. Blennerhassett had failed to side with Parnell and remained within the moderate wing of the Irish Party, which were characterised by a distaste of the politics and radicalism of the Land League.[65] A large number of Catholic priests and poor law guardians were also present on the platform and resolutions were passed calling on landlords to reduce rents.[66] Timothy Harrington, the emerging Parnellite and editor of the *Kerry Sentinel*, attended the meeting. In an editorial in the *Sentinel* leading up to the meeting, Harrington complained that they were unable to amend the proposed resolutions, which avoided radical demands and concentrated on traditional agrarian objectives although he did call for support for the demonstration and declared that 'tenant-right meetings are the new rule throughout Ireland'.[67] Notwithstanding Harrington's grasp of the agitation emerging countywide, the political response in the county remained moderate.

In November a meeting called to meet the distress in Caherciveen remained within the traditional tenant-right demands. A number of Catholic priests, accompanied by Blennerhassett, and some shopkeepers and merchants from the town attended the meeting, as did Daniel O'Connell, a local landowner (17,394 acres, Derrynane), and Captain Needham, the land agent to the Trinity College estates in the region.[68] Needham promised to write to the college asking for them to go lightly on the tenants, and resolutions were passed calling on the government to open public works to meet the distress.[69] The law agent of the college estates later reprimanded Needham and warned him that his comments 'will embarrass you in getting in rents from those who can pay'.[70] The presence of a local landlord and agent at a meeting to address the distress of the period contrasted greatly to the increasingly radical and violent anti-landlord and 'no rent' agitation in the 'west'.

As 1879 came to an end, tensions in the countryside continued to grow. Despite some efforts by landlords to respond favourably to tenant demands by opening relief works and granting rent abatements, many increasingly turned to the threat of eviction. In September the increasingly bellicose land agent Samuel Hussey warned tenants on Lord Headley's estate with legal proceedings if they failed to pay their rent.[71] On Lord Mounteagle's lands the tenants refused to pay rent without a reduction, resulting in legal action being taken against them.[72] By December T. A. Stoughton had issued 60 ejectment notices against tenants for non-payment of rent on his estate.[73] In all, 260 ejectment notices were sought by landlords in the county for non-payment of rent in 1879.[74] In all, 260 ejectment notices were sought by landlords in the county for non-payment of rent in 1879,[74] and the number of evictions had increased to 70 for 1879 compared to 26 in 1878, and 17 in 1877.[75] In late October 1879, tenants of Lord Kenmare attempted to hold a meeting to discuss rent payment only for it to fall through when no leaders attended to address it.[76] The *Sentinel* promulgated the necessity for agitation. In December it observed that 'in Galway, Mayo, Clare, Tipperary, Sligo and other counties vigorous agitation, monster land meetings, and outspoken language' had brought about 'numerous reductions of rent', but complained that in 'Kerry, where no agitation exists . . . there are no reductions'.[77]

By the start of 1880, Kerry lacked a tenant leadership and organisation to orchestrate any form of anti-rent agitation. The demonstrations held were largely of a moderate nature and failed to replicate the tenant mobilisation and adoption of agrarian agitation evident in other parts of Ireland. The divisions within the KTDA made the body redundant. It had not met since July 1879, when supporters of the land agent Samuel Hussey succeeded in passing resolutions favourable to him.[78] Within this leadership vacuum The O'Donoghue attempted to place himself at the head of any emerging tenant movement. In November 1879 he published an open letter in various regional and local newspapers promoting a tenant meeting in Killarney. He called on the 'farmers of the Killarney district to assemble . . . in order to express their determination to hold their farms for ever, subject to the payment of a fair rent'. He also claimed that Parnell and John O'Connor Power MP would attend.[79] The O'Donoghue's political history, which included defeating a home rule candidate in the 1874 general election, and his failure to support either side of the Irish Party, made his attempt to lead a tenant movement in Kerry controversial. One letter published in the county's newspapers noted: 'it is amusing to see him [O'Donoghue] now at war with those who were hand and glove with him at the late county and borough elections'.[80] The *Kerry Sentinel* criticised his role in the House of Commons where it claimed 'the voice of Tralee's member is not once heard in support of the nationalist demands' and The O'Donoghue's nomination was once again a reminder to 'the people of Tralee . . . of the sorry figure they are made to cut in Irish politics'.[81] Opposition to The O'Donoghue from radical figures in the county was also apparent. On the day of the demonstration a band from the Causeway region *en route* to Killarney for the meeting was stopped at Tralee railway station by the ex-Fenian and prominent home ruler John Kelly. The band, on Kelly's advice, returned home without attending the meeting.[82] At the demonstration itself, neither Parnell nor O'Connor Power was present and the Catholic clergy failed to attend. Although the *Kerry Sentinel* reported that 'nothing . . . would testify to general enthusiasm for the meeting', a crowd of over 4,000 attended, including Thomas O'Rourke, secretary of the defunct KTDA, and O'Connor Horgan, a noted Tralee solicitor and 'nationalist'.[83] Individuals attended from other parts of the county such as a J. O'Sullivan from the north Kerry town of Ballylongford, indicating that the meeting's appeal went beyond the Kenmare estate.[84] Despite the *Sentinel*'s opposition and the lack of support from Catholic clergy and local and national home rulers, the meeting was to some degree a success.

In his speech, The O'Donoghue demanded that rents should be set by arbitration between landlord and tenant, that tenants should secure the right to sell their interest, and that landlords should be prevented from increasing rent on tenants' improvements.[85] These demands were closely related to those of Isaac Butt's Land Bill, which still remained the legislative proposal on land of the Home Rule Party.[86] He also directly criticised a number of Kerry landlords including Lord Kenmare, H. E. Herbert and the land agent Samuel Hussey. Resolutions demanding a rent reduction and peasant proprietorship were passed, indicating the influence of the principles of the newly established Irish National Land League.[87] Although The O'Donoghue was an unlikely source of radicalism, and he failed to receive support from various political groupings, his initiative facilitated the most politicised response to the crisis by the start of 1880 in Kerry. Agrarian tensions had yet to develop in the county on similar lines to those in western counties. While 870 agrarian outrages were committed in the country during 1879 of which 180 occurred in Galway alone, a mere 14 were committed in Kerry.[88]

1880 GENERAL ELECTION: THE INTRODUCTION OF PARNELLITE POLITICS

The 1880 general election was fought out not merely between home rulers and anti-home rulers, but within the Home Rule Party by whigs and Parnellites. The Parnellites were associated with the land agitation and parliamentary obstruction while the whigs regarded both movements with contempt and supported the official leader in William Shaw. Much of the public attention of the electoral campaign concentrated on the seven constituencies where the two factions in the Home Rule Party opposed each other (Sligo, Wexford, Dundalk, Louth, Mayo, Cork City and County).[89] In Kerry the politics of Parnellism had yet to affect the county constituencies and the two seats went uncontested. Henry Herbert, long the focus of criticism by tenant activists, retired as MP for the county. R. P. Blennerhassett, originally elected in the famous 1872 by-election, was once again nominated along with another land-lord, Sir Rowland Blennerhassett (8,390 acres, Beaufort).[90] Both had support from traditional tenant-right figures such as the Catholic clerical activist the Rev. Morty O'Connor of Ballylongford (O'Connor was a central figure in the 1872 by-election), who resurrected the defunct North Kerry Farmers' Club for their nominations. Although the two Blennerhassetts were liberal-home rulers who failed to support Parnell, they were elected unopposed as the county representatives and received support from the *Kerry Sentinel* and Timothy Harrington.[91] The parliamentary election for the two county seats failed to lead to any challenge from Parnellites or radical agrarians indicating the weakness of Land League support in the county. This situation was replicated in many constituencies where the Land League remained in its infancy. In King's County the election was marked by a contest between the Edenderry Home Rule Club and a candidate who received support from the Catholic clergy with limited involvement from Parnell and the league.[92] In many Ulster constituencies tenant-righters continued to demonstrate their traditional presence in electoral politics. In Fermanagh a Liberal landlord espousing the cause of land reform and non-sectarian co-operation was put forward by the local tenant association in a contest with no Land League candidate.[93] Other regions did witness indirect league influence, such as Queen's County where the two successful Parnellite candidates, Richard Lawlor and Arthur O'Connor, received funds from the central branch and Parnell addressed a number of electoral meetings although no branch of the Land League had yet been established in the county.[94] In other regions such as Mayo, where the land agitation was at its most intense during early 1880, Parnellites had an extensive organisation. This was reflected in the parliamentary election which witnessed the Fenian John O'Connor Power topping the poll and Charles Stewart Parnell winning the second seat from a landlord named Browne.[95]

Despite the lack of radical Parnellite politics in the Kerry county election, the contest for the borough of Tralee proved somewhat different. The long-standing MP for the town, The O'Donoghue, was opposed by the contentious land agent, Samuel Hussey. When these candidates were announced the *Kerry Sentinel* stated in an editorial: 'the national party have not as yet decided upon their course with regard to the borough but if only The O'Donoghue and Mr Hussey are in the field they will support The O'Donoghue for the chief part though some express their determination to abstain from voting.'[96] Placards were placed in the town, calling on voters to ignore both The O'Donoghue and Hussey in favour of a pro-Parnell candidate yet to be announced.[97] This failed to develop and the election was a direct contest between The O'Donoghue and Hussey. The defunct KTDA was resurrected for the election and had a single meeting. Although Jonathan Walpole, the outspoken opponent of home rule, attended, other prominent nationalists controlled proceedings. The Tralee Fenian Michael Power announced: 'if there is no other man coming forward to oppose Mr Hussey but The O'Donoghue, I will support The O'Donoghue'. The members supported Parnell and a resolution was passed which demanded that The O'Donoghue backed 'the advanced section of the Irish Party'.[98]

The appearance of Hussey, a leading land agent, as a Conservative candidate in the election undoubtedly galvanised and unified support around The O'Donoghue. The editor of the *Kerry Sentinel*, Timothy Harrington, became involved in O'Donoghue's election campaign. Along with Harrington, Thomas O'Rourke, secretary of the KTDA, Michael Power (Fenian and pig merchant), and O'Connor Horgan, a successful solicitor and nationalist, were the principal advocates of The O'Donoghue. These men represented the urban middle class that were attracted to home rule during the 1870s and actively opposed The O'Donoghue in the 1874 general election for the borough. Tensions between such figures and larger tenant farmers who supported The O'Donoghue led to the demise of the KTDA in the late 1870s. Although Harrington's *Sentinel* stressed that The O'Donoghue was widely supported when it stated that 'the most perfect harmony prevails among the different sections of the popular party in Tralee at present', dissensions had clearly arisen between the traditional liberal supporters of The O'Donoghue and the emerging Parnellite nationalists.[99] When The O'Donoghue arrived in Tralee for nominations, he went to the Liberal registration room, accompanied by figures such as Sir Henry Donovan, a Catholic merchant and lower gentry figure. It was reported that the 'nationalists remained aloof' from the nominations.[100] Despite the KTDA's declaration of support for The O'Donoghue, he declined to address the organisation.[101] The leading Parnellites, Harrington and O'Connor Horgan, addressed an election meeting without The O'Donoghue's presence, further demonstrating tension between the traditional whiggish home rulers and the Parnellites.[102]

In a sustained election campaign Hussey obtained the public support of a number of tenants who held land under him, labourers who worked for him, and Griffin, the Catholic Canon of Millstreet, County Cork.[103] The election was marked by sectarian violence. It was reported that at a demonstration O'Connor Horgan 'referred to religious differences and the mob becoming excited rushed away and attacked several Protestant houses and establish-ments'.[104] Further rioting was reported and a force of 30 cavalry was sent to the town.[105] Despite the divisions within The O'Donoghue's camp, the sight of such a controversial land agent as Hussey in the election secured him victory by 187 votes to 133.[106] The election mobilised previous supporters of home rule in the town into political action. Although they actively promoted The O'Donoghue's candidature, they were clearly motivated by the politics of Parnell and the election provided Parnellism with its first popular platform in Kerry. The 1880 election saw the emergence of the Parnellites as a force in the electoral politics of the town and provided a popular platform for the nascent movement. Central to this early Parnellism in Tralee town was the support for traditional liberal and whiggish figures such as The O'Donoghue indicat-ing the continued relevance of such politics to the emerging more radical Parnellite politics.

Following quickly on the electoral success in March, Parnell attempted to further extend his power over the emerging agrarian agitation with the expansion of the Land League. In May 1880 Parnell defeated Shaw for the position of chairmanship of the party, indicating his emergence as the leader of Irish Home Rule.[107] He held a land conference at the Rotunda, Dublin, which was attended by 250 delegates from Land League branches and tenant defence associations from all over Ireland.[108] The delegates from Kerry included the Rev. Morty O'Connor from Ballybunion, Henry Brassill, who was editor of the newly formed *Kerry Independent*, Timothy Harrington, and The O'Donoghue.[109] This conference marked a change in the course of the agrarian agitation and signalled the intervention of middle to large farmers into the affairs of the Land League.[110] Despite opposition from western agrarian radicals, particularly Matthew Harris, who argued that the introduction of graziers into the league platform would harm the small farmer class, the conference consolidated support from larger farmers. The new policy established by the Land League centred on the dual issues of rent and evictions. The conference resolved to demand legislation to suspend evictions on all holdings valued at or below £20, called on rent to be paid at no higher a level than the poor law valuation of the holding (Griffiths), and stipulated that a system for the selling of land to tenants be introduced.[111] These demands transformed the social aspirations of the Land League and attracted the support of the prosperous farmers of Munster and Leinster.

GROWING AGRARIAN TENSIONS AND 'INDIGNANT MEETINGS'

While the Land League was organising on a national level and extending its remit beyond the west, agrarian tensions were rapidly increasing in Kerry. In the first six months of 1880, 104 evictions were carried out by landlords in the county compared to 70 for the previous twelve months.[112] In definite signs of a prevailing agitation, a number of agrarian outrages were committed. In January 1880 The MacGillicuddy (15,510 acres, Whitefield, Killarney) received a threatening letter warning him against evicting any tenants. In the same month a notice appeared on the walls of the Catholic church in Ballyduff threatening the lives of the landlord, T. A. Stoughton (11,710 acres, Ballyhorgan) and his agent George Sandes, to intimidate them from carrying out evictions in the area.[113] During March, violence emerged near Listowel in Moybella as three brothers named O'Connor took forcible possession of a farm that they were had been evicted from. In another incident shots were fired into the dwelling house of an individual who was about to 'grab' an evicted farm. In a different case, an unoccupied house was set alight after Lord Listowel had given the farm to another tenant, having disposed of the original holder when he had become insane. In the same month threatening notices were posted in Newtownsandes which warned individuals against the payment of rent.[114] This indicated the emergence of anti-rent combinations. Within a number of months in 1880, it became apparent that at a local level there was now a systematic campaign based on violent intimidation against rent payment, eviction and 'landgrabbing'.

This grassroots agitation took a public form with a number of 'indignant meetings' which increasingly became intermeshed with an emerging rural and agrarian Fenianism. The first of these meetings was called in late April 1880 at Ballyduff to protest against the eviction of the O'Connor brothers from their holding on an estate owned by an absentee landlord named William Pope

(821 acres).[115] They held a large farm of 161 acres at an annual rent of £80 indicating that the depression was beginning to affect the larger farmers.[116] The brothers, who were amongst the largest farmers in the region, were heavily in debt. They owed their landlord £100 and a number of civil bill decrees from other creditors had been issued against them. In an attempt to reclaim the loss, the landlord's agent offered the tenants the chance to sell their interest in the holding but they declined. The O'Connor brothers were not the archetypical helpless poverty stricken tenants portrayed in Land League propaganda who were victims of capricious landlordism. They were middling farmers who were mired in debt to a range of creditors.

The situation at this farm quickly became radicalised when on the night of their eviction the tenants broke in and took forcible possession of the holding.[117] What was labelled as an 'indignant meeting' in the local newspaper press was held to protest against the eviction and was reportedly attended 'principally [by] young men from the districts of Ballyduff and Causeway'.[118] Resolutions were passed inciting boycotting and calling for no one to bid for the farm. Timothy Harrington attended the meeting and called on the tenants of the county to combine together in clubs and associations to protect their interests.[119] A number of individuals who would later become associated with the Land League, agrarian violence and rural Fenianism in the region addressed the meeting. These included Martin Sullivan and Thomas Dooling (Kiltomey), both farmers' sons, who by the year end were suspected of orchestrating violence and agrarian outrages in the Ballyduff region.[120] As the 1880s progressed Dooling emerged as an important figure in the region and was believed to have been the IRB leader in the nearby Lixnaw area.[121] A few weeks after the meeting, the radicalisation of agrarian relations was evident when a mob resisted the eviction of a tenant named John Kelly on the Harenc estate, which was owned by Samuel Hussey.[122] As the county sheriff, accompanied by a number of bailiffs, attempted to enact the eviction, they were set upon by a large crowd and seriously beaten. Dooling was again a leading figure in this incident and was arrested and accused of orchestrating the riot although he was acquitted at trial.[123]

Dooling was typical of a new strand of agitator who orchestrated the increasing agitation at a local and grassroots level. As a farmer's son he was free of the innate conservatism of much of the rural landholding tenantry and was drawn to the developing Fenianism of the late 1870s. Although Fenianism was particularly weak in most parts of Kerry during the late 1850s and in the 1860s, by the late 1870s the movement had emerged in the county as it began to take an agrarian form. According to IRB records there were 160 members of the society in Kerry by January 1877, although they were poorly armed with a mere 25 rifles.[124] This contrasted greatly to the situation in Connaught where by 1878 there were genuine fears amongst the police that portions of the province were more 'deeply tainted with secret societies than any other division of the country'. Although such societies remained limited in Kerry, there were signs that Fenians had organised in the county and, during April 1878, 'the priests of two parishes warned their congregations against attempts, which they said were being made to revive Fenianism'.[125] By 1879 there was a real growth of Fenianism in certain regions in the county with a Fenian society established in Castleisland town.[126] During the close of the year the resident magistrate for Tralee, Considine, believed that along with Castleisland, Fenianism had spread to Tralee and the rural district of Abbeydorney.[127] Similarly, the magistrate in Killarney town believed that while there was no illicit importation of arms into the region the 'young men . . . do not hide their animosity towards landlords and government, and [it] only requires the coalition of the farming class to cause it to become a terror and danger'.[128] Known Fenians from the 1867 rising such as J. D. Sheehan were suspected of organising Fenianism in the region during 1878–9.[129]

This mix of Fenianism and radical agrarianism appeared to appeal to the large cohort of 'young men' whose social frustrations owing to an abrupt decline in marriage and inheritance opportunities have been highlighted by Joseph Lee as of central importance to the outburst of agrarian outrages during this period.[130] In the pre-Famine period, Kerry along with much of south-west of Ireland was the focus of violent agrarian secret society activity, largely in the form of the Whiteboy and Rockite movements.[131] During the post-Famine period Kerry witnessed limited secret society agrarian activity and agrarian radicals had little if any influence over agrarian relations and were not readily identifiable in the leadership structures of the tenant-right and home rule movements. The emergence of agrarian violence in the developing anti-rent and eviction protests in Kerry during 1880 appeared to revive older violent agrarian traditions. The violence of the late 1870s and early 1880s is seen as centrally connected with previous secret society movements. The historian Paul Bew has highlighted how Ribbonism and Fenianism appeared to coalesce in midland regions such as Westmeath during the violent outbreak of 1870–1. Such organisation also extended into western areas to the extent that the violent organisation of the late 1870s and early 1880s in Connaught has been termed 'Ribbon-Fenianism'.[132] The Whiteboysim of pre-Famine southern Ireland was far less of an underground organisation, and had differing motivations and social composition from Ribbonism, which was prominent in north Leinster, north Connaught and south Ulster.[133] While Ribbonism remained somewhat active in post-Famine Ireland, Whiteboyism, particularly in Kerry, had largely faded away. Throughout the 1860s and 1870s the low number of agrarian outrages reported in the county demonstrated that Whiteboyism and secret society activity were practically non-existent. By 1880, however, it appeared that violent agrarian activity had been reignited as a method in the developing tenant agitation and that this was closely related to a rural Fenianism which had emerged during the previous few years. Although the organisation of such agrarian violence was secret, men suspected of initiating such violence emerged as leaders of the nascent land movement locally.

The socio-economic characteristic of individuals such as Dooling greatly contrasted with the large farmers and shopkeeper and publican axis that dominated the KTDA in the 1870s, and establishment figures such as the MPs, The O'Donoghue and Blennerhassett, and the Catholic priests, who frequently addressed the demonstrations in 1879. This new stratum within the local tenant leadership structure of agrarian society was non-existent in previous tenant-right movements and had not been prominent since the pre-Famine Whiteboyism. These radical agrarians were central to the 'indignant meetings' of early 1880 and closely connected with the Parnellite section of the mainstream tenant and nationalist leadership.

In May 1880 the various sections of the tenant leadership appeared to have coalesced when Parnell addressed a meeting in the centrally located town of Beaufort. Leading figures from the towns of Tralee, Killarney and Killorglin, including publicans, drapers, shopkeepers, merchants and auctioneers along with Catholic clergy and The O'Donoghue, were present on the platform. Parnell promoted the objectives recently adopted at the April Land Convention. He also gave an aggressive, nationalist and radical agrarian speech, which openly promoted extra-constitutional methods. He declared that the 'task of obtaining for our people the land of our native country . . . [was] one of the greatest undertakings that any nation could engage'. He stated that the land question would never be settled 'so long as the institution of landlordism survive[d]'. In what could be interpreted as the promotion of strong-arm tactics, Parnell told his audience that 'if the legislature refuses to step in, this agitation will have to go on. It will increase tenfold in intensity, and the people will do for themselves that which the legislature refuses to do.'[134] Parnell had placed the emerging agitation in Kerry within a broader national movement and allowed for the unification of the various sectional groups under a single banner.

Soon after Parnell's address another 'indignant meeting' was held in the Ballyduff region. The meeting was called to protest against the taking of an evicted farm on the property of Staughton. A number of evictions had occurred on the estate and at least five evicted farms lay unoccupied in the region.[135] Although the former tenant, Matthew O'Flaherty, had emigrated after his eviction, the taking of the farm jeopardised other untenanted land that farmers were evicted from.[136] O'Flaherty's farm was rented to another farmer in the region named John W. O'Connor. The KTDA resolved to hold a meeting on the grounds that O'Connor was a 'greedy land shark' with sufficient lands of his own.[137] Various members of the wider nationalist community were in attendance. T. B. Silles, the large tenant farmer against whom Hussey controversially took protracted legal proceedings in the 1870s, chaired the meeting, indicating the continued importance of traditional tenant right activists. Others on the platform included the Rev. Morty O'Connor, the tenant-right Catholic priest, who was involved in home rule politics during the 1872 by-election. These traditional tenant activists were joined by the new radical element. Thomas Dooling and Martin O'Sullivan, radical agrarians who were directly involved in the orchestration of agrarian violence, were also on the platform. Timothy Harrington also addressed the meeting. During this meeting the 'challenging collectivity' appeared to be in existence. Catholic clergy, large farmers and townsmen aligned with radical figures in the one movement. Harrington outlined several objectives of the agitation. He promoted boycotting by stating: 'they would have to band themselves together and shun every farm from which an honest man had been evicted'.[138] He also called on the people 'not [to] take land from which honest men were ejected for not paying an unjust rent'. Dooling believed: 'if they stood firmly together, and treated with contempt the man who took the farm from which another had been unjustly evicted, they were sure to win the cause, and they not be begging a reduction of rent from the landlords'.[139]

During the following month, July 1880, only one meeting espousing tenant concerns was held. This was in Ballybunion to protest against a local landlord, George Hewson (1,208 acres, Ennismore), who was reclaiming sections of a strand, which tenants had communally used for seaweed and sand.[140] The meeting was addressed by the Rev. Morty O'Connor and was acknowledged by the Land League with a letter from Parnell.[141] The first official meeting of the Land League in Kerry was held in August. Although north Kerry was the centre of agrarian tensions, the meeting was held in the southern Kerry town of Killorglin. In an attempt to gain maximum exposure the meeting coincided with a popular horse fair and festival that dated back to pagan times called the 'Puck Fair'. The *Kerry Sentinel* claimed the location was strategically 'availed of to introduce to the people of Kerry the agitation against eviction and rack rents . . . [the Puck Fair] brings together literally the whole of Kerry'.[142] Timothy Harrington and A. M. O'Sullivan from the central executive of the Land League in Dublin were the primary speakers. Harrington, aware of the innate conservatism of many of the larger tenant farmer class, contended that the motto 'the land for the people of Ireland' was no 'revolutionary cry' and that the league was not unlawful. O'Sullivan called on tenants not to pay rent until further land legislation and to boycott evicted land. He also stated that

the Land League would support evicted tenants.[143] The RIC officer in attendance reported: 'this meeting was a noisy one owing to people having drink
taken. They cheered and shouted for almost everything. There were a great
number of people in town who took no part in the meeting. This meeting was
almost a failure.'[144] No branch of the league was established as a consequence
of the meeting.

By the summer of 1880 no branches of the Land League had yet been
formed in Kerry, but agrarian violence continued to grow and in the four-
month period between May and August 37 agrarian outrages were recorded,
compared to 17 for the previous four months.[145] Much of this violence centred
on untenanted land that farmers were evicted from. In the nine-month period
between January and the end of September 1880 landlords carried out 183
evictions in the county. Of this number 114 tenants were reinstated largely as
caretakers, leaving 69 full evicted farms.[146] Landlords' attempts to use this
evicted land led to much conflict. In late June a body of thirty men armed with
guns and scythes attacked the occupiers of a farm, which had been the scene
of a recent eviction at Moybella near Listowel. The 'grabbers' were forced off
the holding and the evicted tenant was reinstated by the gang.[147] After a
number of arrests for the offence, the prisoners were brought into Listowel
town where they were cheered by a large crowd.[148] Another evicted farm at
Ahabeg in Lixnaw located between Tralee and Listowel was the source of a
number of outrages. In July, two cattle belonging to a bailiff of Samuel Hussey's
were killed on it while in August hay on the holding was destroyed.[149] By late
summer the general north Kerry region was the centre of violence. Attempts
to sell produce (meadowing) from the evicted farm at Moybella was boycotted
at a fair at Clounlogher (on the hinterland of Tralee) attended by many
farmers.[150] There was also agitation outside north Kerry. As early as June
1880, a magistrate sitting at the Petty Session at Aunnascaul, on the western
side of Tralee, warned against ringleaders who were inciting people to pay no
rent in the area.[151] By the start of autumn agrarian unrest had already reached
a level unknown during the previous decade.

CONCLUSION: ORIGINS OF THE LAND WAR IN KERRY

Between 1879 and the autumn of 1880 political and agrarian activity irrevocably altered in the county. While the circumstances behind, and causes of, the
land war have been the focus of much debate, it is clear that a number of
factors were vital to the heightened tensions between landlord and tenants in
Kerry during the first nine months of 1880. Throughout 1879 the depression in
the agricultural economy put the smaller farmers and agricultural labourers in

distress with reports of destitution prevalent amongst this class. Despite this, relations between tenants and landlords failed to become violent and the response to the distress remained moderate. In contrast to the anti-landlord agitation in the 'west' that had emerged concurrently, in Kerry the response largely involved the opening of public relief works, some reductions in rent and the dispersal of private charity which effectively relieved much of the extreme distress of the smaller land holders. Politically, traditional tenant activists such as the Catholic clergy and Blennerhassett, who failed to support Parnell in the Home Rule Party, remained the primary advocates of farmers' concerns. These figures, along with the defunct KTDA, proved incapable of fully expressing the needs of tenants and, in particular, forcing landlords to act accordingly. The anxiety of the tenantry was prevalent when The O'Donoghue held a demonstration in January 1880 that was partially successful despite his failure to achieve support from the clergy or more advanced home rulers. The O'Donoghue, who had long cultivated himself as a tenant activist, received the support of the advanced home rulers in the 1880 election for the Tralee Borough. Samuel Hussey's candidature ensured that old animosities between The O'Donoghue and home rulers in the town were transcended. The election provided a platform for supporters of Parnell, the most important of whom was Timothy Harrington, editor of the *Kerry Sentinel*. The Parnellites took a leading role in the election campaign and called on The O'Donoghue to support Parnell.

The political and agrarian movement in Kerry followed a different trajectory to that of many other regions in the country. Late 1879 and the first nine months of 1880 witnessed the tentative alignment of various groups within non-landlord society behind the Land League and Parnellism in Kerry. In contrast to areas in Connaught where the land war was at its height and the Land League well organised, the influence of Parnellism was still limited in Kerry as late as the 1880 general election. Kerry appeared to fit Bew's timeline of agitation in which Parnell's reaching out to the larger farmers of Leinster and Munster in April 1880 was the catalyst for movement's spread from the 'west' and the subsequent changing of the social objectives of the movement from supporting small and impoverished tenant farmers to one more attuned to the needs of larger tenants who sought rent reductions from their landlords. The movement was undoubtedly more palatable to vital middling-sized tenant farmers who were numerous in Kerry. However, in Kerry these moderate demands became intermingled with an emerging agrarian–Fenian radicalism which orchestrated a campaign of resistance to eviction coupled with intimidation and violence against landlords and 'grabbers'. Farmers' sons who were influenced by Fenianism and were independent of the traditional Catholic middle-class rural power structure appeared to spearhead this violent agitation.

The arrival of Parnell in the county in May facilitated the alliance of these men with the more traditional sections of the tenant leadership such as Catholic clergy, urban merchants, and large tenant farmers. By the autumn of 1880 a range of previously divided interests had united against landlords. This alliance was imbued with a nationalism that appealed to both Fenians and home rulers. This in many ways represented the local and practical implementation of the politics of the 'New Departure'. The emergence of agrarian radicals like Timothy Dooling was highly important. Such figures, who were connected to the IRB and the urban Fenians in Tralee town, represented the emergence of a new element in the local agrarian political spectrum. They were responding at a local level to what was perceived as landlord aggression. While Fenian in outlook, they were attracted to the Land League catch cry of peasant proprie-torship and were able to harness the social frustrations of young, landless and unmarried men into an agitation against landlords and evictions in a way that was surely beyond the more traditional tenant leaders in the county. The general anti-landlordism of the Land League appeared to successfully attract moderates and radicals in mid-1880.

While the role of Fenians in orchestrating the more radical aspect of the land war in County Mayo is well established, in other regions beyond Kerry it is difficult to decipher the importance of Fenianism at a grassroots level. In the south-western region of Skull in County Cork there is definite evidence of Fenian involvement in the anti-landlord agitation.[152] In Queen's County, in contrast, no similar landless Fenian-orientated agrarian radicals emerged in the local leadership structure. In the rural parish of Tullaroan in north-west Kilkenny in the eastern province of Leinster, the leading Land League supporters were mostly middling tenant farmers.[153] The general lack of other systematic research into the nature of grassroots agrarian agitation in the early 1880s and the level of Fenian activity during this period makes it difficult to identify the importance of agrarian Fenians in the local leadership of the Land League beyond areas such as Kerry and Mayo.

In attempting to understand why the land war broke out in the late 1870s and early 1880s as opposed to earlier periods of economic distress such as the early 1870s, the merging of rural agitators (no matter how uneasy) with middle class and traditional local leaders including larger farmers, townsmen, urban Fenians, Catholic clergy and, in the case of Kerry, whiggish figures such as The O'Donoghue was a vital factor in providing the impetus for a widespread anti-landlord agitation. In many ways this alignment, explicitly demonstrated in May 1880, during Parnell's Beaufort meeting, was an embodiment of what the historian Samuel Clark has termed the 'challenging collectivity'. Clark has highlighted how bonds and social ties involving religion, general anti-landlord feeling and nationalist sentiment, combined with the economic benefits for all classes of the redirection of landlord rent money to the non-landlord economy during a period of economic depression, all helped to merge the various interests.[154] In the case of Kerry this must also be tempered by the obvious and widely varying objectives and social outlook of figures as diverse as Dooling, Timothy Harrington, The O'Donoghue and Catholic clerics.[155] The realities of the agrarian economy produced tensions not just between tenants but also with their creditors, many of whom were the urban shop-keepers, publicans and merchants who formed the local leadership of the league. The complicated nature of tenants' debts was illustrated in the initial evictions in Kerry where the tenants were in debt to a range of creditors and not just their landlords. W. E. Vaughan has highlighted such tensions as a bulwark to Clark's thesis and questions how the townsmen leadership could coexist with a tenantry against whom they were issuing a large number of civil bills.[156] Despite such tensions at an economic level, as demonstrated in chapter one, these never dominated the formal agenda of agrarian and nationalist politics in the 1870s, which largely revolved around tenant-right, Fenianism and older Liberal/whig political traditions. Although the intra-tenant tensions which were inevitable in such a litigious economy were bubbling under the surface of anti-landlordism and nationalism, the early 'indignant meetings' which incorporated radical and moderate strains of agrarianism and national-ist politics ignored the issue of non-landlord debt. Quite simply, such socially divisive matters were not included in the political rhetoric of the various sectional interest groups which became aligned during the early days of the land war and any such tensions were channelled into the anti-landlordism which the Land League propagated.

Although immediate local controversies surrounding evictions characterised much of the agitation, it was also propelled by events at a national level. In 1872, politics in the county had responded to that year's Galway by-election and returned Blennerhassett as a home rule MP. By 1880 the agrarian agitation in the west was in full flight and in many ways the rest of the country including Kerry was only beginning to follow suit. The need for Kerry tenant farmers and political activists to be in line with national developments was played on by the Land League organiser, Timothy Harrington, who criticised tenants in the county during early 1880 for their failure to mobilise. The importance of the emergence of a strong national leadership in the form of Parnell and Davitt and the politics of the 'New Departure' have been recognised as crucial factors in the emergence of the land war in 1879 and 1880.[157] Such national developments had a direct influence on events in Kerry. Fenian organisation in the late 1870s in Kerry had penetrated rural regions to a far greater extent than previously and the radical agrarianism surrounding much of the violence can partly be viewed as the local manifestation of the politics of the 'New

Departure'. The influence of wider national politics within the county was further highlighted when Parnell addressed the Beaufort demonstration in May 1880. The meeting allowed for the merging of a local leadership that incorporated the various political and agrarian traditions under a single strong national leadership.

THREE

LAND LEAGUE AGITATION

—

EMERGENCE OF THE LAND LEAGUE, SEPTEMBER TO DECEMBER 1880

By September 1880 the agrarian agitation that had been simmering at a local level over the previous months in the county quickly escalated. Within the first two weeks of September tenants on the properties of Wilson Gunn in Causeway (11,819 acres) and Major James Crosbie in Ballyheigue (13,422 acres) received threatening letters warning them not to pay rents.[1] Another land owner in the Causeway region, Charles W. Stoughton (2,495 acres), became the first landlord in the county to be physically attacked when he had shots fired into his house during the same week.[2] Although Stoughton had not evicted any tenants, he refused to reduce the September rent leading to a rent strike on his property. A number of days before the attack he received a threatening notice demanding a 25 per cent abatement in rent.[3] Within two weeks the tenants of another landlord in the same region, T. A. Stoughton (11,710 acres), refused to pay rent above the government valuation (Griffith's).[4] During the same week tenants on the Mahony estate in Knockanure received a notice threatening death if they paid more than the government valuation as rent.[5] Although the Land League had not established a branch in the county by September 1880, the doctrine of the movement concerning paying rent at the government valuation was becoming a cornerstone for localised agitation. Intimidation and violence were used to enforce rent strikes indicating a significant radical influence in the developing movement.

In September, the land agent Samuel Hussey began adopting stringent measures to fight the nascent agitation. A common practice in the region was for evicted tenants to retake possession of their holdings after they had been evicted. This practice was particularly evident in Kerry, and out of a total of 84 such incidents reported in Ireland as a whole during 1880, 24 occurred in Kerry.[6] In an attempt to counter this practice, Hussey destroyed two houses while carrying out evictions. The first of these was the dwelling of a tenant named Shea on the estate of Arthur Blennerhassett (12,621 acres) in Ballyseedy on the outskirts of Tralee of which Hussey was agent.[7] Within a number of days Hussey burnt down the dwelling of an evicted tenant named Kennedy on the Hickson property (13,443 acres) in the Dingle region.[8] These aggressive measures provided the Land League with the opportune moment to organise in the county. Soon after the burning in Dingle, a meeting was held in O'Sullivan's Hotel in Tralee that led to the establishment of the first branch of the Land League in the county. It adopted Timothy Harrington as president, Thomas O'Rourke (publican and former secretary of the KTDA) as secretary, and M. L. Lyons (shopkeeper) as treasurer. Although all were townsmen, a number of tenant farmers were also present. Jeremiah Leahy and Michael McMahon, a poor law guardian, both large farmers, were elected as committee members.[9] During the first meeting of the Tralee League, Harrington outlined its objectives. He concentrated largely on the rent increases by landlords and, in particular, highlighted Talbot-Crosbie's Ardfert estate. He also condemned 'landgrabbing' and spoke of the recent actions of landlords and their agents:

> the landlords are, it appears, determined to go as far in pushing what they are pleased to call their rights, but what others call their tyranny, as to burn down the houses of the unfortunate tenants that are evicted.[10]

The immediate objectives of the movement were clearly defined as the lowering of rent, preventing landgrabbing and protecting evicted tenants. The emergence of the Land League in Kerry in autumn 1880 was representative of the second wave of league organisation at a national level. Although the league had emerged initially in the 'west' and in particular in Mayo, by late 1880 the movement began to be overcome with internal tensions leading to collapse.[11] During the same period outside the 'west', the Land League was just beginning to organise fully. In Ulster by autumn 1880, Land League branches had been established in Down, Armagh, Tyrone and Derry, and its first membership drives took place.[12]

With the introduction of the Land League into the county the agitation was transformed. During the previous nine months (January–September) six agrarian demonstrations had been held in Kerry. After the establishment of the Land League five land meetings were held in October alone, many of which were addressed by leading league organisers of a national prominence.[13] The leading Parnellite figure Arthur O'Connor MP spoke outside Dingle at Ballingrawn on the site where Hussey had burnt down the house of the evicted tenant, Kennedy. He told tenants to 'keep a grip of your homesteads' and called on them to leave 'the evicted tenants remain in the neighbourhood so they can take the land when possible'.[14] In Castleisland, O'Connor again addressed a meeting, but this time he was accompanied by Joseph Biggar MP.[15] Public Land League meetings were also held in Ballyduff, Kingwilliamstown and

Brosna.[16] During November and December another eleven land meetings were held in the county.[17]

These public meetings provided the impetus for the creation of local branches of the Land League. By the end of December 1880 at least 14 local branches of the league had been established and 41 branch meetings had been reported in the league's mouthpiece, the *Kerry Sentinel*. This unprecedented mobilisation of tenant farmers was concentrated in the northern half of the county. Of the 41 branch meetings held, all but two occurred in the northern three unions. This can only be partly explained by the fact that 66.7 per cent of the county's 201,309 inhabitants lived in the three northern unions. A core-periphery dynamic was at play with the central and northern part of the county acting as the core. The varying circumstances within the county facilitate the analysis of the dynamics behind the emergence of the Land League at a regional level. Although the three northern unions had a greater population, there was a range of socio-economic reasons for the low level of Land League participation in the southern and western parts of the county.

Table.3.1 The number of branch meetings of the Land League reported in the Kerry Sentinel held in each poor law union, September–December 1880

Tralee	Listowel	Killarney	Caherciveen	Dingle	Kenmare
26	8	5	2	0	0

Source: KS, 28 Sept.–31 Dec. 1880.[18]

The north and centre of the county, which witnessed the bulk of Land League activity, was interconnected by an extensive rail network which allowed for the movement of local league organisers from town to town, and likewise the national leaders who campaigned in the region during the final three months of 1880. The railway lines not only facilitated movement of people but also allowed for the effective distribution of the Land League's voice in the county, the *Kerry Sentinel*. The southern and western fringes also had higher rates of illiteracy and monoglot Irish speakers. This too hindered the dissemination of the Land League ideals which were promoted through the English language in newspapers and by the local urban and national leadership. The contrasting social circumstances in the two regions appeared to have been an important influence on the effectiveness of the spread of the Land League. In many ways the emergence of the Land League in north and central Kerry was the product of a modernity which had yet to reach fully into the southern and western region.

Another major difference between the two regions was in landholding and occupational structure. In the western and southern poor law unions, tenant farmers made up the largest class within agrarian society, while in northern and central poor law unions a greater divide existed between tenants and agricultural labourers. Agricultural labourers were an important element in the provision of support for the Land League, although there is little evidence of this socio-economic class within the movement's local leadership structure. Another important structural difference between the two regions was the lack of a middling to large tenant farmer class in the southern and western unions compared to the north and centre. Non-landlord society in the Kenmare, Dingle and Caherciveen Poor Law Unions had few agricultural labourers and was dominated by a small tenant farmer class whose holdings were lowly valued (see table 3.1). Such holdings had a limited economic output and would not have benefited from the prosperity of the 1860s and 1870s to the same extent as in the other regions. In contrast, in the Tralee, Listowel and Killarney Unions an important middle stratum of tenant farmers was in place. This group had been long politicised and were important supporters and local leaders of previous tenant-right and home rule movements, particularly during the 1870s. Such middle-sized tenantry had much to gain from an extensive agitation over the issue of rent compared to smaller farmers of the west and southern regions whose holdings, regardless of rent, were largely unproductive. While the varying political factors outlined in the previous chapter were central to the emergence of the Land League, these were tied to a range of social and economic developments relating to modernisation and land structure typified in the contrasting circumstances in north and south Kerry.

While the Land League clearly mobilised the middle-class tenantry, the movement also employed the supposed 'unwritten law' of agrarian society in its rhetoric. The 'unwritten law' was a complicated and ill-defined agrarian code of practices, which emanated from the customary rights of peasants in the 'moral economy' of the pre-Famine period. These practices were 'based on mutual obligation and shared responsibility' between rich and poor.[19] Despite the emergence of agrarian capitalism in the nineteenth century, contemporary commentators still recognised the 'unwritten law'. A leading British civil servant named George Campbell believed that one of the major threats to British rule in Ireland was the existence of an alternative law and the failure of the official law to always correspond to the realities of Irish life.[20] He was of the opinion that 'in Ireland there are two sets of laws – the English laws, and the laws or customs of the country, which, enforced in a different way, are as active and effective'.[21] By the land war period, the 'unwritten law' was based on a set of principles that gave tenants claims over land regardless of ownership or the ability to pay rents.[22]

In promoting the league, national and local activists frequently invoked the 'natural' rights tenants had under the 'unwritten law'. In Dingle, Arthur O'Connor instructed the people to 'feed your children rather than pay rent and don't pay any rent if you cannot do it without inconvenience to your children, or to those who gave you credit for food when you went without it'.[23] A meeting in Ballyduff resolved that enforced rent payment was 'contrary to law, human and divine, and we emphatically condemn evictions for the non-payment of such rents'.[24] In particular, the destroying of evicted tenants' homes was an affront to this law. The *Kerry Sentinel* clearly played on the sentiments that could be evoked by the burning of a tenant's house. After the burning in Dingle, the newspaper reported that '[this] new and revolting phase in the land war has naturally caused a feeling of horror'.[25] When Hussey repeated the act on the Kenmare estate the newspaper expressed the belief that 'the burning of Rath is not likely to die out of the memory of the people of Kerry for a long time to come'.[26] It went on to state that the act was a 'needless outrage upon the feelings of the people'.[27] This incident demonstrated the presumed breach by landlordism of the customary rights of the tenantry. Lord Kenmare was a Catholic and a widely popular landlord who was considered to have a 'paternal' relationship with his tenantry. His popularity was demonstrated as late as November 1880 when over 5,000 of his tenants led by the local Catholic clergy and largest farmers on his estate met to protest against a threatening letter that he had received.[28] However, the burning of a tenant's house on his lands was something the *Kerry Sentinel* 'deeply regretted' and was at pains 'to see the earl of Kenmare playing the second fiddle for him [Samuel Hussey] while the houses of the property are in ablaze'.[29] In turn, league activists claimed that the official law of the government failed to protect tenants. At a league meeting in Brosna it was resolved that they would 'submit no longer to the unjust law, which had reduced their country to a state of poverty and humiliation'.[30] Similar language and resolutions were common at league meetings. In promoting the movement, Land Leaguers also promoted the principles of the 'unwritten law'. Enforced rent payment, evictions, land-grabbing and the destroying of tenants' homes by landlords were all seen as offences to traditional customary rights. Promoters of the Land League drew on this to some extent when expressing criticisms of landlordism.

THE UNRAVELLING OF THE IDEOLOGY OF THE LAND LEAGUE

The reality of landlord–tenant relations and the agrarian economy was more complicated than the image portrayed by the Land League. Historical research has debunked the nationalist and Land League myth of a rack-renting landlord class in the post-Famine period, yet other factors relating to the agrarian economy are of salient importance in understanding the emergence of the Land League. The level of actual eviction remained relatively low. For example, among the 2,100 occupiers on the Kenmare estate in the county, the permanent-eviction rate was reportedly one in 400 in 1878, one in 500 in 1879 and one in 700 in 1880.[31] Despite Samuel Hussey's belligerent behaviour in burning down a number of evicted tenants' houses, he did not resort to wholesale evictions. During the first six months of 1880, out of the 4,160 tenants under his agency in the county he had evicted a mere 13. Of this number, two were given passage to America by Hussey, while eight were readmitted as caretakers.[32] The practice of readmitting evicted tenants was common. In the 18-month period between 1 January 1879 and 31 June 1880, 152 evictions were carried out in the county. Of this number slightly more than half, 78, were readmitted as caretakers.[33] During the last six months of 1880, a period which corresponded with the growth of the Land League and the agrarian agitation, all but 12 out of 72 tenants who were evicted were readmitted as caretakers.[34] More commonly, landlords initiated legal proceedings against tenants without resorting to any form of eviction. In 1879, 249 ejectment notices were issued against tenants in the county, while 1880 witnessed 279.[35] The total number of evictions in the county in 1880 was 191 of which 101 of the tenants were readmitted as caretakers or tenants on the holdings, leaving a total of 90 fully evicted holdings.[36] While the issuing of ejectment notices reached the highest levels since the Famine years in the county, the majority of the 18,747 agricultural holdings in the county were not directly affected by landlord legal action.[37] These figures support suggestions that evictions were not central to agrarian tensions in the early years of the land war and that the emergence of the Land League in the county was not the direct result of the displacement of large numbers of tenants.[38] Notwithstanding this, evictions whether widespread or not played an important role in the Land League movement. Hussey's burning a number of evicted tenants' homes was propagated by local league leaders with a rhetoric and language of denunciation that emanated from the national leadership.

Other aspects of the Land League ideology failed to represent the realities of the agrarian economy. This was particularly the case concerning the 'unwritten law'. The protection of traditional customary rights motivated a number of violent agrarian movements in the pre-Famine period such as the Thrashers and Whiteboys, although many of these emanated from the lower classes of the agrarian order.[39] In the post-Famine period tenant farmers, particularly middle to large sized ones, were fully incorporated into the emerging agrarian capitalist economy. Tenant farmers became indoctrinated in agrarian capitalism as they took advantage of the increase in agricultural prices. They entered a consumer society and utilised the security of their holdings to obtain credit from various sources. Larger tenants and town shop-keepers frequently bought the interest in holdings and speculated on extra land. Much of this economic activity was regulated by the official law, demonstrated in the large number of claims in the civil bill courts, most of which were initiated by various sections of the non-landlord agrarian community.[40] The principles of the Land League and the 'unwritten law' seemed to be far removed from this economic activity and the reality of agrarian capitalism had the ability to disentangle the unity of the Land League, but many of those who promoted the Land League also participated in agrarian capitalism. As the historian R. V. Comerford has succinctly noted:

> Looking at the enthusiastic league activity of some individual strong farmers and shopkeepers-farmers it is difficult not to be reminded of *converses* making demon-strations of zeal at an *auto-da-fé*. How many of those who joined most vehemently in the attack on landgrabbers were themselves in possession of land that had been scooped up in comparatively recent times?[41]

One of the biggest challenges of the local league leaders was to implement the movement's unilateral principles on the agrarian economy, without disunion and self-interest coming to the fore.

The contradiction between aspects of Land League policy and certain realities of the agrarian economy were highlighted by a Catholic priest who openly opposed the movement, Canon Griffin from the parish of Millstreet (although in County Cork, Millstreet was in the Roman Catholic diocese of Kerry). In a letter published in Kerry's newspapers he commented:

> Why, if the people are indoctrinated with these dangerous dogmas 'no rent for landlords' 'the land for the people', the farmer this day will find very soon that his labourers and servants will say 'you must no longer keep this large farm . . . I have as good a right to this land as you'.[42]

While Griffin noted the potential for radical action against tenant farmers by agricultural labourers, he also concentrated on the payment of non-landlord debts. He objected to the slogan '"pay no rent" as surely the same sentiment applied to all other contracts, the farmer who acted on this nefarious advice might say "I won't pay, or try to pay, my other debts. I won't pay the bank or the butter merchant, or the merchant from whom I got food and clothes".[43] Land League ideology specifically attempted to distinguish between agricul-tural rents and all other debts. In 1879 Davitt and Parnell publicly urged that debts to shopkeepers be given a higher priority than rents.[44] On numerous occasions the issue was dealt with by the Land League organising committee. During one meeting at which Parnell nominated the secretary of the National Bank as a member of the league, the issue of non-landlord debt was addressed. John Ferguson, a leading Land Leaguer, originally from Belfast, stated that

> the shopkeeper must unquestionably be paid and there must be no attempt whatever to meddle with his right to be paid, or his right to exhort payment . . . . They must not sanction the idea that because it was the right to resist an unjust and grasping landlord they had a right to resist the – he would not say unjust because he had a right to his own by every law, human and divine – but the grasping shopkeeper.[45]

Undoubtedly this was an attempt to assure not just the tenants who were rural capitalists, but also merchants, bankers and shopkeepers of the principles of the league.[46] Despite this, non-landlord debt remained a real element in the continual distress of tenants. Throughout 1878 and 1879 shopkeepers and bankers called in many of their loans and refused virtually all applications for additional credit.[47] The credit squeeze by these creditors was seen as a significant factor in the distress of the tenantry.[48]

Another agrarian issue was the competition between tenants for land during the 1870s. As Canon Griffin contended, farmers offered 'immense fines and rents for lands, and even outbid each other for every farm that is put up for sale or let'.[49] Such activity inherently went against the 'unwritten law'. While the league attempted to concentrate on landlord–tenant relations, the reality was that the agrarian economy involved a panoply of complicated and potentially divisive intra-tenant commercial relationships. As early as the second branch meeting of the Tralee League, tensions surrounding such matters, that had little to do with landlord–tenant relations, began to dominate meetings. A tenant named Rooney tried to bring a case before the league against a Tralee merchant for taking his farm. The trader, Patrick Divane, was a grocer in Castle Street and was representative of the class of shopkeeper-farmers who during the latter half of the nineteenth century obtained land through their increased wealth and position as sources of credit. Divane had acquired other lands including a 28-acre holding, which he had acquired in lieu of a £35 loan owed to him from the previous tenant, a Mrs Barton.[50] Rooney's case was an example of the increasing tensions between traders and farmers and between creditors and debtors. Although not evicted by his landlord, Rooney was heavily indebted to various other sources. With a number of decrees against him for repayment of these debts, Rooney was forced to offer a bill of sale on the interest of the farm. Rooney's interest was the only security that his creditors had to recuperate their loans. In a public sale the farm went to Divane for £100. It later transpired that Rooney had organised that the sale should go to a 'Mr Yielding' and that no other person would bid for the farm. In turn, no other bids were offered at the sale and the price of £100, at which Divane had acquired the farm, was considered well under the real value of the interest which was rumoured to be around £500 or £600. A campaign was orchestrated to force Divane to give up the farm. Under the auspices of the local parish priest, Father O'Leary, collections were made for Rooney and a number of public letters were published in the county's newspapers chastising Divane as a landgrabber.[51] In consequence, Divane's trade was harmed and the Ballymacelligot Relief Committee stopped buying Indian meal from him.[52] Divane claimed that he knew nothing of the 'popular feeling' not to bid for the farm and offered to give it back at any time on condition that he was repaid the £100.

During the meeting of the Tralee Land League Thomas O'Rourke attempted to discuss the case, but Timothy Harrington, acting as president, prevented its introduction as it was a case of farmer against trader. He believed that the Land League's 'legitimate business . . . was to interfere in all cases of excessive rent but there was no case here of excessive rent'. Harrington complained that the rent 'seemed low' and each side were merely 'quarrelling with one another for the farm'. He attempted to distance the branch from the affair and claimed that 'in a matter of this kind we may lay ourselves open to grave suspicion by interfering with a trader with whom some of our members may be in competition'.[53] At the next meeting another attempt was made to introduce the case to the league. This time, Michael Power, a pig merchant and Fenian, giving testament to Harrington's fears, proposed that nothing be bought from Divane's store. Harrington again refused to entertain the matter and warned of potential discord. He stated: 'I know if we interfere between farmer and trader we shall yet come to a serious division upon some such case.'[54] It was rumoured in an unsigned letter to the press that Rooney had attempted to keep the price as low as possible in what was known as a 'sham sale' in order to defraud his creditors. Rooney's case exemplified the financial situation of many tenants. They had large personal debts, owing money to merchants and shopkeepers, while the interest in their holdings acted as security for many of these loans. The situation was summarised by an anonymous observer who wrote in the *Kerry Sentinel*:

> many farms are at present mortgaged for large sums, and that the creditors have no security for their loans except the right to turn the mortgages into money. . . these farms may be put up for auction any day.[55]

Despite Harrington's efforts the agrarian agitation began to incorporate resistance to such non-landlord debts. During early November 1880 in the Killarney region, the interest in two farms went up for sale under a sheriff's writ at the instance of Alexander McCarthy, a Cork butter merchant. No bids were made on the farms, which would have had fetched up to £300 two years previously, indicating a level of boycotting.[56] Tenants' attempts to prevent the sale of their holdings to undermine their creditors were not lost on local commentators. The *Tralee Chronicle* observed: 'if the impression generally obtained that farmers could mortgage their farms and spoil the sale afterwards . . . where is the merchant, trader, or banker that would lend him the money?'.[57]

As branches of the Land League emerged in other areas, cases of land sold to reclaim non-landlord debts became prominent. In Castleisland, a case came to the attention of the league concerning the farm of a bankrupt farmer who absconded. When the interest of the farm was sold to pay his debts, another tenant named Brosnan from the townland of Close bought the holding. Brosnan served the absconded tenant's wife, a Mrs O'Sullivan, who still held the land, with an ejectment notice. During a meeting of the Castleisland branch the president, P. D. Kenny, declared it a case of 'landgrabbing' leading to the appearance of a scathing unsigned letter in the press which expounded the fears of the bankers, merchants and farmers. The writer complained that according to the 'gospel of the Castleisland Land League, it is not safe to give any farmer credit as he refuses to pay a decree or execution', concluding that as a result of the inability to reclaim 'lawful debts. . . no well regulated society can exist'.[58]

The doctrine of the Land League was clearly too simplistic for the complexities of the agrarian economy. The heavy debts acquired by farmers from shopkeepers, merchants and banks were central to the financial difficulties farmers were in. When tenants lost their farms due to recovery of these non-landlord debts they were turning to the Land League for protection, although the protection of such tenants and their farms threatened the interests of the middle-class townsmen who made up much of the league leadership. The issue demonstrates the contradictions of the policies promulgated by the Land League.

LAND LEAGUE COURTS

The power of the league at a local level quickly materialised. At only the second meeting of the Tralee branch it was declared that J. W. O'Connor, the farmer who took the farm Flaherty had been evicted from four months previously, had given up the holding.[59] The Castleisland branch also demonstrated its ability to enforce its regulations on agrarian matters. At a meeting of the branch, two tenants named Browne and Keane were accused of taking evicted land. Despite protestations from a local Catholic curate, Father Murphy, that the issue was a family matter and should have nothing to do with the branch, it was decided that 'if his [Browne's] hands are clean let him come before the league'.[60] The two accused men failed to appear before the next meeting to explain their actions and were subsequently boycotted. Within a month, Browne submitted and, accompanied by two armed policemen, attended a league meeting and gave up the holding.[61] The Land League objective of preventing the retaking of evicted land appeared to have succeeded. By the end of October 1880 the RIC county inspector was of the belief that 'land from which tenants may be evicted will not be taken by other tenants, but allowed to remain uncultivated, during the present excited state of the people'.[62]

As the power of local branches grew, the proceedings of branch meetings came to resemble 'land courts'. Aggrieved individuals brought cases before meetings. Complaints dealt with not just landlord activities but also competing claims by tenants over land. In dealing with such disputes local branches of the league achieved a large degree of power and control. These cases also provided the opportunity to put the ideology of the league into practice. However, such disputes were regularly complicated and protracted affairs and often highlighted the failures of the 'law of the league'. In Tralee, a case came before the league in December 1880, which demonstrated the complexity of many agrarian disputes and some of the dynamics behind the activities of the league courts. A man named Edward Ferris complained to the league that two men named Leane and McElligot took a farm from which he was evicted. Ferris claimed that when he was faced with eviction his father-in-law had offered to pay the arrears but that the landlord had refused. Thomas Leane and William McElligott were given the holding on the payment of a fine with a 31-year lease.[63] The Tralee League called the new tenants to appear before the branch. Both Leane and McElligott claimed they got full consent from Ferris to take the land, a claim which he denied. Both parties obtained sworn affidavits from Tralee-based solicitors as evidence in their cases. During the hearing, Harrington asked Leane and McElligott would they give up the farm if they received remuneration for the outlay they spent on the farm. They refused, asking why Ferris had not come to them before they started spending money on the farm and stated 'we did not know this law [of the league] was in place when we took it'.[64] Two central figures in the case were Ferris's father-in-law, William Talbot, and brother-in-law, John Talbot. Talbot senior was a well-established figure within the region. He was a rate collector with connections within local government. He originally held the farm but gave it to Ferris when he married his daughter. Talbot had a number of other agricultural holdings, all of which he claimed his children lived on.[65] His son, John Talbot, who was a butter merchant and had a shop in the town, had also become a leading figure in the league in Tralee, sitting on the committee.[66] Despite Harrington's attempts to deal with the case with caution it became clear that Ferris, with the help of his in-laws' influence, was going to win. Both Leane and McElligott left the meeting before a judgment had been reached.[67] The case illustrates extensive problems within the league. Personal disputes concerning competing tenants' claims over land came to the forefront of branch meetings. These were not directly related to landlord–tenant relations and were potentially divisive. It also appeared that leading members of local branches were using the power of the league to further personal and family interests.

Similar cases involving complicated struggles over land became prominent at meetings. During another meeting a woman named Catherine McMahon applied to the league concerning a farm she had been evicted from in 1868 in the Tralee region. Some time after her eviction the new tenant became 'broken down' and the holding was subsequently let to various other tenants for grazing purposes. Invoking the 'unwritten law', she claimed that two of these tenants, Patrick and Michael McMahon (two brothers who were also her nephews), were already wealthy, had a number of other holdings and could afford to give up the farm which she wanted for her children.[68] Indeed, both men were well established. Patrick McMahon not only grazed farms but was also a butter merchant, while Michael McMahon was a poor law guardian, and a founding member of the league in the town.[69] Although the McMahons were slow to respond, William Hillard of Denny Street, Tralee, gave up part of the lands that he grazed. Patrick Divane, who had been previously targeted for buying the interest in Rooney's farm but had by this stage emerged as a prominent member of the league, said he would give up the 28 acres of the holding which he held.[70] Tenants also turned to the Land League to gain retribution from a past loss of land. At Killarney David Hegarty of Glenflesk brought his brother before the local league. Hegarty had previously handed the farm over to his sibling because he could not pay the rent but was now seeking it back. When the league asked his brother if he would return it to him, he refused. He claimed he had lost money on it and retorted: 'where was the Land League when I came and paid the rent for it two years ago?'.[71]

Issues such as these came to dominate proceedings of meetings. Individuals brought forward claims over land that they had lost to other tenants and had little to do with landlord–tenant relations. These were often complicated intra-tenant affairs with much personal and family rivalry involved. Many of the disputes were born out of the economic activity of tenants and traders who engaged in post-Famine agrarian capitalism and acquired the interest in extra land. Timothy Harrington attempted to prevent local branches of the league becoming embroiled in such affairs. Speaking at a meeting to establish a branch in Ardfert he 'counselled the members . . . to be very careful in the selection of the cases presented to them for consideration at the meetings of the league'. He warned the Ardfert Leaguers that 'it as a very serious danger in other branches of the league, that cases which it was absurd to entertain, and in which it would be impossible to do any good, were being bought forward constantly'.[72] During a branch meeting of the Tralee Land League, Harrington warned of the large number of cases before the branch and complained that someone had recently asked him to take one on that was 15 years old.[73] By January 1880 Harrington bitterly complained that the activities of the Tralee branch 'were such as to seriously injure the character of this league, if not its very existence'. He also warned that he would dissolve the branch if they continued to deal with cases that were out of the remit of the Land League.[74]

The cases that came before the league's branch meetings in the latter half of 1880 demonstrated a number of salient aspects relating to agrarian tensions during the period. The set of grievances around which the Land League officially mobilised and its objectives outlined by the leadership in Parnell and Davitt concentrated wholly on landlord–tenant relations, and failed to acknowledge other underlying economic tensions. When the law of the league came into practice at a branch level, much of the local conflict had little to do with landlords and was based on intra-tenant and family squabbles. This gives validity to David Fitzpatrick's assessment of agrarian disorder which highlights such tensions as primary motivating factors in agrarian disorder.[75] His analysis counters Samuel Clark's premise that the land war was a 'challenging collectivity' of the various sections of the tenant population against landlordism.[76] The evidence from the branch activity of the Land League in Kerry during the later months of 1880 demonstrates the limits of the 'challenging collectivity' thesis. While the varying groups within the broad nationalist community were unified under the Land League banner and its anti-landlordism, the challenges and realities of agrarian capitalism threatened to divide the movement at an everyday level. The ideology of the movement and its failure to acknowledge or address the economic realities of agrarian society led to serious internal divisions. This divisiveness resulted from complicated land disputes which had their origins in tenants' agrarian economic activity during the 1860s and 1870s. From the evidence of Kerry, a modified version of Clark's 'challenging collectivity' is needed to understand the development of the land war. Although the various interest groups in non-landlord society had successfully aligned to form the Land League, collegiality was threatened by a range intra-tenant disputes. While such disputes fuelled everyday agrarian conflict as much as landlord aggression, these tensions did not transcend into the political sphere either at a local or national level. The unwritten law of agrarian society from which the Land League drew inspiration has been viewed as an alternative legal system and set of customs that challenged the official law on agrarian matters. The unwritten law is not only ascribed to the Land League period, but also during the pre-Famine agrarianism and up to the alternative courts of the revolutionary Dáil Éireann.[77] Regardless of the existence of a wider alternative value system in rural Ireland, it would appear from the evidence in the newspaper reports of the Kerry Land League courts that the majority of disputes were between tenants and bound up in post-Famine economic activities.

GOVERNMENT VERSUS LAND LEAGUE: POLARISATION
OF SOCIETY

While the development of the Land League signalled the emergence of extensive hostility towards landlordism, the state and government increasingly became the focus of league criticism. As the agitation wore on, much hostility developed towards the RIC. Clashes between the police and mobs of people became common. As early as July 1880 police accompanying bailiffs at an eviction were attacked by rioters with stones and bottles.[78] During league public meetings there was often a threat of violence against the police. When a meeting of the league was held in Ballyduff in October a full-scale riot broke out after a police reporter attempted to get on to the platform.[79] In December three riots were reported by the RIC in the county. During one of these riots, the house of a man who had prosecuted a member of the Land League for assault in Listowel was set upon by a mob.[80] When the police arrived, they were met with a burning barrel of paraffin oil and stone throwers, and it took them two hours to disperse the crowd.[81] Members of the league were increasingly antagonistic towards the police. In November a confidential report from the RIC county inspector investigated the character of a leading Tralee Leaguer and suspected Fenian, Michael Power. In the report the county inspector commented that until recently the police in the district had not considered Power to be a 'violent or turbulent character'. During the rioting at the election for the Tralee Borough in March 1880 Power 'was a figure holding order and preserving the peace and gave very great assistance to the constabulary in doing so'. By October 1880, during the league demonstration at Ballyduff, the county inspector 'was much surprised he [Power] allowed stones to be thrown at the constabulary' and stated that 'my opinion of him since then is very much altered'.[82] Anti-landlord feeling materialised into antagonism against the police and government.

The politicisation of the agitation into a movement against both landlords and state was fuelled by the government's response. The historian Philip Bull, commenting broadly on the Land League and the later Plan of Campaign and the United Irish League agitations, highlights a strategy of passive resistance common to those three agrarian movements. He states that the substantial advantage of such a strategy 'is the dilemma in which it places government, for it creates a challenge to authority which can be confronted only by methods which often serve to facilitate the agitation'.[83] The degree to which the land agitation can be described as a form of 'passive resistance' is debatable. Bew has written that the 'rent at the point of the bayonet' policy of the Land League was in effect an offensive strategy.[84] The intimidation, outrage and public disorder that dominated much of the agitation were examples of direct action by the protagonists. Bull has shown that governmental responses to the land war exacerbated the situation and propelled the league movement. This was particularly demonstrated by the arrest of the national leaders of the Land League in November 1880 on charges of conspiracy, leading to public outcry.[85] By late January the 'state trial' ended with the acquittal of the Land League leaders owing to a jury disagreement.[86] It has been contended that the real importance of this trial for Gladstone's Liberal government was to demonstrate the impotence of the ordinary law in order to justify the forthcoming coercion legislation.[87] This hinted at official desperation and 'was a lame, hopeless attempt to assert the authority of Dublin authority', which only enhanced the position and popularity of the league and its leaders.[88]

In Kerry, anti-government feeling became even more pronounced with the arrest of the leading members of the Tralee branch of the Land League in January 1881. On 7 January 1881, RIC officers entered a branch meeting of the Tralee Land League and arrested the officers and committee members. They were charged with having

> illegally and seditiously formed themselves into a court for the purpose of trying questions touching the occupation of land in this county and have taken upon themselves to adjudicate, and have adjudicated on such cases, and have made certain orders unlawfully and without any lawful authority so to do, have exercised coercive jurisdiction.[89]

The charges were related to five land cases which had dominated the Tralee Land League in the months since its inception. Likewise, in other regions in the country the government brought legal proceedings against local Land League figures. Within a number of days 12 leading members of the Mullinavat branch of the Land League in County Kilkenny were arrested on boycotting charges.[90] The case of the Tralee Leaguers became a test of the law in the county as did the 'state trials' which were occurring concurrently in Dublin. This ensured that political events in Kerry remained in constant step with those on a national level.

The arrests propelled Kerry to the forefront of the agitation nationally. Two days after the detainments, the Land League leader Michael Davitt arrived in Tralee for a demonstration to protest against the government's action. The parish priest for the area, Father O'Leary, an opponent of the league, urged the government to suppress the meeting on the grounds that it would lead to abusive speeches and boycotting.[91] In consequence of O'Leary's advice and the increasingly volatile situation concerning the arrests in Tralee, the meeting was suppressed. When Davitt arrived at Clogher (five miles from Tralee) for the meeting he was met by a large force of police and army under the control of the resident magistrate, Bodkin. Despite this, Davitt successfully delivered a speech from a wagon. His speech was indicative of the increasing antagonism within the league towards both the police and the state. He stated that as a result of recent police action 'the administration of justice in Ireland would not suffer if the whole of them bag and luggage left the country', although he did contend that 'they are the party in power, they represent the law in this country, and they have bayonets and buckshot and everything else behind them'.[92] He also urged that the traders arrested should receive four times more trade.

Following the arrests, the case of the government quickly turned into farce. In the initial inquiry into the charges brought against the league members, a lack of sufficient evidence to prosecute the prisoners was apparent. The government lawyers relied on information from the individuals called before the league, to provide evidence of the existence of the 'courts'. Under the public glare witness after witness sided with the league. When William Hillard was asked if he had attended a court hearing after being summoned by the league out of a sense of fear, he merely replied: 'I would not expect that I would be injured in my business'. Another witness, Laurence Redmond, secretary to the Tralee Harbour Board, stated he attended the league court on his own free will. When Patrick Divane came before the inquiry as a possible witness for the government, he said that 'he was heart and soul with the objectives of the league'.[93] In an attempt to connect Thomas O'Rourke with handwritten letters summoning people to come before the league, the inquiry called a shop assistant who had previously been in his employment. Despite working for O'Rourke for five or six years, he said: 'I would not know my own handwriting at times' and failed to identify the writing when it was exhibited to him.[94] When a reporter for the *Kerry Sentinel*, who appeared before the inquiry, was asked for his notes on meetings he had reported on, he said that they had been lost. Thereafter he declined to answer the government solicitors' questions of meetings he had attended, on the grounds that the case was a prosecution for conspiracy, and that he would therefore incriminate himself if he gave evidence.[95]

The prosecuting solicitors were further undermined by a robust performance from the prisoners' legal defence. During one cross examination of a witness, the arrested leaguers' solicitor, Broderick, cited the clauses of a supposed lease from Lord Headley to depict the harshness of landlordism. The lease consisted of prohibitive restrictions such as preventing tenants from having more than one dog or giving a neighbour a basket of turf or lime.[96] When the government prosecutors prevailed upon a witness to state that he had received intimidating threatening letters after proceedings in a league meeting concerning him, Broderick suggested that police had sent them. A combination of the hostility of the witnesses called and the effective defence of the prisoners made the inquiry and the government look absurd. Within a month the prisoners were released without charge.[97] This provided the league with a propaganda and moral victory over the police and government which, as Bull has suggested, encouraged the public to identify with the league's methods

The arrests had a decisive effect on the league in the county. Before the arrests the large number of divisive land cases that came before branch meetings threatened to undermine the movement. Many had little to do with landlord–tenant relations and official Land League policy. With the arrest of the Tralee Leaguers, branches quickly turned away from hearing cases in fear of similar action. At the initial meeting of the Ballymacelligot branch it was stated: 'we are not going to hold a court, either civil, religious or ecclesiastic. We have simply to discuss our grievances in an orderly and a peaceful manner amongst ourselves.'[98] During a meeting of the Killarney branch the president, Geoffrey O'Donoghue (son of The O'Donoghue), said that they would not take any cases at present 'but [were] to go on enrolling members and keep the league on its legs'.[99] When a case concerning a land issue came before the Listowel branch, the president postponed hearing it, declaring that 'a discussion of this kind was too loose'. The policy of the league in the Listowel region was clearly defined in the following statement by the president:

> Bodies of tenants ought to come forward where their rents are too high, and let the public see there was good grounds for the present agitation. In fact the principal position of the Land League at present is a machinery of public opinion. In a few months the coercion bill will be passed and it is necessary to be very cautious as the Lord Lieutenant would have the power of putting any man, be he priest or layman, into the body of the gaol without trial. At the same time it is necessary to show that we are not afraid, and to show by public opinion that our

cause is a just one, and that we have reason to complain. We must act bold and determined, but at the same time within the limits of the law.[100]

The effect of the Tralee arrests, and the fear of impeding coercive legislation, discouraged branches from holding league courts not just in Kerry but also countrywide.[101]

NEW DIRECTION OF LAND LEAGUE POLICY: RENT AT THE POINT OF THE BAYONET

Once Harrington was released he set about reorganising the Land League in the county. During February 1881, Harrington, along with Michael Boyton, who had recently been acquitted after the failure of the 'state trials', held a number of demonstrations in Kerry.[102] Their imprisonment provided them with a new level of popularity and status. This was demonstrated when the president of the local league in Caherciveen, Father Lawlor, described Harrington as having 'fearlessly fought the battles of the people, [and] the magistrates have complimented him in their own peculiar fashion by keeping him in jail'.[103] Making use of their prominent status Harrington and Boyton re-shaped the methods of the movement. During a meeting held in Abbeydorney, Boyton outlined new legalistic techniques to undermine landlords. The meeting 'comprised all the principal farmers in the parish'.[104] Large tenant farmers such as Florence O'Sullivan who held a 150-acre farm were reported as in atten-dance.[105] Boyton advised these tenants to fight the landlord for the rent up to a certain point in the courts and then hand in the debt at the last moment. This method placed the legal costs on the landlord, which he said averaged £20.[106] In a definite indication of the large farmer bias of this strategy, Boyton told tenants that they might have to bear some cost. The ability or willingness of small landholders to pay such costs was limited, and this activity paralleled previous patterns of protest carried out by the prosperous tenantry during the tithe war.[107] This policy formulated the offensive strategy of the league known as 'rent at the point of the bayonet'. The new policy also demonstrated the reality of the motivations of tenant farmers, particularly larger ones, for joining the league. Although league activists still called from platforms for a peasant proprietorship and the abolition of landlordism, the policy was essentially moderate and designed to achieve concessions within a continuing landlord–tenant relationship.[108] Boyton and Harrington made similar addresses to meetings of the Land League in Castleisland, Killarney, Dingle, Tralee and Caherciveen.[109] The arrest and subsequent release of the Tralee Leaguers placed Timothy Harrington at the forefront of the movement in the county. This provided him with the platform to concentrate on the official league policy of 'rent at the point of the bayonet'. The arrests also greatly discouraged the holding of league 'courts'. This had the effect of avoiding the complicated land cases that were leading to discord and disunion between league members. Despite the efforts of the government, by February 1881 the Land League in Kerry appeared more unified and stronger than before.

The level of support for the Land League was demonstrated in the 1881 poor law election for the Tralee Board of Guardians. Local branches orchestrated voters ensuring that 26 out of 30 elected guardians supported the league, although this was not enough to unseat the *ex-officio* chairman and landlord, Major Rowan, who retained his position in a vote of the guardians by 29 to 26. After the election Timothy Harrington published the names of voters in the Tralee electoral division and how they voted.[110] This 'snapshot' of voting during the height of Land League influence demonstrate the support for the movement. In a major contribution to the historiography of the period, William Feingold has extensively analysed these election results.[111] Out of a sample of 319 voters of which 76 per cent were shopkeepers and tenant farmers, he uncovered a number of factors concerning those who supported the Land League. While the Land League succeeded in gaining a majority of votes from shopkeepers in Tralee town, it was slimmer than might be expected and it is clear that almost half the Tralee shopkeepers were not ready to throw their weight behind the league. The analysis goes on to show strong support for the league amongst small shopkeepers, but Feingold states that 'these variations are inconclusive and do not establish any significant differences in the degree of support offered to the league by shopkeepers of varying size'.[112] The voting patterns of tenant farmers are indicated to some extent. Although the sample of 56 tenants is limited and, as Feingold contends, 'not representative of all farmers in the region', he does highlight a number of significant trends. Large (valuation of holdings at £50 or more) and small farmers (valuation of holdings between £4 and £19) were more likely to support the Land League than middling farmers (valuation of holdings between £20 and £49).[113] The high support from larger tenants may have been related to the 'rent at the point of the bayonet policy' and the redirecting of the league's objectives towards this group. Despite these developments, the election results demonstrate that the league maintained support from smaller tenants.

Increasingly the Catholic clergy began to emerge at the forefront of the movement. The role of the priests in the Land League branches was initially limited. No Catholic cleric joined the Tralee branch and at times priests failed to attend land demonstrations. Although never outwardly stated, this may have been as a result of the involvement of Fenian and IRB figures in the Tralee League, such as Michael Power. However, by 1881 the clergy emerged as a powerful section of the league's leadership in Kerry. The leading role of the clergy in the local movement was evident during the holding of a mass Land League demonstration in Tralee town in early March 1881. At the meeting, which the *Kerry Sentinel* claimed 25,000 people attended, 20 priests were reported on the platform. In an editorial, the *Sentinel* viewed the clergy's involvement as a positive development and stated that it 'will inspire still more determined enthusiasm into the tenant farmers of Kerry, who confidently look to them for manly and Christian guidance'.[114] The prominence of both large farmers and Catholic clergy illustrated the persistence of pre-land war rural local leadership structures in the Land League.[115] Similarly, the ongoing arrests of the more radical members of the local league leadership under the Protection of Person and Property Act created a vacuum which the clergy filled.[116] The reasserting of the power and influence of the clergy appeared to dampen the initial 'radical' surge of the agrarian agitation. During the last three months of 1880, a large-scale outbreak of agrarian outrages occurred with 220 outrages reported to the police in the county ensuring that Kerry jostled with Mayo and Galway at the top of the outrages table.[117] This escalation of rural outrage, along with an ever more trenchant statement of the league's demand for compulsory land purchase and peasant proprietorship, illustrated that the radical agrarian cause held sway in the wider agrarian agitation.[118] During the first three months of 1881 the number of agrarian outrages dropped significantly to 99.[119] By 1881 the influence of radical agrarians who were willing to use violence and intimidation to carry out the objectives of the league appeared to be somewhat lessened. This was most probably a direct result of the moderation of the league's demands in the 'rent at the point of the bayonet' policy, the increasing role of the Catholic clergy and the anticipation of the forthcoming coercive legislation.

APRIL TO SEPTEMBER: FROM LAND BILL TO SUPPRESSION

The Land League was a far from homogeneous group. The movement's sections had varying stances on its objectives and methods. These divisions were accentuated with the introduction of Gladstone's land bill in April 1881. The bill essentially granted the traditional tenant-right demand of the 'three Fs' which were tenant demands for fair rents, fixity of tenure, and free sale, although large sections of the tenantry – leaseholders and tenants in arrears – were excluded from benefiting from it. The legislation, which provided for the regulation of rent by the Land Commission, attracted support from 'moderate' leaguers and undoubtedly enticed support from the large tenant farmer class. The left-wing and more militant elements of the league, led by

Davitt and John Devoy, rejected the bill.[120] Similarly, John Dillon believed the bill was designed to push small farmers from the Land League, which would lead to its disintegration.[121] In late April 1881 a national convention was held by the Land League to debate the merits of the bill. Branches with over 500 members were entitled to appoint two delegates to the convention.[122] Eight representatives from Kerry branches attended the meeting. In a clear sign of the increasing clerical involvement in the movement, five of the eight were priests.[123] The convention itself was firmly under the control of Parnell (Davitt was imprisoned) and a moderate stance was adopted. Although the bill was vilified by the majority of the speakers at the convention, it was resolved to allow the parliamentary party to attempt to improve the bill through amendments.[124]

The bill was important for leading to the re-emergence of the Catholic clerical hierarchy at the centre of popular politics. Overcoming past divisions in the clergy, a meeting of the bishops was held in Maynooth to discuss the bill. In a unified manner they offered a general approval of the proposed legislation but set out a number of amendments that should be made when the bill passed through parliament.[125] This development, according to William O'Brien, led to Archbishop Croke succeeding 'in winning back the broad basis of the league and also in winning back the clergy's privileged relationship to it'.[126]

In Kerry the bill accentuated divisions between groups loyal to the Land League and Parnell, and more moderate clerics and large tenant farmers. Throughout the 1870s many large tenant farmers had frequently failed to support home rule and had attempted to concentrate the energies of the KTDA on landlord–tenant relations along the parameters of the 'three Fs', leading to extensive divisions within the movement. Although the Land League succeeded in incorporating the support of such farmers, their actual control over these recruits was 'remarkably loose'.[127] By April 1881 the views of this class in Kerry found a voice in the newly established *Kerry Independent*. Although its editor, Henry Brassill, was a leading leaguer and was arrested along with the other Tralee Leaguers in January 1881 over the holding of league courts, his newspaper failed to take the official league policy on the bill and enthusiastically welcomed it. It stated: 'after a careful perusal of the Land Bill introduced by Mr Gladstone we have no hesitation in pronouncing it a great measure, with some very notable shortcomings'.[128] The intervention of the bishops also led to much support for the bill. At a meeting of the Ardfert Land League the president, Father O'Donoghue, stated that the bill was acceptable if the bishops' amendments were granted. He also 'hoped the Irish members would not retard, but rather endeavour to facilitate its passing in an improved state if possible through the House of Commons'.[129] After a meeting of the Abbeydorney League it was reported that 'the general sense of the members present having been taken on the leading principles of the bill, it was found that the measure, if amended, as advised by the bishops of Ireland, would meet the universal approval of the farmers of the country'.[130] The bill, helped by the support of the bishops, received a very favourable response from some sections of the movement in the county.

This favourable reaction was at variance with the official policy of the Land League. The April convention declared that only the abolition of landlordism could be considered as a final solution to the land question although it left the parliamentary party at liberty to accept or reject the bill as they pleased.[131] The *Kerry Sentinel* remained within the parameters of the league's reaction to the bill. Commenting on the convention it observed that 'a large and undoubted majority were in favour of the immediate rejection of the bill'. The newspaper also commented: 'it is difficult for anyone who peruses the new land bill to escape the conclusion that it was specially devised to see Irishmen at variance with one another'.[132] Demonstrating the newspaper's, and Harrington's, loyalty to Parnell it concluded that 'Parnell and his trusted followers in parliament had amply proved themselves worthy, to the fullest extent, of the confidence of the people, and the unanimous vote of the convention assured them of the fact'.[133] There were other negative reactions to the bill in the county. Despite the stance of the bishops, certain Catholic clerical figures condemned it. At a land demonstration in Ballylongford Father Moynihan heavily criticised the act, believing that 'though some persons consider the bill a boon for Ireland, he looked upon it as a strangled, unarmed, and worthless bill'.[134] Furthermore, radical agrarianism remained a constant factor in the ongoing agitation. April witnessed a significant rise in agrarian outrages from any of the previous three months with 52 outrages reported.[135] By the end of April it was apparent that a range of different opinions and interest groups existed within the broad land movement. Reaction to Gladstone's land bill varied from a general approval from Catholic clergy and larger farmers to the much more muted response by the Parnellites. Also, agrarian radicals who were often stimulated by the extreme rhetoric of the league remained prominent in the county.

Notwithstanding the introduction of the land bill into parliament, the agitation continued in the country. By April 1881 landlords had reorganised in the form of the Property Defence Association (PDA) and provided a more effective resistance to the agitation.[136] This signalled the effective landlord counter-offensive to the land war and the actions of the Land League. The organisation was initially established in Dublin in December 1880 by a group of landlords and agents. To counter the league's 'rent at the point of the bayonet' policy, landlords and the PDA began bringing actions against tenants for an ordinary debt to recover rent.[137] Legally creditors could seize removable property from a debtor's land to redeem a bad debt. In the case of tenant farmers, this mainly meant livestock and agricultural produce such as harvested crops. The landlord, agent or bailiffs could seize the goods and enter the tenant's holding by opening gates and crossing fences. The process was cost effective and free of much legal wrangling for the landlord. The greatest advantage of this procedure, however, was the quickness in which it could be enforced. The landlord could seize the tenant's goods one day after a single gale of rent had fallen.[138] This was far quicker than enacting evictions which took anywhere between six to twelve months to carry out. The sheriff was also enabled to sell the tenant's interest in the holding, and if the tenant didn't 'buy in' at the sale he lost all right to redemption and any legal claim to the farm. This effectively undermined the successful league tactic of withholding the rent until the very last moment during a long-drawn-out eviction process. Organised by the PDA, landlords began undertaking the sale of tenants stock and interest at sheriffs' sales in what emerged as one of the most common events in the land war.[139]

In April the PDA became active in Kerry and helped to alter the direction of the agitation. The first significant sale occurred in Killarney when the interest of nine farms on the Kenmare estate was put up for auction.[140] Within a number of days the cattle of two prominent tenants was seized in the Tralee vicinity.[141] One of the tenants, John Kelliher, had been a leading member of the KTDA and was prominent in resisting rent rises on the Kenmare estate during the 1870s.[142] In May the interest of four tenants' holdings was sold in Killarney and fourteen in Listowel.[143] In July the interest in 25 tenants' holdings went for sale in Tralee.[144] Previously the league had simply prevented any bidding at such sales but by this stage the PDA provided agents to bid for the farms. If the tenant failed to 'buy in' the PDA agent would get the interest and employ 'emergency men' as caretakers on the farms. The official league response was to allow the tenants to pay the debt and costs and regain the holding. The league would then reimburse the tenant for the legal costs incurred. This largely failed, however. Out of the first eight sales of interest in the county, the Land League managed to buy only one. During one batch of sales in Killarney, the local league official proposed one shilling above what the 'emergency man' offered but was refused by the sheriff who would only take bids in pounds. The leaguer refused to go higher and the farms were lost.[145] During the Listowel sale in May, the league successfully protected tenants from losing the interest in their holdings. Timothy Harrington, who by this stage had been promoted as the leading league official in Munster, and John Stack, vice-president of the Listowel League, were present. The significance of the sale was heightened by the presence of Goddard, the leading agent of the PDA. Of the 14 sales, two tenants settled before the auction with their landlords, two farms were bought by the PDA, and the remaining eight

were bought by the league. On the farms bought by the league a 20 per cent
abatement, which had been offered by the landlord to the tenants if they paid
their rent, was lost.[146] At the next sheriff's sale in early July in Tralee, the
league bought the interest in all the 25 farms for sale bar one.[147] Evidently the
landlord's policy proved extremely effective. While the process of eviction was
a long and costly affair, the threat of selling the farmer's interest proved to be
an immediate method of getting rents.

The Land League's position of paying the legal fees of tenants was costly.
One large tenant who had his interest sold in Listowel had an annual rent of
£200 and £34 costs.[148] A tenant from the Duagh region who had a debt as low
as £21 had legal costs of £13.[149] The Newtownsandes branch sent a bill of £57 to
the Land League executive after defending five tenants at sales.[150] Although
in May Timothy Harrington claimed that the league had spent over £2,000 in
the county since its formation in October 1880, local branches found it
increasingly difficult to extract money promised by the central authority.[151]
After the Killarney League had failed to receive communication from the
central branch concerning a request to aid tenants who had the interest in
their holdings sold, members became increasingly agitated. During a branch
meeting members 'complained strongly of the delay that had taken place on
the part of the Dublin League. They were tired of that body.' One member
asked, 'where was the money going to?', and another stated that Galway was
getting six times more funds than Kerry.[152] By this stage the central executive
of the league had attempted to regulate the dispersal of funds by creating extra
bureaucracy. By July 1881 claimants had to fill out a document which had the
signatures of the president, treasurer and secretary of the local branch.[153] As
some local leaguers complained of the lack of funds, Parnellite figures
criticised tenants for their over reliance on league money. During a meeting of
the Tralee Land League, John Kelly, who by this stage had emerged as one of
Timothy Harrington's closet allies in the branch, complained that 'it was very
mean of the tenant farmers to be depending on the people of America for
sustenance in the present agitation'. He further criticised tenants for their
reliance on league funds by stating that 'the Irish people in America had to
earn their money by their sweat and the farmers should not expect the Land
League to assist them when they got into some slight trouble'.[154] During
another meeting of the Tralee League Harrington chastised tenants who
failed to pay their subscriptions to the branch. He commented that it was the
farmers 'who were most interested in the present agitation' and that they
'should keep it up and not the men who were going about the country as the
leaders risking a great deal, and in danger of being arrested at any moment'.
Harrington's frustration with such tenants was further demonstrated when he
said that 'the least the farmers ought to do was to pay in the paltry

subscription that was asked each year'.[155] This view of the tenant farmers differed greatly from that of the downtrodden poor tenant in fear of eviction which was central to Land League mythology.

The selling of tenants' interest at sheriffs' sales greatly undermined the league and forced the executive to change policy. From early July the central branch informed local leagues that the legal costs of tenants who 'bought in' would no longer be paid by the league.[156] In early July, the first sales under the new league policy were held in Tralee. The Tralee branch advised that some of the farms should go to landlords and that the cost of emergency men to hold the farms would cripple them.[157] Regardless of this stance, tenants showed a distinct unwillingness to lose the interest in their holdings and 'bought in' in all the 12 sales.[158] In August the interest in 23 farms went for sale in Tralee. The league was partially successful in preventing tenants from buying in. Nine of the 23 went to the PDA. Tensions emerged during the sale when Michael Power, representing the league, chastised tenants for paying the debts.[159] The increasingly militant policy of the league failed to receive support from striking tenants who demonstrated an unwillingness to lose their entire legal rights over their holdings.

Further tensions emerged within the movement after the executive refused to reimburse tenants who had previously 'bought in' at sheriff's sales. By August 1881 the legal costs incurred by two tenants during the sheriff's sale in Listowel in the previous May had not been paid by the central executive, even though on the day of the sale Timothy Harrington 'distinctly and publicly promised them that the costs suffered by them would be made good by the league'.[160] The application from the Listowel branch for their refund was turned down by the central executive, who stated that the tenants received an abatement on account of the actions of the league, which covered their legal expenses.[161] In reply, the president of the Listowel Land League, Father Moynihan, complained that other tenants on the property broke the rent strike and settled with their landlord incurring no legal costs, and those who acted on league advice were being punished. He bitterly informed the central authorities that

> we made promises at the time. Now these men must see they were deceived. We were deceived ourselves and under these conditions it will be impossible to work. This terrible fight has cost me as much anxiety and trouble and work as any other man, but if I am treated in this manner I must lose heart.[162]

By autumn 1881 much of the local structure of the league was divided.

At a national level Parnell was increasingly criticised over the land bill that was being debated in the House of Commons. His abstention from voting on it brought criticisms from the right-wing element of the movement. The

Nation, the *Freeman's Journal* and Archbishop Croke all criticised him sharply over his failure to support the legislation.[163] In Kerry these concerns found voice again in the *Kerry Independent*, a newspaper which previously supported the Land League. After Parnell failed to vote on the bill the paper's editorial stated: 'we are sorry and surprised that his Grace's [Archbishop Croke] advice has not been taken [by Parnell]'.[164] By August, with the enactment of the Land Act just a couple of weeks away, the newspaper's criticism of Parnell and the league's official policy towards the legislation intensified. In an editorial the *Kerry Independent* condemned the league and stated: 'instead of looking for what is practically impossible at present; let all loudly insist on getting what the bill in its present shape confers'.[165] In the next edition the newspaper described itself as 'a thorough land leaguer' but that it was 'ridiculous to reject the land bill' and criticised 'the extreme Parnellite party' for placing 'itself above and before the interest of the people'.[166] In turn, the *Independent* became embroiled in a war of words with the Parnellite *Sentinel*. This schism in the league ranks was significant considering that the editors of both the newspapers, Henry Brassill and Timothy Harrington, had been imprisoned together the previous January on charges of holding league courts in the town. The disintegration of the movement in the county was furthered when The O'Donoghue voted for the bill in parliament. In a retort to Parnell's accusation that those who voted for the bill were 'traitors to their country and the wishes of the party', The O'Donoghue attacked Parnell and the league in an open letter to the *Freeman's Journal* by stating:

> the truth is that the bill is as good as it is in spite of the attitude assumed by Mr Parnell towards the government and the Liberal Party. His bullying tone rendered concessions difficult by giving them the damaging appearance of having been extorted under threat; and I am convinced that to his mismanagement, to the very loathing his conduct must have created in the minds of the government and the Liberal party, we owe the exclusion of leaseholders prior to 1870 from the benefits of the bill . . . Now that the farmers have got a court for the settlement of rent, Mr Parnell advises them not to use it, or at all events to wait till he has manoeuvred so as to obtain some adverse decisions, which may give him an excuse for questioning the impartiality of the tribunal and a pretext for recommending the people not to avail themselves of the only means of getting out of their difficulties. I trust the tenantry will turn a deaf ear to such treacherous council; that every man who feels his rent too high will go before the Commission, and that the farmers as a body will give the Land League executive to understand that their duty is to apply the vast resources at their command to securing an equitable adjustment of rent.[167]

The introduction of the Land Act accentuated the divisions within the broad nationalist movement that the Land League had previously overcome. The whiggish segments of the movement and the more traditional tenant-righters which in Kerry were represented by The O'Donoghue were widely supportive of the legislation which effectively granted the long held tenant-right demand of the 'three Fs'.

The Land League was thrown into further turmoil with the arrest of Parnell in September 1881 under the Protection of Person and Property Act (PPP Act). Following quickly after his arrest, Parnell yielded to radical elements in his party and announced the No Rent Manifesto. In turn the government suppressed the Land League. The structure of the organisation was destroyed and branch meetings prohibited. Police watched the meeting places of branches and prevented any from taking place.[168] The local organisation of the league was wholly undermined. The PPP Act, introduced the previous March, was invoked to detain leading local figures of the movement. By the time of the suppression of the league in October, 21 people had already been arrested under the act in the county.[169] A number of these included the most prominent members of the league. In March, P. D. Kenny, president of the Castleisland branch of the Land League was arrested. By June, Timothy Harrington had also been imprisoned. Other influential league figures arrested in the county included the president of the Tuogh branch and Timothy Dooling.[170] After the suppression of the league more significant figures were arrested in the county. Michael Power and Jeremiah Leahy, leading members of the Tralee and Firies branches respectively, were arrested in the two weeks after the suppression of the league.[171] In late October Timothy Harrington, incarcerated in Galway Gaol, despondently informed Virginia Lynch of the executive of the Ladies Land League of the effect the arrests were having on him:

> To what goal are we standing at present? Tis very hard to say. I am in daily expectation of getting a telegram from Tralee announcing my brother's arrest. If that should happen one branch of home industry, *The Kerry Sentinel*, goes down, as I should make no effort to carry it on if he is arrested.[172]

The suppression of the Land League and imprisonment of its national and local leaders greatly undermined the movement. The suppression compounded its disintegration as tenant farmers increasingly turned away from the league as its radical undercurrents surfaced. The political vacuum created after the suppression of the league placed the militant and violent forces at the fore of the agrarian agitation, which unrealistically promulgated the 'no rent manifesto'. The incidence of agrarian outrage rose (in the three month period of September to November, 118 outrages were committed compared to 70 for the previous three months in the county) as the agitation entered its most violent stage.[173]

Between January and September 1881 the influence of middling to large tenant farmers became increasingly pronounced over the movement. The 'rent at the point of the bayonet' policy and the subsequent successful landlord reprisal of selling the interest in tenants holdings demonstrated that the rent war was being fought against a somewhat solvent tenantry who were ultimately bargaining with their landlords for a significant reduction in rent. The league in Kerry, under the direction of Timothy Harrington, intentionally manoeuvred the agitation in this direction and specifically enticed this middle-class farmer group into a rent strike. By funding the strike through payment of tenants' legal costs, these tenants had little to lose. For the league, the concentration of the movement on an almost mock rent battle removed the socially radical and divisive intra-tenantry problems, which had characterised the local activities of the league during the first three months of its existence. However, the league was never a fully integrated, united movement: various groups and interests existed together in a complex juxtaposition. Large tenant farmers had consistently demonstrated little enthusiasm towards home rule and Parnellism in the late 1870s to the extent that The O'Donoghue successfully reinvented himself as a leader of the nascent agitation in the county. It was not until late September 1880 that the Parnellites created a branch of the Land League in the county, which succeeded in gaining support from tenant farmers. A grassroots radicalism, which had been active since the start of 1880, played a vital part in the emergence of the league, leading to much violence and intimidation. The achievement of the Land League in October 1880 was the unification of these groups into one movement, although from April 1881 it became increasingly evident that tenant farmers were diverging from the official policy of the Land League. As rent strikes were undermined by the success of counter-tactics by landlords, larger tenant farmers, encouraged by the Catholic clergy, increasingly acknowledged the potential benefits of the 1881 Land Act. In an attempt to placate the radical element of the Land League leadership Parnell remained apprehensive towards the legislation. In Kerry, the Harringtons remained loyal to Parnell and promoted the official league policy, although it became increasingly apparent that large sections of the movement would not. The objectives of the larger tenants and clergy were clearly articulated by the *Kerry Independent* and The O'Donoghue voted for the Land Act and called on farmers to enter the courts of the Land Commission. The disintegration of the league was compounded by its suppression in October. The radical agrarian element continued to exist at a local level and began an often violent campaign to enforce the violent No Rent Manifesto.

In many ways, developments in Kerry in these years mirrored the national picture and the wider political developments. The rise of the league in late 1880, the implementation of the 'rent at the point of the bayonet' policies, the ultimate division over the introduction of the 1881 Land Act, and the subsequent extreme violence surrounding the No Rent Manifesto reflected the general development of the land war as outlined by historians such as Paul Bew. Leading Land League figures intervened in directing the agitation through frequent appearances in the county. The league leaders O'Connor and Biggar addressed land demonstrations during the initial surge, Davitt spoke in Tralee after arrest of the Tralee Leaguers, while Boyton promoted the introduction of the 'rent at the point of the bayonet' strategy. A large amount of direction from the league's central branch was forthcoming during the organisation's existence in Kerry, further indicating the importance of the national leadership in directing events beyond the centre. The local playing out of politics along class lines in late 1881 also mirrored the national response to the Land Act, with larger farmers and priests favouring the legislation. Such disintegration of the league along class lines was evident in other regions too, particularly Mayo where the historian Jordan has shown that the moderate and large farmer direction of the Land League led to the sidelining of smaller farmers in a movement that had become divided.[174] Such class divisions were not apparent in other regions that have been the focus of modern research, particularly in Leinster.[175] This outlines the limits to Clark's 'challenging collectivity' thesis which appears to have been largely applicable to the initial emergence of the movement. Although a general anti-landlordism and nationalism undoubtedly existed that attracted all non-landlord classes to the Land League, this unity was easily unravelled by the differing interests of the sectional groups in the movement. The disintegration of the league in Kerry demonstrated the importance of the middle and large farmers and clerical influences to the movement's early success. When these groupings accepted the significant but ultimately conservative 1881 Land Act, the local infrastructure of the Land League was unlikely to survive. Although the radical and Fenian-orientated agitators formed an important aspect of the local leadership structure and often provided the strong arm tactics necessary to enforce an agitation, without more middle-class support any organised mass movement such as the Land League had little opportunity to survive in the mainstream in Kerry and arguably beyond. Along with class differences in the overall nationalist movement, an array of intra-tenant tensions over access to land and credit disputes existed at an everyday level in tenant society.

Although these factors were behind a degree of boycotting and agrarian outrage, they did not become politicised and did not emerge in the political rhetoric of the land war.

FOUR

THE LAND LEAGUE, FENIANISM AND AGRARIAN VIOLENCE

—

Agrarian violence in nineteenth-century Ireland and its level of politicisation have been subject to much historical analysis.[1] It has been argued that Ribbon societies were centres of lower-class nationalism that were imbued with sectarianism and had a lineage to the Defender movement of the 1790s.[2] Similarly, Tom Garvin contends that Ribbonism was a well-institutionalised agitation that was of a proto-nationalist nature and that the basis of these societies was 'assimilated into later organisations of Fenianism, the Land League, Parnell's Irish National League and in particular Hibernianism'.[3] Recent research has countered the supposed link between pre-Famine movements and the violent outbreaks of the latter half of the nineteenth century. Concentrating on County Westmeath during what was widely believed to be the last Ribbon outbreak, in 1870–1, A. C. Murray has pointed out the inconsistencies in definitions of Ribbonism by government officials. Police frequently labelled crimes that they could not solve as acts of Ribbonism. He also contends that there is little evidence of co-operation between localities and concludes that the 'Westmeath case invites great scepticism of the image of Ribbonmen as revolutionary nationalists and doubt of any interpretation which attempted to define true or proper Ribbonism'.[4]

One of the main controversies surrounding Ribbonism concerns the level of nationalist consciousness of those who took part in it. Although County Kerry and much of southern Ireland were never areas of Ribbonism, other forms of agrarian violence occurred in the region. Most commonly in the pre-Famine era this took the form of Whiteboyism. Joseph Lee has noted that class tension between tenant farmers and agricultural labourers over conacre was a significant motivating factor behind such agrarian violence.[5] In contrast, another historian, Michael Beames has posited that Whiteboyism was mainly derived from landlord–tenant tensions. This agrarianism was based on a class consciousness. It was not the typical vehicle of protest for the Catholic rural community but collectively Whiteboys represented the poorer strata of society. They acted beyond the realms of the local and personal. As Beames puts it, 'strangers came together in the Whiteboys movements to pursue common objectives underwritten by a complex web of social, economic and psychological obligations. Essentially, Whiteboyism was the organised expression of a particular social class.'[6] Two central issues concern the historiography of agrarian violence in the pre- and post-Famine period: whether agrarian 'outrages' were an expression of nationalism and/or class-consciousness.

The nature of violence during the 1880s remains ambiguous. This is particularly true of the Land League. There is uncertainty about the emergence of the alliance between constitutional and physical force nationalism in the late 1870s and 'there remains an element of mystery about what precisely transpired between Parnell, Davitt and Devoy in the preparation of the "New Departure"'.[7] When the league applied the moral force of boycotting, the 'connection between ostracism and violence was indirect but pervasive'.[8] Invariably the league's power partially relied on 'a substratum of intimidation and real violence, though it was hard to quantify or apprehend'.[9] Although many league leaders promoted peaceful methods, the perpetration of violence in the wider agitation ensured that agrarian outrage became politicised. As politicians and the organisation of the league adopted agrarian agitation, this had 'the incidental effect of imposing the "peculiar institution" of "Whiteboyism" . . . on the grassroots structure of the first modern Irish political party'.[10] The Whiteboy tradition of local defence and arbitration was politicised in a countrywide nationalist movement. Notwithstanding these assertions, many of the causes of the violence of the pre- and post-Famine period still resonated during the Land League years. Opponents of the league frequently accused the movement of organising this violence from the top down. This culminated in the attempt of the Special Commission of 1888 to portray the Land League and its successor, the National League, as criminal conspiracies directly responsible for the widespread violence of the decade.[11] The level of actual involvement of the Land League in agrarian violence remains uncertain, and the role the IRB played in orchestrating such violence during the land war years also remains difficult to determine. As recently noted, the IRB's secrecy makes it difficult to determine the extent to which Fenian agitation was directed from Dublin or by local leaders.[12] The difficulty in determining the relationship between agrarian violence and Fenianism during this period is reflected in the current literature by Magee and Kelly.[13] Although both works concentrate on the intellectual, political and prosopographical development of Fenianism, little analysis of the IRB's relationship with agrarian violence is offered. This chapter will attempt to address this question by concentrating on agrarian outrages in County Kerry and their relationship with the Land League and Fenianism.

Agrarian violence undoubtedly grew in tandem with the Land League. Although outrages did occur in the immediate post-Famine period they never took the form of a systematic agrarian campaign. As table 4.1 demonstrates, up to 1879 the incidence of agrarian outrage remained low, offering little warning of the portentous violent upheaval that was to follow. Although Kerry was associated with the Whiteboyism of pre-Famine Ireland, this had largely faded away during the post-Famine years. The incidence of agrarian outrage dramatically rose in 1880 when 298 outrages were reported in the county. The majority of these occurred in the final three months of the year, which corresponded with the introduction and growth of the Land League in the county.[14] This provided the police with an inferential link between outrage and the Land League. This appeared particularly the case with Kerry as the widespread distress of the winter of 1879–80 appeared to have subsided by the autumn of 1880 leaving many with the belief that 'the increase in outrage [was] inexplicable except as a consequence of conspiracy'.[15] Joseph Lee has suggested a different explanation and posited that the slower onset of and recovery from the crisis in dairying caused the intensification of the violence in Kerry. This, according to Lee, was compounded by population pressures in the county, which saw the population rise by two per cent in the period 1871–81. The age of marriage rose, leaving a large number of discontented unmarried men consigned to the status of 'boys' willing to participate in Moonlight gangs.[16] Demographic and economic circumstances were undoubtedly important catalysts for the outbreak of violence.

Table 4.1: Number of agrarian outrages reported to the RIC in County Kerry, 1850–79

Years	1850–9	1860–9	1870–9
Number of outrages	48	45	73

Source: Return of outrages, 1879–93 (NAI, CSO ICR, vol. 1)

Notwithstanding these circumstances, a level of Land League complicity and politicisation of agrarian violence was also apparent. During the Special Commission in 1888, RIC Inspector Davis for the Castleisland district claimed that outrages were perpetrated by a secret society under instruction from the league leader, Michael Boyton, in Dublin.[17] The basis of suspicion for this lay in a speech that Boyton had given in Castleisland in September 1880 leading to the establishment of the Land League in the region. In a speech that he was later arrested for under the PPP Act, Boyton openly promoted extra-constitutional action.[18] Although Boyton stressed that no violence on the person was to be committed and that he 'won't encourage anything of that sort' he did promote attacks on landgrabbers' property. He warned grabbers: 'the fences will fall down . . . His corn will be cut down'. He discouraged the 'shooting of landlords and agents' but did state that 'when a man is charged with using violence to a landlord's agent it is the duty of the Land League to see that man gets a fair trial'.[19] The Castleisland region became notorious as a centre of violent upheaval. Other individuals in the region who openly promoted violence included a curate and Land League member named Father Murphy, who in September 1881 was reported as stating that some tenants were paying their rent 'by the back stairs' asking if there were 'no good night boys in the locality'.[20] Captain Plunkett, the Special Resident Magistrate (a senior position in the RIC) for the south-west, wrote of Castleisland that in 'no place in Ireland was as strong language used during the agitation'.[21]

Despite the assumptions of the police, it is difficult to fully establish the level of Land League involvement in agrarian violence. At the Special Commission in 1888 a large amount of evidence was presented that attempted to connect agrarian violence with the Land League in Kerry. Much of this evidence has to be dealt with carefully because of the wider controversy of fraudulent evidence, largely in the form of the infamous Pigott letters, which was presented before the commission.[22] Although the circumstances of the commission were dubious a large amount of evidence was heard in relation to agrarian violence in Kerry. During the commission the District Inspector for the Castleisland region contended that 'in the Land League there was an inner circle which organised the Fenians of the district into a Land League police, to carry out the behests of the league'.[23] A self-confessed Moonlighter named Thomas O'Connor described how he joined a secret society connected to the Castleisland Land League. After becoming a member of the league he was approached by a number of other members who attempted to enlist him to join the society. They 'used to say that I ought to join, that it would be a fine thing, a proud thing to be a soldier of Parnell's, and that I would get a little pay for doing nearly nothing'.[24] The members that approached him, George Twiss and John O'Connor, became renowned Moonlighters, a term for those who committed agrarian violence, in the area but neither belonged to the leadership of the Land League branch. After Thomas O'Connor agreed to join he swore an oath to the secret society in the room of the Land League secretary, Timothy Horan. O'Connor described the first Moonlight act he had undertaken when he, along with a group of 30 or 40 others, reinstated an evicted woman on a farm which had been taken by another tenant named Brown.[25] This particular case of landgrabbing had caused considerable consternation in the Castleisland League. Brown was called before the league in November 1880. When he failed to appear the chairman of the meeting, Father Murphy, called for him to be boycotted.[26] O'Connor claimed that the league's secretary, Timothy Horan, had paid him six shillings for his part in the action. O'Connor went on to allege that after this he was instructed by Timothy Harrington to intimidate voters during the 1881 Poor Law Election into voting for Land League candidates. He stated that Harrington told him he was 'to get them to sign the votes if possible and not to spare them, but not to kill them and not to hurt them too much'. For this O'Connor claimed he was also paid.[27] O'Connor's evidence to the Special Commission suggested that agrarian outrages were carried out on behalf of the Land League to enforce its objectives and regulations.

Although O'Connor's submissions were strongly contested and Harrington vehemently denied the allegations, other informants gave evidence to suggest widespread Land League involvement in agrarian violence. Another self-confessed Moonlighter named Denis Tobin gave evidence concerning secret society activity in the Brosna region. Brosna lay to the east of Castleisland, close to the border with Limerick and the town of Abbeyfeale and the district was the centre of much agrarian violence. During a Land League meeting of the Brosna branch in December 1880, open comments were made in support of the use of force.[28] In Tobin's evidence he stated that a Land League organiser named John McEnery swore him into a Moonlighting secret society in 1880. McEnery told him that 'the Moonlighters were the only support of the league, and were it not for the Moonlighters, the league would be no good'.[29] Tobin described how the district was divided into three different Moonlighter divisions with separate captains. McEnery was the head of the divisions and when he was arrested under the PPP Act another prominent leaguer named William Mangan replaced him.[30] Although Tobin never joined the Land League he spoke about how a member of the secret society 'had to attend the league meetings so as to hear the resolutions that would be passed against the parties who were to be raided on, and condemned by the league'.[31] He took part in a number of Moonlight raids, which seized cattle off evicted land and slaughtered them. He also posted a number of notices threatening a land-grabber named Batt O'Connor. They were posted 'on the ditch of the road . . . so that people going to Mass on Sunday would see them'. For this he received three shillings.[32] Although aspects of Tobin's evidence were questioned during the commission much of what he stated was later reiterated in a history of the area written in 1930.[33]

Another police informer and witness who appeared before the commission gave further insights into the relationship between the Land League and secret societies. James Buckley, an agricultural labourer, testified to joining the IRB in Causeway in November 1880. He went to a public house in the village where he was sworn in by a number of men. Thereafter he attended a Fenian meeting in the Land League rooms where a William Fenix was a central figure in the IRB circle. Fenix was also 'a very active member' on the committee of the Land League.[34] The RM for the region, Considine, believed that the IRB in Causeway was part of a wider organisation and reported to his superiors that 'men in Tralee . . . were directing the organisation who [were] in receipt of certain monies' and who 'undertook' to supply arms'.[35] At the commission, Buckley described how on 31 May 1881 he joined a party of Moonlighters from the surrounding parishes of Ballyduff and Killahan. They proceeded to the house of a tenant named Thomas Sheehy who had taken a farm, which his brother-in-law had previously held. They fired a shot into his house to intimidate him off the land.[36]

Buckley went on to describe how he was ordered to murder an expelled member of the Land League who was suspected of giving information to the police, which had led to the arrests of William Fenix and Thomas Dee under the PPP Act. Buckley was asked to shoot Roche, the suspected informer, and told that he would receive money from the Land League funds to go to America. On the day of the proposed assassination Buckley, who was armed with a revolver, began talking to Roche outside his house. When Roche turned his back to depart Buckley pointed the weapon at him and attempted to shoot. The revolver misfired and failed to shoot after three or four more attempts. Buckley then fled with Roche who was fully aware of the circumstances.[37] When Buckley went to receive the money to flee to America, Thomas Dee told him to go to the president of the Land League in the area, Thomas Pierce. Pierce was a 'gentleman farmer' and part of the middle-class leadership of the league. Pierce brought Buckley 'round to some of the neighbours . . . to collect money to aid me [Buckley] in my escape to America'. They visited a number of the large farmers in the region and received in total a mere four shillings. Some of the farmers 'promised in a few days but did not give it'.[38] Still without enough money he was sent to the secretary of the Lixnaw branch, Thomas Dooling.[39] Dooling was a central Land League figure in the region and was also suspected of being the head of the IRB in the region.[40] Although he obtained another five shillings from Dooling, Buckley failed to receive enough money for his emigration.

The evidence of O'Connor, Tobin and Buckley before the Special Commission must be dealt with a degree of scepticism in view of the infamous circumstances surrounding the evidence of Pigott and the forged Parnell letters. Much of the evidence was contested by the nationalist lawyers and some aspects of it appeared to be fabricated and the likelihood of Timothy Harrington utilising league funds to orchestrate intimidation was tenuous considering Harrington's constant attempts to moderate league activity. In the absence of other evidence into the activities of secret societies, at the very least the evidence would suggest that some individual members central to the leadership of league branches were also leading members of the secret societies. The actual rank and file figures that carried out the agrarian violence were not necessarily members of the Land League. They rarely attended league meetings and were directed by only one or two individuals who were members. All testified that they believed they were carrying out the wishes of the league although only one attested to having been sworn into the IRB, indicating that radical agrarianism was often independent from radical politics. They all received payment for their activities, which suggests that monetary gain was a substantial motivation for taking part. The evidence of Buckley in particular indicates that large tenant farmers, at the very least, sympathised with their activities and patronised them to a certain extent. However, the parsimonious reaction to Buckley's attempt to raise the necessary funds to emigrate suggested that while the farmer class was complicit in the orchestration of outrages they viewed the actual Moonlighters as dispensable. An analysis of those who were suspected by the police of involvement in outrages also shows the level of involvement of farmers. As table 4.2 demonstrates, out of 37 individuals suspected of orchestrating and carrying out outrages only seven were farmers. The largest group were farmers' sons who made up 17 of those suspected. A significant number of town dwellers in the form of office clerks and middle-class figures in the form of two auctioneers, and one editor, hotel keeper and merchant were suspected of involvement in the orchestration and carrying out of agrarian outrages.

Table 4.2: Occupation of individuals suspected by the RIC of being directly or indirectly involved in committing outrages during 1880 in County Kerry

Farmer	7
Farmers' son	13
Labourer	1
Small artisan	3
Office clerk	3
Auctioneer	2
Editor	1
Hotel Keeper	1
Merchant	1
Other	5
Total	37

Source: Lists of persons reasonably suspected of being directly or indirectly connected with outrages, 1880 (NAI, CSO RP, 1880 34686).

Despite the testimonies before the Special Commission, documentary evidence directly confirming Land League complicity in agrarian violence was largely non-existent. As with all secret society activity, little or no paper trail remained as to the inner workings of the Moonlighters. Any analysis of the Land League and its relationship with agrarian violence is further complicated by the lack of any extensive internal records of the Land League organisation.[41] The internal history of the central branch, apart from the reports of meetings regularly published in newspapers, is largely a blank because its records and papers all disappeared before the league was suppressed in 1881.[42] This was a central complaint of the counsel at the Special Commission who claimed that the records were destroyed to cover the illegal activities of the organisation. The lack of evidence proving the league's involvement in agrarian outrage was widely apparent at a local level also. During the commission an RIC officer for the Castleisland region, D. G. Huggins, testified that he believed the leadership of the Land League in Castleisland were behind the agrarian outrages in the area. When pressed for evidence he stated:

> On nearly every occasion on which I heard people, members of the Land League, speak at meetings, I heard landlords and bailiffs and men who had taken evicted farms denounced by those men and I believe that they made the men unpopular in the district and caused a great many outrages.[43]

When pushed for more substantial evidence he admitted he could not produce any positive proof or information linking anybody to secret societies. Despite this, the counsel for *The Times* believed they had unearthed a certain amount of documentary evidence that would prove 'undoubtedly that the National Land League, by which I [the attorney-general] mean the central office, was . . . paying for outrages'.[44] A central element of this evidence was a letter purporting to be from the secretary, Timothy Horan, of the Castleisland Land League to the central branch. In the letter Horan sought money to cover medical expenses of three individuals who were suffering from gunshot wounds. The fact that these individuals were members of a secret society was apparent when he wrote: 'no one knows the persons but the doctor, myself and the members of that society . . . If it were a public affair, a subscription would be opened at once for them, as they proved to be heroes.'[45] The letter concluded by asking for the money to be sent to him or to Father John Halligan, a curate in the district. Written on the back of the letter were the initials P. J. and the amount of £6 that was granted. It was dated 12 October 1881.

This document provided the counsel for *The Times* with the most significant evidence, which suggested that the central branch of the Land League funded agrarian violence. The handwriting of the letter was verified as that of Timothy Horan and its authenticity was never questioned by the nationalist lawyers unlike other controversial material presented at the commission. When John Ferguson, the Scottish businessman who was a founding member of the Land League, appeared before the commission it was deduced that he had attended central branch meetings during the period that the letter was dated.[46]

When the letter was put to him he claimed he knew nothing of it but did contend that the central branch did not publish details of all grants that were made to local branches. He also confirmed that the central branch granted money to support individuals who participated in boycotting. In relation to the Horan letter, after being asked if he morally supported giving money to individuals in those circumstances and whether this formed criminal activity, he replied:

> in Ireland, my Lord, we are bound to sympathise with men who are doing things that under a constitutionally governed country we dare not and would not sympathise with . . .. We cannot accept we are criminal when we are sympathising with our wounded countrymen even when they have gone beyond what is called law.[47]

Although Ferguson stressed that he was not referring to the activities of secret societies but to when individuals were injured by police at public demonstrations such as the infamous 'Mitchelstown Massacre', it did demonstrate a certain favourable attitude amongst certain sections of the leadership of the Land League towards extra-constitutional activity; however, other leading figures did not share Ferguson's views. When Arthur O'Connor was questioned on the Horan letter he stressed:

> I am perfectly aware I never saw it. If I had seen it I should have sent it back to the writer, with an intimation that the Land League funds were not available for such purposes. I think it was a most improper grant.[48]

Such a diversity of opinion represented the omnipresent differences between agrarian radicals and constitutional moderates in the Land League leadership.

The money granted to Horan was authorised by P. J. Quinn. Although Quinn was not a permanent secretary of the executive of the Land League he did grant funds if no other senior member was present at meetings.[49] Quinn, from Claremorris, was the centre of a Fenian IRB circle in County Mayo and an ex-schoolteacher, and had been involved in the Irishtown meeting. By January 1881 he became the head of the clerical staff of the league's central branch.[50] Horan knew Quinn personally, and in the letter referred to a 'private meeting' between the two at the convention of the league in September 1881 in Dublin. This evidence demonstrated that Quinn, a known Fenian, in his position in the league funded agrarian secret society activity in the Castleisland region. This evidence was central to the Special Commission and was one of the few genuine pieces of evidence that demonstrated a direct paper trail connecting the executive of the Land League with the perpetration of outrages.

It should be stressed that there was no evidence that demonstrated that the leadership of the league besides Quinn was complicit in funding violent activity. Also, the level of involvement of even a section of the personnel in the central branch's offices in the mass of outrages that were committed has to be questioned. The efficiency of the office was notoriously poor. In October 1881 Timothy Harrington, who had been recently elevated from his position in Kerry to a more prominent position in the movement, privately advised Parnell on reforms for the central branch. After viewing the office in operation he commented on the understaffing of the office and on 'the terrible pressure that was thrown on the few hands there'. He also complained that the secretary, Brennan, did too much of the writing and that the clerks should do it to a greater extent. He believed that the present clerks were far too political and that they should be non-political with no objective. He also informed Parnell that the legal costs the central branch was granting to tenants were far too high. He stated that much of the costs were being paid to individuals who 'wouldn't go to court unless the league paid his expenses' and that frequently the legal disputes were between tenants themselves as opposed to being against landlords. He stated that measures had to be introduced to reduce the amount of legal costs paid by the central branch.[51] Harrington was clearly demonstrating his organisational and fiscal abilities, which prompted Parnell to appoint him as secretary of the National League 12 months later. Harrington's report on the operational ability of the executive of the league demonstrated the inefficiency of the central office. His comments on the funds of the league concentrated on the cost of tenants' legal fees in relation to sheriffs' sales and evictions. This was in direct reference to the 'rent at the point of the bayonet' policy of the league. Harrington's comments indicate that the Land League was probably too inefficient to orchestrate outrage to any extensive level and that the funds of the league were largely used to provide the legal costs of agitating tenants. For Harrington at least, the funding of secret society activity was not a significant element of the activities of the central branch of the Land League. From the evidence available certain Fenian-orientated figures in the central branch, such as Quinn, may have granted league money to fund secret society activity, although the extent of such funding was limited. Harrington's comments suggest, moreover, that funds were concentrated on supporting the official polices of the league, such as 'rent at the point of a bayonet'.

A number of leading local Land League figures appeared to orchestrate the secret societies. The high level of opposition to outrages from many local leaders corresponded to the divisions within the central branch of the league. As early as August 1880 Timothy Harrington stated: 'the men of Kerry, who followed O'Connell in his monster gatherings, should know how to conduct agitation without outrage or violence'.[52] At the first meeting of the Castleisland branch outrages were condemned and it was argued that violence would 'ruin our cause'.[53] At the inaugural meeting of the Land League in Ardfert Timothy

Harrington explicitly condemned outrage.[54] Similarly, in February 1881, the Listowel branch spoke against the use of violence.[55] Throughout the Land League agitation condemnation of outrages was common in league rooms. League support for outrages was never total and some sections of the local leadership constantly attempted to prevent violence. In some regions a struggle for influence between moderates and radical agrarians was apparent. In Ballybunion the local curate, Father Godley, was of the opinion that:

> I was aware of the existence of a secret society in the parish and they had no sympathy with us [the league] in the beginning, but gradually we weaned them from the secret society, and subsequently they were satisfied with our consti-tutional society.[56]

In several places, only a single member within the leadership of a local branch usually directed secret societies. In Causeway, William Fenix led the secret society while holding the position of secretary in the local branch. In Castleisland, Horan who was also secretary of the league appeared to be the leading member in the secret society. As suggested by R. V. Comerford, individuals in or on the edges of local branches planned physical intimidation in support of league objectives.[57]

A new phase of the land war began with the arrest of Parnell, the announcement of the No Rent Manifesto and the subsequent suppression of the Land League in October 1881. The suppression of the league was followed by a new wave of violent agrarian outrage. Before the suppression of the league in Kerry no agrarian murder had been committed in the county. Although the number of outrages was high, they largely consisted of intimi-dation in the form of threatening letters and offences against property. Much outrage was directly related to the campaigns of rent resistance such as organ-ised protest against seizures, sheriffs' sales and evictions. Attacks on landlords, agents and anti-league tenants were largely a means to strengthening the campaigns against rent.[58] In the 12 months between the emergence of the Land League in Kerry in October 1880 to the suppression of the movement, 12 agrarian outrages which consisted of firing at the person and five of firing into dwellings were recorded by the RIC. For the 13-month period after the suppression of the league between November 1881 and December 1882 four agrarian murders were committed, 12 firings at dwellings and 21 incidents of firing at the person.[59] This was a significant increase in the number of serious agrarian outrages.

The mass imprisonment of 'moderate' league leaders under the PPP Act and suppression of the Land League in late 1881 undoubtedly removed previous restrictions and discipline, leaving, as F. S. L. Lyons has commented, 'agrarian anarchy. . . to operate almost unchecked'.[60] While the instability created after the widespread arrests led to much outrage, government officials also suspected radical and Fenian elements in the league leadership of orchestrating much of the violence for political purposes. They maintained that the increase in crime had the 'object of discrediting the government's decision to suppress the Land League'.[61] The Dublin Metropolitan Police informed the Chief Secretary's office that eight secret society organisers were dispersed around the country to orchestrate violent outrage under the direction of the extremist Patrick Egan. It was believed that £1,000 of league funds, which had previously been given as a 'sop' to the Fenians, was 'now doled out for the purpose of procuring the perpetration of crime'.[62] The police also reported that league activists were told to 'shoot away'.[63] The policed evidently believed that the upsurge in violence after the suppression of the league was politically motivated.

Whatever the assumptions of the police, violence was intense in Kerry and particularly in the Castleisland region. Since the late 1870s Fenians were active in the area and appeared to have been central to the emergence of the local Land League. Evidence suggests that the Land League executive partly funded this violence. In the period between December 1880 and April 1881 a systematic campaign of night raids for arms and intimidation of tenants and landlord employees was under way in the region. According to evidence submitted by a local police constable named D. G. Huggins to the Special Commission, 24 separate attacks by armed gangs were made in this five-month period. They demanded money, weapons, administered illegal oaths and damaged livestock and property.[64]

In one of the more vicious of these attacks both ears were cut off a bailiff named Michael Dennehy in the employment of the landlord Herbert of Muckross on 26 April 1881.[65] The previous day Maurice Murphy, a hotel owner and leading member of the Castleisland League, warned Dennehy to give up serving writs for eviction. Murphy told him to return the writs and go to 'Terry Brosnan and nothing will happen'.[66] Brosnan was another leading league figure in the region and a publican whose son was also the assistant secretary of the Castleisland Land League. Dennehy failed to do as instructed and was subsequently attacked. The DI for the region, Davis, believed that 'Brosnan instigated it' and that his public 'house is the resort of Fenians . . . [and] of all the known disloyal characters about this town'. The police reported that Brosnan was 'generally believed to be the organiser of all the raids for arms which took place in this district in December 1880 and January 1881'.[67] Dennehy also identified one of his attackers, Patrick Quinlan, as the nephew of a farmer who he had previously served a writ on, Lawrence Quinlan. The police believed that the Quinlans' house was 'a meeting place for the night boys' and that Patrick with his two brothers, Lawrence and William, committed the outrage along with one other man named Cornelius Hussey. Hussey had recently returned from America and was a brother of another suspected Moonlighter Edward Hussey who was believed to have previously attacked a house that belonged to a gamekeeper of Drummond's named James Black in January 1881. Black was beaten and two guns and a revolver were stolen from him.[68] It was reported that Hussey 'was constantly seen by the police in company with bad characters and is believed to have been concerned in all the raids for arms made in this district'.[69] Moreover, the Husseys and Quinlans were neighbouring families. In May 1881, the three Quinlan brothers and Cornelius Hussey were imprisoned for committing the attack on Dennehy. Timothy Brosnan and his son were also imprisoned under the Act although not specifically for the Dennehy outrage.[70] The attack on Dennehy demonstrated a complex set of relationships surrounding agrarian violence. Some sections of the local leadership of the Land League appeared to be aware that an attack was imminent, which was indicated by Murphy's warning to Dennehy. The police were of the opinion that Brosnan had orchestrated the attack, while those that had carried it out were a group of neighbouring farmers' sons and were widely suspected of being members of a secret society Moonlight gang. In this case there appeared to be direct evidence that the local leadership of league were aligned with younger famers' sons in the commission of outrages to enforce the law of the league.

During the following months outrages continued, although at a less serious rate. Between May 1881 and the end of September only one shooting occurred in the region.[71] However, the suppression of the league and the No Rent Manifesto in October 1881 led to an unprecedented level of agrarian violence. Threatening letters, illegal oaths and raids for arms continued and tenants who paid their rents were met with violence. In October a tenant named Maloney who paid his rent had his horse mutilated.[72] In November another tenant named Thomas Galvin of Doonane was shot in the thigh for the same offence. The same Moonlight gang which was led by the younger members of the Husseys and Quinlans was involved. Lawrence Quinlan had been released from prison for the previous attack on Dennehy after a number of weeks owing to his young age and was believed to have led the Moonlight gang in the shooting.[73] Bartholomew Hussey (brother of Cornelius and Edward) were suspected of participating in the attack as were two men named Edmond Healy and Jeremiah Reidy. Both Healy and Reidy were suspected of involvement in previous Moonlighting activity in the region but had absconded when the PPP Act came into law.[74] Quinlan, Hussey, Reidy (a farm servant) and two others named John Coffey (a farm servant) and Henry Williams were imprisoned for the attack in December 1881.[75] In the Cordal district of Castleisland another Moonlight gang were in operation. In December several farmers were visited by a group of 12 to 14 men who were disguised and were 'wearing wigs and whiskers of cows' hair'.[76] The farmers were intimidated to maintain the rent strike. During the same month a tenant in the area named Michael Flynn was shot in the leg. On Christmas Day six houses were visited, their inhabitants warned not to pay rent and arms were demanded.[77] In February 1882 threatening notices appeared from 'Captain Moonlight' offering £50 rewards for 'the rentpayers head' in the Castleisland region.[78] During February and March three more tenants were shot at for paying rent in the district indicating the existence of a violent campaign to enforce the No Rent Manifesto.

The first murder of the agitation in the Castleisland district, and indeed in Kerry, occurred soon after when an unpopular local magistrate named Arthur Herbert was attacked on 30 March 1882 and shot three times.[79] He was murdered in the townland of Lissheenbawn, two miles from Castleisland town. While acting as a magistrate he had controversially stated that if he was present at a riot at Brosna that he was investigating he would have used buckshot on the crowd; he concluded that 'there would be no peace in the country until such people would be "skivered"'.[80] He was also a land agent in the region. District Inspector Davis believed that Herbert was killed because of his position as a land agent as opposed to that of a magistrate indicating an agrarian as opposed to political motivation.[81] Herbert had previously been the focus of severe criticism from the Land League. During a Land League meeting in July 1881 at Knockabowl near Castleisland Herbert was publicly threatened during a speech in which it was stated that he 'would be made fly like a redshank'.[82] During another meeting Timothy O'Connor Brosnan, the league leader who the police believed orchestrated the earlier attack on Dennehy, referred to 'skiver'em Herbert' and said that the people were poor because of him.[83] Although the Moonlighter Patrick Quinlan was imprisoned at the time of Herbert's murder he was previously involved in a planned attack on him, which fell through at the last moment.[84] The weapons used to shoot Herbert had been taken in a raid on a farmer's house in April 1881, indicating a connection between previous outrages that the Quinlan and Hussey gang had undertaken and the murder.[85] Although the police failed to identify and imprison any of the perpetrators of the murder it did appear to have emanated from those responsible for the systematic campaign of intimidation and violence in the region, which was carried out by a number of Moonlighters closely associated with local Land League figures. The rise in violent agrarian crime was not confined to Castleisland. By the end of 1882 another three agrarian murders were committed. In June, 65-year-old Patrick Cahill was shot five times with a revolver for working as a herd on an evicted farm near Tralee. In the Killarney region in August a gang of seven men armed with rifles and revolvers dragged a tenant farmer from his bed and shot him three times in front of his wife and stabbed him in the hip and shoulder. He had taken grazing land from an evicted farm. In October another tenant, Thomas Browne, was shot at Drummulton near Castleisland.[86] Moonlighting gangs willing to use violent methods including murder were evidently in existence in several parts of the county.

While much of the violence of the No Rent Manifesto in Kerry and particularly in Castleisland was undoubtedly orchestrated by individuals close to the Land League, the police also suspected Fenian and IRB orchestration. The authorities were certain that, despite the suppression of the Land League, Fenians remained organised and were responsible for much of the violence of the No Rent Manifesto. The police suspected that as late as October 1882 Fenian meetings were held in both Tralee and Castleisland to elect officers and to plan outrages.[87] Some of those who perpetrated outrages claimed to be Fenians. A threatening letter of October 1881 warned that the 'landgrabber must die . . . let him beware a nation['s] curses will be on his head and Irish Fenians will be on his track and the bullet will end his days'.[88] The police believed that the upsurge in violent outrage in Castleisland corresponded with the return of a man named Kenny from America in February 1882, suggesting a connection between events in Kerry with a wider revolutionary campaign. Kenny, whose brother Patrick was a large tenant farmer and formerly president of the Castleisland Land League, was suspected by the police to have been closely connected to the Fenian and leading Land Leaguer P. J. Sheridan. On his return from the United States to Castleisland, the police believed Kenny began orchestrating outrages.[89] This led the resident magistrate for the district to suggest that the Castleisland Fenians were 'connected with similar societies in Tralee and Cork' and were 'in communication with the O'Donovan Rossa party in America, receiving its presumed instructions'.[90] Fenian involvement in agrarian violence was also suspected in other parts of the county. In the Ballybunion region during March 1882 a tenant named Martin Costello was shot in the leg, supposedly for paying his rent. After the arrest of two men for the outrage the police also charged them with being members of a 'treasonable society, having for its object the dethronement of the Queen'.[91] During a magisterial inquiry into the attack the district inspector for the region, Crane, stated that he was 'officially aware of a conspiracy not to pay rent and a conspiracy to establish an Irish Republic'.[92] In 1884 it was again suggested that Fenians in Kerry were connected to a wider international IRB network when a dynamite attack occurred on the residence of the controversial land agent Samuel Hussey at Edenburn on the outskirts of Castleisland. The attack, which failed to injure anyone, was attributed to Fenians from outside the region. Hussey believed that no local person was involved in the attack although the perpetrators were housed in the vicinity.[93] The police were of the opinion that members of the 'dynamite conspiracy' undertook the attack.[94] An investigation into the explosives revealed that the same substances were used in Fenian attacks in Glasgow and Edinburgh in 1883. It was also believed that the explosives were similar to one found on a man named Denis Deasy in Liverpool. Deasy had smuggled the 'infernal machine' from Cork indicating that the one used against Hussey might have originated from there.[95] The attack may have been part of a wider Fenian 'dynamite war' which consisted of attacks in London during late 1883 and early 1884; this was associated with the New York-based Fenian Jeremiah O'Donovan Rossa and the 'Skirmishing Fund'.[96] There were several attempts to plant bombs in the London Underground, which were largely a failure, and no one was killed during any of these attacks.[97] Such involvement by American-based Fenians in local agrarian activity was also evident elsewhere in the southwest of Ireland. Recent scholarship has demonstrated that the Land League in Ballydehob west Cork during 1881 was run by a circle of Fenians which was influenced to some degree by the Fenian John O'Connor of the Cork Land League and were directly involved with O'Donovan Rossa in America.[98]

Although there is much evidence to suggest that the upsurge in agrarian violence in Kerry after the suppression of the Land League was orchestrated by a wider Fenian-related conspiracy, the full extent of IRB and Fenian involvement in agrarian secret society activity in Kerry is impossible to fully determine. The level of Fenian activity was frequently overestimated by the police. This was particularly the case in 1882 when the police apprehended a suspected Moonlighter named O'Connell from Millstreet in northwest Cork near the Kerry border.[99] Acting as an informer, O'Connell told the police that a Fenian body consisting of 1,500 to 1,600 members with over 1,000 arms including dynamite was the source of agrarian outrages in the region. He claimed that the secret society was part of a wider organisation with a hierarchical structure based on a 'district, county and national network' and that it received funds from Land League.[100] The police believed that the 'information he gave was invaluable as it led to the conviction of four men. . . to the arrest of several and to the complete breaking up of the conspiracy'.[101] Considering the extent of O'Connell's claims and that the police had initially arrested 32 individuals, four convictions were a poor return. Moreover, the police did not discover the large stores of arms, which O'Connell claimed were hidden in the area. Some of O'Connell's accusations appeared to have been unfounded and exaggerated. Arguably, the information he gave the police was determined by the fact he was a paid informer who received a full pardon and was later granted expenses and £55 to emigrate to Australia.[102]

The case of O'Connell shows that the police easily believed that much of the agrarian upheaval emanated from Fenianism and the Land League, yet many agrarian outrages attacks were often motivated by complex personal disputes and vendettas. The three Quinlan brothers were arrested for an attack on a process server who had served a writ on their uncle. Similarly, when Lawrence Quinlan was suspected of leading the attack that led to the shooting of Galvin, the police suspected that he had a personal motivation because other tenants in the townland who had also paid their rent were not punished.[103] The police believed that Cahill was murdered as a result of competition between him and another tenant over land, which he was about to take.[104] The murder of Thomas Browne in Drumulton in September 1882 illustrates the complexities that surrounded many agrarian outrages during the period. Shot in the middle of the day by two undisguised men, the police believed it was the work of Fenians.[105] Two men named Poff and Barrett were subsequently arrested and hanged for the murder. Poff was an evicted tenant and had previously been imprisoned for firing a shot at a caretaker of an evicted farm. However, it was widely believed that both Poff and Barrett were innocent of the crime, which most probably emanated from the jealousies of two neighbouring farmers when Brown bought the fee simple in their holdings and in turn became the landlord to his imme-diate neighbours. The murder seems to have had little to do with Fenianism, and resulted from a localised agrarian dispute concerning ownership of land. Although both Poff and Barrett maintained their innocence, and despite signi-ficant public sympathy, they were hanged in January 1883. This further created animosity towards the authorities and greatly embittered their relations with the public.[106]

By the end of 1882 Kerry had become synonymous with agrarian violence and was one of the most disturbed counties in Ireland. During the existence of the Land League, it was apparent that a section of its members had close ties with the IRB and orchestrated much of the agrarian violence and received support from radical Land Leaguers and Fenians outside the county. Although the number of outrages had increased in tandem with the emergence of the Land League's anti-landlord agitation, and appeared to support its objectives, the violence was often based on tightly knit familial and neighbour networks and was not official league policy. In the highly agitated Castleisland region much of the violence appeared to emanate from a Moonlight gang centred on the Quinlan, Hussey and Brosnan families. While those that committed the outrages were not leading league members the police suspected that some leaders such as Timothy O'Connor Brosnan orchestrated the violence. Such a crossover of personal involved in the Land League and in secret society activity undoubtedly existed. However, powerful social groups within the movement, including the Catholic clergy and leading local political figures personified in Timothy Harrington, actively opposed violence. The suppression of the Land League led to a new phase of serious agrarian violence and a number of murders. This surge in violence appeared to be associated with Fenianism and a revolutionary insurgency. The police believed that much of the violence emanated from a combination of local Fenian circles located in Tralee and Castleisland and a wider radical conspiracy with ties in the United States. The dynamite attack on Hussey's house was easily definable as part of a wider 'conspiracy' and demonstrated the ability of Fenians to act in Kerry, yet much of the violence was also a result of internal community tensions over access to land. The violence of 1880–2 was thus motivated by a mixture of an anti-landlord Land League sentiment intermeshed with localised and personal agrarian disputes, which at times appeared to be subject to wider Fenian influences. Moreover, the violence of the Land League and No Rent Manifesto was supported by a significant section of the rural population in pursuit of a combination of immediate agrarian concerns, anti-landlordism and, in some cases, a wider Fenian ideal.

Joseph Lee has argued that demographic circumstances in Kerry partly explain the outbreak of agrarian outrage in the county. Lee highlighted how age of marriage increased more rapidly in Kerry during the 1870s than in any other Irish county, leading to the social frustrations of young males with reduced marriage and inheritance opportunities. In the Listowel Poor Law Union alone during the period 1871 and 1881 there was a 30 per cent increase in the number of single men aged between 20 and 29 compared to a mere seven per cent in Munster. Traditional emigration possibilities to North America were closed off, leaving a potentially large number of recruits for agitation in the active age group.[107] The involvement of younger farmers' sons such as the Quinlans and Husseys in the committal of outrages during the period gives some credence to Lee's assertions. However, the timeline of agitation, with the most serious violence not breaking out until over a year after the establishment of the Land League in the county, demonstrated that other factors besides social frustrations were at play in the pattern of violence. Evidence of orchestration by local Land League leaders and a wider Fenian conspiracy suggests that much of the violence was a political as much as a social phenomenon. While pre-Famine Whiteboyism is viewed as the defence of traditional lower-class agrarian rights, those higher up the social stratum were engaged in agrarian violence in Kerry during the early 1880s. Such political and middle-class involvement in the orchestration of agrarian violence demonstrates that Lee's view that the violence as a product of the social frustrations of young, unmarried and landless males needs to be tempered.

FIVE

THE IRISH NATIONAL LEAGUE AND THE REVIVAL OF HOME RULE

OCTOBER 1882 TO SEPTEMBER 1885

The outcome of the conference of October, 1882, was the complete eclipse, by a purely parliamentary substitute, of what had been a semi-revolutionary organisation. It was, in a sense, the overthrow of a movement and the enthronement of a man, the replacing of Nationalism by Parnellism; the investing of the fortunes and guidance of the agitation, both for national self government and land reform, in a leader's nominal dictatorship.
Michael Davitt, *The Fall of Feudalism in Ireland* (London, 1904), p. 377.

—

With the signing of the Kilmainham Treaty in April 1882 the land war and the agrarian agitation that had dominated previous years were greatly defused countrywide. Within this atmosphere of quietened agrarian tensions the Irish National League was established in October 1882. The new organisation was founded by Parnell and placed him at the head of nationalist politics. The programme and constitution of the new league, drafted by T. M. Healy and Timothy Harrington (recently elevated to the leadership of movement), were clearly influenced by Parnell.[1] The new organisation's main focus was on constitutional politics and attempted to remove agrarian radicalism and the influence of Fenianism from popular politics. The left-wing agrarian radical and Fenian element, which had provided much of the leadership of the Land League, was sidelined in the new organisation. Radical agrarians such as Patrick Egan had departed Ireland by the time of the emergence of the new league. The most agrarian-minded parliamentarian, John Dillon, had also vacated the political scene. Although Dillon cited medical reasons for his departure from Irish politics, many suspected that the conservative new direction of the political movement was a motivating factor.[2] Some attempt was made to placate the agrarian element with the appointment of Thomas Brennan as the National League's honorary secretary, along with Timothy Harrington. The *Kerry Sentinel* recognised this when it wrote about the leading officials of the National League. It commented that Brennan was 'instinctively a radical of the radicals' while Harrington was 'a man instinctively a conservative as Mr Brennan is naturally a radical'.[3] However, Brennan, like

Dillon and Egan, soon left for America too. Davitt remained in Ireland and did accept membership of the organising committee of the new league and supported its programme, but his position in the movement was greatly undermined, if not destroyed, by his division with Parnell over Davitt's policy of land nationalisation.[4] With the radical agrarian and Fenian section sidelined, the leadership of the National League was to be dominated by a central clique loyal to Parnell and intent on replacing any form of radical agrarian agitation with a constitutional movement which was socially conservative and orientated towards parliamentary rather than popular politics.[5] Indeed, the movement attempted to dilute the 'alliance of agrarian, constitutional and physical force nationalism that was Parnellism'.[6] The new Parnellism tried to reinvent itself to become more acceptable to 'Westminster opinion' and the new organisation 'laid great emphasis on its legal and constitutional character' while 'agrarian objectives were downplayed'.[7]

It is generally assumed that Parnell's endeavour succeeded and that the Irish National League under the dominance of the party became the near exclusive forum of nationalism by late 1885. Central to this development was Parnell's charismatic leadership and the leadership's bureaucratic control of the National League.[8] The presumption that the Parnellite leadership was the central agent in disseminating a nationalism that came to dominance in 1885 is an example of historical analysis from 'above'. This analysis counters trends in modern historiography to study events from 'below', concentrating on the importance of social and economic change as determining factors in periods of political upheaval. This approach has been significantly adapted to the modern study of the period, 1878–82. Modern historiography has pointed towards the post-Famine structural changes in Irish society as explanations for the outbreak of the land agitation. The themes emphasised here included the importance of a united rural and urban bourgeoisie, the general rising expectations of the non-gentry population, and class tensions within nationalist Ireland, as explanations for the origins and development of the land war.[9] These understandings are centrally tied to depicting large-scale social and economic changes as catalysts for political transformation. In contrast to this body of work, the historiography of the 1882–5 period largely concentrates on Parnell and 'high politics' and little attempt is made to fully understand the popularity of the political ideology of home rule or Parnellism at a local level.[10] Arguably this is understandable considering that nationalist ideology is inevitably disseminated from 'above' by the leaders and spokesmen of such movements.[11] For the 1882–5 years, this appears particularly true when the autocratic National League acted as the electioneering machine for the successful return of Parnellite MPs in the 1885 general election.[12] Yet this concentration on politics at a high level fails to offer an analysis of how the agrarian semi-revolutionary land war, rooted in local realities and long term economic and social developments, transformed into a broad nationalist and constitutional movement with home rule as its focal point. This chapter looks at the emergence and popularity of the Irish National League between 1882 and 1885 and how it failed to gain any significant support from tenant farmers during its early stages. It also considers how developments such as sports and the creation of butter factories led to alignments between would-be nationalists, gentry figures and unionist middle-class Protestants which appeared to override the objectives of home rule. A split in the National League in Tralee town demonstrates the tensions between the central and local leadership and the contradictions between the conservative and more radical forces that made up the league.

OCTOBER 1882: ESTABLISHMENT OF THE IRISH NATIONAL LEAGUE

With Davitt and radical agrarianism isolated from influencing the National League, Parnell successfully took the mantle of the leadership of Irish Nationalist politics and redirected the focus from the land to the national question. The constitution of the new league placed the attainment of home rule as its principal objective with the land question relegated to secondary importance.[13] This represented a significant move from the farmer-dominated politics of the Land League. The new league intended to incorporate support from the various classes in Irish society. Class antagonisms or allegiances were to be overcome 'for the cause of Ireland'. The *Kerry Sentinel* described this stance of the new league in an editorial:

> the interests of the farmer, the labourer, the trader, and the artisan should be identical, and the cause of all together should be the cause of Ireland . . . branches of the Irish National League will be expected to devote themselves to the encouragement of the labour and trade interests as well as the farming interest.[14]

Despite the National League's pan-class appeal, the new organisation failed initially to develop extensively in Kerry. By January 1883, only four branches existed in the county, at Brosna, Firies, Ballyduff and Listowel. This was a low participation rate compared to neighbouring counties. Cork and Limerick had 15 branches each, although Clare was similar with five. Countrywide, 276 branches had been created by February 1883.[15] The Kerry branches had a similar composition to the previous Land League. In Listowel, the leading members of the new National League were, according to the police, all 'prominent

Land Leaguers'.[16] The new league's secretary, John Stack, and treasurer, Robert Stack, had held the same positions in the town's Land League. Three of the five committee members were also members of the original Land League committee.[17] Similarly, the Firies branch demonstrated a continuity of membership. The newly appointed Special Resident Magistrate (SRM) for Cork and Kerry, Captain T. O. Plunkett, identified Edward Harrington, John Kelly, John McMahon, Jeremiah Leahy, Patrick Murphy and Father O'Connor as the leading members in the Firies branch.[18] Harrington, Kelly and McMahon had been prominent Land Leaguers from Tralee town, while Leahy and Father O'Connor were prominent in the Land League branch in the Firies district. Similarly, in the Ballyduff region, Timothy Dowling, long associated with the local agitation was a leading member.[19] Unsurprisingly, figures that formed the leadership of the Land League branches were central to the new organisation. These formed a core of political agitators who had acted as the local leadership of popular politics during the land war.

Although the new National League branches had the same leading personnel as the Land League, the momentum provided by the economic crisis that had propelled the dramatic emergence of the Land League in the winter of 1880 was not present in the winter of 1882. The agrarian economy had to some degree emerged from the depression which marked the late 1870s and agricultural prices had in general risen.[20] The failure of the National League to develop was further compounded by successive government legislation in the form of Gladstone's 1881 Land Act and 1882 Arrears Act. The decisions and reductions offered by the Land Courts of the Land Commission, created under the 1881 Act, dominated the attention of tenant farmers. Tenant farmers eagerly entered the commission to get rent reductions. During the commission's first statutory year in operation tenants and landlords made 3,335 applications to have rents fixed in the county.[21] The hearings of the vast majority of these applicants were delayed and by August 1882 the commission had fixed only 327 cases.[22] It was not until March 1883 that the commission began to make progress with the massive backlog of cases. From then until the end of the year the commission fixed a monthly average of 130 cases. By the end of December 1883, the commission had set a total of 1,892 new rents for tenant farmers in Kerry.

Table 5.1 Number of rents fixed by the Land Commission in County Kerry, Munster and Ireland, August 1881–December 1883

	Kerry	Munster	Ireland
Aug.–Dec. 1881	66	304	1,313
Apr. 1882	44	726	2,507
May	55	399	1,955

	Kerry	Munster	Ireland
June	68	340	1,781
July	94	604	2,636
Aug.	0	428	1,754
Sept.–Oct.	89	400	1,958
Nov.	80	400	2,759
Dec.	21	386	1,638
Jan. 1883	40	253	1,632
Feb.	79	235	1,990
Mar.	123	791	3,938
Apr.	175	806	3,259
May	173	659	3,954
June	120	717	3,525
July	195	773	3,655
Aug.	63	652	2,405
Sept.	1	115	823
Oct.	225	517	3,578
Nov.	126	482	3,279
Dec.	87	554	2,918
Total	1,924	10,541	53,257

Source: Return, according to provinces and counties, of judicial rents fixed by sub-commissioners and Civil Bill Courts, as notified to the Irish Land Commission, up to 31 Dec. 1881 (up to 31 Dec. 1884).

During this period tenant farmers attentively followed the commission's hearings and subsequent judgments. As early as 1882 a land agent, Simon Little, who attended a number of Land Commission hearings in Kerry, complained to a House of Lords Select Committee established to investigate the workings of the 1881 Land Act that farmers' energy and time were devoted to gaining rent reductions and the business of the Land Commission. He stated:

> it [the Land Act] has disturbed their minds so much that they have all of a sudden found out that their rent is too high, and they come in wholesale clamouring for reduction; and as regards the younger tenants, men from twenty-five to thirty years of age, they have neglected their business terribly; they have all turned legislators; . . . they go in and spend their day in the towns meeting together.[23]

The middle to large tenant farmers availed themselves extensively of the reductions granted by the commission. Of the 1,892 rents fixed in Kerry, tenants whose farms had a government valuation between the valuations of £10 and £50 made up 46.4 per cent of this number, despite representing only 29.6 per cent of the county's holdings. Tenants in Kerry could on average have expected a 23.5 per cent reduction in rent from the courts.[24] For many tenants this was a sizeable reduction in rent and represented a profitable return from their support of the Land League. Smaller tenants availed themselves of the act to a more limited extent. Fifty per cent of the total rents fixed by the Land Commission in Kerry were for farm holdings valued under £10. This was considerably disproportionate to the total number of farms in the county at such a value, which amounted to 67.2 per cent. The reductions these small farmers did receive were often largely undermined by the cost of legal expenses, which reached approximately £3 per case.[25] Only 6.2 per cent of all farm holdings under the £10 valuation received rent reductions compared to 13.1 per cent in the £10 to £50 and eleven per cent in the over £50 bracket. The middle to large farmer group, who held land valued at above £10, benefited mostly from the decisions reached by the Land Commission.

Table 5.2: The number of cases fixed by the Land Commission by valuation, the total number of such holdings, and the proportion of such holdings with rents fixed compared to the overall total in County Kerry, August 1881–December 1883

	Under £10	£10–£50	Over £50
Number and percentage of cases fixed by valuation of the holdings by the Land Commission	946 (50%)	879 (46.4%)	67 (3.5%)
Number and percentage of the total number of holdings in the county	15,225 (67.2%)	6,710 (29.6%)	613 (2.7%)
Proportion of holdings with rent fixed compared to total number of each valuation.	6.2%	13.1%	11%

Source: *Return, according to provinces and counties, of judicial rents fixed by sub-commissioners and Civil Bill Courts, as notified to the Irish Land Commission, up to 31 Dec. 1881* (up to 31 Dec. 1883); *Return of agricultural holdings, compiled by the Local Government Board in Ireland from the returns furnished by the clerks of the poor law unions in Ireland 1881*, pp. 4–7, HC 1881[C 2934], xcii, 793.

The widespread lowering of rents by the Land Commission signified an unheralded gain by tenants over their landlords. It relieved much of the tension between the two groups. In turn, rural society was greatly stabilised and the commission acted as the 'main agent in the deflation of the land war'.[26] The Listowel region, which had been the centre of serious agrarian disorder and as late as August 1882 had parishes proclaimed by the police as a result of outrages committed there, was by October described as 'peaceful and much improved' by Resident Magistrate Massey. He believed that this was due to 'the contentment to a certain extent of the farming class'.[27] Similarly in the Killarney region it was reported by the RM that tenants' 'attention is at present engaged in taking advantage of the Arrears Bill' and rents were paid in 'some instances for the purpose of taking advantage of it'.[28] The National League, with home rule at the forefront of its agenda, failed to compete with the Land Commission in attracting tenants' interest during 1883. The vital group of middle to large sized farmers had little appetite for the National League and such tenants mainly concentrated on gaining rent reductions in the Land Courts.

The new organisation was further undermined by a general apprehension towards potentially violent agrarian agitation. Although the Land League agitation was undoubtedly associated with intimidation and agrarian outrages, no agrarian murder had been committed in the county until 1882 during the violent aftermath of the No Rent Manifesto. This bloody period witnessed an increase in serious violence with three murders and many shootings.[29] By October 1882, many tenant farmers were increasingly apprehensive towards any form of agitation. During that month the RM for the Killarney region stated: 'the more respectable classes of this district express serious apprehension of an increase of outrage during the coming winter. A number of farmers are in the most abject state of terror.'[30] Such hesitancy was also evident in the Ballyduff region. There, the leading figures of the newly formed National League were widely suspected of being heavily involved in violent secret societies. Significantly, two of its principal members had been arrested under the Protection of Persons and Property Act. The police contended that as a result of the branch's radicalism, the farmers in the region had failed to join it and by February 1883 the police believed the branch had collapsed.[31] Condemnation of the violence of the agitation appeared to be widespread. In March 1882 the Land League mouthpiece, the *Sentinel*, condemned Captain Moonlight as 'barbaric' and claimed that agrarian violence exhausted the 'resources of human civilisation'.[32] During June the Roman Catholic Bishop Higgins of Kerry, while speaking in the disturbed district of Castleisland after a recent murder, declared:

> [I] was in Dublin during the past week and in many places I saw to my regret, placarded 'horrible murder near Tralee', 'horrible murder in Kerry'. Why I was ashamed as a Kerryman, and not alone as a Kerryman, but as bishop of the diocese.[33]

After the Phoenix Park murders there was further condemnation of violence, and a number of 'indignation meetings' were held across the county to protest against the assassinations.[34] A certain weariness of the violent outrages during the recent agitation was apparent by the end of 1882. Such violence had alienated many of the middle to large tenant farmers who had previously supported the Land League from the agitation. While Parnell successfully sidelined radical agrarianism in the National League leadership, it was also apparent that tenant farmers were not willing to engage in any political activity that might have led to the re-emergence of the extremism that had marked the No Rent Manifesto.

Apprehension amongst tenants over the implications of agrarian violence was further compounded by the introduction of the 'police tax'. Under the provisions of government legislation stretching back to the 1870 Peace and Preservation Act extra police could be placed in disturbed parishes whose cost was met by the ratepayers of the region in what was known as the 'police tax'. This measure was reintroduced under the Crimes Act of 1882.[35] In July of that year the SRM for the south-west, Captain Plunkett, issued a statement warning that if outrages did not cease in the violent districts he would send extra police to these areas.[36] Over the following months Plunkett carried out his threat. By September 1882 12 parishes in the county had to meet the cost for 70 extra police at a total cost of £557.[37] Fear of the police tax undermined the popularity of the new league. In February 1883 a body of leaguers led by Edward Harrington and John Kelly went to the chairman of the Tralee Town Commissions, John Hayes, to ask him to convene a meeting of the National League.[38] Hayes was a local industrialist and, although never a fully fledged active member of the Land League, had led a fund to pay for Parnell's legal defence in November 1880.[39] He had also acted as a surety for bail for Timothy Harrington after he was arrested in Tralee in January 1881.[40] He was representative of the wealthier, respectable and socially conservative middle class to which Parnell's new movement tried to appeal. Notwithstanding Hayes's past support of the Tralee Leaguers, he refused the request, stating that the establishment of a league branch in the town could lead to agrarian outrage and the subsequent introduction of the police tax.[41] Although the National League was established as a constitutional and parliamentary organisation, apprehension that the new movement would precipitate a renewed violent agitation undermined its progress. Despite the constitutionalist policy of Parnell and rightward shift of the league at a national level, by 1883 many potential supporters in Kerry associated the movement with violent radicalism. In stark contrast to the emergence of the Land League, the National League failed to harness large-scale public support.

The National League was further undermined by other coercive powers provided for by the 1882 Crimes Act. A public meeting of the National League, announced to be held in Causeway in early 1883, was suppressed under the Act. When organisers attempted to hold the meeting it was dispersed by police and led to 15 prosecutions.[42] Police officials regularly cited the Crimes Act as the primary reason for the stabilising of the county from agitation.[43] The powers of the Crimes Act were enforced when the printing press of the *Kerry Sentinel* was seized and its editor, Edward Harrington, was arrested and subsequently imprisoned for six months. By this stage Edward Harrington had emerged as the leading nationalist figure in the county and had taken over the editorship of the *Kerry Sentinel* after his brother, Timothy, had been elevated into Parnell's leadership circle and the national political stage. During May 1883 notices, which referred to the 'bloody English Government' and called for 'death to landlords, agents and bailiffs', appeared on a number of walls in Tralee town.[44] It transpired that they were printed on the printing press in the *Sentinel*'s offices. During the trial, which was held under the Crimes Act, Harrington realistically claimed that two young 'headless' apprentices employed in the offices printed them. Notwithstanding this defence, Harrington received a six month sentence depriving the league of its leading figure in Kerry.[45] The coercive legislation of the Crimes Act undermined the emergence of the National League throughout 1882–4.

As farmers largely avoided the new league, agricultural labourers emerged as a significant group within the movement at a local level. The labourers' question had been formally adopted by the Land League at the September 1881 convention. Following this, many meetings became known as 'Land and Labour' meetings.[46] Before the suppression of the Land League, labour issues became more prominent at local branch meetings. A number of resolutions were passed by branches in the county demanding that farmers give a half acre (conacre) to their labourers at the same rent that they paid their landlord.[47] After the suppression of the Land League, a Labour League emerged in 1882. In Munster alone over 200 branches were formed.[48] There was Labour League activity in Kerry at Ballyduff, Brosna and Knocknagoshel.[49] Despite the name of the organisation, the police believed that it was merely a continuation of the Land League. The Special Resident Magistrate, Plunkett, stated the Labour League was

> simply the Land League over again. They are not organised for the purpose of benefiting the labourers but for the purpose of holding public meetings with a view of forming branches in every place to carry on the work of the [Land] League and to promulgate the same doctrines as before.[50]

An attempt to centralise these Labour Leagues under a Dublin authority was made in August 1882 when the Irish Labour and Industrial Union was established. Although the body espoused labourer causes, the executive was clearly made up of ex-Land Leaguers with little or no record of promoting labourers' rights, and when the National League was established the labour organisation was merged with the new movement.[51] As Pádraig Lane has demonstrated:

> when a Central Labour League Executive appeared it was dominated by Parnell and so that when a National Labour League was formally established that month [August 1882] it was so obviously a subterfuge for the old Land League that when the National League was formed somewhat later it absorbed it.[52]

Although the National League easily overtook the short-lived Labour League, labourers undoubtedly mobilised during this period. While farmers could look at the benefits of the Land Act as a return on their participation in the Land League agitation, labourers had achieved little. This discontentment was recognised by the advocates of the National League in Kerry. Agricultural labourers and their cause featured prominently at initial National League meetings. At the first Ballyduff National League meeting, the Tralee Leaguer and ex-Fenian, John Kelly, announced that 'the labourer interest will be looked to with greater care than it has been before'.[53] During the establishment of the largely town-based Listowel National League, the labourers' cause was championed. Under the chairmanship of Canon Davis the programme for the Listowel League was, firstly, home rule, secondly, the extension of the municipal franchise, and thirdly, that farmers with over 25 acres gave conacre plots to labourers at the same rent as they paid.[54] These objectives contradicted the formal National League constitution, which set the land question before both the extension of the municipal franchise and the labourers' question. The pro-labourer stance of the Listowel League was further evident when a labourer named James Guerin stated during a meeting:

> the farmers alone had benefited by recent land legislation regarding land tenure and the labourers had contributed more than any other class to the success of the late land agitation, yet they had reaped no advantage from them . . . if they [farmers] refuse this [conacre] the labourers as a body will never assist or sympathise with any movement.[55]

Editorial comment in the *Kerry Sentinel* echoed the pro-labourer stance of National League branches. When the National League was established in October 1882, the newspaper claimed that 'the needs of the farmer, once the theme of urgent agitation, pall before the crying necessities of the agricultural labourer'.[56] A month later the newspaper called on farmers to borrow money under the security obtained from the Land Act to make improvements on their farms, which would in turn provide employment for labourers.[57]

Undoubtedly, there was a feeling amongst some National Leaguers that farmers had benefited from the 1881 Land Act and that it was their duty to provide for the agricultural labourer. Although labourer involvement in the local leadership of branches remained minimal, they had a powerful social motive to mobilise and join the new league during 1883–4. In contrast, the position of farmers had improved and the limitations of the Land Act had yet to become fully apparent. Possibly the leaguers were consolidating the support of the agricultural labourers in the knowledge that the farming community was not going to offer the National League substantial support. Such a move further distanced tenants from the league as demands for conacre plots, better housing and more employment were financially detrimental to farmers.

In December 1883 the Divisional Magistrate for the south-west, Captain Plunkett, confidently stated that 'in county Kerry the league is a dead failure, not a single branch exists'.[58] Although many of the leading local Land Leaguers remained active in the county and were committed to establishing the new organisation, they largely failed during 1882–3. An unwillingness of many tenants to commit to what they saw as a renewed agitation, the coercive effects of the Crimes Act and farmer-labourer divisions all undermined the emergence of the National League. The land legislation appealed to many of the middle and large farmers that had previously supported the Land League in the county. With the Land Commission reducing rents by an average of 23 per cent, many of these farmers were willing to forgo political and agrarian agitation to avail of the benefits of the new legislation.

Although the nationalist organisation in the county remained poorly organised, elements that characterised the Land League agitation still prevailed. The Land League's electoral success on boards of guardians continued and in the 1883 poor law election to the Tralee Board of Guardians, 35 of the 42 elected guardians were returned on what the police believed to be a 'Land League ticket'.[59] Although the leaguers had effectively controlled the day-to-day running of the board since 1881, the 1883 election resulted in the successful removal of the *ex-officio* guardians from the controlling positions of the board. Michael McMahon and P. D. Kenny were elected to the positions of chairman and vice-chairman.[60] McMahon was a founding member of the Land League in Tralee and Kenny had previously been president of the Castleisland branch of the league and imprisoned under the PPP Act.[61] By 1883 the Tralee, Killarney and Listowel boards of guardians were all in control of nationalist elected officials. These boards represented an important sphere of local power, patronage and influence, which until the outbreak of the land war were largely in the control of the local landed classes. As originally outlined by the historian Feingold, the advent of nationalist politicians on boards of guardians resulted in a rapid increase in expenditure. Graph 5.1 and graph 5.2 show this trend clearly in relation to the Tralee, Killarney and Listowel boards where expenditure increased significantly since 1871. The control of this expenditure was now largely within the hands of the nationalist guardians and in many regions the *ex-officio* landlord guardians had stopped attending meetings due to harassment. The large increase in expenditure witnessed in 1881, 1882 and 1883 was somewhat curtailed in 1884 on the Killarney and Tralee boards owing to a decrease in destitution and distress and partly as a result of pressure from ratepayers, including tenant farmers, to reduce the burden of local taxation. Regardless of the downward trend, expenditure by local boards remained higher than at any time since the Famine and allowed local nationalists a considerable amount of patronage, and guardians continued to dispense outdoor relief to large numbers. As highlighted in chapter four, this form of relief provided local middle-class nationalists with a source of power and influence that was fundamental to attracting support from the poorer classes. Previously, landlord boards had largely refused to grant the measure and those in need of relief were forced into the highly unpopular and stigmatising workhouse. The distribution of outdoor relief allowed its recipients to remain within their home. This system helped to place local nationalist guardians in an influential position in their communities. Although the level of outdoor relief granted dropped from the peak of 1881–2, the measure remained a constant feature of welfare within the three unions during the mid-1880s.

Graph.5.1 Total annual expenditure in the Tralee, Killarney and Listowel Poor Law Unions, 1871–86

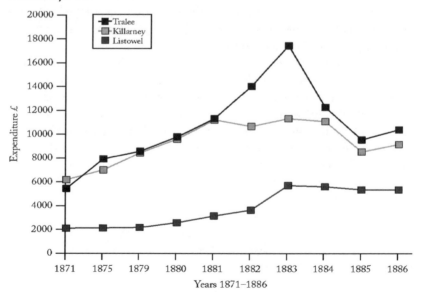

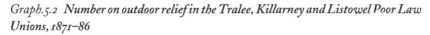

Graph.5.2 Number on outdoor relief in the Tralee, Killarney and Listowel Poor Law Unions, 1871–86

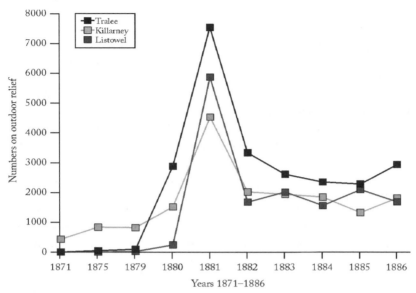

Another central feature of the Land League agitation was the prevention of the retaking of evicted farms by new tenants, popularly known as land-grabbing. By the end of 1883 this policy was still largely adhered to within rural society. As table 5.3 demonstrates, over half of the tenants evicted between January 1881 and October 1883 were reinstated in their original holdings. Of the 270 remaining holdings only 69 were successfully rented to new tenants. One hundred and twenty were farmed by landlords, while a further 81 remained unoccupied and uncultivated. Despite the fact that no open tenant organisation existed, the Land League objective of preventing the retaking of evicted farms remained largely adhered to. In the police district of Castleisland alone thirty farms remained unoccupied. Twenty-eight of these were within the sub-district of Castleisland, an area which comprised only the town and its immediate hinterland. This area had become one of the most disturbed in the country. Although agrarian tensions had generally subsided in the county, this region remained embroiled in agitation until it seemed to have reached a standstill by late 1883. The police believed that

> the tenants are holding out without redeeming knowing that the longer they [unoccupied farms] are useless to the landlords the easier it will be to come to terms with them. No outsider would take these farms as if he did, unless constantly guarded by police, he would unquestionably be assassinated.[62]

Within the Castleisland area secret societies remained active during 1883. Other areas including Tralee and Listowel also experienced agrarian secret society activity. The large number of evicted farms that remained unoccupied or in the hands of the landlord seemed to point towards a systematic organisation in place since the suppression of the Land League, which prevented landgrabbing.

Two significant aspects of the Land League agitation remained within the localities. The middle-class farmers and townsmen who came to prominence during the land war continued to achieve increased local power and influence over local government bodies. Furthermore, the violence, or at the least the threat of violence, that surrounded the Land League agitation, remained a constant force within certain rural localities. The continuation of these two elements demonstrated that while there was general apathy towards the National League, much of the motivation for local political and agrarian action remained in place in 1882 and 1883.

Table 5.3 Return of farms in each police district in County Kerry from which tenants have been evicted or which have been surrendered from 1 January 1881–1 October 1883

	Evicted farms	Occupied by old tenants	Occupied by new tenants	In hands of landlords	Unoccupied and not farmed
Kerry	*624*	*354*	*69*	*120*	*81*
Caherciveen	22	16	7	0	1
Castleisland	80	38	3	9	30
Dingle	58	52	2	2	2
Kenmare	17	8	7	0	2
Killarney	126	83	8	21	14
Killorglin	121	88	7	10	16
Listowel	113	32	29	43	12
Tralee	87	37	6	35	4

Source: Return of farms in County Kerry from which tenants have been evicted or which have been surrendered from 1 Jan. 1881–1 Oct. 1883 (N.A.I., CSO RP, 1883 23534/9127).

By the start of 1884 the National League remained largely unsuccessful in Kerry. The low ebb of nationalist politics in the county was highlighted in January when Edward Harrington was released after his six-month imprisonment. A demonstration in Tralee to mark his release was addressed by T. D. Sullivan and Timothy Harrington, both MPs who were central figures in the movement's national leadership.[63] The demonstration was poorly attended and the RIC reporter commented that only 'the working men, labourers and tradesmen of that town and neighbourhood' attended, while 'very few farmers and with one or two exceptions none of the respectable shopkeepers' were present.[64] Resident Magistrate Heffernan Considine for Tralee commented that 'the meeting was a miserable affair. . . it has shown what little sympathy existed for Mr Harrington'.[65] Such apathy was further highlighted when an attempt to establish a National League branch in Dingle during March failed due to a lack of support from the farmers in the area.[66]

There were further signs of the easing of agrarian tensions. The police noted that the disturbed regions of the county were showing signs of improvement. By February 1884, the SRM, Captain Plunkett, removed the extra police stationed in the Killarney and Molahiffe parishes.[67] Similarly, during March 1884, the 'police tax' was suspended in Castleisland, a region noted for high levels of agrarian violence.[68] The removal of the police tax in these regions was a result of a reduction in the number of agrarian outrages committed. For the years 1880 to 1882, the number of agrarian outrages reported to the RIC in Kerry was 298, 401 and 347.[69] By 1883 this number had dropped to 146, and 1884 witnessed 117 agrarian outrages.[70] Rents were reportedly paid and landlord–tenant relations were improving to some extent. The number of civil bills issued for ejectment, a legal procedure used by landlords to force rent payment, was at its lowest level since 1880, albeit it remained well above the pre-land war norm (in 1879 594 were issued, in 1882 1,676 and in 1884 1,131).[71] By the middle of 1884, social and political tensions in the county appeared to have stabilised.

GROWTH OF THE NATIONAL LEAGUE ON A NATIONAL LEVEL

Despite the apparent tranquillity of the Kerry and Irish countryside, the National League began to emerge in various parts of the country during 1884. The number of branches increased countrywide from 230 in December 1882 to 592 in December 1884. Unlike the initial emergence of the Land League, the National League was at its strongest in the prosperous regions of Munster and Leinster. By the start of 1885 Limerick and Tipperary were the National League's best-organised counties in Munster, with 60 and 49 branches respectively. The league was also active in the south-east, with 33 branches in Waterford and 30 in Kilkenny.[72] These regions were relatively prosperous and were traditionally less violent than the western seaboard. In these areas the increasingly Catholic National League could rely on the support of the middling farmers and shopkeepers who were also loyal sons of the church.[73] Many of these branches provided the parliamentary party with the local strength to return MPs loyal to the party during 1883–4. During this period, 12 MPs were added to the Parnellite party in by-election successes.[74] Central to the success in these elections were the county conventions of the local branches of the league. In December 1884 the chief secretary was informed:

> the county conventions that were summoned at Limerick, Roscommon, Dungarvan and Dublin [were] to exhibit the ready manner in which questions affecting the welfare of the league can be discussed and effectively dealt with and the fact of Mr Power being returned unopposed for county Waterford and recently Mr O'Connor for county Tipperary is sufficient proof of its hold on the votes of the majority.[75]

While these conventions impressed the authorities with their organisational strength, their real value was in effectively providing Parnell and the parliamentary party with hegemony over the selection of candidates. It was a system that 'combined the appearance of local spontaneity with the reality of centralised control'.[76] Other initiatives further strengthened the power and unity of the party. The creation of a party fund to pay elected MPs and the necessity of candidates to take a pledge to the party and vote with it in the House of Commons ensured the return of MPs for 'whom loyalty to the party was a *sine qua non*'.[77] Parnell and the National League's grip on nationalist politics was further strengthened when in October 1884 the Irish Catholic bishops aligned themselves to the movement and formally entrusted the Irish Parliamentary Party to press for their educational demands in the House of Commons.[78] The under-secretary in Dublin Castle commented that the move 'identifies the bishops and priests of Ireland with the people'.[79] The increasing clerical involvement in the new league also helped to contain agrarian violence. In December 1884 the chief secretary was informed that 'it ought in fairness be stated that outrages have not followed the National League as they did the Land League'.[80] These developments have led some historians to see the National League as a 'smooth running national electioneering machinery that had hitherto been lacking to the parliamentary party'.[81] Others have ventured that the Irish parliamentary party together with its localised under body, the National League, was 'among the most remarkable political movements established in a primarily rural European society'.[82]

Although the National League did achieve a degree of success by the start of 1885, it was still not apparent that it would develop into a large-scale mass movement. Areas of traditional Land League activity witnessed little National League organisation. In Mayo only seven branches were established. The Chief Secretary's office commented that 'in Mayo the league has fallen quite flat, rather astonishing considering that this county was the birth place of the Land League'.[83] By 1885 many leading nationalists still had serious doubts whether the demand for home rule could mobilise large sections of the population.[84] Michael Davitt along with the Galway agrarian radical, Matthew

Harris, and Jasper Tully, editor of one of the most radical journals in Ireland, the *Roscommon Herald*, all believed that for tenant farmers home rule paled in significance and importance compared to the land question.[85] Even where branches had been established in regions in the country a degree of apathy was apparent and meetings were at times poorly attended.[86] Although the National League had made significant progress by increasing branch numbers, holding county conventions, and ensuring the successful return of MPs at by-elections, it had yet to develop into a mass movement similar to the Land League.

LOCAL POLITICS IN KERRY, 1885

By the start of 1885 the organisation of the National League began to make some progress in the county. A number of league demonstrations were successfully held, leading to the establishment of local branches. By February a branch was finally established in Tralee, although there was little evidence of the politics of home rule and Parnellism in the wider county. A number of local initiatives emerged, which transcended the nationalist and unionist and largely Catholic and Protestant divisions of home rule politics. In Tralee town a movement which attempted to lower local taxation emerged in the early months of 1885. Local government expenditure had soared since the land agitation had begun. Between 1877 and 1884 the annual expenditure of the county's six boards of guardians and grand jury rose from £64,324 to £109,862. Boards of guardians' expenditure experienced the greatest increase. Land League guardians freely gave outdoor relief to evicted tenants, families of those arrested in the agitation and members of the league.[87] The grand jury, firmly under the control of the landed interest, also witnessed an increase in annual expenditure from £42,434 in 1877 to £55,891 in 1884. This increase was also directly related to the land agitation. In 1880 none of the grand jury expenditure went on extra police in the county. By 1884 extra police cost the grand jury system £6,669 in Kerry.[88] The majority of this police force was employed in protecting landlord's employees and landlords themselves and was considered unnecessary by many.

The land agitation had extensively driven up the cost of local government in the county. This cost was paid by the ratepayers who consisted of landlords and the occupiers of land with a valuation above £4.[89] Attempts were made to establish common ground between these groups of ratepayers. In a letter published in the county's three newspapers, Redmond Roche JP, a small landlord (1,255 acres) from Castleisland, stressed the commonality of interests between landlords and tenants when he wrote:

a large proportion of this [rates] comes out of the rents of the landlord, a larger portion still out of the profits of the farmer and trader, and it is clearly the interest of all, as I submit it is their duty, to do what in them lies to lighten the burden.[90]

Table 5.4 Poor law union and grand jury expenditure in County Kerry, 1877–84

Year	Poor law union £	Grand jury £	Total £
1877	21,890	42,434	64,324
1878	24,609	41,509	65,118
1879	26,701	44,708	71,409
1880	30,079	43,438	73,517
1881	34,430	47,227	81,657
1882	37,454	50,453	87,907
1883	53,225	58,255	111,430
1884	53,971	55,891	109,862

Source: *KEP*, 28 Feb. 1885. Aggregate expenditure of the six poor law unions in the county.

In particular, tenant farmers felt the financial strain of high rates. An unnamed farmer stated to the Cowper Commission that in 1885 he had to pay £17 in poor law rates on a farm of 50 acres. This was a large extra payout on his holding, which had an annual rent of £64.[91] In March 1885, RIC District Inspector William Davis for Castleisland observed that high taxes were a contributory factor to the poverty of tenants in the district. He warned:

taxes are very high and the prices of all sorts of farm produce are low … I fear that if arrangements don't come between landlords and tenants as well as between the latter and their other creditors that there must be a crash among the farmers in this neighbourhood as between rents, taxes, and improvidence most of the farmers around here are on the verge of bankruptcy.[92]

Evidently local taxation was a significant issue which affected all classes. A ratepayers' meeting was held in Tralee in early March, and although no landlords attended those present at the meeting included both nationalists and a number of prominent Protestant Tralee businessmen, who had largely remained outside the arena of local politics through the recent turbulent years. Prominent nationalists, including Edward Harrington, Thomas Lyons and Henry Brassill attended. All were founding members of the National League in the town. The Protestant businessmen who attended included William Hill (leather merchant) Benjamin Piper (shipping agent) and Robert McCowan, a leading Tralee merchant and Methodist.[93] These represented middle-class non-Catholics, whose traditional political allegiance in the town lay largely with Liberalism. The borough constituency remained a Liberal stronghold and no Conservative had been elected since 1837.[94] Many Protestants willingly contributed to the home rule movement of the early 1870s to the extent that under Isaac Butt, Protestants had been largely responsible for instigating the movement.[95] This was evident in Tralee when in 1874 a number of prominent Protestant businessmen signed an election petition supporting the home rule candidate for the borough constituency.[96] The exclusion of these middle-class Protestants from the landed aristocracy and society pushed some of this group towards home rule during the 1870s. Although they shared the same religion as the majority of the ruling class they had limited power. The magistracy remained dominated by landlords. Of the 118 justices of the peace and magistrates in the county in 1884, 86 were Protestants and 32 were Catholics. The gentry's dominance of this group was highlighted in the fact that 106 of the total were landlords, landlords' sons or land agents. The urban middle-class Protestants and Catholics were omitted from this source of power and influence.[97] With the advent of the land war, gentry home rulers such as Rowland Blennerhassett, MP, became alienated from the agitation and failed to support the Land League. Other middle-class Protestants and particularly shopkeepers did offer some support to the Land League. William Feingold's analysis of 24 Protestants who were entitled to vote in the 1881 Tralee Poor Law election shows that eleven did not vote, three remained neutral, three voted for the conservative candidates while the remaining seven voted for Land League nominees.[98] While middle-class Protestants supported the Land League (much of the support most probably because of the economic ties between Protestant shopkeepers and tenants), they failed to become involved in the local leadership of the movement. By 1885 they felt isolated from the increasingly pro-Catholic stance of the new National League movement. Parnell's alliance with the Catholic Church was becoming more apparent at a local level. This was most evident at the county conventions where the Catholic clergy had a large and disproportionate influence.[99]

The meeting of the ratepayers was reportedly a success and a body entitled the Tralee Ratepayers Protective Association was established, which was committed to preventing any further increase in local taxation.[100] With William Hill as president and Maurice Kelliher as vice-president, the organisation was representative of Protestant and Catholic traders.[101] The emergence of the ratepayers' association illustrated the political appetite of middle-class Protestants who were marginalised from the landed ascendancy. Many of these had previously supported the Land League but were alienated by the National League's Catholic emphasis. Significantly, leading members of the National League in the town, such as Edward Harrington, associated themselves with an initiative outside the parameters of the movement. Fenian and radical members of National League, however, opposed the initiative. The measure was opposed by Michael Power and N. J. Nolan, both significant IRB figures in the town, indicating a degree of division in the town's nationalist community.[102]

Another civic endeavour that involved co-operation between members of rival political groupings and traditions was the opening of a butter factory in Tralee town. In February 1885 a public meeting for this purpose was organised by some of the county's leading landlords. The meeting was chaired by Lord Ventry and another large landowner, Colonel Crosbie.[103] Also present were a number of gentlemen farmers long associated with agrarian issues, and Jonathan Walpole, a founding member of the Kerry Tenants Defence Association in 1875 and a prominent tenant-righter before the land war.[104] So too did Michael Whelan, a large farmer who had been involved in the tenant-right movement of the 1870s but had failed to become radicalised during the Land League period.[105] Other figures who attended included Robert McCowan, and Stephen Huggard, who as the Clerk of the Crown and Peace was the leading civil servant in the county. The most prominent National League figure in the county, Edward Harrington, was also present. Many of these men, who represented the political, social and economic elite of the region, were undoubtedly unionist in outlook, although the objective of the meeting was apolitical. The non-partisan nature of the largely unionist gathering was clear when Edward Harrington was offered the position as the group's leading spokesman by Lord Ventry.[106] The coming together of these groups represented a degree of social *détente* amongst landlords and certain National League figures in Tralee town. The objective of the group was to set up a creamery that would improve the standard of production of butter for small farmers.[107]

This was not the only incidence of co-operation between nationalists and the gentry. There was regular social interaction between the two groups at various civic gatherings. By 1884 nationalist traders in Tralee were organising popular horse racing events, together with members of the town's higher orders. The County Kerry Steeplechase Committee consisted of figures such as F. R. Bateman, Lieutenant Colonel Denny and William Denny, all members of the area's gentry. Edward Harrington also sat on its committee as did Thomas Lyons, another founding member of the Tralee Land League.[108] Similarly, a sporting event, known as the Kerry Athletic Sports Day, established originally in 1878, was organised by a combination of Tralee nationalists, urban Protestant traders and gentry. Founding members of the Land League and leading political agitators in the town, such as M. J. Horgan and O'Connor Horgan, sat on the sports day committee with a whole host of gentry luminaries. Thomas Lyons acted as secretary to the group and Edward Harrington was a member of the committee.[109] By 1884 the committee demonstrated its financial clout when it raised £300 for the purchase of a new ground for its sports.[110] Nationalists and unionist landed figures were willing to co-operate over civic issues such as improvement in agricultural techniques and the organisation of local sporting events. Much of this occurred during 1884 and the first number of months of 1885. Even in early 1885 the objectives of the National League evidently did not dominate local politics in Tralee.

THE RE-EMERGENCE OF PARNELLISM AND THE ROYAL VISIT, APRIL 1885

The level of co-operation between would-be National Leaguers and unionists at a local level in Tralee town contradicted the political battle at the level of high politics. Parnellites were engaged in a propaganda battle with the government administration in Dublin Castle. William O'Brien and Tim Healy, through the pages of *United Ireland*, frequently attacked the Lord Lieutenant, Earl Spencer, and his Chief Secretary, Sir George Trevelyan in language that Spencer believed to be 'violent and abusive beyond all precedent'.[111] The political rhetoric used by Parnell's lieutenants to promote the National League and home rule and kind of 'pseudo-revolutionary violence of utterance' became the norm for nationalists during this period.[112] This official language of the movement, which permeated to a local level, drew on nationalist rhetoric dating back to Daniel O'Connell's repeal movement. At a meeting in Milltown in December 1884, a speech by Edward Harrington exemplified this language:

> why should they [Irish people] be slaves to any land or to any nation, no matter how powerful . . . no land or no country where intelligent, educated, and right minded people exist should be without the right and without the principle of having a government of its own.[113]

During the same speech he evoked populist historical grievances with England by claiming that 'the greatest and biggest landgrabber was England . . . for over seven centuries, and the Irish people have always looked on the English as landgrabbers in Ireland'.[114] A few months later in May 1885, at another National League meeting in Lixnaw, a local activist, G. J. Rice, echoed Harrington's words when he claimed: 'Ireland was never created to be the slave or subject of England . . . we don't want England's laws'.[115] Editorials in the league's mouthpiece, the *Kerry Sentinel*, carried on in a similar vein. The National League movement was depicted as 'struggling to be free from a tyrannical misgovernment' and emigration was explained as: 'we see our country depleted to a third of its natural population and we know that British rule caused it'.[116] This denunciation of the government and 'English rule' echoed the rhetoric which emanated from the pages of *United Ireland* and from Parnell's lieutenants promoting the home rule cause. In the spring of 1885, immediate economic and social motivations were absent which might have ignited mass mobilisation. So nationalists turned to this inflammable language designed to sustain a 'high level of popular indignation or sense of grievance – the elementary basis of nationalism – against the "English oppressor"'.[117] This language was used in an attempt by Parnellites 'to shape the nature of Irish national identity itself in one of the most formative periods of modern Irish history'.[118] Notwithstanding the long-term effects of this process on the development and construction of nationalist ideology, in March 1885 the co-operative action of Tralee nationalists and unionists appeared to demonstrate that such rhetoric remained to some extent an abstract concept in the day-to-day affairs of local business.

The failure of the rhetoric of the National League to mobilise anti-government feeling in Kerry was demonstrated during the visit of the Lord Lieutenant, Earl Spencer, to the south-west in September 1884. He received a cool reception in Millstreet where banners proclaimed 'God save Ireland' and 'Parnell for ever'.[119] Similarly, when he arrived in Kerry he was met with a hostile reception in Castleisland where 'black flags with deaths head and cross bones were displayed to welcome him instead of the union jack'.[120] In contrast to this reception in Castleisland, the rest of Spencer's visit to the county was largely a success. With the hierarchy of the Catholic Church in the county were heavily involved in organising the visit, Spencer was welcomed in Killarney, Tralee and Listowel. In Tralee, he was received by Dean Coffey, while in Listowel Canon Davis received him. Those who greeted Spencer were not confined to the county's gentry and higher clergy. He was presented with an address supported by the majority of the town's elected commissioners and traders which demonstrated that his visit was to some extent supported by many of the town's shopkeepers and publicans who were nationalist in outlook.[121] This reception was especially favourable and Spencer was reported as saying that he 'would always remember with pleasant feelings, the kind reception he met in Listowel'.[122] Canon Griffin of Millstreet, who orchestrated the visit, later received a letter from Spencer stating: 'I greatly enjoyed my trip to Kerry and received much kindness from all classes of the people. That some expressions of disapproval should have appeared was but natural, and it is better that they should be made than suppressed.'[123] The visit demonstrated that the 'establishment' in Kerry remained very much intact. In fact, the Catholic hierarchy in the county remained conservative and supportive of the government. This support was augmented by the appointment in late December 1881 of Bishop Higgins whom the government saw as being an opponent of the Land League. His appointment was ensured under British influence at the Vatican.[124] Ties between the leading British government figures in the Vatican and the Kerry Catholic clergy continued into the decade. George Errington, whose 'mission' in Rome gave 'weight to the [British] government view whenever Episcopal succession or precedence was being decided', was in regular contact with Canon Griffin of Millstreet.[125] In June 1883, Errington wrote to Griffin thanking him for a letter explaining circumstances in Kerry, which was shown to the pope and subsequently published in a French Catholic newspaper. Errington warmly stated: 'I assure you it is a very great comfort in the often trying circumstances here to have the support of your great knowledge and experience'.[126] Spencer's visit openly demonstrated the loyal alliance of government officials, gentry and leading Catholic clerics in the county. Edward Harrington's *Kerry Sentinel* heavily criticised the welcoming receptions for the lord lieutenant. It complained that the clergy who greeted Spencer were not representative of the body of priests in the county, and in an editorial stated:

> Be he priest or layman who had mixed himself up in this misrepresentation of the feelings of the people, his tongue or pen can never carry a feather's weight of political influence amongst his people.[127]

The unorganised state of nationalist politics, particularly of the National League, undermined any potential demonstrations against the visit. Of the towns visited by Spencer, both Listowel and Castleisland had branches of the league. However, it was only in Castleisland that any significant opposition to the visit was in evidence. Even there confusion reigned amongst the National Leaguers after the president of the branch P. D. Kenny had an informal conversation with Spencer. The members of the branch then expelled Kenny from the presidency.[128] In all, the visit demonstrated the ineffectiveness of the National League in Kerry in September 1884. No clear policy directed the few branches in existence, and the government aligned with members of the higher Catholic clergy and the unionist gentry orchestrated a successful visit.

The situation had rapidly changed by the time of the announcement of the visit of the Prince of Wales to Ireland in March 1885. At the level of high politics, Earl Spencer organised the trip to arouse popular support for the royalty and undermine Parnellism. In turn, Parnellites, and in particular William O'Brien, saw the need to create and sustain popular opposition to the visit as a means of promoting the National League in Ireland and demonstrating the nationalist demand for home rule to the watching English public.[129] In March the central branch of the National League sent a circular to all branches explaining that the prince was to be treated with 'silent indifference'. Local branches, including those in Tralee and Listowel, responded by passing resolutions to that effect.[130] The leadership of the league believed that this policy would strike a balance between indignation and respect, which would further the constitutional campaign to convince British opinion of the case for home rule, but the prince's arrival in Dublin was a success with a large turnout of loyalists. In consequence, a more aggressive policy was adopted by the Parnellites. Fearing that the visit might prove successful, the league attempted to make the visit an occasion for ideological polarisation or, as William Redmond noted, 'the present was the occasion to draw a line between the nationalists and the anti-nationalists'.[131] When the prince arrived in Mallow in County Cork a mass demonstration was held by William O'Brien (MP for the town), leading to rioting and police baton charges.[132] This demonstration and fracas provided the Parnellites with much propaganda to denounce the visit and promote the National League.

Since Spencer's original visit in September 1884 the National League had progressed somewhat in Kerry. As the New Year began, revival of the league was essential for the forthcoming general election. By the end of 1884 a branch was established in Killarney and the defunct Listowel branch was reorganised.[133] During these months the authorities failed to implement the powers under the 1882 Crimes Act to suppress political meetings, freeing league organisers to promote the organisation.[134] Then, several league public demonstrations were successfully held in the county and by April 1885 12 active National League branches were regularly reporting the proceedings of their branch meetings in the *Kerry Sentinel*.[135] Branches demonstrated a high level of organisation and a degree of influence in their localities. This was demonstrated on the Killarney Board of Guardians when an election for the position of relieving officer arose. Before the meeting both the Castleisland and Killarney branches of the National League agreed on an evicted tenant from Lord Kenmare's estate named Jeremiah Crowley as their candidate.[136] During a guardians' meeting, a circular was handed around calling on them to support 'the victim of landlord tyranny [Crowley]'.[137] Crowley was duly elected.[138] Similarly, the league demonstrated its influence over a ratepayers' election for the position of coroner in Listowel. The Listowel branch put forward Dr Clancy for the position, one of its leading members.[139] During the election, banners appeared in the town which declaring 'vote for Mr Parnell and the Nationalist, Clancy'. Although Clancy received less than half the votes, with 399 out of 856, he did gain a majority and was duly elected.[140] Although the election was a success for the local nationalists, Edward Harrington criticised the Listowel League. In a *Sentinel* editorial he wrote that such localised objectives were not part of the 'national programme'. By concentrating on the election, he accused the branch of neglecting their weekly business and stated that it 'must show some broader national activity'.[141] The reality was that

National League activity at branch level was mired in local concerns and National Leaguers in Kerry demonstrated a preoccupation with controlling patronage over local government positions. In these branches there was little comment on home rule, and the registration of voters – a task which the central branch of the league had determined as being of paramount importance – was largely ignored.

As on the occasion of the successful visit of Lord Spencer the previous September, the local gentry, Protestant community and sections of the county's higher Catholic clergy prepared to welcome the prince in April 1885. In Killarney a total of 200 workmen were employed in painting and decorating the train line in royal regalia and pageantry.[142] In Tralee, Sir Henry Donovan, a Catholic Liberal who had supported The O'Donoghue's election in 1880, ordered 200 flags for the prince's reception.[143] When the royal party arrived in Killarney, a large deputation of the county's gentry, government officials, and some Catholic clergy welcomed the prince.[144] The newly reformed National League organised counter-demonstrations wherever the royal visit went. In Killarney, leading National Leaguers demonstrated and the royal entourage was reportedly hissed as it went through the town.[145] When the royal party arrived in Tralee it was met by members of the gentry, civil servants and some middle-class Protestants such as William Hill. When a band began playing 'God Save the Queen' on the platform of the train station, the nationalist demonstrators outside responded with 'national airs' including 'God Save Ireland'. Similar scenes occurred when the royal party went on to Listowel where the people held up banners with slogans calling on the prince to remember Mallow and Myles Joyce [executed for the Maamtransa murders].[146] The prince was welcomed by unionists while the freshly organised leaguers attempted to upstage the visit with counter demonstrations.

As the historian James Murphy has pointed out, the royal visit had repercussions for the monarchy in Ireland and for the first time many natio-nalist politicians were forced into open displays of hostility and antipathy to the royal family.[147] The prince's visit greatly affected politics in the county for a number of reasons. By April 1885 the success of the National League was still in doubt. Growth in local branches of the league since 1882 had been unimpres-sive and the increase in league activity was still in its infancy with its potential success uncertain. In Kerry, the branch activity concentrated on local issues such as extending patronage over local government appointments. The royal visit of early 1885 provided the 'national' event needed to infuse the movement in the county. The hostile reception of the prince was co-ordinated by local league branches under the influence of the central branch in Dublin. The National League orchestrated similar demonstrations countrywide ensuring that the league's opposition to the visit became the dominant expression of 'popular opinion'. Whereas previously National League activity had been concentrated on specific by-elections, and local branches were preoccupied with parochial issues, these mass demonstrations provided the movement with an immediate 'national' focus. This further instilled the idea of the league as a national and mass movement operating on a countrywide basis. The visit also gave some substance to the rhetoric of the National League. The sight of the prince aligned with the local aristocratic, Protestant and 'loyal' Catholic clerical figures in the trappings of royal regalia undoubtedly gave the league's historic and emotive language a tangible basis. In Kerry, the visit further polarised opinion between on the one hand National Leaguers and on the other the gentry and middle-class Protestants. The visit provided for a popular platform for the spread of the National League. There was also a new emphasis on the division between nationalists and unionists in a county where, since the rise of the Land League's agrarianism, politics had not been dominated by the constitutional question.

THE NATIONAL LEAGUE, THE GAA AND FENIANISM

After the prince's visit to Kerry the National League movement continued to spread. By the end of June 1885 23 branches of the league had been established in the county.[148] By the end of June 1885, 23 branches of the league had been established in the county although internal division threatened to split the movement. A rift developed between Fenian/IRB members of the Tralee League and the branch's president Edward Harrington. Since the emergence of the Land League in the town, a radical Fenian element was a constant force in the movement. One of the faction leaders within the branch was Michael Power who was publicly and widely known as a Fenian.[149] Power was a successful pig dealer and was regularly elected to the Tralee Poor Law Board as a guardian for the town. Other branch members associated with Fenianism included William Moore Stack, whose political origins lay in the 1867 rising, M. J. Nolan who had fled the country after the failed rising in 1867, and John Healy.[150] Stack was a well-known Fenian and by 1879 held a senior position in the organisation and went to Paris on probable IRB business.[151] Stack, Nolan and Healy were archetypical urban Fenian supporters of the 1860s who belonged to the lower middle class of artisans and clerks. Their occupations were respectively law clerk, tinsmith and harness maker. By the outbreak of the land war all these men were prominent supporters of the Land League and, along with Power, were suspected of involvement in agrarian outrages and arrested under the PPP Act, 1881.[152] In 1885 they were still active in local politics and were founding members of the National League in the town.[153]

In July 1885 tensions surfaced in the branch over Gaelic Athletic Association (GAA) sports, highlighting the increasingly divergent directions of Fenianism and Parnellism in the town. These Fenians, along with Maurice Moynihan, were instrumental in creating a branch of the GAA in Tralee. Moynihan, born in 1864, was representative of a new generation of Fenian activists who had limited experience of the Land League. At the age of only 21 he emerged as a leading Fenian organiser in Tralee town and in 1885 was appointed the county secretary of the newly established GAA. Within a few years he was suspected of holding the same position in the IRB.[154] These individuals were also behind the emergence of the Fenian controlled Young Ireland Society in Kerry which expounded a form of cultural nationalism.[155] By 1885 three branches of the Young Ireland Society had been established in the county, which were based in the towns of Tralee, Castleisland and Killarney. Illustrating the diverging nationalist political cultures in Tralee, the leader of the National League in Tralee, Edward Harrington, failed to join the branch of the Young Ireland Society or the new GAA sports organisation. Instead, Harrington remained associated with the organising committee of what was by this stage termed the Tralee Athletic Sports Day. Although pro-National League businessmen from Tralee had previously organised sports days, it remained connected with landlords. The sports days were aligned with the Irish Amateur Athletic Association (IAAA), the Irish wing of a broader English organisation that had been established in Ireland three months previously to counter the rise of the GAA.[156] In Tralee, the newly established GAA specifically challenged the annual athletic sports day and held a competing event on the same date, 17 June 1885. The GAA event proved far more popular and the unionist *Kerry Evening Post* reported that at the athletic sports 'the large stand was filled with the elite of the county. Outside the stand, there was a marked absence of the public who usually support the athletic meeting.'[157] Over 10,000 attended the GAA event along with Michael Cusack, the national secretary of the GAA. The sports participated in included athletics and a hurling match. Reportedly only 500 attended the IAAA sports including Edward Harrington.[158] Evidently, Harrington failed to realise the potential popularity of the nascent GAA.

The large attendance at the GAA sports easily outnumbered political meetings of the National League in the town, indicating that the emergence of the GAA was not necessarily inspired by nationalist politics as has been asserted by many historians.[159] The failure of the public to support the sports event which was connected with the gentry appeared to represent a rejection of the elitism of this group and was not necessarily an endorsement of the IRB or Fenianism. After Edward Harrington failed to support the GAA sports he was chastised for his association with the 'upper classes' and during a National League meeting after the sports day it was said of Harrington that 'the people had lifted him upon their shoulders, and he had kicked the ladder by which he had ascended'.[160] Indeed, a degree of social elitism surrounded the athletic sports, with the county's 'elite' in the 'large stand' and the 'public' outside it. The rules of the Irish Amateur Athletic Association ensured that their games could not be enjoyed by those whose incomes were low or whose social standing made them unwelcome companions for those in control of the association. In contrast the GAA had lower subscriptions with less emphasis on class. In essence the GAA offered an opportunity for large sections of the population to participate in the late Victorian sporting revolution.[161] Many could readily identify with a sporting organisation which met their social and economic position and rivalled the elitism of the landed classes.

Within the National League the division between the sports represented a broader struggle between Harrington and the more Fenian inspired-members of the movement. The Franchise Act of 1884 and the Redistribution Act of 1885 greatly altered the nature of parliamentary electoral politics, increasing the Irish electorate from 225,999 to 737,965, many of whom were small farmers and agricultural labourers.[162] Also, many of the smaller boroughs were abolished and single seat constituencies were created.[163] In Kerry, the two county seats and the Tralee borough were replaced by four constituencies, North Kerry, West Kerry, South Kerry and East Kerry. By 1891 the combined parliamentary electorate for Kerry was 20,793 compared to 5,582 in 1880.[164] The increase in the franchise made the successful election of league-supported candidates a formality. Whoever the Tralee branch of the National League nominated for the newly created constituency of West Kerry would inevitably win the Westminster seat. The branch prepared intensively for the election – in April it established a registration committee to ensure parliamentary voters were registered.[165] Within a few weeks the committee identified a large number of unregistered potential voters and set about enrolling them.[166] The branch also initiated efforts to hold a county convention of the league to nominate candidates for the election. The Tralee branch communicated with other branches about the issue and proposed to hold the convention in July. Timothy Harrington, who by this stage was secretary of the National League at a national level, wrote to the Tralee branch agreeing to a convention. Perhaps anticipating that the Tralee branch was attempting to exert its influence over the convention, he warned that no one branch was to assume predominance and that the central branch should remain in control over such proceedings. He said that he would attend as a representative of the central branch and that it would provide him with 'an opportunity of meeting my friends in Kerry upon such an occasion'.[167] However, before the convention was held the disagreement over the sports occurred. At the meeting of the

National League following the sports day, Edward Harrington was removed from his position as president of the Tralee League for his failure to support the GAA event. His removal was orchestrated by the radical faction in the league who elected William Moore Stack, a well-known Fenian, as its new president.[168]

Harrington's expulsion took on a broader significance and threatened the unity of the newly developed politics of home rule. In a public letter to Edward Harrington, Archbishop Croke distanced himself from the actions of the Tralee GAA and leaguers, and wrote that when he promoted the revival of the 'national' sports he 'had no idea of extending or discouraging all other sports whatever'.[169] The actions of the Tralee Leaguers antagonised the organising committee of the National League. The Committee, spearheaded by Timothy Harrington, condemned the expulsion of his brother Edward.[170] In an increasingly public and widely reported split, Timothy wrote to the national newspapers denying any connection between the National League and the GAA in an attempt to debase the legitimacy of the actions of the Tralee Leaguers. Timothy wrote that 'those who have used the name of the National League, in connection with the GAA have done so without authorisation'. He claimed that the prominent members of the GAA were not members of the league and 'have never in any way so identified themselves with national politics as to establish a claim upon members of that organisation'.[171] The matter had the potential to exacerbate tensions between Fenians and the more constitutionally minded National League. By 1885, the IRB's organisation was greatly undermined by the arrest of a number of high profile Fenians by the Crime Special Branch, directed by the zealous Under-Secretary E. G. Jenkinson. Also, a number of other prominent IRB men, including two Cork city IRB leaders, James Christopher Flynn and John O'Connor, were won over by Parnell and 'defected' to constitutional politics.[172] However, the GAA had emerged as a large-scale sporting movement, which was to a considerable extent infiltrated by Fenians and linked to the advanced separatist tradition.[173] By publicly claiming that the GAA and the National League were separate organisations, Timothy Harrington aggravated these potential divisions. Michael Cusack, the founder and secretary of the GAA, saw Harrington's actions as a threat to his organisation. In another published letter, this time written to the Tralee Fenian and GAA organiser Michael Power, Cusack bitterly criticised the Harrington brothers by stating:

> Timothy Harrington is supreme dictator of Ireland – if people submit . . . He has attempted to bolster up his brother and to crush us with a brutality and bad taste which would appear the chief characteristics of the family. Either the Harringtons must go or the people must go.[174]

A few weeks later he wrote privately to Michael Davitt, deploring that 'Timothy Harrington . . . will no longer say anything good of the GAA'.[175] He concluded that they will have to 'face any party that shows its hostility to the GAA. We don't care how formidable the thing may be.'[176] The divisions in the Tralee League clearly had wider ramifications for the nationalist movement with potential dissension between the GAA and the National League.

In Kerry the situation came to a head when Edward and Timothy Harrington both addressed a demonstration in Abbeydorney under the auspices of the local National League branch, headed by the parish priest, Father Brosnan. Both Harringtons spoke and were met by a chorus of boos and cheers. In the middle of the demonstration a contingent of the Tralee Leaguers arrived, led by William Moore Stack and Michael Power.[177] A tirade of insults and accusations followed between the two groups and the meeting broke up in disorder. After these scenes Timothy Harrington and the central branch of the National League dissolved the Tralee branch reputedly for disrupting a National League meeting.[178]

Opponents of the league seized on the opportunity to criticise what some saw as the increasingly hierarchical and autocratic nature of the organisation. The unionist *Dublin Evening Mail* commented in its editorial:

> the summary fashion in which the Central Branch of the National League snuffed out the Tralee branch of that association on Tuesday, will probably serve as a warning to similar bodies throughout the country not to flatter themselves that they possess the smallest portion of independence in the matter of home rule.[179]

The Times of London, pointing to the episode in Tralee, complained that 'Parnell's despotic will is enforced by his subordinate officers'. It went on to state that local branches were subject to the central branch and 'are ruled with a rod of iron and are not allowed to do or say anything which does not accord with the instructions of Mr Harrington'.[180] Accusations that the league acted in a dictatorial fashion had become one of the chief criticisms of Parnell and the movement. Much of this criticism emerged after the failure of the Irish parliamentary party to create a governing council of the National League. The council, which was to be made up of elected MPs and 32 delegates elected by county conventions of the local branches, never materialised and power remained in the hands of the non-elected organising committee.[181] Condemnation of the league's hierarchical nature was not confined to the exponents of unionist and Conservative opposition. During August, Michael Davitt called for the proposed council to be established and for it to 'meet in Dublin occasionally, and direct the attention of the Irish race'.[182] This policy was an alternative to the centralisation of power within the hands of the leading figures of the Irish Parliamentary Party. By 1885 that centralisation had been achieved in the National League and was now a leading tendency of Parnellism.

Davitt who was personally close to many of the Tralee Leaguers, was before the Harringtons episode undoubtedly aware of the schism in the town's politics between Harrington and the other members of the league. In July 1884 he had spoken at an event in Tralee organised by William Moore Stack.[183] The proceeds of the event went to a printer named Brosnan, who had been discharged by Edward Harrington from the offices of the *Sentinel*. During Davitt's visit in 1884, Harrington unsurprisingly made no appearance.[184] By this stage Davitt's relationship with the National League had greatly deteriorated. His policy of 'land nationalisation' ostracised him from the heart of Irish politics. Since the inception of the National League, a campaign orchestrated by figures loyal to Parnell such as T. M. Healy and Timothy Harrington had attempted to – in the words of Davitt – 'push me to the wall'.[185] The same month as Davitt delivered his speech in Tralee, he was informed by William O'Brien that his leading opponents in the league were Timothy Harrington along with the other leading Parnellites and national figures, T. P. O'Connor and Dr Joseph Edward Kenny.[186] The actions of Davitt's opponents and his disillusionment with what he saw as the increasingly dictatorial nature of the league led to Davitt leaving the country to undertake a worldwide trip. When in Rome during March 1885 he wrote to another dissenting nationalist, Alfred Webb, stating that if he had stayed 'I would have collided with the organising committee' and that he could 'never participate in it so long as two or three men are allowed to boss it in the name of nationality and democracy'.[187] While Davitt was defiant during these months he did return to the political stage in Ireland sooner rather than later.

By July 1885 Davitt, had returned to Ireland. Although a member of the organising committee of the league, he frequently criticised aspects of the movement. Along with calling for the formation of the elected councils, he condemned the constant focus of the movement on the return of MPs. He wrote in July 1885:

is there another field in which men, who have both personal and political objections to membership of the British Legislature, can labour more effectively for Ireland than in Parliament? . . . I strongly object to the theory implied by *United Ireland*, that an Irish nationalist is only suitably equipped for service against Ireland's enemy when he is armed with the letters 'MP' . . . Carry on the fight here at home on the lines of the Land League against the enemy that will outnumber the Irish phalanx in Westminster.[188]

He continued his tirade by evoking his Fenian past when he wrote that he would not seek election for the House of Commons because of the necessity to take the oath of allegiance.[189] The following week he delivered a lecture at the Rotunda in Dublin to raise money for James Stephens. In his lecture, entitled: 'Fenian movement and the Land League: twenty years of Irish history', he continued to outline his ideas on political action. While acknowledging that the 'prudence and moderation' being professed by the parliamentary party were necessary for political struggle, he contended that 'advice that is calculated to damp that enthusiasm without popular forces can never be brought into the field of national politics and can only give encouragement to our enemies.' He reiterated that politics must not be confined to the House of Commons by stating that 'diplomacy may avail for something in Westminster; but it has never achieved anything but defeat for the popular cause in Ireland'.[190] Although Davitt had disassociated himself from the IRB by this stage, his comments clearly appealed to Fenian sentiments and criticised the dominance of the parliamentary effort over local concerns.[191] His comments on these issues along with his negative response to the 1885 Land Purchase (Ashbourne) Act were 'an unmistakable attack on the authority and policy of Parnell and his lieutenants'.[192] In particular, Davitt deplored the dominance these figures had over the nomination of parliamentary candidates through the county conventions. This was demonstrated at two conventions in Tipperary and Galway when locally nominated candidates were discarded in favour of nominees that Parnell forced on the constituencies.[193] Davitt's severe and public criticisms were related to the main issues in the case of the suppression of the Tralee League. The enforcement of Parnellism over local concerns and disputes was apparent in the Tralee case. Although Davitt did not directly comment on the situation in Tralee, many of the dissenting leaguers may have taken encouragement from his comments, which were made during the period of the upheaval in the branch. Despite the undermining of the IRB by Dublin Castle, Fenianism in general also appeared to have received a degree of public support in Ireland during 1884–5. In September 1884 a crowd of 15,000 marched through Dublin city for the funeral of an old Fenian named Denis Duggan. In April 1885 a subscription was raised for the Fenian leader James Stephens, which in time collected £2,000. Another Fenian leader, John O'Leary, made a triumphant return to Ireland and was greeted by 10,000 people when he arrived in Limerick during March 1885.[194] With Davitt's criticisms of the National League and parliamentary party, and some degree of popular support for Fenianism, it seemed possible for the Tralee Fenian-Leaguers to gain support from these sources.

The Tralee Fenian members of the National League quickly concentrated on gaining support within the county. The Tralee branch appeared to have had some support from other regions. On the day the dissolution of the branch was announced, the Tralee Leaguers met members from both the Killarney and Castleisland branches.[195] The next meetings of both branches condemned the actions of the organising committee. The Castleisland branch, under the influence of a section of radical agrarian activists, whom the police believed to be members of the IRB, passed a resolution condemning Timothy Harrington and the organising committee.[196] In Killarney an attempt was made to pass a similar resolution but was prevented by Jeremiah D. Sheehan. Sheehan was involved in the 1867 Fenian Rising and was still suspected of being a Fenian during the 1880s by the police.[197] Notwithstanding his suspected links with Fenianism, Sheehan was unwilling to back the Tralee Fenian-Leaguers, probably out of a desire to obtain the candidacy for the East Kerry constituency.[198] Other areas of known Fenianism also failed to back the actions of the Tralee Leaguers. The Causeway National League contained a number of known IRB suporters. Its secretary, Thomas Dee, and a member of its committee, William Fenix, were both arrested under the PPP Act and were widely known as Fenians, although the branch failed to comment on the controversy and completely ignored the events.[199] Other areas of National League activity such as Listowel and its surrounding district, which had a number of branches, remained silent on the issue. Any belief by the Tralee Fenian-Leaguers that they could count on widespread support in the county was quickly dispelled. When the secretary of the Tralee branch, Timothy McEnery, condemned the central branch for not funding evicted tenants in Kerry, and called for all subscriptions to be returned to the county, both the Duagh and Firies branches publicly contradicted him and said they had received large grants.[200] Other branches demonstrated further support for Harrington. Resolutions in favour of Harrington were passed at the Killorglin and Dingle Leagues.[201] At a National League public meeting in Knockagree on the Cork border between Castleisland and Millstreet, the speakers expressed strong support for Harrington.[202] Within a number of weeks Edward Harrington demonstrated his continued presence in the county by speaking at a National League demonstration in the south Kerry village of Glenbeigh.[203]

Support for the actions of the Tralee Fenian-Leaguers was concentrated in Tralee and Castleisland. Since the inception of the National League in Castleisland, outrage and boycotting were on the increase in the region. Reporting for July 1885, District Inspector Davis for Castleisland commented: 'boycotting and intimidation, both by notice and from the National League rooms, are beginning to be very much resorted to particularly when persons having anything to do with evicted farms are brought under the notice of the organisation [league]'.[204] While radical agrarian agitators were present in the Castleisland branch, moderate and constitutional influences began to exert control over the body. In June a new parish priest, Archdeacon Irwin, was appointed to Castleisland by the bishop in the belief that his 'quiet, firm, sympathetic temper fits him eminently for the post'.[205] Soon after his appointment, members of the Castleisland League approached Irwin and asked him to preside over the branch. Irwin replied in the affirmative and stated the curates of the town could join if they pleased.[206] At the next meeting of the league, which had a 'crowded attendance', Irwin demonstrated the qualities that his superiors believed made him an ideal parish priest for the volatile district. A letter from the Tralee League was read seeking support for its position against the Central Branch. Although the branch had previously passed resolutions in favour of the Tralee League, Irwin heavily criticised Edward Harrington's expulsion and refused to allow any further communication with the dissolved branch. Irwin also condemned excessive boycotting and refused to sanction a proposed resolution supporting a certain candidate for the position of dispensary doctor. The militant members of the league were enraged and 'a rather discreditable scene followed' leading to the meeting ending in confusion.[207] Although not mentioned in the newspapers, the RIC county inspector reported that Irwin was assaulted by 'a member named Quinlan who is an infidel and a reputed dynamiter'.[208] Quinlan was indeed a known radical whom the police suspected of orchestrating agrarian intimidation and violence.[209] Despite Irwin's difficulties, he achieved a degree of influence over the branch and prevented the radical elements from dominating its proceedings. By early September Davis believed: 'boycotting has received a check by the appointment of Archdeacon Irwin'.[210]

Although the Tralee Fenian-Leaguers continued to meet weekly, the branch's prospects of success had significantly lessened. With the general election looming, leaders of radical nationalism began to offer their full support to Parnell. Michael Davitt settled any ambiguity over his political stance and gave his full backing to Parnell when he said in late August 1885 at a demonstration in Longford: 'I declare that there is only one parliamentary policy in Ireland, and that is the policy of Mr Parnell'.[211] Several other Fenian leaders also gave their support to Parnell. In Mullinahone, County Tipperary, John O'Leary, while giving a speech over the grave of Charles Kickham to commemorate the third anniversary of his death, declared that Parnell 'should now be allowed to decide when and how to take the fence' and that opposition to him was 'unworthy of patriotic men'.[212] Within a number of days the former IRB leader for Cork city and recently elected MP for Tipperary, John O'Connor, visited Tralee and met with William Moore Stack. Since January 1885, O'Connor had become the chief instrument of the Irish Party in Munster to persuade other IRB men to follow his example and join the Parnellites.[213] He persuaded Moore Stack to support the Parnellites and explained to him that if the officers of the branch resigned and a re-election occurred the organising committee would consider reinstating the branch.[214] At the next meeting of the league, Moore Stack outlined these conditions and demonstrated his new conversion to Parnellism by condemning agrarian outrages. The members in attendance failed to support a resolution to this effect, illustrating their continued radicalism, although it was decided to agree to O'Connor's proposals. Thomas O'Rourke depicted the influence Fenianism had over the Tralee Leaguers when he contended:

> he thought it would be a very patriotic duty on their part to do so [support Parnellism], looking at the pronouncement of Mr Michael Davitt at Longford, the speech of John O'Leary over the grave of Charles Kickham and seeing the interview which the *Freeman* correspondent had with James Stephens . . . all of which tended towards one thing, the promotion of unity.[215]

With such Fenian leaders supporting the parliamentary effort for home rule, the Tralee Fenian-Leaguers capitulated. The officers of the branch resigned and in the re-election the Fenians John Power and Maurice Moynihan were elected to leading positions and it is significant that Edward Harrington did not feature. The Central Branch refused to sanction this move. Another election was finally held and in September Edward Harrington was reappointed as president and the branch was officially recognised by the Central Branch.

The debacle within the Tralee League illustrates a number of factors influencing popular politics in the county. The Tralee Fenians were willing to challenge the Irish Party and the constitutional nationalism represented by Edward Harrington and the leaders of the Irish National League. The public's overwhelming support for the GAA sports, which were orchestrated by Fenians, demonstrated the scale of popularity these individuals had. Edward Harrington's continued support of the 'landlord' sports showed that he underestimated this popular sentiment. The resulting divisions between the central branch of the league and the Tralee Leaguers had larger implications. A growing unrest was apparent amongst many nationalists, including Michael Davitt, with the increasingly autocratic nature of the parliamentary party. The suppression of the Tralee branch led to more such criticisms. The episode showed that the National League leadership was trying to create a centralised nationalism against the claims of local organisations and personalities. The failure of the league in the years 1882–4 demonstrated the predominance of local issues and the apathy amongst many to home rule. Davitt's criticisms of the league, which concentrated on its failure to adopt the proposed council of delegates and the constant focus on the return of MPs, astutely played on this danger. There were signs that local disquiet, as in Tralee, could develop into a broader competing movement. Michael Cusack's private and public comments illustrated his willingness to defy the National League to protect the increasingly popular GAA. The Fenian undertones in Davitt's comments demonstrated another threat to the National League's hegemony over popular politics. Popular demonstrations for Fenianism and Fenian leaders were evident in 1884–5. These developments undoubtedly encouraged and gave confidence to the Tralee Leaguers in deposing Edward Harrington and replacing him with a publicly known Fenian, William Moore Stack. However, with the collapse of the Liberal government and the ever increasing prospects of a hung parliament further facilitating Parnell's ability to deliver home rule, any challenge to the leadership of the National League was undermined. When the Tralee Leaguers capitulated to the central branch they cited as influences the pronouncements by Davitt, O'Leary and Stephens, which supported Parnell. The failure of the Fenian-inspired Tralee Leaguers to secure any support outside the Castleisland Branch demonstrated the IRB's limited ability to orchestrate political action in the county. Although the leaders of the move against Edward Harrington in Tralee were well-known Fenians their influence in areas outside the town was cripplingly limited. The vast majority of branches either failed to comment on the issue or openly supported Edward Harrington. Even in regions where Fenians were active in branches, such as Killarney and Causeway, there was no solid support for the Tralee branch. The IRB network that appeared to co-ordinate violent outrages during the land war years could not overcome the moderate and constitutional forces that prevailed locally in the National League.

SIX

THE OPERATION OF THE
NATIONAL LEAGUE

—

THE LAND QUESTION IN 1885

Agrarian matters rather than home rule were ultimately at the heart of the transformation of the league and the political reawakening of the tenant farmers. The reason for the new popularity of the National League in 1885 was the increasing anxiety amongst tenant farmers over the continuing depression in the agricultural economy. A renewed agricultural depression began to take full effect on the rural community in 1885. The prices of both cattle and butter plunged in 1884 and 'no Irish agricultural export commodity was more affected by the downward plunge of prices after 1883 than butter'.[1] Imports of butter into Britain from France, the Netherlands, and the Scandinavian countries undermined the traditional supremacy of Irish butter. This directly diminished the financial return farmers received for their butter. For example, a farmer with 30 dairy cows under the north Kerry land agent George Sandes saw his return for 80 firkins of butter drop from £292 in 1883 to £247 in 1885.[2] Kerry farmers were largely dependent on butter as their main produce. They were further financially squeezed with high county taxes, poor law rates and the taxes for extra police. One farmer from the Castleisland region who had an annual rent of £64 for fifty acres paid £17 for poor rates alone.[3] The fall in the prices of agricultural produce in general, and butter in particular, compounded with the high taxation of tenants undermined the economic viability of the farming class. As early as March 1885 RIC District Inspector William Davis for Castleisland warned: 'taxes are very high and the prices of all sorts of farm produce are low . . . Most of the farmers around here are on the verge of bankruptcy'.[4] By August he feared the worst when he reported:

> the condition of the county is far from promising just now and all classes are in such a bad financial plight that I fear it will be a long time [until] they are in working order. . . I have it from a good number of the largest most intelligent and hard-working farmers in the district that they cannot hold out if matters do not improve.[5]

The precarious financial position of the tenant farmers undermined the gains they had made through rent reductions from the Land Commission.

Despite the farmers' increasing anxiety, no anti-rent combinations or systematic rent strikes had emerged by August 1885, although for a number of months it had been apparent that a renewed clash with landlordism over rent was strongly in the minds of league organisers. As early as April 1885, the Tralee branch warned landlords not to demand rents from tenants.[6] In June the branch sent a circular to all the other league branches in the county calling on them to 'consider. . . some feasible means of averting the extraction from [tenants] of impossible rents'.[7] A leading member of the branch, Thomas O'Rourke, radically advocated that tenants not pay any rent, because of the depression in agricultural prices.[8] In June, the Barraduff National League in the Killarney region urged farmers to first look after themselves and their families, and then pay their landlords. Invoking the 'unwritten law', farmers were informed at the meeting that 'we have natural rights and claims to live in our native soil and they [landlords] want to exterminate us'.[9] Anxiety over the deepening crisis in agricultural prices appeared to be a primary motivation behind the emergence of the National League at a local level during the first two-thirds of 1885.

The agrarianism of the local branches of the National League contradicted the official policy of the movement, which promoted home rule as its primary objective. It has often been contended that, as a result of the land war, the issues of land and nationality were deeply interconnected and from then on land agitation had become a valuable aspect of future nationalist and political activity.[10] Although the leadership of the movement did promote land reform, it was second to home rule in importance in the league's official programme. This was demonstrated in June 1885 when Timothy Harrington (acting as secretary to the central branch) attempted to discourage any potential agrarian agitation and informed local branches that the new league would not dispense funds to evicted tenants as the Land League did. He wrote in a public letter that the league would not wholly discard the claims of evicted tenants but 'when the league was established it was purely and simply as a political organisation, and the relief of evicted tenants had no place in its programme'. He stated that the high cost of the registration of voters undermined the league's ability to fund evicted tenants.[11] At the level of high politics Parnell was preoccupied with politicking for home rule with members of the newly appointed Tory caretaker government. Any renewed agrarian agitation had portentous consequences for the newly established, although largely informal, alliance that Parnell achieved with the Conservatives.[12] In the summer of 1885, despite the realities of the worsening agricultural economy and the simmering tensions in rural society, there was still no impetus from the leadership of the national movement for an agrarian agitation.

Similarly, in Kerry, some elements in the league attempted to prevent agrarianism from dominating the local movement. Edward Harrington, reflecting the objectives of the national leadership, frequently focused on home rule when organising the National League at public demonstrations in the county. At a league meeting in Lixnaw in May 1885, he was pressed by members of the crowd to condemn landgrabbing but refused to dwell on the topic and continued his speech, which spoke of the 'dawning daylight of Irish independence'.[13] The widespread presence of the clergy in the new league attracted a more conservative element, who wished to avoid agitation and its potential excesses. This unwillingness to inflame agrarian tensions was demonstrated at the inaugural meeting of the league in Dingle during May. The meeting's chairman, Canon O'Sullivan, clashed with the Tralee Leaguer, Thomas O'Rourke, who attempted to criticise recent evictions on Lord Ventry's estate. Canon O'Sullivan commented that the evictions were not unjust and only took place where six or seven years rent were due and that Ventry 'is always ready to do justice'. O'Rourke, an established agrarian agitator, replied that they should 'uproot landlordism root and branch'.[14] When Archdeacon Irwin was appointed to the Castleisland parish in August 1885, he succeeded in diluting radical elements in the local branch of the league. During the first meeting he presided over he condemned excessive boycotting and prevented a radical resolution being passed.[15] While agrarianism did influence local league activity and the circumstances were present for a renewed agitation against rent payment, the lack of any initiative from the national leadership and the increasing role of conservative-minded clergy in the movement undermined any potential agrarian agitation.

Parnell's policy of concentrating politics and the National League on home rule rather than on the potentially radical land question was jeopardised with the passing of the new land act in August 1885. The new act attempted to promote the sale of land from landlords to tenants.[16] Easier terms of purchase were offered to tenants, and the government provided £5,000,000 credit for tenants to buy their holdings. Popularly known as the Ashbourne Act, the legislation attempted to overcome the defects of the purchase clauses of the 1881 Land Act. The legislation appeared to meet the National League's policy over land, which amounted to the socially conservative objective of land purchase with the radical Land League cry of compulsory purchase set aside.[17] Editorial comment in *United Ireland*, the National League newspaper, claimed the Land League goal of tenant ownership had been obtained under the act. The newspaper declared:

> the Land League principle of making the tiller the owner of the soil . . . has been
> legislatively admitted, there is room for no other dispute amongst Land Leaguers

except as to the price at which the transfer of property is to take place. This as we have shown is not a matter of principle but of detail, and can be discussed without passion.[18]

The comments illustrated the eagerness of the editors of the newspaper to quell any potential radical agitation. By claiming that the Land League objective of peasant proprietorship had been achieved and that the remaining details did not involve 'principle' or 'passion', the newspaper clearly advocated a moderate reaction to the act, although it contended that some form of organisation orchestrated by the league was necessary:

it is open to the tenants to make their own market for their holdings, and by a little combination and forethought they can regulate the price to the pocket [and] the number of years purchase to be given on any estate must come up for discussion in the local branches of the league everywhere.[19]

The newspaper's reaction to the act reflected an increasing schism within the nationalist movement over the legislation and the increasing potential for rural unrest. Parnell initially failed to recognise the increased significance of the agrarian situation and continued to concentrate on home rule.[20] Similarly, when William O'Brien, T. M. Healy and Justin McCarthy addressed a meeting in Cork on 14 August, little or no comment was made on the land question.[21] However, there was serious criticism from the agrarian left. In early August, Davitt stated at Ardboe, County Tyrone, that the Land Purchase Act had 'for its object the robbing of the public purse and of the tenant farmers, in order to pay the debts of bankrupt landlords' and branded it a 'landlord relief bill'.[22] Within a week, Jeremiah Jordan, soon to be Parnellite MP, pronounced against purchase in much the same vein as had Davitt.[23]

The introduction of the act had the effect of introducing agrarianism into the nationalist movement in a period when the emphasis from Parnell and his leadership was on preparing for the forthcoming general election and the ultimate objective of home rule. Throughout the summer of 1885 the concern with the agrarian question in the localities, owing to the effects of the agricultural depression, was not reflected in the actions of the National League leadership. The introduction of the new legislation transformed the direction of the nationalist movement. While some form of agitation against the payment of rent in the customary September gale was inevitable due to the depressed agricultural economy, the situation was irrevocably altered with the passing of the act. Now the demand and resistance of rent were inextricably linked with the much larger and more significant issue of purchase. With the commonly held Irish nationalist goal of tenant proprietorship apparently on the horizon, attention shifted sharply towards the land question. The more moderate and constitutionally minded Parnellites began concentrating on the issue. John Redmond promoted tenant combination at Castleblaney when he advised tenants to be patient and if 'they waited they would get the land for half what they would have to pay for it if they rushed into the snare in too great a hurry'.[24] At Gorey, County Wexford, William O'Brien promoted National League involvement in agrarian agitation when he stated: 'I see no reason why the branches in their districts should not meet and fix the minimum number of years purchase on the valuation. . . and I see no reason why they should not boycott anyone who went beyond that figure as a landgrabber of the worst stamp'.[25] Parnell continued his political dexterity from the Land League period when he 'had to identify himself (at least superficially) with the pre-eminent cause' within the movement and realigned his policy.[26] He quickly reaffirmed the movement's agrarianism and promoted anti-rent combinations. At the end of August he stated:

> I trust that the example of the settlement that the Tottenham tenants and other tenants have obtained by standing together in a body will instruct the rest of the Irish tenantry and that they will come forward suitably at the commencement of the winter, and subscribe to the funds of the league, which are mainly used for the relief of evicted tenants.[27]

His claim that National League money would fund evicted tenants contra-dicted Timothy Harrington's statement the previous June, which emphasised the use most of league funds for registration and electoral expenses. Harrington also adopted the new-found agrarianism of the leadership when he boasted that 47 evicted tenants on the Tottenham estate were supported by the National League over the previous four years at a total cost of £4,859.[28]

In late August 1885, the recrudescence of anti-rent combinations with support from the national leadership was compounded in Kerry by a large demonstration in Killarney. Over 10,000 attended the meeting, which was addressed by both T. M. Healy and William O'Brien along with the president of the Killarney National League, J. D. Sheehan. Healy and O'Brien were the most prominent national figures to have attended a political demonstration in the county for many years. Healy, long identified as one of the most constitu-tionally minded of all the Parnellite MPs, gave an extremely radical agrarian speech laced with vituperation towards landlords. He condemned those who were grazing on evicted land on the earl of Kenmare's estate, and complained that 'in no part of Ireland was landlordism so odious as in Kerry'. He claimed that the National League's objective was to 'expedite the departure of vultures and harpies from this district' and that tenant farmers should be 'secure in their holdings without having to pay any rent'. Healy stoked tensions between tenants by commenting that 'rich farmers are to be distrusted' and during the Land League era such tenants 'sneaked into the [rent] office, and paid behind backs'. He advised the tenants to 'enter into a combination, to take proper precautions that no man breaks the line' and called on them to 'bank your rents in the name of trustees'.[29] This advice to bank rents until the strike was successful foreshadowed the agrarian agitation announced in October 1886 in the form of the Plan of Campaign.[30] Healy went on to condemn violent outrage and called on the people to employ boycotting to enforce the rent strike. He also deemed that no tenant should purchase under the Ashbourne Act without consulting the local branch of the National League.[31] Healy's comments clearly advocated rent strikes in extreme and violent agrarian rhetoric.[32] Such words urged a renewal of agitation, both against the payment of rent and to lower the purchase price of holdings. This was to be orchestrated by local branches of the National League. Although the meeting also passed resolutions on home rule, and William O'Brien criticised the government, the tone of the meeting was agrarian.

The injection of agrarianism from the nationalist leadership encouraged the emergence of agitation in Kerry. Tenants combined and sought large reductions from their landlords. At a meeting of the Ballyheigue branch of the National League in September, tenants on the Busteed estate were told to seek an abatement in rent of 35 per cent. During the same meeting, tenants on Colonel James Crosbie's 13,422-acre estate decided to demand a 25 per cent reduction.[33] Following on the direction of the league, tenants led by the parish priest, Father McCarthy, who was also the president of the branch, went to Crosbie and demanded this reduction.[34] Tenants on an estate managed by George Trench threatened a 'solid strike . . . against the payment of rent unless [granted] an abatement of forty per cent'.[35] In Ardfert, tenants of Lord Listowel came together at a meeting of the local branch of the National League where 'they debated . . . their claim to a respectable reduction . . .[and] they agreed to demand a reduction of twenty-five per cent'.[36] In nearby Causeway, tenants of Captain Oliver's 1,369-acre estate embarked on a rent strike having been refused an abatement of 25 per cent.[37] Tenants on Sir Edward Denny's 21,479-acre estate near Tralee sought an abatement of 35 per cent in rent.[38] In the autumn of 1885, tenants on many Kerry estates, encouraged and organised by local branches of the National League, sought a general abatement.

The landlord reaction to the tenants' demands varied. Some of the smaller landowners granted reductions. On William Pope's 821-acre estate in Ballyheigue a 30 per cent reduction was granted to the tenants.[39] In the Castleisland region Catherine Clotsman (2,016 acre estate) gave a 25 per cent reduction.[40] Another small landlord in the same region, Captain Fagan (840-

acre estate) offered his tenants a sizeable 40 per cent reduction.[41] Some larger landlords also significantly reduced rents. On the 94,983-acre Lansdowne estate at Kenmare a thousand tenants reportedly marched to seek reductions.[42] The agent, Townsend Trench, offered terms of reduction that the tenants accepted.[43] The ability to reach agreement was partly a result of the fact that landlord–tenant relations on these estates were benign and they were not in centres of previous agrarian disturbance. Such magnanimity was non-existent in other regions. With the prospect of abatements reducing any potential purchase price under the Ashbourne Act, coupled with previous landlord losses experienced through the land courts and Arrears Act, many landowners were determined to withstand tenants' demands. James Crosbie of Ballyheigue refused a reduction on the grounds that he had fixed a judicial rent with two-thirds of his tenantry in 1882.[44] The north Kerry landlord Wilson Gunn informed his tenants that he was aware of the depression in prices 'but that he with the other landlords in the adjoining properties were bound by combination not to give their tenants one penny reduction'.[45] In the perpetually disturbed Castleisland region the majority of landlords flatly refused any rent abatements.[46] Many landlords were heavily in debt and unable to grant reductions.[47] This was particularly evident in the Killarney area where the two major estates of the earl of Kenmare (91,080 acres) and H. A. Herbert of Muckross (47,238 acres) were out of the control of the landlords and in the hands of trustees.[48] In early October 1885 300 tenants sought a 30 per cent rent reduction from Kenmare. The earl, sequestered in his stately Killarney House, offered his sympathy to the tenants but said he had no ability to reduce their rents. In 1882 the estate was £227,000 in debt to Standard Life Assurance Company (a mortgage body) who placed the estate under the control of four trustees who in 1885 refused to reduce rents.[49] The Herbert estate was in a similar financial predicament and the trustees also refused any reduction.[50]

The issue of rent payment was further complicated by the looming question of land purchase. Under the terms of the Ashbourne Act it was recommended that tenants purchase their holdings at a price of between 17 and 20 years of their rent. Tenants were advised by nationalist leaders to wait and combine through branches of the National League to attain lower purchase prices. Landlords and agents, however, appeared anxious to push the sale of holdings at prices that were invariably unacceptable to tenants. The increasingly insolvent Sir Rowland Blennerhassett of Killorglin (8,390 acres) offered his tenants purchase of their holdings, less ten per cent of their current rents.[51] They refused and continued their demand for a 30 per cent reduction. On the Hickson lands near Causeway, the land agent, Samuel Hussey, offered a 20 per cent temporary reduction if tenants bought their holdings at a purchase rate of 20 years, which they promptly refused. In the Castleisland area a small landlord named Richard Meredith (1,839 acres) refused any reduction but offered his tenants purchase of their holdings at 20 years at a price that was Griffith's Valuation and a quarter.[52] The tenants responded by demanding purchase at Griffith's valuation only.[53] In Abbeydorney, tenants on the Hurley estate were offered purchase of their holdings at 20 years. They refused and instead demanded purchase at 15 years.[54] Tenants were encouraged by a general belief that better terms would be easily achieved through combination. This was compounded by the popular opinion that purchase legislation was still in a nascent state and that further incentives to purchase were likely. The Cowper Commission reported that 'so much has been already gained for the tenants that most of them are easily led to believe that, by waiting, they may get more. They are said to be advised by the nationalist party to take this course.'[55] The land agent Townsend Trench told the same commission that the land acts of 1881 and 1885, 'created expectations that still further advantages could be obtained by continued agitation and by the spread of an organisation for resistance to the payment of rent'.[56] In September 1885, police District Inspector Davis for Castleisland described the motivations behind the impending agitation as:

> the people believe that the land question is but in a transition state, and that at any moment a fresh resistance to present rents may become advisable. This feeling is evidenced in the first place by the frequent and almost general refusal on their part to accept the terms (generally about twenty years) on which landlords have offered to sell farms and in the second by the readiness with which they seem disposed to grasp the excuse afforded by the present rather adverse season, in order to demand considerable reduction on even judicial rents. [57]

With the finality of purchase not far from the minds of tenants and landlords a renewed agitation was inevitable. When landlords and their agents refused reductions, the advice of T. M. Healy was heeded and rents were lodged with tenant representatives as defence funds. In Ballyheigue the local league established a defence fund to protect tenants against eviction. Similarly in Ballydonoghue the branch of the National League called on all members to pay 6s in the pound on the valuation of their farms, 'to protect any tenant or tenants who may be put to their costs by their landlord'. Two members of the league were appointed to each townland for the purpose of collection.[58] After Samuel Hussey refused abatements to the earl of Kenmare's tenantry, a defence fund was established and rents were lodged with trustees of the tenants. Within weeks, £850 of tenants' rent was in the hands of the parish priest of Firies and president of the local league, Father O'Connor.[59] Landlords retaliated by re-adopting tactics employed during the land war. As early as September the largest tenants on Captain Oliver's estate were served with writs for eviction.[60] Tenants to a man were reportedly served with writs on a number of estates in Castleisland.[61] On the Kenmare estates 40 of the largest tenants were served with writs.[62] Within several weeks cattle from a number of tenants on the estate were decreed for rent. In a scene reminiscent of the first phase of the land war the cattle were put to public auction. The National League demonstrated against the sale and J. D. Sheehan, acting as the league representative, bid against an 'emergency man' and bought the stock for the tenants.[63] In another tactic revived from the 1879–82 era, tenants in Duagh had the interest in their holdings sold by the landlord to recover rent.[64] The Property Defence Association re-emerged and in October 'proposed to offer help to boycotted farmers, landowners, traders and others by arranging sales of stock, hay, and all kinds of farm produce'.[65] In all, 391 writs were issued for rent in the county during 1885, a significant increase on the 235 issued during the previous year.[66] It was clear that, once again, there was widespread conflict between landlords and tenants.

By the late autumn of 1885 a renewed agrarian agitation was under way in Kerry and large parts of Ireland. Although some landlords willingly reduced rents to a level acceptable to tenants, many refused any abatement. Landlords were anxious to avoid further financial losses after the reductions in many rents in the land courts and the wiping away of rent arrears. On certain estates, such as the earl of Kenmare's, landlords were so much in debt that they were unable to help their tenants. The situation was further complicated by the implications of the Ashbourne Act as landlords and tenants both attempted to influence the purchase price of holdings. By late 1885 the land question remained as intractable as ever. Central to the emergence of rent strikes was the role of local branches of the National League. Local leagues organised tenants, advised them on what reductions to seek and orchestrated defence funds. Despite the constitutional objectives of the leadership of the league, agrarian issues were central to the emergence of the movement at a local level.

GROWTH OF THE NATIONAL LEAGUE AND ITS SOCIAL COMPOSITION

By the time of the county convention in November 1885 the National League had developed into a mass movement. The league was propelled by the re-emergence of agrarian agitation. The organisation received widespread clerical support leading to the establishment of over 50 branches in the county. Utilising the structure of the Roman Catholic administration and the organisational skills of its clergy, branches were established on a parish basis. According to

RIC County Inspector Moriarty, as the convention approached 'there [was] a branch of the National League in full swing in every parish in Kerry'.[67] This level of local activity was unprecedented in Irish politics. In Kerry, during the height of the land war period (1879–82) a total of only 17 different Land League branches were reported as active in the *Kerry Sentinel*. The level of political activity was represented in the large number of branch meetings held. A table 6.1 shows, the number of branch meetings rose from 48 in the first four months of 1885 to 110 for the second four months.

Table 6.1 Number of branch meetings of the Irish National League by poor law union, 1 January 1885–31 December 1885

Poor Law Union	Jan.–Apr.	May–Aug.	Sept.–Dec.	Total
Cahirciveen	0	1	16	17
Dingle	0	4	15	19
Glin	0	0	3	3
Kenmare	0	0	11	11
Killarney	18	32	29	79
Listowel	16	42	66	124
Tralee	13	31	60	105
Total	48	110	200	358

Source: KS, 1 Jan. 1885–31 Dec. 1885.

During the final third of the year, 200 branch meetings were reported in the *Kerry Sentinel*. In all, branches of the league were reported as meeting on 358 occasions in Kerry during 1885. The organisation appeared to have the support of the mass of the non-landlord Catholic population. During a single meeting of the league in September at Ballyduff 200 new members reportedly joined.[68] At another branch meeting in Ballydonoghue up to 600 were present while in Ballybunion 352 attended.[69] By December 1885 Timothy Harrington, in an interview with the Central News Agency, confidently stated that 1,600 branches were in existence in the country which had on average 300 members each.[70] Local communities in their entirety joined the league. A tenant farmer of the earl of Kenmare named Denis McCarthy commented in 1888 that he was a member of the 'National League as were all his neighbours around him'.[71] It was undoubtedly one of the most extensive mass political mobilisations in recent times in Ireland.

Although the league gained support from the mass of the Catholic and non-gentry population, vital to its success was the politicisation of middle to large tenant farmers. As the Land League period demonstrated, this group was pivotal to the success of any large scale agrarian movement. The large farmers supported the Land League until the radicalism of the No Rent Manifesto threatened their position. They widely availed of the 1881 Land Act and entered the Land Commission to receive rent reductions. At the end of 1882 they were avoiding the new National League which soon atrophied into a defunct organisation, further illustrating their importance as a political group. The renewal of the land agitation combined with the increasing spectre of home rule propelled this group back on to the political stage. Farmers are often seen as a class unlikely to become active participants in politics due to more pressing and unavoidable duties on the farm. In nineteenth-century Ireland, their most important contribution in politics often remained who they supported at election time.[72] While this was invariably true in relation to national and electoral politics, the localised and parish based organisation of the National League harnessed this group into political activity.

During the growth of the National League in the latter half of 1885, it was clear that a middle class of tenant farmers aligned with Catholic priests was central to the leadership of league branches. The leading members at a branch level shared a number of social characteristics. Similarities occurred in age, marital status and acreage of farms. This is evident from a sample of leading members (officials and committee members) from four branches (table 6.2). From the Abbeydorney, Ardfert, Firies and Kilflynn branches, 21 individuals were traced in the 1901 census returns to create a sample of the age of leading members of the league. This age profile demonstrates that most of the leading members of local league branches were aged above 30. The largest age group were between the years of 30 and 39. These signified a new generation of community leaders who had recently elevated their position within society. Many men in this age group had acquired their farm holdings, making the transition from farmers' sons to occupiers of land. In many cases they were recently married. Of the Abbeydorney branch leaders' households, seven had children cited as living in the family home in 1901. All of these families bar one had a child aged sixteen years or over indicating that the head of the household was married and had children by the time they joined the branch of the National League in 1885.[73] The opportunity to marriage was increasingly restricted in post-Famine Ireland. Restrictive marriage practices emerged as subdivision of farm holdings was avoided and parents, largely concerned with the economic advantages of the match, controlled the marriage of children.[74] The men who became the leading members of branches of the National League were the favoured sons within families whose succession to land was rapidly followed by marriage.[75] By 1881 the majority of men in Kerry were married by the time they were 40 with only 693 of the county's male population over that age unmarried, although later marriage had become increasingly prevalent by this time. During the 1870s the age of marriage rapidly increased in the county. Between 1871 and 1881 the number of unmarried males aged between 20 and 29 had risen 27 per cent.[76] Those in the sample who formed the leadership of the National League at a local level appeared to avoid this tendency and marry young. These men had married at a relatively young age because they inherited the family farm, assuming an elevated position in their communities.

Table 6.2 Age of leading members from four branches of the National League, 1885

Age	20–29	30–39	40–49	50–59	60–69
Abbeydorney	1	4	0	1	1
Ardfert	0	2	3	0	0
Firies	1	2	0	0	2
Kilflynn	0	1	2	1	0
Total	2	9	5	2	3
Percentage of total	9.5%	42.8%	23.8%	9.5%	14.3%

Source: For Abbeydorney see, *KS*, 8 May, 30 June, 28 Aug. 1885, *Guy's*, pp. 5–6, 1901 Census returns, roll 129, 135, 136 (NAI); for Ardfert see, *KS*, 12 May 1885, *Guy's*, pp. 77–9, 1901 Census returns; for Firies see, *KS*, 20 Oct. 1885, *Guy's*, p. 471, 1901 Census returns; for Kilflynn see, *KS*, 23 Oct. 1885, *Guy's*, p. 542, 1901 Census roll 122, 164.

Many of these leading figures were also prosperous middle to large sized farmers. This is demonstrated by a different sample. Concentrating on the leadership of the Abbeydorney, Ardfert and Firies branches, information was obtained on 14 individuals. Of this group, three had a tenant farm with a valuation of over £100, four had valuations from £50 to £99, while seven ranged between £10 and £49. Only one had a holding valued below £10.[77] Many of these men were typical of the large farmer class who were long-standing leaders within their communities and formed the leadership of the farmers' clubs and tenant right clubs in the 1870s.[78] During the pre-land war period they also made up the body of elected poor law guardians whose positions were 'status symbols' and allowed the 'aggressive farmer or shopkeeper . . . both social and political advancement'.[79] Prominence in a local National League branch, like becoming a Poor Law Guardian, provided individuals with a degree of prestige and status within their local communities.[80] The leadership of the league was soon swollen with members of the rural middle classes – those who had access to land and marriage and formed the elite of the non-landed rural population.

Modern historians have long established the leading role of publicans and shopkeepers in the local leadership of the Land League.[81] The prominent role of this group continued with the emergence of the National League. This was particularly evident in towns where merchants were prominent in the movement. In Listowel the branch president, John Stack, was a draper. At least two other members of the branch's committee were merchants in the town.[82] The middle-class leadership of the league was further illustrated with the appointment of a schoolteacher named John Fitzpatrick as the branch vice-president while a doctor, John Clancy, was a committee member.[83] In the highly disturbed Castleisland area, the league was controlled by a group of large farmers and town traders. During a meeting of the branch in September 1885 fourteen names were published as in attendance.[84] Of this group three were large farmers, five were traders (two vintners, two provisional dealers and one grocer), one was a hotel owner and another was an auctioneer.[85] An RIC district inspector named David Huggins, who had served in Castleisland, believed that the 'respectable class of farmers and shopkeepers' led the Land and National League in the region.[86]

In Tralee, shopkeepers, publicans, newspaper editors and solicitors formed the core of the leadership of the National League. This middle-class grouping had been heavily involved in political action before the emergence of the National League. They acted as the local leadership of the 'Catholic people of Ireland [who] were ambitious for power-power of a social as well as political kind'.[87] By the 1880s this class had become integrated in public life with access to a range of local government positions from poor law boards, dispensary committees and sanitary authorities along with town commissions in urban areas. The leading local officials of the National League were typical of the mid to late Victorian 'public man' who participated in an ever-expanding civic culture brought about by wider transformations in local government.[88] Participation of the 'respectable classes' in the local leadership of the National League not only allowed such men power and patronage but also status in a Victorian culture where local newspapers and directories constantly noted who was important in local society.

THE 'LAW OF THE LEAGUE'

The National League's new mass organisation incorporated various socio-economic groupings. The leadership of the movement, as shown above, was largely made up of middle-class figures and clergy, including the vital middle to large tenant farmers who were politicised by the interconnected matters of rent payment and purchase in the autumn of 1885. While this socio-economic group was vital to the strength of any nationalist movement, the National League was not established solely to meet their needs; the primary objective of the movement officially remained home rule. There were also demands from within the league to address the objectives of the rural poor. An analysis of 360 resolutions passed at local branch meetings in Kerry between January and December 1885 illustrates the range of issues that came to the fore during branch meetings (table 6.3).

Table 6.3 A breakdown of 360 resolutions passed at National League branch meetings reported in the Kerry Sentinel, 1 January 1885–31 December 1885[89]

	Jan.– Apr.	May– Aug.	Sept.– Dec.	Total/ %
National issues and demands				40
				11.1%
Pro Parnell/IPP/NL	3	9	5	17
Land reform/Condemnation of 1881 Land Act/				
Landlordism	0	3	1	4
Praising/commenting on popular nationalist figures	2	8	2	12
Cattle company	0	0	5	5
Buy Irish manufactures/goods	0	0	2	2
Rents/ Evicted land				82
				22.7%
Lower rents/defence funds/ tenant combinations	1	6	20	27
Warning not to break rent strikes	0	2	7	9
Condemning Land Commission judgements	0	1	0	1
Condemning Landlords/ agents	0	0	2	2
Condemning land/grass grabbing	2	8	4	14
Don't hold social/economic intercourse with				
anyone connected with evicted land	4	15	10	29
Enforcing law of the league				84
				23.3%
Don't hold social/economic intercourse with				
non-members of the league	1	14	3	18
Asking/demanding people to join the league	3	4	5	12
Warning expulsion for breaking rules of league	2	7	13	22
Condemning/calling individuals before the league	1	2	5	8
Condemning of outrage	1	3	11	14
Other	3	7	0	10
Agricultural labourers				46
				12.7%
Conacre/ score ground	4	3	20	27

	Jan.– Apr.	May– Aug.	Sept.– Dec.	Total/ %
Calling on boards of guardians to implement				
Labourers Act	0	4	7	11
Other	0	2	6	8
Local government				31
				8.6%
PLU elections	4	2	0	6
PLU appointments/jobs	4	1	0	5
Criticising/ directing guardians	0	4	1	5
Condemning local action of police and government	4	0	1	5
Condemning royal visit	10	0	0	10
Parliamentary elections				23
				6.4%
Registration of voters	1	5	0	6
County convention	0	3	1	4
Supporting Irish Party candidates/ General election	0	0	13	13
Internal branch administration				34
				9.4%
Warning about non-attendance	2	1	4	7
Bringing resolution/ new member before				
committee first	4	1	3	8
Support/sending subscriptions to central branch	4	1	3	8
Calling on members to pay subscriptions	0	3	3	6
Order in local branch meetings	0	1	2	3
Other	0	2	0	2
Other				20
				5.5%
Resolutions that do not fit into the above categories	3	11	13	20
Total				360

Source: These resolutions were derived from a systematic examination of reports of 360 branch meetings of the National League that appeared in the *Kerry Sentinel*, 1 Jan. 1885–31 Dec. 1885.

As depicted in table 6.3, 40 of the resolutions passed dealt with 'national issues and demands'. The most numerous in this category were resolutions passed declaring loyalty to Parnell, the Irish Parliamentary Party and the National League. Branches also praised and commented on other nationalist figures, often when they were in the public eye. In late July the Abbeydorney branch 'hailed' the reintroduction of John Dillon into the political scene.[90] After Walsh, the leading nationalist Catholic cleric, was appointed Archbishop of Dublin, a number of branches passed resolutions offering him congratulations.[91] Local branches also offered support to broader national and provincial campaigns, such as the attempt by the Southern Cattle Association to boycott the Cork Steam Packet Company.[92] Other resolutions called for reform of the land law and particularly the 1881 Land Act. There was a limited amount of local activity in support of the National League's call to support Irish manufacturing and to buy only goods made in Ireland.[93] In total, 11.1 per cent of all resolutions passed at branch meetings dealt with issues that had significance beyond the realm of local life. To some degree members of local branches placed their political activity within the context of the broader home rule and nationalist movement. With reference to the leaders of the parliamentary party and nationalist members of the Catholic hierarchy, local branches placed and viewed these figures as the political and spiritual leadership of their movement.

Local branches of the league were also concerned with the administration of local government, and passed 31 resolutions concerning the topic. Considerable attention was given to boards of guardians. Branches attempted to orchestrate elections, influence appointments and direct policy on the boards. Other resolutions criticised certain actions of the police and government and opposed royal visits. Twenty-two resolutions concerning these issues were passed in the first four months of the year. This period corresponded with the annual poor law union elections and the controversial visit of the Prince of Wales.[94]

Twenty-one resolutions passed at branch meetings were related to the 1885 general election. Six of these dealt with the registration of voters. In Tralee a registration committee was established to ensure voters were on the electoral roll while the Duagh branch warned its members to pay their poor law rates to ensure their right to vote.[95] Only four resolutions were passed regarding the county convention to nominate candidates for the general election. This was demonstrated when the Ballybunion branch proposed John Stack, vice-president of the neighbouring Listowel branch, to the convention.[96] Despite the limited number of resolutions regarding the convention, the issue was discussed extensively which was demonstrated by the large number of branch members attending the county convention that selected candidates. Also 13 resolutions were passed supporting and congratulating the candidates that ran and were duly elected in the 1885 general election.

Although branches did deal with national issues, local government and parliamentary elections the overriding concern of local branches of the National League remained agrarian. Most activity in branches was related to rent, agricultural labourers and the enforcement of the law of the league, which made up 212 of the total 360 resolutions passed. The most significant resolutions affecting landlord–tenant relations and the state of the countryside were those related to rent strikes. These resolutions regulated the demands of tenants, organised defence funds, and warned against tenants breaking the strikes and paying their rents. For example, in early September 1885 the Ballyheigue branch resolved that tenants should pay rent only with a 35 per cent reduction on the Busteed estate and an abatement of 25 per cent on the Crosbie lands.[97] Branches also organised funds for the defence of striking tenants. To enforce anti-rent combinations, branches passed resolutions warning against payment by tenants.[98] The prevention of the retaking of evicted land or, as it was popularly known, landgrabbing, was strongly connected to rent strikes. The protection of evicted land was essential for the success of the anti-landlord agitation. The overall strategy was to undermine the landlord's weapon of eviction by making evicted land economically non-viable by preventing it being re-let. Many resolutions – 29 – warned against social or economic intercourse with anyone connected with evicted land, which openly advocated boycotting. These resolutions forbade not just the taking of evicted land but also labourers working on such land, the buying of hay and the grazing on evicted farms (popularly known as grass-grabbing). The interrelated issues of rent strikes and evicted land were the subject of much of the activity of local branches of the National League, demonstrating the dominance of agrarian issues in its proceedings.

Although the demands of tenant farmers were the most prominent topic at branch level, matters of concern to agricultural labourers was frequently dealt with. Forty-six resolutions were passed promoting the cause of labourers. The most common issue was the agricultural labourer's right to rent farmers' land for the taking of a single crop, most commonly for potatoes, in what was known as conacre.[99] Totalling 27 resolutions, this number equalled the other highest single issue in the sample. The most common theme of these resolutions was that farmers grant all labourers who were members of the league conacre at the same rent that the tenant paid the landlord.[100] Other resolutions called on poor law guardians to implement the terms of the 1883 Labourers Act and build labourers' cottages.[101] Eight more resolutions were passed which concentrated on the creation of employment by calling for public works and the banning of the use of agricultural machinery.[102] One meeting in Ballyduff resolved to condemn 'the action of farmers, who have mowing machines and let them out on hire to others as we consider it prevents the poor workingman from getting employment and a chance of getting their hire during the busy harvest time'.[103] The substantial number of resolutions passed concerning agricultural labourers demonstrates that local branches of the league did attempt to promote the rights of that class often to the detriment of farmers.

This reflected the new electoral power of agricultural labourers who were enfranchised for the first time in 1884.

The observance of rent strikes, the protection of evicted land and the rights of agricultural labourers were the social aims of the National League at branch level. Branches passed 82 resolutions attempting to enforce the 'law of the league'. These frequently declared that members must only deal socially and economically with fellow members. This was often cloaked in nationalism, as when the Currans branch resolved: 'for the purpose of displaying our patriotism in a practical manner, we . . . pledge ourselves today to hold intercourse with no farmer, trader, shopkeeper, or labourer except a member of the National League'.[104] Similarly, the Kilcummin branch declared that its members must 'remain aloof from those who failed to join the league and treat them as supporters of landlordism'.[105] Some branches issued forceful decrees calling on people to join the movement. In November the Knocknagoshel branch declared that everyone in the community had to join the league by the following week.[106] In Lixnaw the league warned that those who failed to become enrolled would have their names published outside the chapel door on Sundays.[107] Branches demanded the full co-operation of the non-landlord community to the extent that the Ballymacelligot branch agreed that boys under the age of 16 would be admitted as members at a reduced subscription fee of sixpence.[108] Branches frequently warned members with expulsion if they broke the rules of the league, and this accounted for 22 resolutions.

Local branches of the league constantly reinforced the political and social divisions between 'unionist' landlords and 'nationalists'. Resolutions passed by local branches were made up of a potent mix of nationalist fervour, anti-landlord sentiment and Catholicism. Those who failed to join the league or abide by its rules were made pariahs and derided as grabbers and traitors to Ireland. Local branches were largely successful in the enforcement of the 'law of the league' over agrarian society. By December 1885, RIC County Inspector Moriarty despondently reported that 'regarding the National League, I may say what every one knows that its laws and not those of the British government are governing this unfortunate country'.[109] A month later he echoed these sentiments when he reported: 'the National League has superseded British law, which is a thing of the past in Kerry and is now ruling the county completely'.[110] These assertions were undoubtedly a gross exaggeration, since the league attempted to legislate over agrarian matters only and the 'ordinary law' still regulated other aspects of life, although the comments did reflect the power of the league over agrarian matters. A significant aspect of the attempt to enforce the 'law of the league' was the development of 'league courts'. These courts had emerged during the Land League period but were largely undermined with the arrest of the Tralee Leaguers in January 1881 and thereafter discouraged by the leadership of the movement.[111] Some historians have suggested that the formation of league courts provided the basis for alternative agrarian legal systems from the official law that would emerge during the later periods of the United Irish League and Sinn Féin (1916–21).[112] These league 'courts' adopted the forms, methods and language of legal tribunals. The committees of local branches summoned defendants and witnesses, heard cases, issued judgments and assigned penalties. Proceedings were begun in cases when complaints against individuals were raised orally at a meeting.[113] In doing so these courts did not offer a radical alternative from the existing law institutions of the petty sessions but closely modelled themselves on the established forms.[114] Cases were usually heard at the next meeting of the branch where the accused could contest the charges or offer an explanation and the committee would give its verdict. Failure to attend or offer an adequate response would lead to the defendant being declared obnoxious and subsequently punished, which usually meant boycotting. The Cowper Commissioners described the process of the National League courts:

> the methods of passing resolutions at National League meetings, causing their proceedings to be reported in the local newspapers naming obnoxious men and then boycotting those names. Tenants who have paid even the judicial rents have been summoned to appear before self constituted tribunals, and if they failed to do so, or appearing failed to satisfy these tribunals have been fined or boycotted. The people are more afraid of boycotting, which depends for its success on the probability of outrage, than they are of the judgments of the courts of justice. This unwritten law in some districts is supreme.[115]

As these league courts emerged, boycotting spread rapidly. As early as May 1885 the Divisional Magistrate for the south-west, Captain Plunkett, believed that 'the system of boycotting is decidedly on the increase owing entirely to the teaching of the Irish National League'.[116] In the next eight months the number of individuals boycotted in the county rose from 37 in June to 97 by January 1886 (out of this number only seven were wholly boycotted, while the remaining 90 were partially boycotted).[117] By and large the threat of the boycott was enough to force individuals to obey the regulations of the league and those who went against the league frequently caved in and sought forgiveness.[118] The league proved extremely effective in preventing the re-taking of evicted land. By the autumn of 1886 there were 1,680 acres of derelict evicted land in the police district of Killarney alone.[119] Similarly, in the Castleisland region, where by December 1885 60 evicted farms lay uncultivated, the RIC district inspector believed that 'the whole community are in league to have reprisals from any person, be he landlord or tenant who interferes with, or attempts to derive any benefit from a farm from which a tenant has been evicted'.[120] Local branches of the league also implemented rent strikes successfully. The league succeeded in enforcing its edicts on large sections of the community.

A further analysis of the cases that came before the league courts demonstrates the practical implementation of the 'law of the league'. Table 6.4 provides a breakdown of 66 cases that came before league branches. This number is based on any charge, hearing or outcome that arose during meetings. The protection of the interests of tenant farmers by punishing, firstly those who broke rent strikes (28.8%), and secondly those who grabbed land (19.7%), accounted for almost half of the cases that came before the league. The matter of paying rent was particularly common at league courts. During a branch meeting in Keelgarrylander the leadership resolved that a number of tenants were 'in violation of agreement with their fellow tenants to pay no impossible rents, are guilty of a breach of faith going separately and unknown to the rest'.[121] Similarly, the Ballyduff branch passed 'a vote of censure' against three tenants who paid their rents on the Hickson estate.[122] When 13 tenants broke a rent strike and paid their rents openly on Crosbie's estate in Ballyheigue, the local league immediately expelled them.[123] A significant number of cases of landgrabbing also came before league meetings. Like the cases that arose during the Land League period, these landgrabbing cases were often complicated and varied. They were frequently based on disputes between neighbours and family members over competing claims on land. [124]

Table 6.4 Breakdown of cases before National League 'courts' in Kerry, 1 August–31 December 1885

Issue	Cases	Percentage
Breaking rent strikes	19	28.8
Land and grass grabbing	13	19.7
Dealing with obnoxious people	23	34.8
Breaking rules relating to agricultural labourers	7	10.6
Other	4	6.1
Total	66	100

Notes: This information is gleaned from reports of National League meetings between 1 August 1885 and 31 December 1885 published in the *Kerry Sentinel*. These reports do not offer a full account of every case before local leagues. Any charge, hearing or outcome is therefore used in the statistics.

The most prominent issue before the league courts was the punishment of offenders of the rules of the league, and particularly those that broke boycotts. Offenders of the 'law of the league' were frequently charged with social or economic interaction with boycotted individuals. For example, in August 1885 two members of the Ballyduff branch were charged with buying hay and meadowing from a boycotted landlord. In the same week five members of the Causeway branch had similar charges brought against them.[125] And at a league court in Dingle during September 1885 charges were issued against four shopkeepers for selling to 'landlords' men'. In another case, a carman, who was working for Lord Ventry and was ordered to appear at the previous meeting on a complaint, offered an apology to the court and pleaded that 'he would rather to go to the workhouse than to work for [Ventry]'.[126] These enquiries into cases where individuals were accused of breaking the rules of the league were the most common matters before the league courts. While this was done to enforce boycotting, branch members also attempted to influence and use the 'law of the league' for personal advantage. In the Dingle region, for example, a hotel owner and leading league member, John Lee, orchestrated the boycott of a competing hotel owner in the town. It transpired that the intended boycotted individual, a Mrs Benner, had not transgressed the league, and was a personal friend of Timothy Harrington who intervened and warned that the branch would be dissolved if it continued to pursue such cases.[127] The league agitation in the Millstreet region – just over the border with County Cork – may have involved similar motives. Canon Griffin, the local parish priest, believed that 'any disturbances that took place in [Millstreet] were not caused so much by disputes between landlords and tenants as trade jealousies, which caused much boycotting'.[128] Griffin described to the Cowper Commission a case where a large shopkeeper who was also a farmer fell out of favour with a number of league members over road-building contracts. The members subsequently 'took advantage of the league for the purpose of ruining him'.[129] Under the surface of the action and rhetoric of the league lay an undercurrent of trade disputes and personal vendettas. League members sometimes attempted to manipulate the 'law of the league' to gain an advantage in such disputes although the league courts were essentially designed to protect evicted land (that is, prevent landgrabbing), organise tenants and enforce rent strikes.

While the National League branch structure developed rapidly in 1885, the national leadership tried to contain the organisation as a constitutional body. Despite this, agrarian issues dominated at a local level and in the spread and popularity of the new league.[130] Although the nationalist leaders appeared to support this agrarian agitation in August 1885, this rapidly changed in September with the publication of Gladstone's manifesto for the forthcoming general election. Although the manifesto did not openly declare support for home rule it did grant 'an expression of qualified approval for "every grant to portions of the country [i.e. United Kingdom] of enlarged powers for the management of their own affairs"'.[131] In October, Gladstone further hinted at favouring home rule when he said that if the majority of MPs in the new parliament were to demand strong local powers of self-government then the question would have to be dealt with.[132] This was all carried out in the context of a strengthening bond between the Tories and Parnell, which served to further inflate nationalist aspirations concerning home rule.[133] During October and November the election campaign gained momentum when the league held county conventions across the country to nominate candidates. Home rule appeared omnipresent on the political arena. By the start of November, 23 National League conventions had been held nominating 52 candidates.[134]

The home rule question re-emerged to dominate the electoral campaign at a national level, and a clash with the inherent agrarianism of the local branches of the league was inevitable. The increase in boycotting and agitation, a result of the upsurge in branch activity and agrarian tensions, was deleterious to the prospects of home rule. During the election campaign the parliamentary party and the National League leadership thought it essential to appear as moderate and 'reasonable' as possible before a sceptical British public. Opponents of home rule made political capital from reports of the National League's enforcement of the 'law of the league'. As early as September, the leadership of the league moved to counter the excesses of local branches. There was criticism of the practice of publishing lists of names of those individuals who failed to join branches. The rise in boycotting was directly related to punishments ordered by local branches to those who broke their rules. Despite the potential dangers of implementing the 'law of the league', the leadership still recognised the local realities of the movement, while stressing moderation. An editorial of the *United Ireland* announced:

> the social government of the country is to a great extent carried on by over a thousand branches and is upon the whole carried on with a tranquillity, moderation and fair play, as well as effectiveness . . . [Such power] ought to be accompanied by a deep sense of responsibility, and a resolute determination to banish all personal spleens and petty disputes.[135]

A week later at a meeting of the central branch, T. M. Healy dealt tentatively with the issue. Always the practitioner of *Realpolitik*, Healy refused to condemn boycotting. Anxious to avoid tension and possible alienation of the league's local leadership, he contended that the nationalist community in Ireland had been the victims of freemason boycotting in which the government, civil service, the railway companies and the Bank of Ireland had all participated. He claimed that the only difference was that this conspiracy had been done in secret and he urged branches to follow suit and not publish names of offenders.[136] In contrast to Healy's soft attitude towards local leagues,

Timothy Harrington, the increasingly authoritarian secretary of the central branch, chastised local branches for extreme actions. At a meeting of the central branch of the National League's organising committee Harrington highlighted that he

> wished to point out in the most distinct manner that they could have no sympathy with a movement to coerce men to become members of an organisation from which, if they did not follow out all its programme, they might at any time be expelled, and as a matter of fact were being expelled in many localities.[137]

Harrington, evidently less concerned with his popular standing than some of his peers, announced that the central branch would 'separate themselves from the action of the local branch, and if the local branch did not discontinue practices of the kind they would take steps to dissolve the local branch of the National League'.[138] Although the leadership of the league attempted to prevent the excesses of boycotting, in the countryside the power and status of the local branches depended on their ability to enforce their laws and regulations. The league courts often adjudicated over local disputes, while boycotting was the lynchpin of local league power. This agrarian activity and aims were fundamental to the success of local branches.

While the national leadership was able to exert pressure on branches to maintain a moderate course, the threat remained of an outbreak of serious violence similar to that of the land war, 1879–82. The radical and Fenian influences that had permeated the original Land League leadership were purged from the new movement by Parnell and his loyal inner circle. The organisation had condemned agrarian outrages since its foundation. In Kerry, outrage was denounced from National League platforms and branches resolved to act constitutionally. The impetus for this largely emanated from the leadership. In August 1885, Timothy Harrington sent a circular to all branches, instructing members to stop committing outrages.[139] In fact, as the National League had grown in strength, outrages appeared to decrease in some regions. By October 1885 the police County Inspector Moriarty for Kerry believed that 'outrages have decreased in number and I am of [the] opinion such is attributable to the league leaders, who are anxious to keep down outrage for the present as far they can'.[140] The influence of radical agrarians and Fenians in the National League was countered to some degree at a local level by the Catholic clergy. This was particularly evident in the Castleisland region where the appointment of Archdeacon Irwin appeared to moderate the branch's activities. Similarly, in the neighbouring Ballymacelligott branch, local priests had the same effect. District Inspector Davis stated that [the branch is] composed of the worst characters in the district and ripe for any mischief. Father O'Leary PP is constantly working to counteract the evil effects of the Ballymacelligott one and I have no doubt he has up to the present been the means of preventing a good deal of outrage which was hatched at the league rooms.[141]

In Tralee Edward Harrington successfully sidelined his radical Fenian opponents in the town's branch of the league.[142] Parnellite politics was primarily concerned with controlling such radical forces and maintaining the constitutional nature of the movement. The move to isolate radical and Fenian elements in the movement became apparent at the county election convention in November 1885.

Several men associated with radical agrarianism attended the convention. William Fenix was one of the Causeway contingent who had a history of involvement in Fenian and secret society activity and had been arrested under the 1881 PPP Act. Thomas Dooling was one of the Lixnaw branch's delegates. Although not arrested under the 1881 PPP Act, he took part in secret society activity during the Land League period.[143] By 1890 the police believed Dooling was an IRB centre and had orchestrated the murder of a tenant named Fitzmaurice in 1888.[144] Despite Michael Power's opposition to Edward Harrington in the Tralee League, he was one of the four representatives of the branch at the convention, indicating that he still maintained a degree of influence.[145] Of the four men who represented the Castleisland branch, two – Hussey and Quinlan – were considered as perpetrators of agrarian violence in the region during the Land League period. Quinlan's radicalism persisted and in 1885 he physically assaulted Archdeacon Irwin after he condemned boycotting during a meeting of the Castleisland National League.[146] It was rumoured that during 1886 he had provided weapons for an attack on cattle belonging to an absentee landlord, Standish O'Grady, in the Brosna region.[147] These men were deeply involved in the agrarian violence of the early 1880s and in 1885 were still connected with radical agrarianism.

The county convention was held in late November 1885 at the premises of the Christian Brothers School in Tralee town. Of the 277 delegates, 60 were from the Catholic clergy who were present as *ex-officio* members. Predictably, no clergymen of other nominations were present at the convention. The lay delegates were representatives of the 60 Kerry branches of the league. The central branch of the National League had a strong influence over the convention which was chaired by T. D. Sullivan and James O'Kelly, two MPs who were loyal to Parnell.[148] Eight nominations were put forward for the four seats in the county. Five of them – W. J. O'Doherty, John O'Connor, John Stack, Edward Harrington and J. D. Foley – were each proposed by a lay and clerical delegate. The remaining three candidates, Michael Healy, J. D. Sheehan, president of the Killarney branch, and the Castleisland radical Lawrence Quinlan failed to receive any clerical backing and were proposed by lay members only.[149] In a private meeting, which according to the *Kerry Sentinel* passed off with the 'entire absence on anything approaching dissension in the slightest degree', Doherty, O'Connor, Stack and Harrington were all nominated as election candidates.[150] Only Stack and Harrington lived in the county and both were considered moderate nationalists with no past in agrarian secret societies; both were committed to Parnellism. Stack was vice-president of the Listowel National League and was widely considered 'moderate' and even the unionist *Kerry Evening Post* commented that he 'has the reputation of being an "honest" nationalist, a title, we may remark, given to very few in this county'.[151]

The other two candidates, O'Connor and Doherty, both from outside the county, clearly had the support of the central branch of the league and as a result received the nominations. Of the nominations that failed, only J. D. Foley had any clerical backing. Foley was the most prominent league organiser in the south Kerry town of Killorglin and was credited with organising five branches in the region.[152] A civil engineer and the son of a respectable farmer, he would probably have been successful, had the seat not been earmarked for O'Connor. Sheehan, president of the Killarney League, and a central organiser of the movement in the region, failed to get nominated for East Kerry. Although he had not been prominent in the Land League, he had emerged as the most active National Leaguer in the Killarney region by 1885. During the Fenian rising in 1867–8 he had been arrested, and in 1878–9 was suspected by the police of promoting Fenianism in Killarney, which may explain his failure to gain any support from the clergy at the convention.[153] By 1885 he appeared to have converted to Parnellism and he actively condemned outrage. His apparent transformation to moderate politics was confirmed when he successfully received the candidature in December after Doherty dropped out of the election. Of all the initial nominations Lawrence Quinlan was undoubtedly the most committed radical agrarian agitator with a history of using physical force. The moderate lay nationalists committed to Parnellism combined with the priests to overcome any individuals connected with radical agrarianism. The hierarchical structure of the National League succeeded in providing candidates completely loyal to Parnell for the 1885 general election and isolated radical agrarians within the movement. The Catholic clergy, too, had a leading role in the selection of candidates and only those who received clerical backing were successfully nominated. The *Kerry Evening Post* sarcastically noted the isolation of radicals at the convention when it commented:

there is however, a powerful body in Kerry who have been treated very unfairly, and who now have a big grievance to brood over. We mean the Moonlighting body, which occupies a foremost rank in the politics of the county. Their interests have been entirely overlooked, and owing to their apathy in the matter, the Kerry Moonlighters will have no staunch advocate in the House of Commons.[154]

By the National League's county convention in late 1885 the movement and popular political activity had significantly changed in the county. The National League had developed into one of the largest mass mobilisations of the later nineteenth century. Vitally for the success of the movement at a local level, priests, tenant farmers and shopkeepers were attracted to its leadership en masse. This middle-class grouping provided the organisational abilities necessary for such a mass mobilisation and also the social status, influence and power to attract large numbers to the movement. Other groupings, including radical agrarians and Fenians, lacked the ability to organise such a large movement on their own. Rent and the purchase of holdings, which emerged as central agrarian concerns in the autumn of 1885, were also concerns of such middle-class groupings and played an important part in motivating them to organise the new movement. However, the outbreak of renewed agitation inevitably led to boycotting and intimidation. The central authority of the National League, largely in the form of its secretary, Timothy Harrington, attempted to restrain such agrarian excesses. The prospect of home rule, brought about by the December general election, further necessitated moderation at a local level. Such a course of action was introduced in the county election convention when candidates that were associated with agrarian radicalism and violence were sidelined in favour of proven moderate nationalists. This emerged as a result of a combination of influences, including the central branch Parnellites, priests and local moderate National Leaguers, although the power of the moderates was far from complete. Boycotting, intimidation and violence continued to persist.

SEVEN

THE IRISH NATIONAL LEAGUE AND MOONLIGHTERS

AGRARIAN VIOLENCE DURING THE HOME RULE PERIOD, 1885–6

—

One of the main aims of Parnell and the National League was the isolation of radical and Fenian elements within the leadership of nationalism at a local and national level. As the 1885 general election approached this had, to a large degree, been achieved throughout the country and particularly in Kerry, as was demonstrated in the county convention in late 1885. Notwithstanding the attempts of the local and national leadership to restrict the movement along a constitutional path, agrarian outrage increased in tandem with the emergence of the National League. In Kerry, the number of outrages rose from 71 committed in the last six months of 1884 to 127 for the corresponding period in 1885.[1] Kerry was the most violent part of the country throughout this period. This is demonstrated in the final quarter returns of agrarian outrages. For the final three months of 1885, out a total of 279 outrages committed countrywide, 63 were carried out in Kerry. This was by far the highest of any county. Other districts which had high agrarian outrage rates included other Munster counties including Clare (30), Cork East and West Ridings (36) and Tipperary North and South Ridings (38) along with the Connaught Galway East and West Ridings (20). The number of agrarian outrages did not reach above double figures for the four-month period in any other county. Agrarian violence was mostly a southern phenomenon in the period with limited outrages recorded in Leinster, Ulster and most Connaught counties.[2] In Munster, Kerry was the most violent county.

The RIC recorded 339 outrages in an 11-month period between August 1885 and June 1886. An analysis of their location demonstrates that outrage prevailed in districts where the National League was most active. As demonstrated in table 7.1, 283 outrages were committed in the RIC districts of Castleisland, Killarney, Listowel and Tralee. This area corresponded directly to regions of high National League activity (in 1885, 305 out of a total of 358 branch meetings of the league in the county were held in these areas).[3]

Table 7.1 Number of outrages committed in RIC districts in County Kerry, August 1885–June 1886

RIC district	Castleisland	Killarney	Listowel	Tralee	Rest	Total
Total	76	73	73	63	55	339

Note: Rest comprised the RIC districts of Dingle, Kenmare and Killorglin. *Source:* NAI, CSO RP 1887 box 3310.

Much of the motivation for these outrages was analogous to the objectives of local branches of the National League, which is illustrated in table 7.2 in a breakdown of the issues at stake behind the outrages. Of all 339 outrages, 105 were directly related to landlords, evicted land, rent strikes and enforcement of boycotts. These matters were also those that the local branches of the National League attempted to control, demonstrating a widespread use of violence and intimidation to enforce the 'law of the league'. Thirty-nine outrages were committed relating to disputes within agrarian society, many of which came before the courts of the National League.

Although many of these outrages appeared to correspond with the aims of the National League the entangled nature of many land disputes ensured that the motives for much violence lay in complicated private disputes. The complex nature of such disputes was evident in an apparent Moonlight raid on two tenants in the Kilcummin district near Killarney in late 1885. At night, four armed and disguised men forced a tenant named Denis O'Sullivan out of his bed. The gang demanded to see his rent book, and he was forced on to his knees to swear an oath to give up possession of a neighbouring farm from which the tenant had been evicted four years previously. Although the evicted tenant had emigrated to America the local branch of the league was trying to persuade O'Sullivan to give up the land. The gang also fired a shot into the roof and asked for money for gunpowder. On the same night a neighbouring farmer named O'Callaghan was also attacked and shots were fired into his house. It was believed the motive for this outrage was that O'Callaghan and his sons had refused to join the National League.[4] These attacks appeared to have been committed to enforce the power of the league in the region. However, O'Sullivan identified two farm servants named Leary and Coakley as his attackers. These two servants were employed by two neighbouring farmers named Fleming and Courane who had grazed the evicted farm before O'Sullivan had taken it. The police believed that these two farmers orchestrated the outrage to intimidate O'Sullivan off it and regain access to the land. They organised the attack on Callaghan while trying to disguise the outrages as part of a wider conspiracy and hide their own motives.[5] As this case illustrates, outrages attributed to the National League were often the actions

of aggrieved individuals. As demonstrated by A.C. Murray, many such personal disputes lay behind violence during the broader outbreak of Ribbonism
in County Westmeath between 1868 and 1871.[6]

Table 7.2 Objectives of 339 outrages committed in County Kerry, August 1885–June 1886

	Castleisland	Killarney	Listowel	Tralee	Rest	Total
Landlord–tenant relations	29	23	26	14	12	104
Against landlords	3	3	7	3	2	18
Holding evicted land	8	3	4	3	5	23
Grazing evicted land	10	4	4	1	0	19
Dealing with 'obnoxious' people	5	12	4	3	2	26
Rent strikes	3	1	7	4	3	18
Other disputes	13	9	4	7	6	39
Farmer/ labourer	4	1	0	1	0	6
Disputes between farmers/ family/traders	9	8	4	6	6	33
Non-agrarian	34	41	43	42	37	196
Elections	3	0	0	0	0	3
Against police	4	3	4	1	2	13
Robbery/ levying contributions	12	19	23	16	16	86
Other	0	5	2	8	6	21
Ordinary	15	14	14	17	13	73
Total	76	73	73	63	55	339

Source: Précis of agrarian outrages committed in Kerry, Aug. 1885–June 1886 (NAI, CSO RP 1887 box
3310).

The complex relationship between agrarian violence, the National League
and the wider community was illuminated in November 1885 with the murder
of a farmer named John O'Connell Curtin. The renewed agrarian agitation in
the autumn of 1885 inevitably led to an increase in outrage. In September RIC
County Inspector Moriarty reported that large sections of the county were
disturbed. He stated that not only were the continuously disaffected regions
of Castleisland, Killarney and Killorglin disturbed, but that 'the spirit of
lawlessness has manifested itself in portions of the Tralee district around
Ardfert and Abbeydorney and the Dingle district around Castlegregory and
Kilgobbin, hitherto the most tranquil in the county'.[7] The killing and stealing
of cattle, demanding of money and arms, and the sending and posting of
threatening notices all occurred regularly in various regions in the county. By

November the increased violence led Moriarty to report to Dublin Castle that 'I do not exaggerate when I say that things generally could not possibly have been worse. . . . Nothing but lawlessness and sympathy with crime prevails [in] the rest of Kerry.'[8] The number of outrages reported rose from 34 for the month of October to 44 in November. Of these outrages the most violent and significant was the murder of John O'Connell Curtin by a band of Moonlighters at Firies, which was located between Killarney, Castleisland and Tralee. Curtin belonged to the gentleman farmer class and was one of the largest tenant farmers in the county with a farm of over 160 acres. Born in County Limerick in 1820, he was educated at Clongowes Wood Jesuit College. In 1847 he married Agnes De Courcey, the youngest daughter of Maurice De Courcey, another gentleman farmer in the Firies district.[9] Although never a member of the Land League, he joined the National League and was appointed as treasurer to the Firies branch.[10] Together with the president of the branch, Father O'Connor, Curtin led the local tenants of Lord Kenmare's estate when they sought a reduction in rent from the land landlord in October 1885.[11] Despite Lord Kenmare's refusal of any rent reduction and the subsequent outbreak of a general rent strike on the estate, Curtin paid his rent. Strong denunciations of those who paid rent were commonly heard at National League meetings in the weeks leading up to the attack.[12] By breaking the rent strike Curtin had violated the 'law of the league' and could have expected punishment by the branch. Before the branch took any action against Curtin, the Moonlight gang attacked him.

Although Curtin had broken the rent strike, the motive of the gang of Moonlighters appeared to be solely to demand guns and money. Demands for money or arms were the most common motive for outrage during this period. Out of a total of 339 outrages for which details are available for the period between August 1885 and June 1886, 86 involved such demands (only 18 outrages were committed in relation to rent strikes). Curtin had previously been the target of a raid for arms in 1881 when he was forced to give up a gun. These raids appear to have had a degree of legitimacy within communities. When demanding money, Moonlighters frequently sought a 'contribution' rather than enacting a full robbery. Despite the extreme violence to which Moonlighters often resorted, at times they were welcomed in the houses they raided. After a Moonlight raid on a number of farmers' homes in Duagh near Listowel, it was reported that the Moonlighters were 'extremely jovial' and on entering a house where a 'wedding was taking place they feasted on the good things supplied to them and joined in the festivities'.[13] Indeed, the practice of groups of men dressing up in disguise and visiting neighbouring farms under the direction of a 'captain' paralleled aspects of local rural customs. When a marriage took place the younger men of the neighbourhood who did not attend the ceremony dressed up as 'strawboys' and visited the party during the night. One contributor to the Folklore Commission, which collected information in the 1930s, described rural traditions in the Ballyseedy area, a few miles from Firies: as 'at night the [wedding] party is surprised by a large number of straw boys called "sursufs"' who were disguised with 'straw helmets' and under the direction of a 'captain' and 'remained for an hour singing and dancing and taking refreshments and then they left'.[14] The intersection of Moonlighting and agrarian customs was demonstrated in 1886 when a police night patrol intersected a group who they believed were a gang of Moonlighters. After a fracas the offenders claimed they were not on a Moonlight raid but were attending a wedding party. A number of young men were arrested and appeared at the subsequent petty sessions where the bench agreed with the suspects and acquitted them. However, the arrest of George Twiss, a known Moonlighter, on this occasion suggested a crossover in the personnel of the Moonlighters and those individuals who took part in such customs.[15] The practice of young men joining Moonlighting gangs paralleled certain accepted roles undertaken by this social group. Moonlighting also had similarities to peasant festive customs such as the 'wren boys' which occurred on St Stephen's Day. In the Munster region groups of up to twenty disguised 'wren boys' visited neighbouring houses seeking money and drinks.[16] Moreover the rise in Moonlighting activity in late autumn and early winter corresponded to the peasant feast-day of Halloween which was 'an occasion of emotional release involving numerous customs and superstitions'.[17] Like the Whiteboys in the pre-Famine period, Moonlighters seemed linked to 'the cycle of peasant life and rural custom'.[18] Moonlighters clearly drew on cultural practices that were common to the rural peasant agrarian society in which they lived.

The motive of the gang of Moonlighters raiding Curtin's house was most probably simply to seek money or arms. When they broke in, Curtin refused to submit and defended himself by fetching his gun and reportedly saying 'well now boys'.[19] A number of shots were fired by both parties after which one of the intruders, a neighbouring farmer's son named Timothy O'Sullivan, lay mortally wounded.[20] A melee broke out between the remaining intruders and three of Curtin's children, Lizzie, Norah and Daniel. Two guns were seized from the attackers, one of whom lost his disguise in the struggle. As the Moonlighters fled the house, Curtin followed them and shouted 'be gone with you now boys', at which point one of the attackers turned around and shot Curtin a number of times, mortally wounding him. It was widely believed that a brother of the dead Moonlighter fired the shots.[21]

The murder had significant repercussions in national politics and quickly entered the discourse of the general election campaign. *The Times* of London commented that if the 'desperados' could not be 'restrained in [Timothy]

Harrington's own county which has the advantage of being instructed under his special guidance, in his own [news]paper, what becomes of the claim of the league to be regarded as a peaceable and constitutional body'. The newspaper also claimed that the murder demonstrated the inability of the National League 'to control the purpose of the people and keep the nationalist movement within legal bounds'.[22] The central branch of the National League condemned the murder and offered its condolence to the Curtin family.[23] Nationalists, while eager to condemn the murder of Curtin, also criticised the use of it as propaganda. *United Ireland* typified the nationalist reaction:

> Captain Moonlight has again come to the rescue of the landlord faction in their sorest need. The conspiracy to represent the country as in a state of veiled massacre had completely collapsed. . . . At this dismal moment the abominable slaughter at Castlefarm in Kerry cropped up in the nick of time to cheer the drooping spirits of the landlord defence union and to give [opponents to home rule] another convenient text for preaching to England that ours is a race of incurable barbarians, and that to hand over the control of the police to such a nation would be to give the sword of justice to the masked monsters who brought death and horror upon O'Connell Curtin's peaceful home.[24]

While the murder entered the rhetoric of the general election the situation quickly deteriorated in the Firies district. The killing of one of the Moonlighters and the subsequent identification of a number of the attackers by Curtin's children created a groundswell of local antagonism towards the Curtin family. There was considerable sympathy for the dead Moonlighter, O'Sullivan. At a branch meeting of the Firies National League a vote of condolence was offered to O'Sullivan's mother. A collection of £35 was gathered for her in 'a number of hours' and the branch called on neighbouring parishes to follow suit.[25] Bitterness over the shooting of O'Sullivan quickly grew and Curtin's funeral was poorly attended. When the local Catholic priest, Father Murphy, attempted to speak highly of Curtin during mass, uproar followed in the church.[26] The family became the target of boycotting and intimidation and Curtin's daughter, Lizzie, later said that whenever the family drove on the roads 'we were hooted and booed and called murders and informers and all sorts of things as we drove along'.[27] The situation reached fever point when the arrested Moonlighters were convicted at the Cork Winter Assizes, largely on the evidence of Curtin's daughters in late December 1885. The boycotting against the family became extensive and all the servants in their employment left them. In one case a herd who had worked for the family for the previous 32 years said he was too afraid to remain in the family's employment.[28] In January 1886, the Curtins were intimidated while attending Sunday mass.

The RIC reported that as the 'young [Curtin] ladies passed up through the chapel a derisive cheer was raised by six or eight shameless girls'. The police report stated that the 'shameless girls' took advantage of their sex 'in misconducting themselves, believing that the police [would not] interfere with them'. The authorities noted that 'though the parish priest was in the chapel while this was going on he never uttered a word in condemnation'.[29] After the mass the Curtin family were booed at and rushed by a crowd. Despite the intimidation the region's District Inspector Crane believed that the 'family [were] more determined than ever not to give their provocateurs the satisfaction of hunting them out of the country'.[30] The family again attended mass the following Sunday, but this time protected by twenty-five policemen. They were accompanied by Alfred Webb, the Quaker nationalist and member of the organising committee of the National League. During mass Father O'Connor read a letter from the Bishop of Kerry warning the parishioners that further scenes like those of the previous week would lead to the suspension of services in the church. Despite the bishop's warning, the Curtin family were again booed and hissed after mass by the sections of the congregation, leading to stone throwing and police intervention. When the Curtins left the grounds, Alfred Webb attempted to address the crowd. After being introduced by Father O'Connor, the president of the Firies National League, Webb began to say that the Curtin family had every right to defend themselves on the night of the killings at which 'he got hooted and [was] glad enough to get away'.[31] Webb believed his 'life would not have been worth much but for the police'.[32] During Webb's speech a number of women took the Curtins' family pew from inside the church and proceeded to smash it into pieces.[33] After this the bishop carried out his threat and mass at Firies church was suspended.[34]

The events at Firies and in other parts of Kerry were in these months constantly in the focus of the wider national press and political debate on home rule. The leadership of the league tried to curtail the excesses in the Firies district. When the president of the branch, Father O'Connor, sought to gain funds from the central branch to fund litigation between tenants and landlords, Timothy Harrington refused and said that Curtin's murder 'has shocked the whole civilised world, and must do incalculable injury to the cause of the people in the district'.[35] Several months later the same branch applied for grants for evicted tenants in the region. Harrington refused the request stating that the central branch was 'compelled to refuse a grant, owing to the very disturbed and lawless state of Kerry at the present time'. While Harrington explained that he did associate the Firies branch with 'lawless outrages', the central branch 'wish[ed] to save the general organisation from even the suspicion of sending funds to places where outrages of this kind have been occurring'.[36] Sections of the movement in Kerry also attempted to distance the league from the actions in Firies. At the county convention in November resolutions were passed condemning the attack on Curtin.[37] In February the newly elected MP for East Kerry, J. D. Sheehan, warned the people of Firies that 'if you wish to cripple the action of the Irish Party it is only by the repetition of those unseemly acts that you can impede the progress they are making'.[38] Despite this extensive pressure from both the league's county and national leadership, powerful sections of the community in Firies continued their hostility towards the Curtin family. In 1887 the family was still being extensively boycotted. Curtin's wife Agnes told a reporter that 'I can never live here in peace but they won't let me go. I tried to sell it [the farm] at auction but notices were posted that any purchaser would get the same treatment as old Curtin.'[39] The depth of animosity towards the Curtins was clear from comments made by 'widow' Casey, the mother of one of the men arrested and given penal servitude for the offence. She said that, 'if those boys did that thing they merely went for arms; a foolish thing, but it has been done throughout Ireland, and is done today. . . . As long as I am alive and my children, and their children live, we will try to root the Curtins out of the land, now I will do it. Wasn't the young man more the equal to that old codger?'[40] The Curtin family eventually left Firies in 1888, receiving a price that amounted to half the farm's value.[41]

The Curtin murder and the events that followed demonstrated the paradoxes that characterised agrarian violence and its relationship with not just the broader league movement but also with communities. The Moonlight attack may have been in response to Curtin paying his rent, an act that had been condemned by the Firies League the previous week. However, the incident was more probably a regular Moonlight raid for money and weapons. That such raids had a degree of legitimacy in communities was demonstrated by the widespread hostility exhibited towards the Curtins after the death of one of the attackers and the subsequent prosecution of two others. A groundswell of sympathy for the Moonlighters and bitterness towards the Curtins soon drove the family out of Firies. Those who intimidated the Curtins resisted attempts by both the regional and national leadership of the league, and by the religious authorities, to stop the hostility towards the family.

After the parliamentary party's success in the general election of December 1885 Parnellite MPs were returned in all four Kerry constituencies as the parliamentary party dominated the vast majority of nationalist constituencies. Parnell's subsequent alliance with Gladstone meant that the granting of home rule was a realistic aspiration. To ensure there was sufficient support for home rule, Parnell and other party leaders thought it necessary to contain the ongoing agrarian agitation and violence in rural Ireland. In spite of these efforts, the agitation intensified during January 1886 as landlords attempted to break the rent strikes which had been under way since the previous September. *United Ireland* commented that 'we regard the state of Ireland from an agrarian point of view to be as serious today as ever it was during the century'.[42] The situation was deteriorating in Kerry in particular. During the quarter sessions in Killarney alone 230 ejectment notices for non-payment of rent were granted.[43] Tensions were further exacerbated with a number of evictions. In the continually disturbed Firies region a number of evictions took place in early January. The evictions were accompanied by the customary demonstrations, with large crowds assembling at eviction and large numbers of police enforcing the evictions. During the eviction of Billy Daly of Droumraig, a tenant on the Kenmare estate, 200 police and troops were at hand. As the eviction party approached, the assembled people began blowing horns, 'which were heard in every direction and attracted large crowds of people of both sexes'. Stone throwing followed and the Riot Act was read as the police dispersed the crowd with force.[44] The January evictions increased agrarian tensions and County Inspector Moriarty commented that they 'tended to a great extent in further inflaming the minds of the people'.[45] In this atmosphere outrages continued. A gang of 15 to 20 Moonlighters forcibly obtained four guns and one revolver from a number of farmers in the Listowel region. Similarly, armed men entered several farm houses at Crotta, near Tralee, and demanded guns. Cattle stealing continued around Castleisland. The most serious outrage during January occurred in Castlegregory where a 72-year-old process server, who was serving writs for eviction, named Giles Rae, had an ear sliced off by a gang of Moonlighters. The Divisional Commissioner for the south-west, Captain Plunkett, reported that 'in Kerry the districts of Dingle, Killarney, Listowel and Tralee are in a most lawless state'.[46] In north Kerry a new wave of rent strikes began in January 1886. George Sandes, a notorious land agent who managed a number of properties in the area, refused to meet the tenants' demands to reduce the spring rents.[47] This was followed by a widespread rent strike in the north Kerry region, which further increased tensions.

The National League's relationship with this violence is difficult to ascertain. In the Killarney region the district inspector firmly believed that the league orchestrated outrages. In January 1886 he reported that 'it is idle to think the National League discourages outrage. It does not except in words.... The National League and the perpetrators are all one.'[48] A month later he was of the same opinion and believed that the influence of the league had 'rendered the detection of crime an utter impossibility'.[49] After an increase in outrages in the Listowel area the district inspector commented: 'I entirely attribute nearly all the serious outrages recently perpetrated in this district to the evil teachings of the National League.'[50] Representatives of landlordism also believed that the league was responsible for outrage. Maurice Leonard, the land agent on the Kenmare estate, wrote to the *Freeman's Journal* claiming that all the members of the Kilcummin branch were active Moonlighters.[51] Among the violent methods used to enforce the laws of the league was the practice of cattle maiming and killing which became frequent in Castleisland in the latter half of 1885. In the Castleisland district there were 60 evicted farms on which landlords and organisations such as the Land Corporation attempted to stock this boycotted land with cattle to derive some financial gain from the holdings.[52] A campaign of stealing and cutting up cattle on such evicted land was orchestrated to counter the landlords' actions. Again the Quinlans of Farran were apparently involved in the practice, and when cattle stocked on an evicted farm by the Land Corporation went missing in October 1885 the hides and entrails of the animals were found in a cave on the family's farm.[53] The police believed that because the practice did not endanger human life it was 'probably countenanced by the higher branch of the organisation [National League]. It has hitherto been planned and carried out in safety, it has not involved any tax on the people, and it is most injurious to the landlords'.[54] The police were of the opinion that the motives of such attacks were not just to uphold the agitation but also out of 'the desire to become possessed of the meat'.[55]

The practice nevertheless appeared to have been supported in the Castleisland region to the extent that District Inspector Davis informed his superiors that the 'whole community are in league to have reprisals from any person be he landlord or tenant who interferes with . . . a farm from which a tenant has been evicted'. Davis went on to complain that the police had to protect such farms and declared that for the 'past six months they have acted more in the capacity of herds than policemen and the result is that the men are becoming completely worn out, disgusted with their duty and demoralised'.[56] This form of outrage also emerged in the Listowel region where in October 1885 six bullocks went missing from a farm. No trace of the cattle could be found and the police believed that 'this class of outrage is becoming prevalent in this parish and is most difficult to prevent, as the ill disposed can watch their opportunity to take the cattle over which a constant watch could not be kept except by a very much larger force of police than is available'.[57] Significantly, cattle stealing appeared to be another method of enforcing the National League policy of boycotting evicted farms.

In contrast to this increasing agrarian protest at a local level, the political pendulum further swung towards constitutionalism and home rule, and at the end of January 1886 Parnell attempted to curtail all agrarian activity in Ireland. On 21 January 1886 he told the House of Commons that tenants were combining to resist payment of rents but claimed that these movements were spontaneous and had received neither encouragement nor financial assistance from the National League. He declared that the Irish Party was doing all in its power to stamp out boycotting and curb anti-rent combinations.[58] Despite the differences within the nationalist movement, Parnell secured support for home rule over agrarianism by assuring the party that he 'had parliament in the hollow of his hand'.[59] Parnell appeared to have succeeded in sacrificing agrarian concerns for the cause of home rule when the radical parliamentarian John Dillon publicly stated that restraint and silence within the movement was vital. He proclaimed that farmers and labourers would have to make sacrifices for the success of home rule.[60] Correspondingly, when newly elected Irish MPs arrived back from London after attending the House of Commons and meetings of the Irish Party, they condemned agrarian outrage. Speaking at the Killarney branch of the league, the East Kerry MP, J. D. Sheehan, appealed to the people 'to desist once and for all from those foolish and senseless outrages'. He contended that if they continued they would 'tie our hands and wreck us and cripple and damage the National League which embraces a plank for legislative independence as well as land reform'.[61] The central branch continued to threaten branches that were involved in conflict that could result in extreme actions. When in late January 1886 the Glenbeigh branch of the league in south-west Kerry consulted the central branch over a land dispute, Timothy Harrington warned:

> we must take strong measures to put an end to the discussion of extreme subjects of this kind in our local branches. . . . I am directing the presidents not to receive any notices upon discussions of this kind; and if these instructions not be carried out, we shall deem it our duty immediately to dissolve any such branches. Strong measures of this kind are absolutely necessary, if the great cause of the country is to be allowed to succeed.[62]

Soon after, when the Knocknagoshel branch published a resolution threatening anyone who did not join the movement, Harrington excoriated the branch for publishing such a resolution that would 'do the organisation and the national cause serious injury. . .. We [central branch] are determined to suppress branches that are a danger to the organisation'.[63] The central branch also began to stop sending money to local branches to assist evicted tenants. The Scartaglin branch applied several times for grants but received no reply.[64] The central branch appeared to have, to some extent, curtailed the excesses of local branches. In early March, the Killorglin branch resolved to meet only monthly on the grounds that 'in such an emergency [home rule] silence is recommended to us as good'.[65] The district inspector for the region commented that although five branches existed in his division they were now far less active. He believed that the 'executive' of the local branch hardly ever met 'owing to the central branch having directed' the branches to 'meet as seldom as possible' and to refrain from 'topics that might provoke discussion'. He also stated that the central branch instructed that branch if any divisions did 'prevail . . . they were not to meet at all'.[66]

Branches also tried to prevent outrages. The Firies branch resolved to 'fight within the lines of the constitution, felonious landlordism'.[67] After a Moonlight raid resulted in the robbery of money 'under the guise of nationalism' in Ballyhar, the local branch condemned the action and offered £5 from the funds of the branch to bring the culprits to justice and the police authorities.[68] The Duagh branch condemned the 'misguided and reckless men who are . . . propping up the enemies of this country, by taking arms, or doing any other act that could be termed an outrage'.[69] The Castleisland branch, previously renowned for its radicalism, further condemned outrage when it stated that 'the person who committed a crime now meant to ruin this poor and unfortunate country'.[70] The Ballyferriter branch similarly condemned all outrage and resolved that 'the branches of the league in these districts should exert their whole influence against the commission of these dastardly acts'.[71]

Many outrages were still committed despite these attempts. Those who committed Moonlighting ignored the intense political pressure to prevent outrages. Michael Davitt, on behalf of the central branch of the league, spoke in Castleisland town in February 1886 to condemn violence. The police drew attention to his ineffectiveness when reporting: '[Davitt] denounced outrages in very strong terms but there were very few persons in attendance at the meeting – about 500 – and most of the bad boys went away while he was denouncing them. I am afraid at some of the districts they are not under control.'[72] In Killorglin, the district inspector commented in March 1886 that despite the decrease in league activity the district continued in a lawless state. This was 'owing to the operation of a regular organised gang which it is almost impossible to break up'. He believed that the people were 'afraid of their lives' to give the police the slightest information concerning those who committed agrarian outrages.[73] During the same month the district inspector in Listowel contended that a new secret society 'exists for the perpetration of crime and that it has been extensively joined by farmers' sons and on pain of death to carry out the orders of the heads of the society'.[74]

By the start of 1886 it was clear that the national leadership and sections of the local leadership of the National League had little control over the actions of radical and violent agrarian elements. This reality was recognised by the Divisional Magistrate for counties Cork and Kerry, Captain Plunkett, when he reported that attempts by the National League 'to put a stop to outrage . . . have only partially succeeded'. He observed how 'younger members of the community are so thoroughly demoralised that they are beyond control . . . [and] they know that the denunciation of crime lately is only because it appears to suit the purposes of the National League at present having regard to the all important measures soon to be discussed in Parliament'.[75]

In league branches power struggles between radical and moderate influences were common. The police believed that 'some of the worst characters in the Castleisland branch of the National League have left in consequence of Archdeacon Irwin curbing them so much' and that they would in turn form their own league.[76] During the controversial incidents in Firies it was evident that elements, out of the control of the leadership of the local league were behind much of the intimidation of the Curtin family. The parish priest and president of the National League Branch, Father O'Connor, was the most prominent leaguer in the area during the upheaval. However, the treatment received by the Curtin family was beyond his control. During the mass, when he read the bishop's letter threatening closure of the church, he told the congregation that while he was 'on their side and was never on the side of landlords, agents or bailiffs . . . [and] that he considered that the Curtins had done the wrong [but] that the people of Firies should bear with the wrong'. He pleaded with the people to show Christian faith towards the Curtin family but his attempts at restrain failed.[77] O'Connor later revealed he could not pass a resolution condemning Moonlighters at league meetings out of fear of being attacked.[78]

Edward Harrington thought that in areas where agrarian outrage was common the National League was not at its strongest. He believed that 'in some of those districts there must have been some other feeling – possibly some Moonlight or secret society – and the league used not to get a grip in those districts at all'.[79] In the Dingle branch there were tensions between moderate and radical influences which led to its suppression by the central branch. In 1886 the secretary of the branch, M. W. Murphy, a publican from Dingle town, complained to Timothy Harrington that members of the league were enforcing boycotting for 'any or every cause' and that the branch was 'ruled by force rather than reason'.[80] Murphy represented moderate nationalists who were loyal to Parnellism and informed Harrington that he only joined the movement for 'the national cause'. On the advice of Murphy, Harrington dissolved the Dingle branch of the National League in September 1886.[81] An editorial in the *Kerry Sentinel* described what it believed was the relationship between agrarian radicals and local branches of the National League. It stated that 'fanatics are more formidable than ordinary disciples. . . it is certain three of these men in a branch make their influence more felt than the remaining three hundred'.[82] Throughout the Land League period, local agrarian violence seemed to have been organised by one or two of the leading members of each branch with little other involvement from the rest of the local leadership.[83] During the Land League phase this was accepted by the leadership of the movement and arguably seen as an integral element of the agitation. By 1885 agrarian violence had again emerged in parallel with the National League, indicating that at the very least it was used to some extent to enforce the 'law of the league'. Men long associated with radical agrarianism remained in leading positions in many branches; they remained a powerful and influential presence at a local level. The recent developments in parliamentary politics had placed these forces in direct confrontation with Parnellism and local moderate elements. The Curtin murder and the subsequent occurrences in the Firies district, together with the general continuance of outrages, demonstrated that radical agrarianism continued during the high point of the politics of home rule. Many local branches of the league were now divided between moderate constitutionalists and radical agrarians who were prepared to use violence.

A range of explanations have been offered for agrarian violence in nineteenth century Ireland. Much of this violence, particularly the Whiteboy movement that was prominent in the south of Ireland before the Famine, was the mode of protest of the smaller tenants and those on the fringes of rural society. According to Michael Beames, in a major study of this movement, the Whiteboys were solely the social expression of this class, with no direction and allegiance from dissident gentry or larger tenant farmers.[84] The emergence of the land war appeared to politicise such violent agrarian agitators under the middle-class leadership of the Land League. 'Radical' and 'moderate' influences vied for power within local branches of the National League. These internal divisions were not necessarily class based and many figures that were involved in radical agrarian activity were drawn from segments of the middle-class leadership of the league. Men such as Michael Power, a pig merchant and Fenian in Tralee, were pivotal to the leadership of their respective branches as well as being suspected of involvement in committing outrages. It was apparent that sections of the middle class local league leadership were committed to radical agrarianism, including the orchestration of violence to uphold the objectives of the National League. This was demonstrated in the large number of outrages committed to regulate landlord–tenant relations in accordance with the 'law of the league'. Agrarian violence in mid-1880s Kerry was evidently an important method of protecting the rights of middle-sized farmers whose interests were largely reflected in the anti-landlord rent agitations of the National League. While not all agrarian violence could be described in such terms, violence such as occurred in Castleisland to prevent the graving of evicted land was extremely close to official National League policy.

Although agrarian violence often conformed to the objectives of middle and larger sized tenants, those who actually committed the outrages and formed the rank and file of the Moonlighters were invariably drawn from the lower classes of the agrarian order. A number of cases where Moonlighters were apprehended by the police illuminate the background of these agitators. In January 1886, a gang of Moonlighters attacked the house of a farmer named Patrick Doyle at Brida bear Killorglin. Doyle, along with his sons, fought the attackers, and was later able to identify them; the police arrested nine men believed to have made up the raiding party. All were under the age of 30, with two of the nine under 25 years. Occupationally, the gang was made up of five farmers' sons, two servant boys, a labourer and a cabinet-maker. Six of the group, four of whom were brothers, had worked together the previous week shearing sheep on a farm, and had stayed in a two-bed dwelling. The police optimistically believed that they had arrested the 'most celebrated gang of desperadoes in Kerry.'[85] In another incident in February 1886, the police arrested 19 individuals in the district of Cordal on suspicion of Moonlighting. Cordal, which neighboured Castleisland, witnessed a high level of violent agrarian activity during the period. Like the Brida Moonlighters they were relatively young and all but three were under the age of 30 while four were in their teens. Their occupations also mirrored those of the Brida gang of nine farmers' sons with seven labourers and three artisans (a tailor, a mason and a carpenter).[86] Rural tradesmen were arrested on a number of other occasions for Moonlighting. In April 1886, two shoemakers were arrested when they were recognised as part of a gang which had raided a farmer's house at Gortatlea between Tralee and Castleisland.[87] Another Moonlighter, named Patrick Moynihan, brought before the Spring Assizes in Tralee for attacking the house of a gamekeeper at Inch on the eastern side of Dingle, gave his occupation as a weaver.[88]

For the class the Moonlighters came from – the farmers' sons, labourers and tradesmen – life chances were limited in the 1880s. Sharp demographic changes in 1870s Kerry limited marriage opportunities.[89] The system of late marriages often left those farmers' sons who were actually going to inherit dissatisfied with a system which required that they often remained 'boys', subservient to their fathers until they finally married.[90] Denied the opportunity to marry, this group also had little access to land. The increasing unwillingness of farmers to subdivide holdings left non-inheriting sons landless. In November 1886 Canon Griffin described to the Cowper Commission the predicament of those who took part in Moonlighting:

I do not know what is to be done with the children of the farming classes that are growing up, because the lands cannot be sub-divided, and then they are disconnected when they are not marrying as they used. . . . The eldest is not as dissatisfied as the others, because he thinks he is to get the land by and by, but there are three or four others, the younger members of the family, who are by no means satisfied, and one thing with another they do not see why they should work when there is no final benefit in prospect for them.

He considered that such young men along with 'those who have no stake in the country' such as 'small artisans', 'shoemakers' and 'servant boys' were the principal participants in boycotting and Moonlight raids.[91] Other witnesses to the commission gave similar evidence. A large tenant farmer named James Sullivan, who held a hundred acres with a government valuation of £82, claimed that the 'respectable' classes would like a return to 'law and order' and believed that those who committed agrarian outrages were 'the young fellas . . . no sensible man takes any part in it'.[92] Another large farmer with 80 acres in the Castleisland district (his name was not published) contended that Moonlighters were 'reckless careless fellows, who have nothing to lose, who maraud from place to place. They have nothing else to do.'[93] The *Kerry Sentinel* echoed similar sentiments in February 1886 when it attempted to explain the ongoing Moonlight activity. It claimed that the majority of Moonlighting outrages were 'committed by unemployed labourers and young sons indicating that they are not wholly due to agrarian causes . . . [they] are only Moonlight robberies and mischievous freaks of unemployed labourers'.[94] A number of years later Edward Harrington maintained this view when asked at the Special Commission who the Moonlighters were. He replied that he presumed that they were 'working men and poor men, who under the influence of drink, or under any other influence, might be bought into it [a secret society]'.[95] He was also of the opinion that 'the respectable people of the country-were in great terror of the Moonlighters'.[96]

The middle-aged and middle-class 'respectable' leadership of the National League chastised Moonlighters when the league failed to control agrarian violence during the critical home rule stage. There were several reasons for the inability of the local league leaders to control Moonlighters. The league provided middle to large tenant farmers with an avenue to further their socio-economic status within their local communities. The leading positions in branches were largely confined to the 'respectable' middle classes, a situation that was compounded by the official recognition of the role of the Catholic clergy in the movement. In contrast to these officers of local leagues, Moonlighters were young and landless. Indeed, the demand for arms and money seemed to be perpetrated against the very class of which the local leadership of the league was composed. In April 1886, a Moonlight party comprising 25 to 30 armed and disguised men raided a number of houses in the townland of Droumcrunnig in north Kerry.[97] The gang visited 12 house-holds in one night. Of these, six had a government valuation between £20 and £29 while four were valued between £30 and £39. Only two of the tenants raided had a valuation under £20.[98] Another instance of Moonlighting, in Kerries in the hinterland of Tralee, further illustrated that Moonlighters frequently targeted larger tenants when searching for arms and money. During April 1886 a disguised and armed party of up to 20 Moonlighters stole eight guns from a number of farmers in the district.[99] Out of five households visited in one night all the tenants raided had holdings valued at above £50, while one, William Barrett, had a tenant farm valued at £149.[100] These were some of the wealthiest tenants in the county. When a number of tenants were raided in the parishes of Kilmeaney and Knockanure in north Kerry it was reported that 'the people whose houses were visited belonged to the respect-able farming class. . . . The Moonlighters are said to have been of the lower order.'[101] The contrast in social status between those who took part in Moonlighting and those who were subject to raids suggests at some level a degree of tension between the two groups.

The inability of the National League local leadership to restrain the Moonlighters could also have been due to age differences between older tenant farmers and the younger landless agitators. The secretary of the Killarney National League, 'a respectable auctioneer', explained the attitude of many within the local leadership towards agrarian violence: 'When Moonlighting first began it was difficult not to sympathise with some outrages that were excited by injustice . . . but now they are absolutely opposed to any outrage, as they are sure of getting their ends by legal methods.'[102] Indeed, divisions existed between the younger and older members of families. One example was the Quinlan family in Farran, Castleisland. After the PPP Act was introduced in 1881, their father, Maurice, refused the three Quinlan brothers money to escape to America, which led to their imprisonment.[103] Maurice Quinlan was a 'res-pectable farmer' with a long history in nationalist politics tracing back to the 1872 home rule by-election when he was a public supporter of Blennerhassett.[104] By 1882 the local RIC commented that 'though Quinlan's sons [are] very bad characters, Maurice Quinlan himself is a very respectable man'. He also gave the police 'information' concerning the murder of Herbert in 1882.[105] Undoubtedly the younger generation of farmers' sons were prone to more radical action than the older landholding generation.

The Moonlighters appeared to have been rooted in local communities and networks based on personal relationships such as families and co-workers. Much of the violence committed in the Castleisland area originated from the younger members of neighbouring families, the Quinlans and Husseys, who were also related. As we have seen, nine young men, six of whom had spent the previous week labouring together on a farm and living in the same accommodation, committed the Moonlight attack on Patrick Doyle. The similarity between Moonlighting and certain peasant customs suggests that these gangs provided to some extent an opportunity for the interaction of young male members of agrarian society. Like those who joined the IRA in County Cork during the later revolutionary period of 1916–23, 'the "boys" who "strawed", played, worked, and grew up together became the "boys" who drilled, marched, and raided together'.[106]

Despite the differences between Moonlighters and the leadership of the league, and the fact that this leadership derided those who took part in secret society activity as being social idlers, Moonlighters appeared to have wielded much power and influence within their local communities. The events in Firies demonstrated that the mass of the people sympathised with the dead Moonlighter and the men who were subsequently prosecuted for the killing of Curtin. This popular support for Moonlighters was apparent on a number of other occasions. When the crown solicitor, Murphy, went to a magisterial inquiry in Killorglin town after the arrest of a number of Moonlighters he intended to 'remain there until the inquiry closed but having been twice "interviewed" and observing that a concourse of people remained about the court house, displaying their sympathy with the defendants when the opportunity occurred', he returned to Tralee.[107] Considine, the resident magistrate for large parts of north Kerry, believed that there was 'a very widespread sympathy of an undefined character' for Moonlighters among the people. He contended that 'they have it in their mind that Moonlighting helps them to withstand the landlord'.[108]

Although Moonlighters and the mainstream local leadership of the National League were disconnected, known radicals remained in the league. During the Land League period, elements of this radicalism seemed to have emanated from a network of Fenians working inside the movement. By 1885, whatever organisation of Fenians existed in provincial Ireland appeared to have been completely superseded by the National League. In Kerry this was best illustrated when Fenian elements of the Tralee League broke from the central authority of the movement in 1885. Their attempts to gain support from other regions utterly failed, although known Fenians were at the time active in other local leagues and the Tralee branch soon fell into line with the central branch of the National League. The National League had superseded Fenians to the extent that during September 1885 a police spy in north Kerry expressed astonishment that the most extreme members of the IRB in the area had fallen into line with Parnell's policy and joined the league.[109] Although, as Owen Magee has demonstrated, leading IRB figures such as John O'Leary had attempted to prevent the organisation's members from participating in agrarian outrages since the winter of 1880–1, there is some evidence of Fenian complicity in a number of outrages by 1885.[110] A rifle seized from Casey, one of the Moonlighters who had attacked Doyle at Brida, was believed to have been part of shipment of guns sent to Kerry from London by Fenians a number of years previously.[111] During the land war period the IRB had purchased and imported 4,018 firearms. The loyalty of many members of the movement was dependent on their continuing to receive arms in return for their subscriptions.[112]

Some anecdotal evidence suggests that some Moonlighters considered themselves Fenian in outlook by 1885 and 1886. When a jury at the Kerry Spring Assizes acquitted Patrick Moynihan of outrage offences in March 1886, despite compelling evidence against him, he shouted out the Fenian catch cry 'God Save Ireland' as he left the dock.[113] On another occasion a group of Moonlighters informed a farmer from whom they were demanding a gun that they believed that 'they were doing [their country's cause] immense good'.[114] During this period, this feature of agrarianism was inspired by Fenianism although it was characterised by little coherent objectives or leadership beyond the local. Considine was of the opinion that the practice of robbing arms was partly based on a 'vague idea that at some future time there will be occasion to use these arms for their national aspirations'.[115] However, Fenianism remained popular with certain social groups despite the apparent success of the National League and Parnellism. In November 1885, a monument to the Manchester Martyrs was unveiled in Tralee. A large procession of 8,000 marched to Rath graveyard in a procession 'as the bands played the dead march in Saul'. Michael Davitt gave a speech that was loaded with republican rhetoric. He said that 'we are assembled to honour three men of the people who proudly died and offered up their lives as sacrifices on the altar of Irish liberty'. He further evoked republican sentiment when he said that it was the people's' 'holy duty to emulate them and prove if necessary that death alone will be welcome to you in the cause of Irish liberty'.[116] No reference was made to the National League movement, or to the 1885 general election, which was to be held the following week made. The Fenian members of the Tralee League were present although the clergy and leading leaguer in the county, Edward Harrington, did not attend. The meeting demonstrated that even at the height of Parnellism, Fenianism remained popular at a local level, especially amongst tradesmen. As Matthew Kelly has recently posited, the 'Fenian Ideal' of separatism transcended the small and limited organisation of the IRB and attracted a large degree of sympathy in Ireland.[117]

UNDERSTANDING RURAL VIOLENCE AND POLITICAL ACTIVITY IN 1880s KERRY AND ITS BROADER SIGNIFICANCE

—

This book has concentrated on the dynamics behind political and agrarian activity in County Kerry during one of the most formative periods in Irish history. Although the work concentrates on one particular area, it has a wider significance and relevance and provides a range of insights into the underlying motivations of political activity in nineteenth and early twentieth century Ireland. Of particular importance is the exploration of the tensions and divisions internal to nationalism, which marked the land agitation in Kerry and what these understandings reveal about wider political and agrarian actions. The dissonance within the ranks of the general nationalist and land movements in Kerry came to a head during the high point of home rule politics in 1885 and 1886. The largely conservative clerical and middle-class local leadership of the movement along with national figures attempted to contain and limit violent agrarian activity during what was a delicate moment in the high politics of home rule. The radical and more violent section of the land and political movement had already been isolated during the convention to select candidates for the general election in November 1885. All four nominations for the county went to moderate nationalists who were committed to constitutionalism. Despite this sidelining of radical agrarianism in Kerry, violent outrages continued throughout 1885 and 1886. The powerful social forces surrounding Moonlighting and radical agrarian activity were painfully depicted in the Firies region after the murder of John O'Connell Curtin. The local and national leadership of nationalism failed to curtail the harassment of the bereaved Curtin family after the shooting dead of one Moonlighter and subsequent prosecution of two others by members of the Curtin family. Nor could the religious authorities restrain the treatment of the family, which resulted in the temporary closure of the Catholic Church of the parish by the bishop. This episode demonstrated that the constitutional nationalism of Parnellism and the influence of traditional clerical power brokers were not strong enough to overcome the influence of Moonlighting in the area.

A range of factors undermined the ability of the formal nationalist organisation, the National League, to control Moonlighting and radical agrarian activity. The contrast between young landless Moonlighters and the more middle-aged landholding local league leadership ensured that each group was disconnected, leaving the latter group with little or no power or influence over the former. The argument that a generational gap between Moonlighters and the local leadership of the mainstream nationalism was an underlying factor in the agrarian violence of the Kerry Moonlighters has wider implications for the understanding of political violence during not just the 1880s, but also throughout the pre-land war era, and the subsequent violence that engulfed much of Ireland in the years between 1916–23. Moonlighting drew on a range of agrarian customs and rituals which were common to younger males in Irish agrarian society. Peter Hart's work on the war of independence in County Cork makes a similar connection between the volunteers of the IRA and rural male youth culture during the period of 1916–23. Hart highlights how younger adult males were often cut off from the more formal older men's social and political circles. Kept outside the adult male world, young men formed their own, somewhat marginal subculture, much of which revolved around being 'the boys' that led to informal but stable cliques often based on a territorial basis of neighbourhoods, parishes, or townlands. Although these young men were in many ways cut off from formal society, Irish folk culture contained an accepted element of ritualised rebellion, which allowed for a temporary and largely symbolic reversal of roles. In a similar way to the Moonlighters, male youth culture in early twentieth-century Ireland allowed young men the customary right to wear masks, disguise and decorate themselves and demand money, food or entrance to a house.[1] It would appear that in Kerry during the 1880s a similar dynamic was at play. Moonlighters' actions clearly replicated folk customs common to the lives of young men not just in Kerry but throughout much of provincial Ireland. Hart's view of the violence of the IRA as being in some ways a product of intergenerational tensions in local communities has obvious relevance to the Kerry Moonlighters. The Hart generational thesis has even greater resonance in Kerry considering the demographic challenges that this particular social group met in the 1880s, with the sudden and dramatic increase in the age of marriage. Joseph Lee's important analysis of the outbreak of the land war (1879–82) in Kerry also highlights such social frustrations as an underlying factor in the agrarian violence of the period.

The role of demographic, intra-generational and intra-tenant tensions in the phenomenon of agrarian violence in Kerry during the 1880s has parallels in Irish historiography, which explains agrarian and political violence through the lens of immediate socio-economic circumstances and personal motivation.

Such understandings have tended to dilute the importance of nationalism and social radicalism. This is particularly evident in A. C. Murray's important analysis of Ribbonism.[2] For the revolutionary period (1916–21), Peter Hart highlights that the violence of the IRA cannot be explained by 'wealth' or 'class' and that IRA activity did not follow 'poverty'.[3] For Hart, social radicalism was not an important factor in understanding the political violence of the IRA.

Unsurprisingly, such perspectives have been the focus of historiographical debate. As early as 1982, the historian and political scientist Tom Garvin has argued against what he viewed as the 'economic perspective' of historians such as Joseph Lee, who viewed pre-Famine agitations as 'apolitical' and due to 'local agrarian and socio-economic tensions'. Garvin viewed pre-Famine Ribbonism as the proto-nationalism of a Catholic lower middle class and working class, which went beyond the local and was characterised by a wider national infrastructure and organisation.[4] While Ribbonism never emerged in the southern half of Ireland, the proposition that agrarian violence in the Munster region had a wider political and social consciousness that went beyond the local has been put forward by Beames in relation to the Whiteboy movement. The Whiteboys were violent agrarian secret societies in Munster during the later eighteenth and early nineteenth centuries; Whiteboy activity has been viewed by Beames as the social expression of the poorer strata of peasant society. Such agrarian activity has been seen as an attempt to enforce an alternative set of codes and values concerning access to land and to regulate the employment of labourers, which ensured that Whiteboyism was marked by a social radicalism and class consciousness.[5]

In many ways Beame's historiographical interpretation was influenced by developments in British history surrounding the writings of E. P. Thompson and George Rude, which viewed protest movements as the protection of what has been termed the 'moral economy'.[6] Such perspectives have provided historians with an alternative basis set of understandings towards the development of popular politics, which counter the emphasis on the immediate and local. For the 1880s some historians have laid much emphasis on the 'unwritten law' of the 'moral economy' of tenant society as an important motivating factor in the activities of the National League.[7] It has been argued that agrarian violence, boycotting and the land courts of the Land and National League were methods of upholding the 'written law', which regulated tenants' right and access to land. This is particularly evident in the work of Heather Laird who has argued that the 'unwritten law' of the period was based on a combination of 'social radicalism and subaltern discontent'.[8] Such perspectives place local popular politics and agrarian activity within a radical context and as being representative of a widespread nationalism, which was integrated with preconceived 'natural rights' concerning tenants access to land. The influence of E. P. Thompson is also reflected in Fergus Campbell's micro-study of the evolution of politics in the east Galway village of Craughwell during the period 1891–1921. Campbell's extensive research on the rank and file of the United Irish League and Sinn Féin movements allows for an exploration of the motivations, ideas and activities of the ordinary people who engaged in popular politics.[9] Importantly, Campbell's thesis challenges the perception that popular politics in early twentieth-century Ireland did not contain a serious attempt to change the existing social balance of power. Instead, the period was marked by a small farmer and landless labourer radicalism that was determined to achieve a degree of land redistribution from landlords and graziers, which was imbued with nationalism and republicanism.[10] According to Campbell, such objectives unified nationalism and he rebuts the proposition that popular agrarian politics were marked by intra-tenant class tensions.[11] At a broader level Campbell's analysis subscribes to the thesis that throughout nineteenth and early twentieth-century Ireland popular political activity involved a social radicalism closely connected with a wider nationalist perspective.

The evidence of agrarian activity in Kerry during the 1880s suggests that a combination of these approaches is needed to fully appreciate the dynamics behind the Moonlighters and the perpetration of agrarian outrage. In Kerry it was evident that youth culture – social frustrations of young adult males along with personal grudges – were behind much agrarian activity during the 1880s. It was also apparent that much of this violence coalesced with the objectives of the formal local nationalist organisations in the form of the Land League and National League. Agrarian violence was clearly used to uphold the 'law of the league', perhaps most obviously in the Castleisland region where the stealing of cattle directly enforced the National League objective of preventing the use of evicted land. The analysis of resolutions passed at National League meetings in Kerry (see chapter six) corresponded closely to the motives behind a large number of agrarian outrages (see chapter seven). Although much of the local league leadership objected to agrarian violence, individuals drawn from the middle classes were often directly involved in its orchestration. Such middle-class involvement in agrarian violence was an important departure from previous secret society movements such as the Ribbonmen and Whiteboys, which have been largely viewed in the historiography as the preserve of the lower classes. The involvement of middle-class figures in Moonlighting demonstrated that a certain degree of pan-tenant unity existed. Echoing Campbell's analysis, class divisions, which revolved around labourers, small farmers and larger farmers, were not the most important dynamic in agrarian violence and political activity. As explained in chapter six, the National League's agrarian objectives were limited to a landed settlement, which removed land-lords but maintained the status quo within tenant society. The issue of land redistribution or the attempt to break up large or grazier farms, which marked later agrarian agitations, failed to materialise to any extent in Kerry during the 1880s. Agrarian violence was not used as a means to systematically redefine access to land along class lines beyond the spectrum of landlord–tenant relations. Although much of the league leadership undoubtedly opposed the use of violence, this appeared to have been based on differences in opinion on methods and tactics as opposed to wider social divisions within tenant society. Usually agrarian radicalism in 1880s Kerry amounted to the use of violence to enforce the 'law of the league' in an attempt to regulate landlord–tenant relations, and was not reflective of a potentially more radical aim to force the claims of smaller uneconomic tenants and labourers over those of middling to larger tenant farmers.

However, the proposition that the major motivation of agrarian violence committed by the Kerry Moonlighters was primarily 'anti-landlord' has to be treated with caution as intra-tenant tension was a factor behind much agrarian activity including violence. In chapters two and three the agrarian violence of the early land war period is partly explained by intra-tenant tensions brought about by the failure of the agrarian economy, the issuing of civil bills, and tenants competing for access to land. During the National League period similar motivations underpinned much agrarian violence. This was demon-strated in the O'Callaghan case in January 1886, where a farmer tried to disguise an outrage as part of the wider agrarian agitation while in reality it was committed to intimidating a neighbouring tenant off the holding. Agrarian outrages were often mired in complicated disputes within tenant society. These forms of intra-tenant disputes did not usually represent any particular class interests and were largely between neighbours, family members and competitors for land. Such conflicts had little if anything to do with protecting the rights of the agrarian lower classes, in contrast to Garvin's view of the Ribbonmen and Beames's analysis of the Whiteboys. Similarly, Campbell's anti-grazier agitation by small farmers and labourers in the United Irish League after 1898 is not applicable to Kerry in the 1880s. The importance of personal grudges as an undercurrent in agrarian violence in Kerry demonstrates the worth of Murray's analysis of the Ribbonmen of Westmeath. While such motivations were important features of agrarian violence and Moonlighting, it would appear that the overarching reason behind the use of violence remained the continual anti-landlord agitation that marked the period. From the sample of outrages analysed in chapter seven, the issues of rent, taking of evicted land and dealing with boycotted individuals formed the motivation for the majority of violent acts. Arguably the motivation behind much of the violence of the period was a combination of factors, with anti-landlordism the most important.

An important feature of Moonlighting was its relationship with Fenianism. It did appear that Moonlighters identified themselves with a Fenianism that merged with the inherent agrarianism of the countryside. As shown in chapter three, Fenians had organised in rural regions in the county since the late 1870s and there was evidence of the orchestration of some violent outrages by individuals from outside the county, such as in the case of the 1884 bombing of the land agent, Samuel Hussey. While little is known of wider Fenian structure and influence in the agrarianism of the 1880s, it would be inaccurate to suggest that the majority of agrarian violence in 1880s Kerry was a result of a Fenian conspiracy. Nevertheless, many of the Moonlighters viewed themselves as Fenians and integrated their agrarianism with a form of advanced nationalism which was an important development within the political and agrarian culture in Kerry. While the traditional urban working-class Fenians who were synonymous with the 1867 rising were present in Tralee town, Fenianism and violent agrarianism integrated at a grassroots level in the Kerry countryside for the first time during the land war. By the mid 1880s the level of outside Fenian involvement in the county had dissipated and many leading Fenian figures nationally had committed themselves to the Parnellism of the National League. However, many of the Moonlighters in Kerry continued to connect their violent anti-landlordism with a Fenian ideal, albeit vague in definition, indicating the level at which it had permeated local rural society. Although this study has concentrated on County Kerry, the prominence of agrarian violence in a range of Irish counties suggests that a similar form of agrarian–Fenianism was an important dynamic in other parts of the country. The 1880s marked the emergence of a form of rural Republicanism, which had previously been of little relevance in the Kerry and Irish countryside.

Although this study stops when home rule was at its high point in 1886, the National League and agrarian violence continued in Kerry for a number of years. In October 1886 the nationalist movement refocused its attention on agrarian agitation through the Plan of Campaign after it became apparent that home rule was dampened as a political objective with the election of majority Conservative government. The 'Plan' amounted to specific rent strikes on a limited number of high profile estates throughout the country. While Kerry had for much of the early and mid 1880s been one of the foremost counties in terms of agrarian agitation, the Plan was not widely adopted in the county.[12] However, agitation continued on a number of estates, including the Kenmare property, ensuring that the county remained the focus of attention. In the autumn of 1887 the new Chief Secretary, Arthur Balfour, introduced a new Crimes Act which revived the coercive legislation of the 1882 Act. Although the National League was not outlawed outright, provisions in the legislation allowed for specific regions to be declared proclaimed and the organisation suppressed. Most of Kerry along with parts of Clare, Donegal, Mayo, Queen's County, Tipperary and Waterford were proclaimed, leading to the suppression of the movement. In contrast to the suppression of the Land League, this did not lead to the outbreak of serious violence and by the late 1880s the number of agrarian outrages had dropped to their lowest levels since before the first phase of the land war. Notwithstanding the dampening of political and agrarian tensions, Moonlighting continued, albeit at a much lower rate than in the early and mid 1880s. The Parnellite era came to a conclusion in the early 1890s with the split in the movement after the divorce case of Katharine O'Shea from Captain O'Shea with Parnell cited as co-respondent; nationalist Ireland was divided into pro and anti Parnellite camps. In Kerry, Edward Harrington, mirroring his brother, Timothy Harrington, remained loyal to Parnell and promoted the cause in the pages of the *Kerry Sentinel*. However, the clergy backed anti-Parnellites who succeeded in gaining the majority of support in the county, which was demonstrated in the 1892 general election when anti-Parnellites won all of the four seats in the county.[13]

Notes

—

INTRODUCTION

1   G. G. Iggers, *Historiography in the Twentieth Century: From Scientific Objectivity to the Postmodern Challenge* (2nd edn, Middletown, Conn., 2005), p. 7.

2   A large amount of research has been published in relation to women's and gender history in the nineteenth century, for example see Maria Luddy, *Women and Philanthropy in Nineteenth-Century Ireland* (Cambridge, 1995); Margaret MacCurtain and Mary O'Dowd, 'An agenda for women's history in Ireland, 1500–1900: part I: 1500–1900', *IHS* XXVIII: 109 (May, 1992), pp. 1–19. History of the poor and welfare is a nascent area of research; for latest publication in relation to the topic see, Virginia Crossman, *Politics, Pauperism and Power in Late Nineteenth Century Ireland* (Manchester, 2006); Crossman recently led a major ESRC research project entitled 'Welfare regimes under the Irish poor law 1850–1921' see, www.brookes.ac.uk/historyofwelfare; Significant research is also under way on the history of medicine at the Centre for the History of the Body (UCD) with a number of monographs forthcoming, see www.ucd.ie/history/body.htm. Furthermore, extensive research on the history of landed estates in Ireland is carried out by the Centre of the Study of Irish Historic Houses and Estates (NUI, Maynooth), see www. historicirishhouses.ie.

3   Central to the study of local history has been the annual publication Maynooth Studies in Local History which to date has over 70 titles. Another significant set of local history publications include the Irish County History and Society series which to date has published 17 volumes of essays dedicated to a prescribed county. The latest in this series is William Nolan and Thomas McGrath (eds), *Kildare History and Society: Interdisciplinary Essays on the History of an Irish County* (Dublin, 2006).

4   Raymond Gillespie and Gerard Moran 'Land, politics and religion in Longford since 1600' in idem (eds), *Longford: Essays in County History* (Dublin, 1991), p. 7.

5   Barbara Solow, *The Land Question and the Irish Economy* (Cambridge, Mass., 1971); William Vaughan in *Landlords and Tenants in Mid-Victorian Ireland* (Oxford, 1994). For other expositions of Vaughan's work see, idem, 'Farmer, grazier and gentlemen: Edward Delany of Woodtown, 1851–99', *Irish Economic and Social History* IX (1982), pp. 53–72; idem, *Landlords and Tenants in Ireland, 1848–1904* (Dublin, 1984). For further analysis of rent levels during this period see Terence Dooley, *The Decline of the Big House in Ireland: A Study of Irish Landed Families, 1860–1960* (Dublin, 2001).

6   Michael Turner, *After the Famine: Irish Agriculture, 1850–1914* (Cambridge, 1996); K. T. Hoppen, *Ireland since 1800: Conflict and Conformity* (2nd edn, London, 1999), pp. 97–9.

7   J. S. Donnelly Jr, *The Land and the People of Nineteenth-Century Cork: The Rural Economy and the Land Question* (London, 1975), p. 250.

8   Philip Bull, *Land, Politics and Nationalism: A Study of the Irish Land Question* (Dublin, 1996), p. 80.

9   Samuel Clark, 'The social composition of the Land League', *IHS* XVII: 68 (Sept. 1971), pp. 447–69; idem, *Social Origins of the Irish Land War* (Princeton, 1979).

10   Paul Bew, *Land and the National Question in Ireland 1858–82* (Dublin, 1978).

11   David Fitzpatrick, 'Class, family and rural unrest in nineteenth-century Ireland' in P. J. Drudy (ed.), *Ireland: Land, Politics and People* (Cambridge, 1982), pp. 37–75; idem, 'Review essay: unrest in rural Ireland', *Irish Economic and Social Review* XII (1985), pp. 98–105; Other important works on the landlord question in the post-Famine period include, Philip Bull, *Land, Politics and Nationalism: A Study of the Irish Land Question* (Dublin, 1996); Terence Dooley, *The Decline of the Big House in Ireland: A Study of Irish Landed Families, 1860–1960* (Dublin, 2001).

12   Vaughan, *Landlords and Tenants in Mid-Victorian Ireland*, p. x; Fergus Campbell, *Land and Revolution: Nationalist Politics in the West of Ireland, 1891–1921* (Oxford, 2005), p. 292.

13   Donald Jordan, *Land and Popular Politics in Ireland: County Mayo from the Plantation to the Land War* (Cambridge, 1994).

14   Ibid.; J. S. Donnelly Jr', *The Land and the People of Nineteenth-Century Cork* (London, 1975); Frank Thompson, *The End of Liberal Ulster: Land Agitation and Land Reform, 1868–88* (Belfast, 2001); J. W. H. Carter, *The Land War and its Leaders in Queen's County, 1879–82* (Portlaoise, 1994). Important doctoral research has recently been undertaken by Walter Walsh on County Kilkenny at NUI Maynooth. A number of important albeit smaller localised studies have appeared on the period in question. These include: Edward Kennedy *The Land Movement in Tullaroan, County Kilkenny, 1879–91* in Maynooth Studies in Local History, no. 48 (Dublin, 2003); D. S. Lucey *The Irish National League in Dingle County Kerry, 1885–92* in Maynooth Studies in Local History, no. 48 (Dublin, 2003). For another important article on the land war in Ulster see, R. W. Kirkpatrick, 'Origins and development of the land war in mid-Ulster, 1879–85' in F. S. L. Lyons and R. A. J. Hawkins (eds), *Ireland under the Union: Varieties of Tension: Essays in Honour of T. W. Moody* (Oxford, 1980), pp. 201–36.

15   C. C. O'Brien, *Parnell and His Party* (5th edn, Oxford, 1974), p. 128.

16   Joseph Lee, *The Modernisation of Irish Society, 1848–1918* (Dublin, 1973), p. 106.

17   A.C. Murray, 'Nationality and local politics in late nineteenth century Ireland: the case of County Westmeath', *IHS* XXV: 98 (Nov. 1986), p. 146; James Loughlin, 'Nationality and loyalty: Parnellism, monarchy and the construction of Irish identity, 1880–85' in D. G. Boyce and Alan O'Day (eds), *Ireland in Transition, 1867–1921* (London, 2004), pp. 35–56.

18   Alvin Jackson, *The Ulster Party: Irish Unionists in the House of Commons, 1884–1911* (Oxford, 1989); James Loughlin, *Ulster Unionism and British National Identity since 1885* (London, 1994).

19   See Michael Beames, *Peasants and Power: The Whiteboy Movements and Their Control in pre-Famine Ireland* (Sussex, 1983); J. S. Donnelly Jr, 'Pastorini and Captain Rock: millenarianism and sectarianism in the Rockite movement of 1821–24' in Samuel Clark and J. S. Donnelly Jr (eds), *Irish Peasants, Violence and Political Unrest, 1780–1914* (Manchester, 1983), pp. 102–39; Tom Garvin, 'Defenders, Ribbonmen and others: underground political networks in pre-Famine Ireland', *Past & Present* 96 (1982), pp. 133–55; K. T. Hoppen, *Elections, Politics and Society in Ireland, 1832–85* (Oxford, 1984), pp. 341–78.

20   R. F. Foster, *Modern Ireland, 1600–1972* (London, 1988), p. 408.

21   Margaret O'Callaghan, *British High Politics and a Nationalist Ireland: Criminality, Land and the Law under Forster and Balfour* (Cork, 1994), p. 2.

22 For an analysis of agrarian and political activity in east Galway from the United Irish League to the war of independence, see Campbell, *Land and Revolution*. For an analysis of the IRA campaign in Cork during the revolutionary period see, Peter Hart, *The IRA and its Enemies: Violence and Community in Cork, 1916–23* (Oxford, 1998).

23 See M. J. Kelly, *The Fenian Ideal and Irish Nationalism, 1882–1916* (Woodbridge, 2006), Owen McGee, *The Irish Republican Brotherhood from the Land League to Sinn Féin* (Dublin, 2005). The only systematic study of the role of the IRB at a local level in the land war period is Frank Rynne's chapter 'Permanent revolutionaries: the IRB and the land war in West Cork' in James McConnel and Fearghal McGarry (eds), *The Black Hand of Republicanism: Fenianism in Modern Ireland* (Dublin, 2009), pp. 55–71.

24 Hart, *The I.R.A. and its Enemies*; Joost Augusteijn, *From Public Defiance To Guerrilla Warfare: The Experience of Ordinary Volunteers in the Irish War of Independence, 1916–21* (Dublin, 1996).

25 *Journal of the Kerry Archaeological and Historical Society.* The first volume of this journal was published in 1968.

26 J. S. Donnelly Jr, 'The Kenmare estates during the nineteenth century', *JKAHS* 21 (1988), pp. 5–41; idem, 'The Kenmare estates during the nineteenth century', *JKAHS* 22 (1989), pp. 61–98; idem, 'The Kenmare estates during the nineteenth century', *JKAHS* 23 (1990), pp. 5–45.

27 G. J. Lyne, *The Lansdowne Estate in Kerry Under the Agency of William Stuart Trench, 1849–72* (Dublin, 2001).

28 W. L. Feingold, 'Land League power: the Tralee poor-law election of 1881' in Samuel Clark and J. S. Donnelly Jr (eds), *Irish Peasants: Violence and Political Unrest, 1780–1915* (Manchester, 1983), pp. 285–310; idem, *The Revolt of the Tenantry: The Transformation of Local Government in Ireland, 1872–86* (Boston, 1984).

29 Maura Cronin, 'Local history' in Mary McAuliffe, Katherine O'Donnell and Leeann Lane (eds), *Palgrave Advances in Irish History* (London, 2009), p. 152.

30 Raymond Gillespie and G. P. Moran, *Longford: Essays in County History* (Dublin, 1991), p. 7.

31 Ibid.,, p. 5. For a full examination of the problems of 'nationalising local history' and merely viewing local events through the prism of national frameworks see Charles Phythian-Adams, *Re-thinking English Local History* (Leicester, 1987), pp. 1–15.

32 Campbell, *Land and Revolution*; Marie Coleman, *County Longford and the Irish Revolution* (Dublin, 2003); Michael Farry, *Sligo, 1914–21: A Chronicle of Conflict* (Trim, 1992); *The Aftermath of Revolution: Sligo, 1921–23* (Dublin, 2000); John Callaghan, *Revolutionary Limerick: The Republican Campaign for Independence in Limerick, 1913–21* (Dublin, 2010); Robert Lynch, *The Northern IRA and the Early Years of Partition, 1920–22* (Dublin, 2006).

33 For a general outline of the geography of the land war see Tom Garvin, *The Evolution of Irish Nationalist Politics* (Dublin, 1981), pp. 72–3.

34 O'Callaghan, *British Politics and a Nationalist Ireland*.

ONE: BACKGROUND TO THE LAND WAR IN COUNTY KERRY

1 Michael Turner, *After the Famine: Irish Agriculture, 1850–1914* (Cambridge, 1996), p. 15.

2 *Return of agricultural produce in Ireland in the year 1848*, p. vii, HC, 1847–8 [923], lvii, 1; *Return of agricultural statistics for the year 1880*, p. 33, HC 1881 [C 2932], xciii, 685.

3 *Agricultural statistics part ii–stock, table viii–showing the number of holdings and quantity of live stock in each county in Ireland in 1870*, p. 131 [C 880] HC 1872, lxix, 119.

4 Ibid.

5 Alvin Jackson, *Ireland: Politics and War* (Oxford, 1999), p. 82.

6 It has been argued that tenants benefited mostly from the post-Famine increase in agricultural prices. See generally Vaughan, *Landlords and Tenants in mid-Victorian Ireland.* In contrast, other works suggest that landlords were the main beneficiaries of the post-Famine increase in agricultural prices, see Turner, *After the Famine.*

7 Donnelly, *The Land and the People of Nineteenth-Century Cork*, p. 138.

8 Ibid., p. 148.

9 J. S. Donnelly Jr, 'The journals of Sir John Benn-Walsh relating to the management of his Irish estates, 1823–64', *JCHAS* 80 (1975), p. 39.

10 *TC*, 11 Aug. 1871.

11 *TC*, 8 Feb. 1876.

12 *Report of her majesty's commissioners of inquiry into the working of the Landlord and Tenant (Ireland) Act, 1870, and the acts amending the same, vol. iii: minutes of evidence*, p. 761 [C 2779–11], HC 1881, xix, 1 [hereafter cited as *Bessborough comm. . ., vol. iii:.. evidence. . .*].

13 Ibid., p. 759.

14 For a full account of the Cork Butter Market see, J. S. Donnelly, 'Cork market: Its role in the nineteenth-century Irish butter trade', *Studia Hibernica* 11, 1971, pp. 130–63.

15 T. W. Freeman, *Ireland: A General and Regional Geography* (4th edn, London, 1969), p. 360.

16 *Return of agricultural holdings, compiled by the local government board in Ireland from the returns furnished by the clerks of the poor law unions in Ireland 1881*, p. 4 [C 2934], HC 1881, xcii, 793.

17 J. S. Donnelly, 'The Kenmare estates during the nineteenth century', *Journal of the Kerry Archaeological & Historical Society* 21 (1988), p. 13.

18 *Return of agricultural holdings. . ., 1881*, p. 4.

19 *Return showing, with regard to each electoral division in Ireland, the gross rateable valuation per acre, the total population, the rateable valuation per head of the population, and the average poor rate for the last five years*, p. 33, HC 1887 (27), lxxi, 51.

20 *Bessborough comm. . ., vol. iii:.. evidence. . .* , p. 771.

21 Ibid., p. 774.

22 Joseph Lee, *The Modernisation of Irish Society, 1848–1918* (Dublin, 1973) p. 82.

23 *Census of Ireland 1881: area, population and number of houses; occupations, religion and education vol. ii: province of Munster*, pp. 523–29 [C 3148], HC 1882, lxxvii, 1.

24 *Bessborough comm. . ., vol. iii:.. evidence. . .*, p. 774.

25 Ibid.

26 S. J. Connolly, *Religion and Society in Nineteenth-Century Ireland* (Dundalk, 1985), p. 55. In this work Connolly offers an overview of the various arguments concerning the development of the Roman Catholic Church in the post-Famine period.

27 Congested District Board: Base Line reports, County Kerry, Castlegregory, p. 641 (TCD).

28 Ibid.

29 Congested District Board: Base Line report, Killorglin, p. 653.

30 Return of outrages, 1879–93 (NAI, CSO ICR, vol. 1)

31 *Return, by Provinces and Counties, of Cases of Evictions under Knowledge of RIC, 1849–80*, pp. 19–22, HC 1881 (185), lxxvii, 725.

32 Donnelly, *The Land and the People of Nineteenth-Century Cork*, p. 218.

33 Vaughan, *Landlords and Tenants*, p. 80.

34 D. E. Steele, *Irish Land and British Politics: Tenant-right and Nationality, 1865–70* (Cambridge, 1974).

35 Donnelly, *The Land and the People of Nineteenth-Century Cork*, p. 217. Donnelly offers this as evidence of landlord restriction on tenant-right. It must be noted that Hussey only attempted to control sales after the economic depression took effect, indicating that the rule had not previously existed.

36 Drummond Estate papers (NAI, Rental Book, 1025/1/29).

37 *Bessborough comm . . ., vol. iii:.. evidence. . .*, p. 815.

38 Ibid., p. 763.

39 Donnelly, *The Land and the People of Nineteenth-Century Cork*, p. 210.

40 *Bessborough comm . . ., vol. iii:.. evidence. . .*, p. 808.

41 Robert McCarthy, *The Trinity College Estates 1800–1912: Corporate Management in an Age of Reform* (Dundalk, 1992), p. 65.

42 G. J. Lyne, *The Lansdowne Estate in Kerry under the Agency of William Stuart Trench, 1849–72* (Dublin, 2001), p. 194. This example was given before the Devon commission by a Tralee solicitor.

43 Lyne, *The Lansdowne Estate in Kerry*, p. 194.

44 For example see *TC*, 14 Mar. 1876.

45 *TC*, 25 Jan. 1876.

46 *TC*, 30 Jan. 1877.

47 Finlay Dun, *Landlords and Tenants in Ireland* (London, 1881), p. 79.

48 Knight of Kerry, *Irish Landlords and Tenants: Recent Letters to 'The Times' and Further Correspondence on the Above Subject* (Dublin, 1876), p. 28.

49 *Bessborough comm. . ., vol. iii:.. evidence. . .*, p. 818.

50 Knight of Kerry, *Irish Landlords and Tenants*, appendix.

51 Lyne, *The Lansdowne Estate in Kerry*, p. 195.

52 Dun, *Landlords*, p. 79.

53 *TC*, 30 Nov. 1875.

54 *Bessborough comm . . ., vol. iii:.. evidence. . .*, p. 803.

55 Ibid., p. 756.

56 Ibid., p. 760.

57 Ibid., p. 775.

58 *TC*, 6 July 1875.

59 Thomas O'Rourke to John Sweetman, 4 Mar. 1879, (NLI, Sweetman Family papers, MS 47573/4).

60 Fergus Campbell, *Land and Revolution: Nationalist Politics in the West of Ireland, 1891–1921* (Oxford, 2005), p. 19.

61 Talbot-Crosbie Ledger Book p. 431 (NLI, MS 5037).

62 D. S. Jones, *Graziers, Land Reform and Popular Conflict In Ireland* (Washington, 1995), p. 127.

63 Ibid., pp. 89–135. In a chapter entitled 'The land market' Jones extensively examines the supply of rented property, particularly focusing on the emergence of graziers and the eleven month system. However, he fails to recognise the sale of tenant interest as a significant factor in the land market.

64 *KEP*, 29 Sept. 1880.

65 *Bessborough comm..., vol. iii:... evidence...*, p. 808.

66 *Thom's Directory 1863*, pp. 1007–9.

67 *Thom's Directory 1871*, pp. 1224–2248; *Thom's Directory 1881*, pp. 984–9.

68 *Royal Commission on depressed condition of agricultural interests; minutes of evidence, part I*, p. 628 [C 2778–I], HC 1881, 25 [hereafter *Richmond comm... evidence...*].

69 Ibid., p. 94.

70 Ibid., p. 811.

71 Donnelly, 'Cork market', pp. 133–41.

72 *Richmond comm... evidence...*, p. 999.

73 Ibid., p. 89.

74 Peter Gibbon and M. D. Higgins, 'Patronage, tradition and modernisation: The role of the Irish "Gombeenman"', *Economic and Social Review* VI (1974), p. 32.

75 Congested District Board: Base Line reports, County Kerry, p. 362 (TCD).

76 *Thom's Directory 1871*, p. 909.

77 *Thom's Directory 1878*, p. 659.

78 *Return of number of original civil bill processes served in quarter session districts in each county in Ireland 1876*, p. 3, HC 1877 (62), lxi. 329.

79 *KS*, 16 Apr. 1879.

80 *KS*, 21 Oct. 1879.

81 Donnelly, *The Land and the People of Nineteenth-Century Cork*, p. 148.

82 For the emergence of this class in Mayo see Donald Jordan, 'Merchants, "strong farmers" and Fenians: the post-Famine political elite and the Irish Land War' in C. H. E. Philpin (ed), *Nationalism and Popular Protest in Ireland* (Cambridge, 1987), pp. 320–48.

83 H. A. Herbert began his career as a Peelite in 1847 and became one of the few Irish-born chief secretaries, although his appointment was short lived from 1857 to 1858. See Brendan O'Cathaoir, 'The Kerry "Home Rule" by-election, 1872', *JKAHS* 3 (1970), p. 155; B. M. Walker, *Parliamentary Election Results in Ireland, 1801–1922* (Dublin, 1978), pp. 284–5; J. F. Mangan, 'H.A. Herbert as Chief Secretary for Ireland, 1857–58' (unpublished MA thesis, NUI Maynooth, 2005)

84 O'Brien, *Parnell and his Party*, p. 8.

85 Walker, *Parliamentary Election Results in Ireland, 1801–1922*, pp. 284–5. The Independent Irish Party succeeded in winning seats in many constituencies that were traditionally Liberal, for example see Gerard Moran, 'Politics and electioneering in County Longford, 1868–80' in Raymond Gillespie and Gerard Moran (eds), *Longford: Essays in County History* (Dublin, 1991), p. 173.

86 K.T. Hoppen, 'Landlords, society and electoral politics in mid-nineteenth-century Ireland', *Past & Present* 75 (May 1977), p. 67.

87 Thompson, *The End of Liberal Ulster, 1868–86*, p. 61.

88 Ibid., p. 68.

89 For an examination of politics in King's County see Gerard Moran, 'Political developments in King's County, 1868–1885' in William Nolan and T. P. O'Neill (eds), *Offaly: History and Society* (Dublin, 1998), pp. 767–98.

90 Jordan, *Land and Popular Politics in Ireland: County Mayo*, p. 171

91 Hoppen, *Ireland since 1800*, p. 159.

92   Hoppen, *Elections, Politics and Society in Ireland 1832–85*, p. 289.

93   Ibid., p. 273.

94   Moran, 'Politics and electioneering in County Longford, 1868–80', p. 174; idem, 'Political developments in King's County, 1868–1885' in William Nolan and T. P. O'Neill (eds), *Offaly: History and Society*, p. 768.

95   Alvin Jackson, *Home Rule: An Irish History, 1800–2000* (London, 2003), pp. 26–7.

96   Ibid., p. 29.

97   R.V. Comerford, 'Isaac Butt and the Home Rule Party, 1870–77' in W.E. Vaughan (ed.), *A New History of Ireland, VI Ireland under the Union, II 1879–1921* (Oxford, 1996), p. 8.

98   Hoppen, *Elections, Politics and Society in Ireland*, p. 466.

99   See *Tralee Chronicle*, 9 Jan. 1872, 26 Mar. 1872.

100 Samuel Clark, *Social Origins of the Irish Land War* (Princeton, 1979), p. 255.

101 Hoppen, *Elections, Politics and Society in Ireland*, p. 469.

102 Frank Thompson, *The End of Liberal Ulster: Land Agitation and Land Reform, 1868–86* (Belfast, 2001), p. 66.

103 Clark, *Social Origins of the Irish Land War*, p. 215.

104 David Steele, *Irish Land and British Politics: Tenant-right and Nationality, 1865–70* (Cambridge, 1974), p. 313.

105 W. E. Vaughan, *Landlords and Tenants in Mid-Victorian Ireland* (Oxford, 1994), p. 214.

106 *TC*, 4 Aug. 1871.

107 Ibid.

108 Clark, *Social Origins of the Irish Land War*, p. 217.

109 Walker (ed.), *Parliamentary Election Results in Ireland, 1801–1922*, p. 114.

110 See *TC*, 6. Feb. 1872, 9 Feb. 1872.

111 Brendan O'Cathaoir, 'The Kerry "Home Rule" by-election, 1872', *JKAHS* 3 (1970), pp. 154–77, p. 165.

112 *TC*, 12 Jan. 1872, Valuation records, E.D. Ardfert (Valuation Office, Dublin). The three farmers were James O'Connell, Knockenagh, Florence O'Sullivan, Ballymacquinn, Thomas Egan, Tubrid.

113 O'Cathaoir, 'Kerry "Home Rule" by-election', *JKAHS*, p. 161.

114 Ibid., p. 156; *TC*, 19 Jan. 1872.

115 *TC*, 19 Mar. 1872.

116 Walker (ed.), *Parliamentary Election Results in Ireland, 1801–1922*, p. 114.

117 O'Cathaoir, 'Kerry "Home Rule" by-election', p. 165.

118 O'Brien, *Parnell and his Party*, p. 125.

119 Gerard Moran, 'The emergence and consolidation of the home rule movement in County Cavan, 1870–86' in Raymond Gillespie (ed), *Cavan: Essays on the History of An Irish County* (Dublin, 1995), p. 224.

120 For a brief overview of The O'Donoghue's life see R.V. Comerford, http://www.oxforddnb.com/view/article/47769 (1 June 2006). For a comprehensive analysis of his early political career see, idem, 'Churchmen, tenants and independent opposition, 1850–56' in W. E. Vaughan (ed.), *A New History of Ireland, V Ireland under the Union, I, 1801–1870* (Oxford, 1989), pp. 396–414.

121 Walker, *Parliamentary Election Results in Ireland, 1801–1922*, p. 119

122 Ibid., p. 315.

123 Clark, *Social Origins of the Irish Land War*, p. 263.

124 Jackson, *Ireland*, p. 110.

125 Hoppen, *Elections, Politics, and Society in Ireland*, p. 464.

126 Moran, 'Political developments in King's County, 1868–1885' in Nolan and O'Neill (eds), *Offaly: History and Society*, p. 777.

127 R. V. Comerford, *The Fenians in Context: Irish Politics and Society, 1848–82* (Dublin, 1985), p. 115.

128 Comerford, 'Patriotism as pastime: the appeal of Fenianism in the mid-1860s', *IHS* xxii: 87 (Mar. 1981), p. 242.

129 Fenianism index of names, 1861–5, vol. 1 (NAI, CSO ICR). This list was drawn up by the government after the suspension of habeas corpus in Ireland in February 1866 and included anyone suspected of supporting Fenianism.

130 'List of persons now undergoing sentences of penal servitude under conviction of offences in connection with Fenianism, Jan. 1869': Fenian Arrests and discharges, no. 18 (NAI, Fenian Papers).

131 Maura Cronin, *Country, Class or Craft? The Politicisation of the Skilled Artisan in Nineteenth-Century Cork* (Cork, 1994), p. 106.

132 Comerford, *Fenians*, p. 41.

133 Ibid. Seán O'Luing, 'The Phoenix Society in Kerry, 1858–9', *JKAHS* 2 (1969), p. 6. This article provides an extensive account of the society in Kerry.

134 Index of names 1861–5, Fenian Papers (NAI, Police and Crime Records); O'Luing, 'Phoenix Society', pp. 14–18.

135 For an account of the Fenian uprising in Kerry see O'Luing, 'Aspects of the Fenian rising in Kerry, 1867: I. The rising and its background', *JKAHS* 3 (1970), pp. 131–53; idem, 'Aspects of the Fenian rising in Kerry, 1867: II. Aftermath', *JKAHS* 4 (1971), pp. 139–64.

136 Comerford, *Fenians*.

137 Clark, *Social Origins of the Irish Land War*, p. 204.

138 Jackson, *Ireland*, p. 110.

139 *TC*, 19 Mar. 1872.

140 Comerford, *Fenians*, p. 193.

141 *TC*, 3 Feb. 1874; Return of persons arrested and discharges in connection with the Fenian conspiracy 1866–8, John Kelly (NAI, Fenian Arrests and Discharges 1866–9, Carton 1).

142 Jordan, *Land and Popular Politics in Ireland: County Mayo*, p. 188; idem, 'John O'Connor Power, Charles Stewart Parnell and the centralisation of popular politics in Ireland', *Irish Historical Studies* 25 (1986), pp. 49–53.

143 Hoppen, *Elections, Politics, and Society in Ireland*, p. 468.

144 Jackson, *Ireland 1798–1998*, p. 110.

145 Gerard Moran, 'The radical priest of Partry: Fr Patrick Lavelle (1826–1885) in Gerard Moran (ed.), *Radical Irish Priests, 1660–1970* (Dublin, 1998), p. 127.

146 O'Brien, *Parnell and his Party*, p. 123.

147 *FJ*, 22 Jan. 1875.

148 Frank Thompson, *The End of Liberal Ulster: Land Agitation and Land Reform, 1868–86* (Belfast, 2001), p. 158.

149 For a discussion on Kerry landlords and rent increases in the county see Donnelly, 'Kenmare', 21, pp. 15–19.

150 For a discussion on increases in rent on a countrywide-scale see Vaughan, *Landlords and Tenants*, pp. 44–52.

151 Donnelly, 'Kenmare', 21, pp. 18–19.

152 *TC*, 15 Jan. 1875 and 12 Feb. 1875.

153 Talbot-Crosbie ledger book (NLI, MS 5037).

154 *TC*, 13 Apr. 1875. This was the beginning of a campaign that witnessed Hussey increase the annual rents from £24,393 to £27,312 between 1875 and 1879, see Donnelly, 'Kenmare', 21, p. 38.

155 *TC*, 14 Dec. 1875.

156 *TC*, 2 July 1875.

157 Quoted in Bryan MacMahon, 'George Sandes of Listowel: land agent, magistrate and terror of north Kerry', *JKAHS* 2nd series, 3 (2003), p. 15.

158 *TC*, 23 Mar. 1875 and *TC*, 6 Apr. 1875.

159 *TC*, 30 Mar. 1875.

160 *TC*, 16 Apr. 1875.

161 *TC*, 13 July 1875 and *TC*, 6 Aug. 1875.

162 Cited in *TC*, 13 July 1875.

163 *Bessborough comm. . ., vol. iii:.. evidence. . .*, p. 573.

164 Studies such as Carter's *The Land War and its Leaders in Queen's County* offer little exploration of tenant politics in the years leading up to 1879.

165 *TC*, Jan. 1874; *Land Owners in Ireland* (Baltimore, 1988), pp. 141–2.

166 *TC*, 27 Apr. 1875 and 24 May 1875.

167 *TC*, 15 June 1875.

168 Ibid.

169 *TC*, 17 Aug. 1875.

170 Rules of Ballinasloe Tenants' Defence Association, Sweetman Family Papers (NLI, MS 47573/3).

171 Thompson, *The End of Liberal Ulster*, p. 157.

172 *Bessborough comm. . ., vol. iii:.. evidence. . .*, p. 805–7.

173 *TC*, 25 Jan. 1876; Francis Guy, *Guy's Munster Directory* (Cork, 1886).

174 Jordan, *Land and Popular Politics in Ireland: County Mayo*, p. 180.

175 William Feingold, *The Revolt of the Tenantry: The Transformation of Local Government in Ireland* (Boston, 1984), p. 72.

176 Ibid., p. 71.

177 Thompson, *The End of Liberal Ulster*, pp. 158–9.

178 *TC*, 3 Aug. 1875.

179 *TC*, 14 Dec. 1875.

180 *TC*, 12 May 1876 and 19 May 1876. The chairmen of both the Listowel and Caherciveen boards refused to allow a vote on the issue.

181 John Kelly was arrested for his involvement in Fenianism in 1865 at the age of 20. At the time of his arrest he had no stated occupation; see Fenian Arrests and Discharges 1866–9 (NAI, Fenian papers). In 1880 the police believed that Power always took the lead in Fenian demonstrations, see, Report on the character of Michael Power, 30 Dec. 1880 (NAI, CSO RP, 1881, 1221).

182 *TC*, 12 Jan. 1877.

183 *TC*, 2 Jan. 1877.

184 *TC*, 14 Dec. 1875.

185 *TC*, 12 May 1876.

186 *TC*, 18 Aug. 1876.

187 Ibid.

188 *TC*, 12 Sept. 1876.

189 *TC*, 20 Feb. 1877.

190 *TC*, 6 Mar. 1877.

191 *TC*, 20 Feb. 1877.

192 In this case the agent Hussey attempted to sell the holdings at a price that was unacceptable to the tenants, see *TC*, 23 Nov. 1877, 3 Sept. 1878.

193 *TC*, 8 Oct. 1878.

194 Although a major landowner in Kells, County Meath, Sweetman was an advocate of agrarian reform and took a prominent part in the 1870s tenant-right movement. He was also a founding member of the Land League's national committee. For Sweetman's biography see Patrick Maume, 'John Sweetman', in *Dictionary of Irish Biography* (Cambridge, 2009), pp. 185–7.

195 Thomas O'Rourke to John Sweetman 4 Oct. 1878, Sweetman Family Papers (NLI, MS 47573/4).

196 Ibid.

197 O'Rourke to Sweetman, 9 Oct. 1878, Sweetman Family Papers (NLI, MS 47,573/3).

198 'Prospectus on Irish Farmers Union', Sweetman Family Papers (NLI, MS 47,573/9).

199 O'Brien, *Parnell and his Party*, p. 126.

200 Moran, 'The emergence and consolidation of the home rule movement', p. 170; idem 'Political developments in King's County', p. 780.

201 For the *Sentinel*'s first editorial which concentrated on the education question see, *KS*, 26 Apr. 1878. For an outline of Harrington's long and distinguished career see Patrick Maume, 'Timothy Harrington' in *Dictionary of Irish Biography*, pp. 475–7.

202 *KS*, 5 Nov. 1878.

203 *KS*, 22 Oct. 1878.

204 *TC*, 24 Sept. 1878.

205 T.W. Moody, *Davitt and the Irish Revolution* (Oxford, 1981), p. 254; Comerford, *Fenians*, p. 225.

206 *TC*, 19 Nov. 1878.

207 *TC*, 22 Oct. 1878.

208 *TC*, 12 Nov. 1878.

209 Mr Parnell's speech at Tralee, 10 Nov. 1878, Sweetman Family Papers (NLI, MS 47573/3)

210 *TC*, 19 Nov. 1878.

211 Ibid.

212 Paul Bew, *The Politics of Enmity, 1789–2006* (Oxford, 2007), p. 310.

213 Ibid.

214 Gerard Moran, 'James Daly and the rise and fall of the Land League in the west of Ireland, 1879–82', *IHS* xxix: 114 (Nov. 1994), p. 191.

TWO: AGRICULTURAL DEPRESSION AND THE EMERGENCE
OF RADICAL AGITATION

1   *Thom's Directory 1881*, p. 659.

2   *KS*, 2 Jan. 1879.

3   A firkin is equal to 40.91 litres.

4   *KS*, 25 Feb. 1879.

5   *KS*, 6 June 1879.

6   Ibid.

7   *Thom's Directory 1881*, p. 691.

8   *KS*, 21 Oct. 1879.

9   RIC County Inspector report on the condition of the country, 31 Oct. 1879 (NAI, CSO RP, 1880, 34686).

10   *Preliminary report on the returns of agricultural produce in Ireland in 1879*, p. 14 [C 2495], HC 1880 lxxvi, 893.

11   *KS*, 16 Sept. 1879.

12   *KS*, 21 Oct. 1879. Article reprinted from the *Freeman's Journal*.

13   *KS*, 29 July 1879.

14   Donnelly, 'Cork market', p. 135.

15   *KS*, 25 Nov. 1879.

16   Donnelly, *The Land and the People of Nineteenth-Century Cork*, pp. 170–2.

17   *Bessborough comm . . ., vol. iii:. . . evidence. . .*, p. 811.

18   RIC County Inspector report in the condition of the country, 31 Oct. 1879 (NAI, CSO RP, 1880, 34686).

19   *KS*, 21 Oct. 1879. Figures republished from *Stubb's Gazette*.

20   *Annual report of the Local Government Board for Ireland, being the eighth report under the Local Government Board (Ireland) Act, 35 & 36 Vic., with appendix*, p. 75 [C 2603] HC 1880 xxviii, 1.

21   *KS*, 10 Oct. 1879, *KS*, 18 Oct. 1879, and *KS*, 1 Nov. 1879.

22   David Fitzpatrick, 'The disappearance of the Irish agricultural labourer, 1841–1912', *Irish Economic and Social History* VII (1980), p. 70. This work highlights the similarities and overlap in the lives of small farmers and agricultural labourers.

23   *Annual report of the Local Government Board for Ireland, being the eighth report*, p. 77.

24   Ibid., p. 122.

25   Ballybunion relief committee to Mansion House Relief Committee, 17 Feb. 1880 (Dublin City Archive (DCA), Mansion House Relief Fund Papers, Ch 1/52/320 letter no. 5).

26   Firies relief committee to Mansion House Relief Committee, 20 Jan. 1880 (DCA, Mansion House Relief Fund Papers, Ch 1/52/513 letter no. 1).

27   *Special Commission act, reprint of the shorthand notes of the speeches, proceedings, and evidence taken before the commissioners appointed under the above act, vol. i* (London, 1890), p. 544.

28   *Return, arranged according to counties, showing the number of accounts of depositors in Post Office Savings Banks in the U.K. remaining open on the 31 Dec. 1879, with the amount, inclusive of interest, standing to the credit of those accounts*, p. 41, HC, 1881 (24), lvii, 335.

29   Firies relief committee to Mansion House Relief Committee, 20 Jan. 1880 (DCA, Mansion House Relief Fund Papers, Ch 1/52/513 letter no. 4).

30 Gerald Moran, 'Famine and the land war: relief and distress in Mayo, 1879–1881, part 1', *Cathair na Mart: Journal of the Westport Historical Society* 5: 1 (1985); idem, 'Famine and the land war: relief and distress in Mayo, 1879–81, part 11', *Cathair na Mairt* 6: 1 (1986), pp. 111–28; T. P. O'Neill, 'Minor famines and relief in Galway, 1815–1925', *Galway: History and Society: Interdisciplinary Essays on the History of an Irish County* (Dublin, 1996), pp. 465–72, Donnelly, *The Land and the People of Nineteenth-Century Cork.*

31 Carter, *The Land War and its Leaders in Queen's County.*

32 *KS,* 8 July 1879. These included Daniel Coltsmann of Glenflesk, J. R. Leahy, Daniel Brennan of Droumhall, M. J. O'Connell of Lake View, D. J. O'Connell of Grenagh, Wilson Gunn of Ratoo, G. R. Brown of Caherdown,

33 Ibid.

34 *KS,* 1 Aug. 1879.

35 Virginia Crossman, '"With the experience of 1846 and 1847 before them": the politics of emergency relief, 1879–84' in Peter Gray (ed.), *Victoria's Ireland? Irishness and Britishness, 1837–1901* (Dublin, 2004), p. 175.

36 *Return of applications from landed proprietors and sanitary authorities in scheduled unions for loans under notices of Commissioners of Public Works in Ireland, 22 Nov. 1879–12 Jan. 1880, with result,* p. 4, HC 1880 (154), lxii.

37 *KS,* 6 Jan. 1880.

38 Returns of relief of distress: County Kerry, 23 Oct. 1880 (NAI, CSO RP, 1880, 26726/25850).

39 Ibid.

40 *KS,* 20 Jan. 1880; *Land Owners in Ireland,* p. 142.

41 *KS,* 20 Jan. 1880; *Land Owners in Ireland,* p. 142.

42 Crossman, 'The politics of emergency relief, 1879–84' p. 178.

43 *Return of numbers in receipt of relief in the several unions in Ireland on 1 Jan., 1 Mar., and 1 June, in 1878, 1879, and 1880,* p. 23, HC 1880 (420), lxii, 289.

44 Crossman, 'The politics of emergency relief, 1879–84', p. 175; *Circular of 7 Feb. 1880, issued by the Local Government Board for Ireland to boards of guardians, relating to the relief to families of persons occupying land,* HC 1880 (9), lvii, 705.

45 *Annual report of the Local Government Board for Ireland, being the eighth report.*

46 Moran 'Famine and the land war, part 11', p. 112.

47 *Annual report of the Local Government Board for Ireland, being the ninth report under the Local Government Board (Ireland) Act, 35 & 36 Vic., with appendix,* p. 127, HC 1881 [C.2926], xlvii, 269.

48 Ibid., p. 129.

49 Mansion House Relief Committee, *The Irish Crisis of 1879–80: proceedings of the Dublin Mansion House Relief Committee, 1880* (Dublin, 1881), pp. 307–8.

50 Carter, *The Land War and its Leaders in Queen's County,* p. 34.

51 For a full analysis of the role of the Catholic clergy in relief measures during this period see G. P. Moran, '"Near famine": the Roman Catholic Church and the subsistence crisis of 1879–82', *Studia Hibernica* 32 (2002–3), pp. 155–78.

52 Mansion House Relief Committee, *The Irish Crisis of 1879–80,* p. 311.

53 Ardfert Relief Committee to Mansion House Committee, 1 Jan. 28 1880 (DCA, Mansion House Relief Fund Papers, Ch1/52/206 letter no. 1).

54 Ibid., Ch1/52/513 letter 1; Valuation Office (Dublin, Valuation records).

55 Ballybunion Relief Committee to Mansion House Committee (DCA, House Relief Fund Papers, Ch 1/52/320 letter no. 1).

56 Gerard Moran, 'Near famine: The crisis in the West of Ireland, 1879–82', *Irish Studies Review* 5: 18 (1997), p. 18.

57 Carter, *The Land War and its Leaders in Queen's County*, p. 32.

58 Jordan, *Land Popular and Politics in Ireland: County Mayo*, pp. 209–29.

59 *Land Owners in Ireland*, p. 141.

60 Butt's land bill was tabled in 1876 and remained the policy of the moderate section of the Irish Party.

61 *KS*, 14 Feb. 1879.

62 *KS*, 6 June 1879.

63 *KS*, 13 June 1879 and 17 June 1879.

64 *KS*, 13 June 1879.

65 Comerford, *Fenians*, p. 232.

66 *KS*, 26 Sept. 1879.

67 *KS*, 23 Sept. 1879.

68 *Land Owners in Ireland*, p. 144.

69 *KS*, 7 Nov. 1879.

70 McCarthy, *Trinity*, p. 58.

71 *KS*, 30 Sept. 1879.

72 *KS*, 12 Sept. 1879.

73 *KS*, 23 Dec. 1879.

74 *Return of number of families evicted other than for non-payment of rent, 1877–79; Return of number of civil bill ejectments entered, tried and determined in Ireland, 1877–79*, p. 5, HC 1880 (132), lx, 379.

75 *Return of cases of eviction which have come under the knowledge of the constabulary in each of the four quarters of 1877, 1878, 1879, and the first quarter of 1880 and up to the 10 June 1880*, pp. 2–4, HC 1880 (245), lx, 361.

76 *KS*, 21 Oct. 1880.

77 *KS*, 5 Dec. 1880.

78 *KS*, 8 July 1880.

79 *KS*, 18 Nov. 1880.

80 Ibid.

81 Ibid.

82 *KS*, 6 Jan. 1880.

83 Ibid.

84 Ibid.

85 *TC*, 6 Jan. 1880.

86 For an explanation of Butt's solution to the land question see, David Thornley, *Isaac Butt and Home Rule* (2nd edn, London, 1976), p. 274; Philip Bull, *Land, Politics and Nationalism: A Study of the Irish Land Question* (Dublin, 1996), pp. 66–7.

87 *KS*, 6 Jan. 1880. The Irish National Land League was established on 21 October 1879. See, Comerford, *Fenians*, p. 231.

88 *Return of all agrarian outrages which have been reported by the RIC between the 1st day of Jan. and the 31st day of Jan. 1880, giving particulars of crime, arrests, and results of proceedings*, pp. 199–290, HC 1880 (131), lx.

89 O'Brien, *Parnell and his Party*, p. 24.

90 *Land Owners in Ireland*, p. 141.

91   *KS*, 16 Mar. 1880.

92   G. M. Moran, 'Political developments in King's County, 1868–85' in Nolan and O'Neill (eds), *Offaly: History and Society*, p. 783.

93   R.W. Kirkpatrick, 'Origins and development of the land war in mid-Ulster, 1879–85' in F. S. L. Lyons and R. A. J. Hawkins (eds), *Ireland under the Union: Varieties of Tension. Essays in honour of T. W. Moody* (Oxford, 1980), p. 226.

94   Carter, *The Land War and its Leaders in Queen's County, 1879–82*, pp. 48–51.

95   Parnell was also elected in Meath and Cork City and took the Cork seat. The Mayo seat was taken by a Parnellite Presbyterian Minister, the Rev. Isaac Nelson. See Jordan, *Land and Popular Politics in Ireland: County Mayo*, pp. 260–1.

96   *KS*, 12 Mar. 1880.

97   *TC*, 19 Mar. 1880.

98   *TC*, 16 Mar. 1880.

99   *KS*, 23 Mar. 1880.

100 *TC*, 23 Mar. 1880.

101 *KS*, 30 Mar. 1880

102 *KS*, 26 Mar. 1880.

103 *TC*, 30 Mar. 1880.

104 'Police report on disturbances in Tralee, 31 Mar. 1880' (NAI, CSO RP, 1880, 8384).

105 Ibid.

106 *KS*, 2 Apr. 1880.

107 O'Brien, *Parnell and His Party*, p. 25.

108 Moody, *Davitt*, p. 375.

109 *KS*, 30 Apr. 1880.

110 Bew, *Land and the National Question*, p. 101.

111 Moody, *Davitt*, p. 374.

112 *Return of cases of eviction which have come under the knowledge of the constabulary in each of the four quarters of 1877, 1878, 1879, and the first quarter of 1880 and up to the 10 June 1880*, pp. 2–4, HC 1880 (245), lx, 361.

113 *Return of agrarian outrages reported by the RIC between 1st Feb. 1880 and 31st Oct. 1880*, p. 48 HC 1881 (6), lxxvii, 273; *Land Owners in Ireland*, p. 145, 148.

114 *Return of agrarian outrages reported by the RIC between 1st Feb. 1880 and 31st Oct. 1880*, p. 48.

115 Pope had an address in France, see *Land Owners in Ireland*, p. 144.

116 *TC*, 13 Apr. 1880.

117 *Return of agrarian outrages reported by the RIC between 1st Feb. 1880 and 31st Oct. 1880*, p. 48 HC 1881 (6), lxxvii, 273.

118 *KS*, 27 Apr. 1880.

119 *KS*, 27 Apr. 1880.

120 Report of RIC county inspectors on the condition of Ireland, 1880: lists of persons reasonably suspected of being directly or indirectly connected with outrages during the latter quarter of 1880 (NAI, CSO RP, 1880, 34686).

121 'File on Thomas Dooling' (TNA, CO 904/15: microfilm, NLI, p. 153).

122 *KS*, 11 May 1880.

123 *KS*, 16 July 1880, *Return of agrarian outrages reported by the RIC between 1st Feb. 1880 and 31st Oct. 1880*, p. 49, HC 1880 (6), lxxvii. 273.

124 'Select documents: XXXII The IRB supreme council, 1868–78', eds T.W. Moody and Leon O'Broin in *IHS* XIX: 75 (Mar. 1975), p. 322

125 Fenian files (NAI, CSO Fenian A Files, Carton 4, A 574).

126 T. D. Sullivan, *A Popular History of East Kerry* (Dublin, 1931), pp. 88–9.

127 Report of county inspectors of the RIC, 31 Oct. 1879 (NAI, CSO RP, 1880, 34686).

128 Ibid.

129 File on J. D. Sheehan (TNA CO/904: microfilm, NLI, p. 956). Sheehan was arrested for partaking in the 1867 rising.

130 J. J. Lee, *The Modernisation of Irish Society, 1848–1918* (Dublin, 1973), p. 82.

131 J. S. Donnelly Jr, *Captain Rock: the Irish Agrarian Rebellion of 1821–24* (London, 2009); Beames, *Peasants and Power*.

132 Bew, *Land and the National Question, 1858–82*, pp. 38–45, 60–1, 97, 103.

133 Tom Garvin 'Defenders, 'Ribbonmen and others: Underground political networks in pre-Famine Ireland' in C. H. E. Philpin, *Nationalism and Popular Protest in Ireland* (Cambridge, 1987), p. 227

134 *KS*, 14 May 1880.

135 *KS*, 22 June 1880.

136 For O'Flaherty's emigration see, *KS*, 6 Aug. 1880.

137 *TC*, 8 June 1880.

138 *KS*, 22 June 1880.

139 Ibid.

140 *Land Owners in Ireland*, p. 143.

141 *KS*, 16 July 1880.

142 *KS*, 13 Aug. 1880.

143 Ibid.

144 Report of Land League meeting, Killorglin 11 Aug. 1880 (NAI, CSO RP, Queen *versus* Parnell, Carton v).

145 *Return of number of agrarian offences in each county in Ireland reported to the RIC 1880* ,pp 199–290, HC 1881 (12), lxxvii, 619.

146 *Return of cases of eviction under knowledge of constabulary in Ireland, 1880*, pp. 2–5, HC, 1881 (2), lxxvii, 713.

147 *KS*, 29 June 1880.

148 Notes on the *Kerry Sentinel*, Jan.–Sept. 1880, (NLI, Harrington papers, MS 8933). This source is a ledger of notes taken by Timothy Harrington from the *Sentinel* concerning the emerging land agitation from Jan-Sept 1880. Although undated these notes were complied some time after the events. On a number of occasions Harrington refers to the occurrence of violent outrages before the emergence of the league. This would indicate he was gathering evidence to defend the organisation against claims that it was a violent conspiracy, most probably at the Special Commission of 1888.

149 *KS*, 30 July, 20 Aug. 1880.

150 *KS*, 30 July 1880.

151 Ibid.

152 Frank Rynne, 'Permanent revolutionaries: the IRB and the Land War in West Cork' in McConnel and McGarry (eds), *The Black Hand of Republicanism*, pp. 55–71

153 Carter, *The Land War and its leaders in Queen's County*; Edward Kennedy, *The Land Movement in Tullaroan, County Kilkenny, 1879–91* in Maynooth Studies in Local History: no. 55 (Dublin, 2004), p. 10.

154 See Clark, *Social Origins of the Irish Land War*.

155 The differing social aspirations of the various classes in tenant society have been extensively explored by Bew in *Land and the National Question in Ireland*.

156 Vaughan, *Landlords and Tenants in mid-Victorian Ireland*, p. 210.

157 Ibid., pp. 215–16.

THREE: LAND LEAGUE AGITATION

1   *KS*, 14 Sept. 1880; *Land Owners in Ireland, 1876* (Baltimore, 1988), pp. 141–2.

2   Outrage Returns 1880 (NAI, CSO ICR); *Land Owners in Ireland*, p. 145.

3   *KS*, 14 Sept. 1880 and *Return of agrarian outrages reported by Royal Irish Constabulary, Feb.–Oct. 1880*, p. 52, HC 1881 (6), lxxvii, 273. Although Staughton and his daughter were in the house at the time of the attack neither were injured.

4   *KS*, 1 Oct. 1880 and *Land Owners in Ireland*, p. 145.

5   Ibid.

6   *Return of number of agrarian offences in each county in Ireland reported to the constabulary office, 1880*, p. 3, HC 1881 (12), lxxvii, 619.

7   *KS*, 24 Sept. 1880; *Land Owners in Ireland*, p. 141.

8   *KS*, 28 Sept. 1880; *Land Owners in Ireland*, p. 143.

9   *KS*, 28 Sept. 1880; Leahy was a tenant to Lord Kenmare and paid an annual rent of £104, see, *KS*, 11 June 1880.

10   *KS*, 5 Oct. 1880.

11   Jordan, *Land and Popular Politics in Ireland: County Mayo*, pp. 264–83.

12   Kirkpatrick, 'Origins and development of the land war in mid-Ulster, 1879–85', p. 228.

13   *Return showing for each month of the years 1879 and 1880 the number of Land League meetings held and agrarian crimes reported to the Inspector General of the RIC in each county throughout Ireland*, p. 5, HC 1881 (5), lxxvii, 793

14   *KS*, 8 Oct. 1880.

15   *KS*, 12 Oct. 1880.

16   *KS*, 15 Oct. 1880, 19 Oct. 1880, 26 Oct. 1880.

17   *Return showing for each month of the years 1879 and 1880 the number of Land League meetings held and agrarian crimes reported to the Inspector General of the RIC in each county throughout Ireland*, p. 5, HC 1881 (5), lxxvii, 793.

18   The following is a list of the locations of branches and the number of meetings held: Tralee 12, Ballyduff 3, Castleisland 5, Brosna 4, Milltown and Listry 2, Firies 2, Caherciveen 2, Lixnaw 1, Listowel 2, Knocknagoshel 1, Ardfert 2, O'Dorney 2, Newtownsandes 1, Killarney 3.

19   Thomas Bartlett, 'An end to moral economy' in C. H. E. Philpin, *Nationalism and Popular Protest in Ireland* (Cambridge, 1987), p. 195. The work of E. P. Thompson is the standard bearer on the 'moral economy'; see E. P. Thompson, 'The moral economy of the English crowd in the eighteenth century', *Past & Present* 50 (Feb. 1971), pp. 76–136.

20   For a brief outline of Campbell's career see, G. Le. G. Norgate, revised by David Steele, 'Sir George Campbell' in http://www.oxforddnb.com/view/article/4499.

21   Quoted in Bull, *Land, politics and Nationalism*, p. 50, see also George Campbell, *Irish Land* (London, 1869); for an explanation of this work in relation to the 'unwritten law' see, Heather

Laird, *Subversive Law in Ireland, 1879–1920: From 'Unwritten Law' to the Dáil courts* (Dublin, 2005), p. 21.

22 Donald Jordan, 'The Irish National League and the "unwritten law": rural protest and nation building in Ireland 1882–90', *Past & Present* 158 (Feb 1998), p. 148.

23 *KS*, 8 Oct. 1880.

24 *KS*, 15 Oct. 1880.

25 *KS*, 28 Sept. 1880.

26 *KS*, 1 Oct. 1880.

27 Ibid.

28 *KS*, 16 Nov. 1880.

29 *KS*, 1 Oct. 1880.

30 *KS*, 26 Oct. 1880.

31 J. S. Donnelly, 'The Kenmare estates during the nineteenth century', *JKHAS* 22 (1989), p. 68.

32 *KS*, 5 Oct. 1880.

33 *Return of the number of families evicted in Ireland for non-payment of rent, and re-admitted as caretakers, 1877–June 1880*, pp. 2–5, HC 1880 (317), lx, 367.

34 *Return of cases of eviction under the knowledge of the constabulary in Ireland, 1880*, pp. 4–5, HC 1881 (2), lxxvii, 713.

35 *Return of number of civil bill ejectments entered, tried and determined in Ireland, 1877–80*, pp. 2–6, HC 1881 (90), lxxvii, 685.

36 *Return of cases of eviction under the knowledge of the constabulary in Ireland, 1880*, pp. 2–8.

37 *Agricultural Statistics of Ireland, 1880*, pp. 55–6, HC 1881[C 2932], xciii, 685.

38 A. D. Orridge, 'Who supported the land war? An aggregate-data analysis of Irish agrarian discontent, 1879–82', *Economic and Social Review* 12: 3 (Apr. 1981), p. 221.

39 A range of historical research has been undertaken on these movements, for example see Beames, *Peasants and Power*, for contemporary pre-Famine observations on such agrarianism; see George Cornewall Lewis, *Local Disturbances in Ireland* (London, 1836).

40 For a full description of the agrarian economy in the 1870s see ch. one.

41 Comerford, *Fenians*, p. 237.

42 *KS*, 14 Sept. 1880.

43 Ibid.

44 Hoppen, *Elections, Politics, and Society in Ireland*, p. 472

45 *FJ*, 20 Oct. 1880.

46 Comerford, *Fenians*, p. 234.

47 Donnelly, 'The Kenmare estates during the nineteenth century', 22, p. 67.

48 See ch. two.

49 *KS*, 8 Oct. 1880.

50 *KS*, 24 Dec. 1880.

51 See *TC*, 7 May 1880, 20 Aug. 1880, 3 and 10 Sept. 1880.

52 *TC*, 20 Aug. 1880.

53 *KS*, 12 Oct. 1880.

54 *KS*, 26 Oct. 1880.

55 *KS*, 21 Sept. 1880.

56 *KEP*, 6 Nov. 1880.

57 *TC*, 21 Sept. 1880.

58 *KS*, 30 Nov. 1880

59 *KS*, 5 Oct. 1880.

60 *KS*, 19 Nov. 1880.

61 *KS*, 21 Dec. 1880.

62 Reports of county inspectors of the RIC, 28 Oct. 1880 (NAI, CSO RP, 1880, 34686).

63 *KS*, 7 Dec. 1880.

64 *KS*, 14 Dec. 1880.

65 *KS*, 14 Dec. 1880; *KS*, 24 Dec. 1880.

66 *KS*, 7 Jan. 1880.

67 *KS*, 24 Dec. 1880.

68 Ibid.

69 *KS*, 28 Sept. 1880.

70 *KS*, 24 Dec. 1880.

71 *KS*, 21 Dec. 1880.

72 *KS*, 21 Dec. 1880.

73 *KS*, 24 Dec. 1880.

74 *KS*, 7 Jan. 1881.

75 David Fitzpatrick, 'Class, family and rural unrest in nineteenth-century Ireland', pp. 37–76.

76 For an overview of both arguments see Samuel Clark, 'The importance of agrarian classes: agrarian class structure and collective action in nineteenth-century Ireland' in P. J. Drudy (ed.), *Land*, pp. 11–36; Fitzpatrick, 'Class, family and rural unrest', pp. 37–76.

77 Laird, *Subversive Law in Ireland, 1879–1920*, p. 23.

78 *KS*, 16 July 1880.

79 *KS*, 15 Oct. 1880.

80 *Return of all agrarian outrages reported by the RIC between 1 Jan. 1880 and 31 Jan. 1881, giving particulars of crime, arrests, and results of proceedings*, pp. 38–44, HC 1881 (6) lxxvii, 273.

81 *KS*, 1 Feb. 1881. This information was given before an inquiry into the riot in Listowel.

82 Report on the character of Michael Power, 30 Dec. 1880 (NAI, CSO RP, 1881, 1221).

83 Bull, *Land, Politics and Nationalism*, p. 118.

84 Bew, *Land and the National Question*, p. 124.

85 O'Callaghan, *British High Politics and a Nationalist Ireland*, pp. 62–70.

86 Bew, *Land and the National Question*, p. 145.

87 Ibid.

88 Jackson, *Ireland: Politics and War, 1798–1998*, p. 120.

89 *KS*, 7 Jan. 1881. Those arrested were: Timothy Harrington (president of the league and editor of the *Kerry Sentinel*), Michael Lyons (draper), Thomas O'Rourke (secretary of the league and publican), John Kelly (draper), Henry Brassill (editor of *Kerry Independent*), John Talbot (butter merchant and shopkeeper), Jeremiah Leahy (tenant farmer), and Michael Leahy.

90 *FJ*, 10 Jan. 1880.

91 Fr O'Leary to Chief Secretary's Office, 3 Jan. 1881(NAI, CSO RP, 1881, 1702/632).

92 *FJ*, 10 Jan. 1881.

93 *FJ*, 12 Jan. 1881.

94 *FJ*, 13 Jan. 1881.

95 *FJ*, 15 Jan. 1881.

96 *FJ*, 12 Jan. 1881.

97 *KS*, 12 Feb. 1881.

98 *KS*, 28 Jan. 1881.

99 *KS*, 8 Feb. 1881.

100 *KS*, 1 Feb. 1881.

101 Bew, *Land and the National Question*, p. 124

102 Michael Boyton was an Irish-American nationalist who had spent much of his youth on a farm near Kildare town. By 1881 he was one of the first to be arrested under the 1881 Protection of Person and Property Act leading to much outcry in the USA over the arrest of an American citizen. He is credited with playing a significant role in giving the Land League a firm foothold outside Connaught; Thomas Nelson, *The Land War in County Kildare* in Maynooth Historical Series, no. 3 (Maynooth, 1985), p. 18; Bew, *Land and the National Question*, pp. 237–8.

103 *KS*, 8 Mar. 1881.

104 *KS*, 18 Feb. 1881.

105 *Bessborough comm. . . , vol. iii:. . . evidence. . .*, pp. 767–76.

106 *KS*, 18 Feb. 1881.

107 Bew, *Land and the National Question*, p. 122.

108 Vincent Comerford, 'The land war and the politics of distress, 1877–82', in W. E. Vaughan (ed.), *A New History of Ireland, VI Ireland under the Union, II 1879–1921* (Oxford, 1996), p. 47.

109 *KS*, 22 Feb. 1881.

110 *KS*, 29 Mar. 1881. This provides a valuable insight into voting behaviour during poor law elections. Although such elections were under open voting no poll books have been discovered, see Feingold, *Revolt of the Tenantry*, p. 128.

111 William Feingold, 'Land League power: the Tralee poor-law election of 1881' in Samuel Clark and J. S. Donnelly (ed.), *Irish Peasants: Violence and Political Unrest, 1780–1914* (Manchester, 1983), pp. 285–310, idem, *Revolt of the Tenantry*, pp. 123–37.

112 Feingold, *Revolt of the Tenantry*, p. 134.

113 Ibid.

114 *KS*, 8 Mar. 1881.

115 Bew, *Land and the National Question*, p. 128.

116 Emmet Larkin, *The Roman Catholic Church and the Creation of the Modern Irish State, 1878–86* (Philadelphia, 1975), p. 113.

117 *Return of number of agrarian outrages in each county in Ireland reported to the RIC, 1880*, pp. 11–4, HC 1881 (12), lxxvii, 619; Lee, *Modernisation*, p. 80.

118 Alvin Jackson, *Home Rule: An Irish History 1800– 2000* (London, 2003), p. 51.

119 *Return of number of agrarian offences in each county in Ireland reported to the RIC, 1881*, pp. 4–6, HC 1882 (8), lv, 1.

120 Feingold, *Revolt of the Tenantry*, p. 139

121 Bew, *Land and the National Question*, p. 163.

122 *FJ*, 3 Feb. 1881.

123 *KS*, 26 Apr. 1881.

124 Jordan, *Land and Popular Politics in Ireland: County Mayo*, p. 306–7.

125 Larkin, *The Roman Catholic Church and the Creation of the Modern Irish State*, p. 111.

126 Bew, *Land and the National Question*, p. 168

127 Ibid., p. 126.

128 *KI*, 14 Apr. 1881.

129 *KS*, 10 May 1881.

130 *KI*, 9 May 1881.

131 Larkin, *The Roman Catholic Church and the Creation of the Modern Irish State*, p. 111.

132 *KS*, 26 Apr. 1881.

133 Ibid.

134 *KS*, 29 Apr. 1881.

135 *Return of number of agrarian offences in each county in Ireland reported to the RIC, 1881*, p. 7, HC 1882 (8), lv, 1.

136 L. P. Curtis, 'Landlord responses to the Irish Land War, 1879–87', *Eire-Ireland* xxvii (2003), p. 172.

137 Bew, *Land and the National Question*, p. 156; Adam Pole, 'Sheriffs' sales during the land war, 1879–82', *IHS* xxxiv: 136 (Nov. 2005), pp. 386–402.

138 Thomas de Moleyns, *The Land Owners and Agents Practical Guide* (8th edn, London, 1899), p. 375.

139 Bew, *Land and the National Question*, p. 156; Pole, 'Sheriffs' sales during the land war', p. 387.

140 *KEP*, 9 Apr. 1881.

141 *KEP*, 13 Apr. 1881.

142 *Guy's Munster Directory 1886*, p. 215; *TC*, 13 Apr. 1875 and 25 Jan. 1876. His rent was raised from £67 to £100 by Hussey.

143 *KEP*, 14 May 1881, *KEP*, 21 May 1881.

144 *KEP*, 2 July 1881.

145 *KEP*, 9 Apr. 1881, *KEP*, 14 May 1881.

146 *KEP*, 21 May 1881.

147 *KEP*, 2 July 1881.

148 *KEP*, 2 July 1881.

149 Duagh Land League to Land League executive, 28 July 1881 (NLI, Land League papers, MS 8291).

150 Newtownsandes to Land League executive (NLI, Land League papers, MS 8291).

151 *KEP*, 18 May 1881.

152 *KEP*, 11 May 1881.

153 Irish National Land League form of application for costs and expenses (NLI, Land League papers, MS 8291).

154 *KI*, 27 June 1881.

155 *KEP*, 18 May 1881.

156 Bew, *Land and the National Question*, p. 172.

157 *KS*, 3 July 1881.

158 *KEP*, 2 July 1881.

159 *KEP*, 3 Aug. 1881.

160 Rev Arthur Moynihan to the Land League executive, 8 Aug. 1881 (NLI, Land League papers, MS 8291).

161 Land League executive to Rev. Casey, Listowel, 4 Aug. 1881 (NLI, Land League papers, MS 8291).

162 Rev Arthur Moynihan to the Land League executive, 8 Aug. 1881 (NLI, Land League papers, MS 8291).

163 Feingold, *The Revolt of the Tenantry*, p. 139.

164 *KI*, 12 May 1881.

165 *KI*, 4 Aug. 1881.

166 *KI*, 8 Aug. 1881

167 Reprinted in *KEP*, 6 Aug. 1881.

168 After the suppression of the Land League a number of branches attempted to hold meetings but were disrupted by the police, for example see *KS*, 23 Oct 1881.

169 *Return of persons who have been or are in custody under the Protection of Person and Property (Ireland) Act, 1881, up to 31 Mar. 1882,* p. 156, HC 1882 (156) lv, 635.

170 Dooling was central to the league in the northern half of the county. He was a prominent at the first indignant meeting held in April 1880 in Causeway. He was also a significant member of the Lixnaw Land League. See ch. one.

171 *KI*, 24 Oct. 1881, *KI*, 10 Nov. 1881. A number of days before his arrest Leahy had written to the central executive of the Ladies Land League stating that he was awaiting their instruction for the course of action to be taken, see Leahy to Virginia Lynch, 3 Nov. 1881 (NLI, Land League papers, MS 17,699 (2)).

172 Timothy Harrington to Virginia Lynch, 28 Oct 1881 (NLI, Land League papers, MS 17,699 (1)).

173 *Return of number of agrarian offences in each county in Ireland reported to the RIC, 1881,* pp. 9–14.

174 Jordan, *Land and Popular Politics in Ireland: County Mayo*, p. 283.

175 Kennedy, *Tullaroan*; Nelson, *The Land War in County Kildare.* In Carter's study of Queen's County, moderate and die-hard leaguers are identified but they are not characterised along social or political lines, idem, *Queen's*, p. 214.

FOUR: THE LAND LEAGUE, FENIANISM AND AGRARIAN VIOLENCE

1   See Beames, *Peasants and Power*; J. S. Donnelly, 'Pastorini and Captain Rock: millenarianism and sectarianism in the Rockite movement of 1821–4' in Samuel Clark and J. S. Donnelly (eds), *Irish Peasants, Violence and Political Unrest, 1780–1914* (Manchester, 1983), pp. 102–39; Tom Garvin, 'Defenders, Ribbonmen and others: underground political networks in pre-Famine Ireland', *Past and Present* 96 (1982), pp. 133–55; Hoppen, *Elections, Politics and Society in Ireland, 1832–1885*, pp. 341–78.

2   Michael Beames, 'The Ribbon-societies: lower-class nationalism in pre-Famine Ireland', *Past and Present* 97 (1982), p. 128.

3   Garvin, 'Defenders, Ribbonmen and others: Underground political networks in pre-Famine Ireland', p. 140.

4   A. C. Murray, 'Agrarian violence and nationalism in nineteenth-century Ireland: the myth of Ribbonism', *Irish Social and Economic History* 13 (1986), p. 73.

5   Joseph Lee, 'The Ribbonmen' in T. D. Williams (ed.), *Secret Societies in Ireland* (Dublin, 1973).

6   Beames, *Peasants and Power*, p. 62.

7   R.V. Comerford, 'Republicans and democracy in modern Irish politics' in Fearghal McGarry (ed.), *Republicanism in Modern Ireland* (Dublin, 2003), p. 14.

8   Charles Townshend, *Political Violence in Ireland: Government and Resistance since 1848* (Oxford, 1983), p. 116.

9   R. F. Foster, *Modern Ireland, 1600–1972* (London, 1988), p. 408.

10   Tom Garvin, *The Evolution of Irish Nationalist Politics* (Dublin, 1981), p. 77.

11   Margaret O'Callaghan, *British High Politics and a Nationalist Ireland: Criminality, Land and the Law under Forster and Balfour* (Cork, 1994), p. 113.

12   Fearghal McGarry and James McConnel, 'Introduction' in McGarry and McConnel (eds), *The Black Hand of Republicanism*, p. xvii.

13   Magee, *The IRB*; Kelly, *The Fenian Ideal*.

14   Return of outrages, 1879–93 (NAI, CSO ICR, vol. 1).

15   Joseph Lee, *The Modernisation of Irish Society, 1948–1918* (Dublin, 1973), p. 80.

16   Ibid., p.84; Townshend, *Political Violence*, p. 174; For a further analysis of this social group see Donnelly, *The Land and the People of Nineteenth-Century Cork*, pp. 249–50.

17   *Special Commission . . . vol. ii*, p. 414.

18   List of persons prosecuted under the PPP (Ireland) Act nos 1–206 (NAI, CSO/ICR 5).

19   *KS*, 12 Oct. 1880.

20   *Special Commission . . . vol. ii*, p. 335. Night boys was a common phrase for Moonlighters.

21   Report to Lord Spencer Chief Secretary concerning why Castleisland is the worst district in Ireland (NAI, CSO RP, 1883, 24113).

22   Richard Pigott had forged a number of letters which fraudulently claimed Parnell was behind the Phoenix Park murders in 1882 of the Chief Secretary Lord Frederick Cavendish and the Under-Secretary Thomas Henry Burke.

23   *Special Commission . . . vol. ii*, p. 413.

24   *Special Commission. . . vol. iii*, p. 12.

25   Ibid.

26   *KS*, 23 Nov. 1880.

27   *Special Commission. . . vol. iii*, p. 14. The election was for the Killeentierna electoral division. Jeremiah McSweeney, a member of the league, was running against a landlord candidate named Bourke. McSweeney won the contest.

28   *KS*, 21 Dec. 1880.

29   *Special Commission. . . vol. iv*, p. 135.

30   Ibid.

31   *Special Commission. . . vol. iv*, p. 136.

32   Ibid., p. 139.

33   M. G. Murphy, *The Story of Brosna* (Brosna, 1977), pp. 22–3.

34   *Special Commission. . . vol. iii*, p. 366.

35   Considine to Plunkett, Police reports Oct. 1882 (NLI, H. F. Considine papers, unsorted collection).

36   *Special Commission. . . vol. iii*, p. 366..

37   Ibid., p. 370.

38   Ibid., p. 374.

39   Dooling was a shoemaker in the region and was imprisoned under the PPP Act on suspicion of writing threatening notices and of being a Fenian. See, Arrests under the PPP Act (NAI, CSO ICR).

40 RIC file on Thomas Dooling (TNA, CO/904/15: microfilm, NLI, p. 153).

41 Some Land League papers are located in the National Library of Ireland but these are of a limited nature.

42 T. W. Moody, *Davitt and the Irish Revolution* (Oxford, 1981), p. 36.

43 *Special Commission . . . vol. ii*, p. 371.

44 *Special Commission . . . vol. i*, p. 109. These were the words of the attorney-general in his opening address to the commission.

45 *Special Commission . . . vol. ii*, p. 409.

46 *Special Commission . . . vol. viii*, p. 269.

47 *Special Commission . . . vol. viii*, p. 285.

48 Ibid., p. 484.

49 Ibid., p. 275.

50 Moody, *Davitt*, p. 360.

51 Harrington to C. S. Parnell, 12 Oct. 1881 (NLI, Harrington Papers, MS 8578).

52 *KS*, 13 Aug. 1880.

53 *KS*, 19 Nov. 1880.

54 *KS*, 21 Dec. 1880.

55 *KS*, 25 Feb. 1881.

56 *Special Commission . . . vol. viii*, p. 576.

57 R. V. Comerford, 'The Land War and the politics of distress', in William Vaughan (ed.), *A New History of Ireland, VI Ireland under the Union, II 1879–1921* (Oxford, 1996), p. 45.

58 Bew, *Land and the National Question*, p. 200.

59 Return of outrages (NAI, CSO ICR, vol.1).

60 F. S. L. Lyons, *Charles Stewart Parnell* (London, 1977), p. 177.

61 Bew, *Land and the National Question*, p. 201.

62 Report on Irish National Land League (NAI, CSO ILLNLP, carton VII).

63 Stephen Ball, 'Policing the Land War: official responses to political protest and agrarian crime in Ireland, 1879–91' (University of London, PhD thesis, 2000), pp. 156–7.

64 For a description of these outrages see *Special Commission . . . vol. ii*, pp. 328–30.

65 *Special Commission . . . vol. ii*, p. 330.

66 Outrage report: attack on Dennehy (NAI, CSO PPP Act carton 1).

67 Ibid.

68 *Special Commission . . . vol. ii*, p. 329.

69 Report on Edward Hussey (NAI, CSO PPP Act carton 1).

70 List of warrants for arrests issued under PPP Act (NAI, CSO PPP Act carton 11).

71 In June a labourer and process server named John McAuliffe was attacked by a gang of 10 to 15 men. MacAuliffe's sister was beaten and John was shot in the arm leading to amputation, see *Special Commission . . . vol. ii*, p. 333; Outrage returns (NAI, CSO ICR, vol. 1).

72 *Special Commission . . . vol. ii*, p. 339.

73 Arrests under the PPP Act (NAI, CSO PPP Act, carton II); Outrage report of attack on Thomas Galvin, 13 Nov. 1881 (NLI, H. F. Considine papers box 5, unsorted collection).

74 Outrage report of attack on Thomas Galvin, 13 Nov. 1881 (NLI, H. F. Considine papers box 5, unsorted collection).

75 Lists of persons arrested under the PPP Act (NAI, CSO PPP Act, carton 1).

76 Outrage report Dec. 1881 (NLI, H. F. Considine papers box 5, unsorted collection).

77 *Special Commission. . . vol. ii*, p. 339. John Twiss, brother of George, was arrested and imprisoned for one of the Christmas attacks, see, Pat Lynch, *They Hanged John Twiss* (Tralee, 1982), p. 27.

78 *Special Commission . . . vol. ii*, p. 340.

79 Return of outrages (NAI, CSO ICR, vol. 1).

80 Skivered meant sliced and cut up.

81 *Special Commission . . . vol. ii*, p. 411.

82 Ibid., p. 334.

83 Ibid., p. 335.

84 Tim Donovan, *A Popular History of East Kerry* (Dublin, 1931), p. 102

85 *Special Commission. . . vol. ii*, p. 335.

86 Return of outrages (NAI, CSO ICR vol. 1).

87 South Western Division, RM's fortnightly report ending 14 Oct. 1882 (NAI, CSO RP, 1882, 41261).

88 Outrage report: threatening notice (NAI, CSO ILLNLP Carton VIII, Special Commission of 1888).

89 Report to Lord Spencer Lord Lieutenant concerning why Castleisland is the worst district in Ireland, 14 Nov. 1883 (NAI, CSO RP, 1883, 24113).

90 Ibid.

91 *KEP*, 22 Mar. 1882.

92 *KEP*, 15 Apr. 1882.

93 Hussey, *Reminiscences of an Irish Land Agent*, p. 246.

94 South Western Division: Monthly police report, Nov. 1884 (NAI, CSO RP, 1884, 26604).

95 *Report on explosion at Edenburn, private residence of S. M. Hussey, in County Kerry, Nov. 1884*, p. 6, HC 1885 [C. 4289], xiv, 927.

96 For a description of Fenian use of dynamite see, Niall Whelehan, "'Cheap as soap and common as sugar': the Fenians, dynamite and scientific warfare' in McGarry and McConnel (eds), *The Black Hand of Republicanism*, pp. 105–20.

97 For an outline of this 'dynamite' campaign see, Magee, *The IRB*, p. 120; Townshend, *Political Violence*, pp. 158–66.

98 Frank Rynne, 'Permanent revolutionaries: The IRB and the Land War in West Cork' in McGarry and McConnel (eds), *The Black Hand of Irish Republicanism*, pp. 55–71.

99 Millstreet is in County Cork but borders Kerry and was in the Roman Catholic diocese of Kerry.

100 Files relating to O'Connell's case, 15 Feb. 1882 (NAI, CSO RP, 1883, 7756).

101 Ibid.

102 Ibid.

103 RIC Outrage Report of attack on Thomas Galvin, 13 Nov. 1881 (NLI, H. F. Considine papers box 5, unsorted collection).

104 Return of outrages (NAI, CSO ICR, vol. i).

105 South Western Division RM's fortnightly police report ending 14 Oct. 1882 (NAI, CSO RP, 1882, 41261).

106 For an account of the Brown murder and the subsequent trial and hanging of Poff and Barrett see, Peter O'Sullivan, 'Murder at Drommulton: An incident in the land war in Kerry' (MA in Local History, NUI, Maynooth, 1996).

107 Lee, *Modernisation*, p. 82.

FIVE: THE IRISH NATIONAL LAND LEAGUE

1 Moody, *Davitt*, p. 543.

2 F. S. L. Lyons, *John Dillon: A Biography* (London, 1968), p. 68.

3 *KS*, 17 Nov. 1883.

4 For a discussion on Parnell's views on the land question see, Liam Kennedy, 'The economic thought of the nation's lost leader: Charles Stewart Parnell' in D. G. Boyce and Alan O'Day (eds), *Parnell in Perspective* (London, 1991), pp. 171–200.

5 Carla King, *Michael Davitt* (Dundalk, 1999), p. 43.

6 D. G. Boyce, *Nationalism in Ireland* (3rd edn, London, 1995), p. 207.

7 Paul Bew, *Ireland: The Politics of Enmity 1789–2006* (Oxford, 2007), p. 340.

8 Alan O'Day, 'Max Weber and leadership, Butt, Parnell and Dillon' in Boyce and O'Day (eds), *Ireland in Transition*, p. 28.

9 Samuel Clark, *Social Origins of the Irish Land War* (Princeton, 1979); Bew, *Land and the National Question*; Donnelly, *The Land and the People of Nineteenth-Century Cork*.

10 Notable exceptions include, Frank Thompson, *The End of Liberal Ulster: Land Agitation and Land Reform, 1868–86* (Belfast, 2001); Edward Kennedy, *The Land Movement in Tullaroan, County Kilkenny, 1879–91* in Maynooth Studies in Local History: no. 55 (Dublin, 2004).

11 E. J. Hobsbawm, *Nations and Nationalism* (2nd edn, Cambridge, 1992), p. 11. Hobsbawm goes on to state the necessity of understanding the view from 'below' in interpreting nationalism and those it was ultimately aimed at.

12 C. C. O'Brien, 'The machinery of the Irish Parliamentary Party, 1880–85', *IHS* v: 17 (1946), pp. 55–85; B. M. Walker, 'The 1885 and 1886 general elections: a milestone in Irish history' in Peter Collins (ed.), *Nationalism and Unionism: Conflict in Ireland, 1885–1921* (Belfast, 1994), pp. 1–15.

13 The official objectives of the National League can be summarised as: (1) national self government, (2) land-law reform, (3) local self government, (4) extension of the parliamentary and municipal franchises, (5) the development and encouragement of the labour and industrial interest of Ireland, with emphasis on improving the conditions of agricultural labourers; see Moody, *Davitt* p. 543.

14 *KS*, 27 Oct. 1882.

15 Report on progress of Irish National Land League from 1 Jan.-28 Feb. 83 (NAI, Irish Land League and National League Papers (ILLNLP), carton vi: Irish National League proceedings, 1883–4).

16 Ibid.

17 *KS*, 14 Jan. 1881, *KS*, 20 Feb. 1883.

18 Report on progress of Irish National League, 1 Apr.–31 Apr. 1883 (NAI, CSO ILLNLP, carton vi). In December 1881 a new grade of police officers was created with the appointment of six Special Resident Magistrates. They were responsible for directing and co-ordinating the activities of the forces of law and order in specific groups of counties. In 1883 they were reduced to four and termed Divisional Magistrates; see R. B. McDowell, *The Irish Administration, 1801–1914* (London, 1964), p. 142; Crossman, *Politics, Law and Order in Nineteenth-Century Ireland*, p. 142; For an account of the activities of a zealous SRM in the counties Clare and Limerick see, Clifford Lloyd, *Ireland Under the Land League: A Narrative of Personal Experiences* (Edinburgh, 1892).

19   Report on progress of Irish National Land League from 1 Apr.-31 Apr. 1883 (NAI, CSO ILLNLP, carton vi).

20   Donnelly, *The Land and the People of Nineteenth-Century Cork*, pp. 293–5.

21   *Irish Land Commission report for the period 22 Aug. 1881 to 22 Aug. 1882*, p. 8, HC 1882 [C 3413] xx, 265.

22   A number of reasons were cited for this 'block'. The most common was that large numbers of tenants applied to enter the Land Courts immediately because reductions were to be granted from the date of application as opposed to when the case and decision were made. See *Select committee of House of Lords on land law (Ireland): first report, proceedings, minutes of evidence, appendix, index*, p. 83, HC 1882 (249), xi, 1; *Irish Land Commission report for the period 22 Aug. 1881 to 22 Aug. 1882*, p. 8.

23   *Select committee of House of Lords on Land Law (Ireland): first report, proceedings, minutes of evidence, appendix, index*, p. 147, HC 1882 (249), xi, 1.

24   By December 1883 a total rental of £62,036 was reduced to £48,070 by the Land Commission making a 23.5 per cent reduction.

25   Donnelly, *The Land and the People of Nineteenth-Century Cork*, p. 299.

26   R. V. Comerford, 'Land Commission' in S. J. Connolly (ed.), *The Oxford Companion to Irish History* (Oxford, 1998), p. 296.

27   South Western Division: RM's fortnightly report, 14 Oct. 1882 (NAI, CSO RP, 1882, 41261).

28   Ibid.

29   Returns of outrages, 1882 (NAI, CSO ICR, Returns of outrages, 1879–93 (annual printed statistics) vol. 2). For a full analysis of agrarian violence during this period see ch. VI.

30   South Western Division: RM's fortnightly report ending 31 Oct. 1881 (NAI, CSO RP, 1882, 42882).

31   Report on progress of Irish National Land League from 1 Jan. to 28 Feb. 83 (NAI, ILLNLP, carton vi: Irish National League proceedings, 1883–4).

32   *KS*, 21 Mar. 1882.

33   *KI*, 3 July 1882.

34   *KI*, 11 May 1882; the Tralee Chamber of Commerce and Killarney Town Commission met to denounce the assassinations.

35   Crossman, *Politics, Law and Order in Nineteenth-Century Ireland*, p. 142.

36   South Western Division, RM's fortnightly report ending 16 July 1882 (NAI, CSO RP, 1882, 34011).

37   *KEP*, 25 Nov. 1882.

38   *KEP*, 3 Feb. 1883.

39   *KS*, 9 Nov. 1880.

40   *TC*, 11 Feb. 1881.

41   *KEP*, 3 Feb. 1883.

42   *KS*, 9 Jan. 1882 and *KS*, 29 Jan. 1882.

43   For example see, South Western Division: RM's fortnightly reports ending 31 Oct. 1882 (NAI, CSO RP, 1882, 42882).

44   *KS*, 22 May 1883.

45   In a follow up search of the *Sentinel's* offices letters were found dating from the height of the Land League agitation asking for threatening notices to be printed for rent strikes. Harrington

retorted that he received letters like these all the time but didn't act on them, see NAI, CSO, Protection of Person and Property Act, 1881, carton VI. This carton contains documents relating to the prosecution of newspapers under the aforementioned Act.

46 For two examples see meeting at Currow *KS*, 13 Sept. 1881, and meeting at Fenit *KS*, 27 Sept. 1881.

47 See Ardfert Land League, *KS*, 11 Oct. 1881. Farmers were frequently accused of charging labourers inflated con-acre rents.

48 Pádraig Lane, 'Agricultural labourers in Ireland, 1850–1914' (unpublished PhD thesis, UCC, 1980), pp. 84–90.

49 *KS*, 9 May 1882, 15 Sep 1882 and 20 Oct. 1882.

50 South Western Division: RM's fortnightly report ending 31 Aug. 1882 (NAI, CSO RP, 1882, 37029).

51 Fintan Lane, 'Rural labourers, social change and politics in later nineteenth century Ireland' in Fintan Lane and Donal Ó Drisceoil, *Politics and the Irish Working Class, 1830–1945* (Houndmills, 2005), p. 133.

52 Lane, 'Agricultural labourers in Ireland', p. 85.

53 *KS*, 19 Dec. 1882.

54 *KS*, 20 Feb. 1883.

55 Ibid.

56 *KS*, 13 Oct. 1882.

57 *KS*, 10 Nov. 1882.

58 Report on the progress of the Irish National League 1 Oct. to 31 Dec. 1883 (NAI, CSO ILLNLP, carton VI). Structural changes in the police administration of the country led to disbandment of the positions of Special Resident Magistrates and the creation of the Divisional Magistrates.

59 RM's reports regarding recent poor law elections, Apr. 1883 (NAI, CSO RP, 1882, 2289).

60 *KS*, 27 Mar. 1883.

61 For McMahon see *KS*, 27 Sept. 1880 and for Kenny see *KS*, 19 Nov. 1880.

62 Return of farms in County Kerry from which tenants have been evicted or which have been surrendered from 1 Jan. 1881 to 1 Oct. 1883 (NAI, CSO RP, 1883, 23534/9127).

63 *KS*, 8 Jan. 1884. Timothy Harrington had cemented his position at the forefront of the movement when elected as MP for Westmeath in the 1883 by-election. T. D. Sullivan was editor of the *Nation* and was a central figure in the National League. Both Sullivan and Harrington were closely connected with a number of other MPs associated with Sullivan and T. M. Healy. This group, which later included Edward Harrington were known as the 'Bantry Band' owing to their political ambitions and their origins in west Cork. The Harrington's were from Berehaven as opposed to Bantry. The ten members of the Irish Party in the group were T. M. Healy, Maurice Healy, Thomas J. Healy, A. M. Sullivan, T. D. Sullivan, Donal Sullivan, Timothy Harrington, Edward Harrington, William Martin Murphy, and James Gilhooly; see Frank Callanan, *The Parnell Split, 1890–91* (Cork, 1992), p. 236.

64 Report on the release of Edward Harrington, 6 Jan. 1884 (NAI, CSO RP, 1884, 741).

65 South Western Division: RM's fortnightly report, 3. Feb. 1884 (NAI, CSO RP, 1884, 3333).

66 South Western Division: DI's monthly police report, Mar. 1884 (NAI, CSO RP, 1884, 8788).

67 *KS*, 15 Feb. 1884.

68   South Western Division: DI's monthly police report, Mar. 1884 (NAI, CSO RP, 1884, 8788).

69   *Return of number of agrarian offences in each county in Ireland reported to the constabulary office, 1880*, p. 3, HC 1881 (12), lxxvii, 619; *Return of number of agrarian offences in each county in Ireland reported to the constabulary office, 1881*, p. 3, HC 1882 (8), lv.1; *Return, by provinces, of agrarian offences throughout Ireland reported to Inspector General of Royal Irish Constabulary, 1882*, pp. 8–9, HC 1883 (12), lvi, 1.

70   *Return, by provinces, of agrarian offences throughout Ireland reported to Inspector General of Royal Irish Constabulary, 1883*, pp. 8–9 [C 3950], HC 1884, lxiv.1; *Return, by provinces, of agrarian offences throughout Ireland reported to Inspector General of Royal Irish Constabulary, 1884*, pp. 8–9 HC 1884–5 [C 4500], lxiv, 1.

71   *Returns showing, for the counties of Clare, Cork, Kerry, Galway, and Mayo respectively, the number of civil bills entered at quarter sessions in ejectment on title for non-payment of rent, or overholding in the years from 1879 to 1888 inclusive*, p. 5, HC 1889 (211), lxi, 417.

72   Report on progress of Irish National League from 1 July to 31 Dec 1884 (NAI, CSO ILLNLP, carton VI: Irish National League proceedings, 1883–84).

73   Jackson, *Ireland 1798–1998*, p. 125; Tom Garvin, *The Evolution of Irish Nationalist politics* (Dublin, 1981), p. 78.

74   Walker, *Parliamentary Election Results in Ireland, 1801–1922*, pp. 128–9.

75   Ibid. The Dungarvan convention decided to pay Mr Power £200 a year for his position as MP. The money was to be levied on the county branches.

76   Garvin, *The Evolution of Irish Nationalist Politics*, p. 81.

77   R. V. Comerford, 'The Parnell era, 1883–91' in W. E. Vaughan (ed.), *A New History of Ireland, VI Ireland under the Union, II 1879–1921* (Oxford, 1996), p. 54.

78   For a detailed analysis of the high politics of Catholic Church and its evolving relationship with the forces of nationalism during the period see Emmet Larkin, *The Roman Catholic Church and the Creation of the Modern Irish State, 1878–86* (Philadelphia, 1975).

79   Report on progress of Irish National League from 1 July to 31 Dec. 1884 (NAI, CSO ILLNLP, carton VI, Irish National League proceedings, 1883–84).

80   Ibid.

81   O'Brien, *Parnell and his Party*, p. 128.

82   Lee, *The Modernisation of Irish Society, 1848–1918*, p. 106.

83   Report on progress of Irish National League from 1 July to 31 Dec 1884 (NAI, CSO ILLNLP, carton VI, Irish National League proceedings, 1883–4).

84   James Loughlin, 'Constructing the political spectacle: Parnell, the press and national leadership, 1879–86' in Boyce and O'Day (eds), *Parnell in Perspective*, p. 231.

85   James Loughlin, *Gladstone, Home Rule and the Ulster Question* (Dublin, 1986), pp. 27–8. During July 1885 Harris highlighted continued class tensions in tenant society when he publicly declared that graziers were the 'enemies' of the peasantry, see *UI*, 11 July 1885.

86   For an example of local apathy towards National League meetings during September 1884 in County Westmeath see A. C. Murray, 'Nationality and local politics in late nineteenth-century Ireland: the case of County Westmeath', *IHS* xxv: 98 (Nov. 1986), p. 146.

87   Expenditure on relief differed greatly between boards controlled by pro league elected guardians and those controlled by landlord *ex-officio* guardians. For example, the Dingle Board of Guardians, under the control of the parsimonious Lord Ventry, spent a mere £9 on outdoor relief in 1877 which rose to £13 in 1884. In stark contrast, the Tralee Board's expenditure on relief

soared from £30 to £2,534 after league guardians gained control during the corresponding period. For more on poor law expenditure in Kerry during the period, see the evidence given by the LGB inspector for Kerry, Colonel Spraight, to a House of Lords Select Committee, *Report from the Select Committee of the House of Lords on the Poor Law Guardians (Ireland) Bill; with the proceedings, evidence, and index*, pp. 68–74, HC 1884–5 (297), x, 281.

88 *Return of local taxation in Ireland for 1880*; p. 13, HC 1881 [C 3097], lxxix, 125 and *Return of local taxation in Ireland, for 1884*, p. 13, HC 1884–5 [C 4544], lxvii, 429.

89 Virginia Crossman, *Local Government in Nineteenth-Century Ireland* (Belfast, 1994), p. 41.

90 *Land Owners in Ireland, 1876*, p. 144; *KEP*, 28 Feb. 1885.

91 *Report of the Royal Commission on the Land Law (Ireland) Act and the Purchase of Land (Ireland) Act, 1885: Minutes of evidence, and appendix*, p. 540, HC 1887, xxvi, 25. (Hereafter *Cowper Commission; Evidence*).

92 South Western Division: DI's monthly report, Mar. 1885 (NAI, CSO RP, 1885, 7273).

93 All these regularly attended meetings in the town's Protestant Hall, see *KWR*, 25 Apr. 1885.

94 The Conservative candidate, John Bateman, was unseated on petition soon after his election and replaced by a Liberal-Repeal candidate named Maurice O'Connell, see Walker, *Parliamentary Election Results in Ireland, 1801–1922*, p. 315.

95 James Loughlin, 'Irish Protestant Home Rule Association and nationalist politics, 1886–93', *IHS* 25 (1985), p. 341.

96 Such names included Richard Latchford, a leading Protestant miller in Tralee. Latchford attended meetings at the Protestant Hall in Tralee.

97 The occupations of the other JPs were: two medical doctors, two military officers, three gentlemen farmers, two barristers/solicitors and one merchant, see *Return for each county, city, and borough in Ireland, of the names of persons holding the Commission of the Peace, with date of appointment and designation at time of appointment; and number that are Protestants, Roman Catholics, and of other religious persuasions*, pp. 44–6, HC 1884 (13), lxiii, 331.

98 With the lack of census material, Feingold, using local knowledge, identified the religious affiliation of 120 voters of which 24 were Protestant. These were all either shopkeepers or farmers. Of those that voted for the leaguers, six were shopkeepers and one was a farmer, see Feingold, *The Revolt of the Tenantry*, p. 135.

99 For further analysis of Protestant alienation from the parliamentary party and the National League during this period, see; Loughlin, 'The Irish Protestant Home Rule Association and nationalist politics 1886–90', pp. 341–63.

100 *KEP*, 11 Mar. 1885.

101 *KEP*, 1 Apr. 1885. Maurice Kelliher was listed as a flour dealer, see *Guy's Munster Directory 1886*, p. 883.

102 *KEP*, 11 Mar. 1885.

103 Crosbie owned 13,422 acres near Ballyheigue and Lord Ventry had 93,629 acres mostly on the Dingle peninsula. Other landlords present included F. R. Bateman (1,259 acres, Tralee), Redmond Roche (1,255 acres, Castleisland), and John White Leahy (5,511 acres, Killarney), see *Land Owners in Ireland, 1876*, pp. 141–5.

104 Walpole was always an out spoken critic of landlordism. However, he opposed home rule during the 1870s and by the 1880s he had never supported the Land League. He was well respected within agrarian society and had formerly given evidence to the Bessborough Commission in 1880. Furthermore, he was one of the first tenants in the county to have a judicial

[104 *cont.*] rent fixed when he had his rent reduced from £400 per annum to £360 in December 1881; see *TC*, 15 June 1875; *Bessborough Commission* . . . p. 803; *Return, according to provinces and counties, of judicial rents fixed by sub-commissioners and Civil Bill Courts, as notified to the Irish Land Commission, up to 31 Dec. 1881*, p. 76, HC 1882 [C 3120], lvi.1

105 Both were present at the large KTDA demonstration in Tralee in January 1877, see *TC*, 12 Jan. 1877.

106 *KEP*, 21 Feb. 1885.

107 *KWR*, 21 Feb. 1885.

108 *KEP*, 10 May 1884.

109 For a long list of those who organised the Kerry Athletic Sports see *KEP*, 21 Jan. 1885.

110 *KEP*, 30 Apr. 1884.

111 Sally Warwick-Haller, *William O'Brien and the Irish Land War* (Dublin, 1990), p. 73.

112 Frank Callanan, *T.M. Healy* (Cork, 1996), p. 93.

113 *KS*, 16 Dec. 1884.

114 *KS*, 16 Dec. 1884.

115 *KS*, 26 May 1885.

116 *KS*, 1 May 1885.

117 James Loughlin, *Gladstone, Home Rule and the Ulster Question, 1882–93* (Dublin, 1987), p. 28.

118 James Loughlin, 'Nationality and loyalty: Parnellism, monarchy and the construction of Irish identity, 1880–5' in Boyce and Day (eds), *Ireland in Transition, 1867–1921* (London, 2004), p. 35.

119 J. H. Murphy, *Abject Loyalty: Nationalism and Monarchy in Ireland during the Reign of Queen Victoria* (Cork, 2001), p. 226.

120 A. E. Turner, *Sixty Years of a Soldier's Life* (London, 1912), p. 187.

121 *KS*, 12 Sept. 1884.

122 *KWR*, 13 Sept. 1884.

123 Spencer to Griffin, 16 Sept. 1884 (Kerry Diocesan Records Killarney (KDRK), Priests Papers: box 3/ Griffin, A.S./Correspondence).

124 When the bishopric of Kerry became vacant, Lord Granville, the British government's head of the Foreign Office, informed Rome that Higgins was a far better candidate than his competitor, Archdeacon O'Sullivan, who was described as a 'man of extreme political views'. See C. J. Woods, 'Ireland and Anglo-Papal relations, 1880–85', *IHS* 18 (Mar. 1972), 69, p. 30; Larkin, *The Roman Catholic Church and the Creation of the Modern Irish State, 1878–86*, pp. 143–4.

125 Woods, 'Ireland and Anglo-Papal relations, 1880–85', p. 42.

126 Errington to Griffin, 5 June 1883 (KDRK, Priests papers: box 3/ Griffin, A. S. /Correspondence).

127 *KS*, 12 Sept. 1885.

128 *KWR*, 27 Sept. 1885.

129 For a comprehensive analysis of the political motivations around the visit see, Murphy, *Abject loyalty*, pp. 228–42; James Loughlin, 'Nationality and loyalty: Parnellism, monarchy and the construction of Irish identity, 1880–5' in Boyce and O'Day (eds), *Ireland in Transition, 1867–1921* (London, 2004), pp. 35–56.

130 For examples of resolutions passed in Kerry see Listowel National League meeting, *KS*, 17 Mar. 1885 and Tralee League meeting *KS*, 24 Mar. 1885.

131 Murphy, *Abject Loyalty*, p. 234.

132 Loughlin, 'Nationality and loyalty', p. 52.

133 For the inaugural meeting of the Killarney National League, see *KS*, 28 Oct. 1884; For Listowel see *KS*, 16 Dec. 1884.

134 The Liberal government remained divided over the retention of the Crimes Act which was due to pass in 1885. Spencer was in favour of maintaining elements of the Act, including the right to suppress meetings. However, the legislation was withdrawn in its entirety in July after the government resigned in June 1885, see Virginia Crossman, *Politics, Law and Order in Nineteenth-Century Ireland* (Dublin, 1996), pp. 150–1.

135 For National League meeting at Milltown, see, *KS*, 16 Dec. 1884, at Ballydonoghue, see *KS*, 30 Dec. 1884, and at Ballylongford, see *KS*, 27 Jan. 1885. The branches existed in Killarney, Ballydonoghue, Milltown, Knockanure, Tralee, Barrowduff, Ballymacelligott, Listry, Castlemaine, Currans, Ballyduff and Ballylongford.

136 At a meeting of the Killarney branch a deputation from the Castleisland League attended seeking support for Crowley, see *KS*, 23 Dec. 1884.

137 *Report from the Select Committee of the House of Lords on the Poor Law Guardians (Ireland) Bill; with the proceedings, evidence, and index*, p. 70, HC 1884–5 (297), x, 281. This information was part of the evidence given to the commission by Colonel Spraight, the Local Government Board Inspector for Kerry. He was present at the board meeting.

138 *KS*, 16 Jan. 1885. The position of relieving officer contained extensive patronage as they decided on the merits of individuals applying for relief. In this case the position was for the Coom Dispensary District. This district lay between Killarney and Castleisland.

139 Clancy was one of the founding members of the Listowel League. When the branch was reorganised in December he chaired the meeting, see *KS*, 23 Dec. 1884.

140 *KS*, 27 Feb. 1885.

141 *KS*, 6 Mar. 1885.

142 *KEP*, 4 Apr. 1885.

143 *KEP*, 22 Apr. 1885.

144 Landlords who attended included Lord Kenmare and Daniel Clotsman, along with several justices of the peace, the RIC County Inspector, Local Government Board Inspector Colonel Spraight, the Crown Solicitor Charles Morphy, and the Clerk of the Peace, Stephen Huggard.

145 Figures such as J. D. Sheehan, a hotel owner, Daniel Shea, a general smith, and a vintner named Michael Warren led the demonstration, see *KWR*, 4 Apr. 1885. The occupations of these figures are given in *Guy's Munster Directory*, pp. 561–7.

146 *KWR*, 25 Apr. 1885; Murphy, *Abject Loyalty*, p. 238.

147 Murphy, *Abject Loyalty*, p. 241.

148 Report on progress of Irish National Land League, 1 Jan.–30 June 1885 (NAI, ILLNLP, Carton VII, Irish National League proceedings 1885–90).

149 In the pre-land war period Power frequently organised the annual Manchester Martyr demonstrations in Tralee. By December 1880 he was commonly referred to in Tralee as Captain Power. See Capt. Phibbs to Chief Secretary's Office, 30 Dec. 1880 (NAI, CSO RP, 1881, 1221). He was one of the main activists behind the Land League in Tralee and was imprisoned under the PPP Act.

150 Nolan died in October 1885. His exile was referred to in newspaper obituaries, see *KS*, 30 Oct. 1885.

151 J. A. Gaughan, *Austin Stack: Portrait of a Separatist* (Dublin, 1977), p. 14.

152 *Return of persons who have been or are in custody under the Protection of Person and Property (Ireland) Act, 1881, up to 31 Mar. 1882*, p. 156, HC 1882, (156) lv, 635. See 'Lists of persons arrested under the PPP Act', nos 210–420 (NAI, CSO RP/ ICR 6).

153 *KS*, 24 Feb. 1885.

154 A teacher in the school that Maurice Moynihan attended, St Michael's College, Listowel, influenced him to become involved in Fenianism. Deirdre McMahon (ed.), *The Moynihan Brothers in Peace and War, 1909–1918: Their New Ireland*, (Dublin, 2004), p. xiv; J.A. Gaughan, *A Political Odyssey: Thomas O'Donnell, MP for West Kerry* (Dublin, 1983), p. 22–3; RIC file on W. M. Stack (TNA, CO 904/18/50).

155 For an outline of the cultural nationalism of the Young Ireland Society and its links with Fenianism see Kelly, *The Fenian Ideal*.

156 Magee, *The IRB*, p. 164.

157 *KEP*, 20 June 1885.

158 Danny Curtin, 'Edward Harrington and the first GAA event in Kerry', *Kerry Magazine* 11 (2000), p. 12.

159 For an account of the role nationalism played in the emergence of the GAA see Marcus de Burca, *The GAA: A History* (2nd edn, Dublin, 2000), pp. 15–33. For an outline of the historiography of the GAA and the importance of its link with nationalism see Neal Garnham, 'Accounting for the early success of the Gaelic Athletic Association', *IHS* xxxiv: 133 (May 2004), pp. 65–78.

160 *KEP*, 24 June 1885.

161 Garnham, 'Accounting for the early success of the Gaelic Athletic Association', p. 78.

162 Hoppen, *Elections, Politics and Society in Ireland*, pp. 87–8.

163 Comerford, 'Tipperary representation at Westminster, 1801–1918' in T.G. McGrath and William Nolan (eds), *Tipperary: History and Society* (Dublin, 1985), p. 335.

164 Walker, *Parliamentary Election Results, 1801–1922*, pp. 353–5, p. 284, p. 315.

165 *KS*, 28 April 1885.

166 *KS*, 12 May 1885. Registering voters became one of the main objectives of the organising committee in Dublin.

167 *KS*, 9 June 1885.

168 *KS*, 6 July 1885.

169 *KS*, 3 July 1885.

170 *KS*, 30 June 1885.

171 *UI*, 27 June 1885.

172 For an account of the blows dealt to the IRB by the government and police during 1882–4. See Magee, *The IRB*, pp. 119–34. For IRB defections to Parnell, ibid., p. 139–40; James McConnel, 'Fenians at Westminster: the Edwardian Irish Parliamentary Party and the legacy of the New Departure', *IHS* xxiv: 133 (May, 2004), p. 51.

173 Alvin Jackson, *Ireland 1798–1998: Politics and War* (Oxford, 1999), p. 183.

174 *KWR*, 4 July 1885.

175 Cusack to Davitt, 23 July 1885 (TCD, Davitt papers/9346/469).

176 Ibid.

177 *UI*, 11 July 1885.

178 *KWR*, 18 July 1885.

179 Reprinted in *KWR*, 18 July 1885.

180 *The Times*, 17 Aug. 1885.

181 O'Brien, *Parnell and his Party*, p. 127.

182 *UI*, 8 Aug. 1885.

183 *KWR*, 26 July 1884.

184 The purpose of the meeting was not given in the local newspapers during the visit. The motive of assisting a discharged printer of Harrington's was later discussed at a meeting of the Tralee National League after Harrington's expulsion. See *KS*, 30 June 1885.

185 Entry in Michael Davitt's personal diary, 4 July 1884 (TCD, Davitt papers/9541).

186 Ibid.

187 Davitt to Webb, 5 Mar. 1885 (TCD, Davitt papers/9490/4959).

188 *UI*, 25 July 1885.

189 Ibid.

190 *UI*, 1 Aug. 1885.

191 For Davitt's relationship with the IRB after the Land League see Owen Magee, 'Michael Davitt and the Irish Revolutionary movement' in Fintan Lane and Andrew Newby (eds), *Michael Davitt: New Perspectives* (Dublin, 2009), pp. 102–6.

192 Alan O'Day, *Parnell and the First Home Rule Episode* (Dublin, 1986), p. 81.

193 Davitt, *The Fall of Feudalism in Ireland*, p. 469.

194 Marcus Bourke, *John O'Leary: A Study in Irish Separatism* (Tralee, 1967), p. 174.

195 *KWR*, 18 July 1885.

196 *KWR*, 1 Aug. 1885.

197 RIC file on J. D. Sheehan (PRO CO/904, microfilm in NLI, p. 956).

198 *KWR*, 22 Aug. 1885.

199 During the Special Commission in 1888 both Fenix and Thomas Dee were identified by an informer from the region as being Fenian leaders in the area. The informer gave a large amount of evidence relating to Fenianism in the Causeway region, much of which was disputed by Henry O'Connor, a former secretary of the National League. However, O'Connor, a hostile witness, admitted that Fenix was a member of a Fenian society. See *Special Commission. . . vol. iii, pp.* 364–72 and *Special Commission. . . vol. ix*, p. 90.

200 *KWR*, 18 July 1885; The Firies branch claimed it received 33 grants amounting to £100, see *KS*, 31 July 1885; The Duagh branch claimed that since its inception the branch received two £30 cheques for evicted tenants despite only subscribing a fraction of that amount to the Central Branch, see *KWR*, 25 July 1885.

201 *KS*, 30 June 1885.

202 *KS*, 3 July 1885.

203 *KS*, 11 Aug. 1885.

204 South Western Division: DI's monthly report, Aug. 1885 (NAI, CSO RP, 1887, box 3310).

205 Bishop Higgins to Dean Coffey, 20 June 1885 (KDRK, Parish Correspondence/ St John's, Tralee, letter no. 6).

206 *KS*, 21 Aug. 1885.

207 *KWR*, 29 Aug. 1885.

208 Report on Maurice Murphy, Castleisland (NAI, CSO RP, 1885, 19125).

209 For a full analysis of Quinlan and the radicalism of the Castleisland League see ch. four.

210 South Western Division: DI's monthly report, 1 Sept. 1885 (NAI, CSO RP, 1887, box 3310).

211 *UI*, 22 Aug. 1885.

212 Bourke, *John O'Leary*, p. 175.
213 Magee, *The IRB*, p. 138.
214 *KWR*, 29 Aug. 1885.
215 *KWR*, 5 Sept. 1885.

SIX: THE OPERATION OF THE NATIONAL LEAGUE

1   Donnelly, *The Land and the People of Nineteenth-Century Cork*, p. 308.
2   *Report of the Royal Commission on the Land Law (Ireland) Act, 1881 and the Purchase of Land (Ireland) Act, 1885: minutes of evidence, and appendix*, p. 536, HC 1887, xxvi, 25 (hereafter *Cowper Commission: evidence*).
3   *Cowper Commission: evidence. . .*, p. 540.
4   South Western Division: monthly report, Mar. 1885 (NAI, CSO RP, 1885, 7273).
5   South Western Division: monthly report, Aug. 1885 (NAI, CSO RP, 1887, box 3310). In this box there is a full set of RIC police reports for County Kerry for the period of Aug. 1885–July 1886.
6   *KS*, 14 Apr. 1885.
7   *KS*, 16 June 1885.
8   *KS*, 16 June 1885.
9   Ibid.
10   Philip Bull, *Land, Politics and Nationalism: A Study of the Irish Land Question* (Dublin, 1996), p. 93.
11   *UI*, 6 June 1885.
12   R.V. Comerford, 'The Parnell era, 1883–91' in W. E. Vaughan (ed.), *A New History of Ireland, V Ireland under the Union, I, 1801–1870* (Oxford, 1989), pp. 59–61; Alan O'Day, *Parnell and the First Home Rule Episode* (Dublin, 1986), pp. 56–80.
13   *KS*, 26 May 1885.
14   *KS*, 8 May 1885.
15   *KWR*, 29 Aug. 1885.
16   The new legislation gave the Land Commission power to make advances to tenants for the purchase of their holdings. *Purchase of Land (Ireland) Act, 1885*, 48 & 49 Vict., c. 73.
17   Alvin Jackson, *Home Rule: An Irish History, 1800–2000* (London, 2003), p. 56.
18   *UI*, 15 Aug. 1885.
19   Ibid.
20   O'Day, *Parnell and the First Home Rule Episode*, p. 82.
21   *UI*, 15 Aug. 1885.
22   *UI*, 8 Aug. 1885.
23   O'Day, *Parnell and the First Home Rule Episode*, p. 82.
24   *UI*, 15 Aug. 1885.
25   *UI*, 29 Aug. 1885.
26   Jackson, *Home Rule*, p. 51.
27   *KS*, 28 Aug. 1885.
28   *UI*, 29 Aug. 1885
29   This section of the speech was emphasised in the opening address of the attorney general at the Special Commission in 1888. See, *Special Commission act, reprint of the shorthand notes of the*

speeches, proceedings, and evidence taken before the commissioners appointed under the above act, vol. i (London, 1890), p. 277.

30 Healy, William O'Brien and, by October 1885, John Dillon seemed determined to promote this form of agitation. Within a number of weeks, Healy advised tenants in County Monaghan to bank rents in a 'war chest' to fight landlords and advised that such methods should be adopted nationally. In October John Dillon, marking his return to the political scene, completely ignored home rule and promoted the idea of banking rents, as did O'Brien in the pages of *United Ireland*, see L. M. Geary, *The Plan of Campaign 1886–91* (Cork, 1986), p. 8; F. S. L. Lyons, *John Dillon, A Biography* (London, 1968), pp. 74–5.

31 *Special Commission act . . . vol. i*, p. 277.

32 It has been posited by Healy's modern day biographer, Frank Callanan, that Healy used such extreme language in promoting a proprietorial solution to the land question to surpass the agrarian 'left'. Callanan terms this the 'agrarianism of the right'. For a full analysis of Healy's opinions on the land question see Frank Callanan, *T. M. Healy* (Cork, 1996), pp. 107–13.

33 *KS*, 8 Sept. 1885; *Land Owners in Ireland, 1876* (Baltimore, 1988), p. 141.

34 *Cowper Commission: evidence . . .*, p. 497; *KS*, 18 Sept. 1885.

35 *Cowper Commission: evidence . . .*, p. 502.

36 *KS*, 4 Sept. 1885; Lord Listowel owned 25,964 acres in the northern half of the county, see *Land Owners*, p. 143.

37 *Land Owners*, p. 145; *KWR*, 19 Sept. 1885

38 Denny was an absentee landlord with an address in London, *Land Owners*, p. 142; *KS*, 23 Oct. 1885.

39 *Land Owners*, p. 144; *KWR*, 19 Sept. 1885.

40 *Land Owners*, p. 141; *KWR*, 26 Sept. 1885.

41 *Land Owners*, p. 142; *KWR*, 31 Oct. 1885.

42 *Land Owners*, p. 143.

43 *KWR*, 14 Nov. 1885.

44 *Cowper Commission: evidence. . .*, p. 502.

45 *KS*, 2 Oct. 1885.

46 *KWR*, 31 Oct. 1885.

47 For an analysis of landlord debt during the period see, L. P. Curtis, jr, 'Encumbered wealth: Landlord indebtedness in post-Famine Ireland', *American Historical Review* 85 (Apr. 1980), pp. 332–67; Terence Dooley, *The Decline of the Big House in Ireland: A Study of Irish Landed Families, 1860–1960* (Dublin, 2001), pp. 79–111.

48 *Land owners*, p. 142–3.

49 J. S. Donnelly, 'The Kenmare estates during the nineteenth century: Part 11', *JKAHS* 22, 1989, pp. 81–95.

50 *KS*, 2 Oct. 1885.

51 *Land owners*, p. 141; Blennerhassett was one of a number of landlords who held their estates under perpetuity from Trinity College Dublin. He was in precarious financial position and owed up to £18,000 to mortgage companies, see R. B. MacCarthy, *The Trinity College Estates, 1800–1923: Corporate Management in an Age of Reform* (Dundalk, 1992), p. 175.

52 *Land Owners*, p. 143.

53 *KWR*, 31 Oct. 1885.

54 *KS*, 27 Oct. 1885.

55 *Report of the Royal Commission on the Land Law (Ireland) Act, 1881, and the Purchase of Land (Ireland) Act, 1885*, p. 9, HC 1887 [C 4059], xxvi, 1.

56 *Cowper Commission: evidence . . .*, p. 473.

57 South Western Division: DI's monthly report, Sept. 1885 (NAI, CSO RP, 1887, box 3310).

58 *KS*, 2 Oct. 1885.

59 *KS*, 24 Nov. 1885.

60 *KWR*, 19 Sept. 1885.

61 *KWR*, 31 Oct. 1885.

62 *KWR*, 24 Oct. 1885.

63 *KWR*, 14 Nov. 1885.

64 Outrage report: burning of crops belonging to Foster Fitzgerald, Sept. 1885 (NAI, CSO RP, 1885, 17636). Fitzgerald's crops were burnt in retaliation for selling the interest in a number of holdings.

65 Report on Property Defence Association, 18 Oct. 1885 (NAI, CSO RP, 1885, 19248/ 18946).

66 *Returns for Clare, Cork, Kerry, Galway and Mayo of number of civil bills entered at quarter sessions in ejectment on title for non-payment of rent, or overholding, 1879–88*, p. 4, HC 1889 (211), lxi, 417.

67 South Western Division: DI's monthly report, Nov. 1885 (NAI, CSO RP, 1887, box 3310).

68 *KS*, 18 Sept. 1885.

69 *KS*, 13 Oct. 1885.

70 *KS*, 18 Dec. 1885.

71 *Special Commission. . . vol. ii*, p. 205.

72 D. G. Boyce, *Nineteenth Century Ireland: The Search for Stability* (3rd edn, Dublin, 1990), p. 172.

73 1901 Census returns, roll 129, 135, 136 (NAI).

74 Jordan, *Land and Popular Politics in Ireland: County Mayo*, p. 126.

75 David Fitzpatrick, 'Marriage in post-Famine Ireland' in Art Cosgrove (ed.), *Marriage in Ireland* (Dublin, 1985), p. 118.

76 Joseph Lee, *Modernisation of Irish Society* (Dublin, 1973), p. 82.

77 Valuation records (Valuation Office, Dublin).

78 Clark, *Social Origins of the Irish Land War*, p. 214.

79 Feingold, *Revolt of the Tenantry*, pp. 64–5.

80 Crossman, *Politics, Pauperism and Power in late Nineteenth-Century Ireland*, p. 47.

81 Samuel Clark, 'The social composition of the Land League', *IHS* 17: 68 (Sept. 1971), pp. 447–69.

82 *KS*, 31 March 1885. J. J. Nolan was a vintner and R. Browne a victualler, see *Guy's*, p. 692.

83 Fitzgerald, originally from Mountrath, County Laois, taught in St Michael's Listowel. He had achieved an MA from Queen's College, Galway. See Gaughan, *Listowel and its Vicinity*, p. 109.

84 *KWR*, 26 Sept. 1885.

85 *Guy's*, pp. 224–5.

86 *Special Commission. . . vol. ii*, p. 365.

87 Boyce, *Nineteenth-Century Ireland*, p. 173.

88 For an outline of the growth in Victorian local government structures see K.T. Hoppen, *The Mid-Victorian Generation, 1846–88* (Oxford, 1998).

89 For a similar analysis of reolutions passed at Land League meetings in Ireland and County Mayo, see Clark, *Social Origins of the Irish Land Wart*, p. 298; Jordan, *Mayo*, p. 231. For an analysis of resolutions passed at branch meetings of political organisations in County Clare during 1913–21, see Fitzpatrick, *Politics and Irish Life*, p. 237

90 *KS*, 21 July 1885.

91 See Listowel NL, *KS*, 3 July 1885; Ballydonoghue NL, *KS*, 7 July 1885. Walsh replied and thanked the Ballydonoghue branch for the resolution; see *KS*, 14 July 1885.

92 See Abbeydorney NL, *KS*, 27 Oct. 1885; Knockane NL, *KS*, 13 Nov. 1885.

93 See Ballybunion, *KS*, 2 Oct. 1885. The promotion of Irish industry was one of the objectives set out in the constitution of the INL.

94 For National League activity during the first four months of 1885, see ch. five.

95 *KS*, 28 Apr. 1885; *KS*, 23 June 1885.

96 *KS*, 17 Nov. 1885.

97 *KS*, 8. Sept. 1885.

98 For example see Firies branch, *KS*, 20 Oct. 1885.

99 S. J. Connolly, 'Conacre' in idem (ed.), *The Oxford Companion to Irish History* (2nd edn, Oxford, 2002), p. 114.

100 For example, see Knockane branch, *KS*, 13 Oct. 1885.

101 For example, see Keelgarrylander branch, *KS*, 30 Oct. 1885.

102 For examples see Listowel branch, *KS*, 14 July 1885 and Ballyduff branch, *KS*, 15 Dec. 1885.

103 *KS*, 21 July 1885.

104 *KS*, 12 May 1885.

105 *KS*, 3 July 1885.

106 *KS*, 27 Nov. 1885.

107 *KS*, 22 Sept. 1885.

108 *KS*, 15 May 1885.

109 South Western Division: DI's monthly report, Dec. 1885 (NAI, CSO RP, 1887, box 3310).

110 South Western Division: DI's monthly report, Jan. 1886 (NAI, CSO RP, 1887, box 3310).

111 See ch. two.

112 Bull, *Land, Politics and Nationalism*, p. 131; Fergus Campbell, *Land and Revolution*, p. 126.

113 Donald Jordan, 'The Irish National League and the "unwritten law": rural protest and nation building in Ireland 1882–1890', *Past and Present* 158 (Feb. 1998), p. 162.

114 S. A. Ball, 'Policing the Land War: official responses to political protest and agrarian crime in Ireland, 1879–91' (unpublished PhD thesis, Goldsmith's College, University of London, 2000), p. 229.

115 *Cowper Commission: report. . .*, p.7.

116 South Western Division: DI's monthly report May 1885 (NAI CSO RP, 1885, 10841).

117 Return showing persons wholly and partially boycotted on June last [1885] and January 86 (NAI, CSO RP, 1886, 830). In January 1886 a total of 908 people were boycotted in the whole country.

118 For a comprehensive description of National League courts and boycotting in the Dingle region, see Lucey, *The Irish National League*, pp. 21–5.

119 *Cowper Commission: evidence . . .*, p. 501.

120 South Western Division: monthly report, Dec. 1885 (NAI, CSO RP, 1887, box 3310).

121 *KS*, 2 Oct. 1885.

122 *KS*, 3 Nov. 1885.

123 *Cowper Commission: evidence. . .*, p. 513; *KS*, 22 Dec. 1885.

124 See ch. two.

125 *KS*, 28 Aug. 1885.

126 Lucey, *The Irish National League in Dingle*, p. 22.

127 Ibid., pp. 36–7.

128 *Cowper Commission: evidence . . .*, p. 515.

129 Ibid., p. 518.

130 For the circumstances surrounding the emergence of the National League in Kerry, see ch. v.

131 R.V. Comerford, 'The Parnell era, 1883–91' in W. E. Vaughan (ed.), *A New History of Ireland, VI Ireland under the Union, II 1879–1921* (Oxford, 1996), p. 60.

132 Ibid., p. 61.

133 Jackson, *Home Rule*, p. 64.

134 *UI*, 7 Nov. 1885.

135 *UI*, 19 Sept. 1885.

136 *UI*, 26 Sept. 1885.

137 *KS*, 25 Sept. 1885.

138 *KS*, 25 Sept. 1885.

139 South Western Division: monthly police report, Aug. 1885 (NAI, CSO RP, 1887, box 3310).

140 South Western Division: monthly police report, Sept. 1885 (NAI, CSO RP, 1887, box 3310).

141 South Western Division: monthly police report, Aug. 1885 (NAI, CSO RP, 1887, box 3310).

142 See ch. five.

143 See ch. three.

144 File on Thomas Dooling (TNA CO/904: microfilm, NLI, p. 153).

145 The other representatives of the Tralee branch were Thomas O'Rourke, Edward Harrington and Garrett Fitzgerald.

146 C. I. Moriarty to Chief Secretary's Office, 19 Oct. 1885 (NAI, CSO RP, 1885, 19125).

147 Murphy, *The Story of Brosna*, p. 22.

148 James O'Kelly was elected as a Parnellite MP for Roscommon in 1880 and T. D. Sullivan was a Parnellite MP for Westmeath, see Walker, *Parliamentary Election Results in Ireland, 1801–1922*, pp. 310, 320.

149 *KWR*, 21 Nov. 1885.

150 *KS*, 20 Nov. 1885.

151 *KEP*, 21 Nov. 1885.

152 *KS*, 16 Oct. 1885.

153 File on J. D. Sheehan (TNA CO/904: microfilm, NLI, p. 956).

154 *KEP*, 21 Nov. 1885.

SEVEN: THE IRISH NATIONAL LEAGUE AND MOONLIGHTERS

1 *Return of number of agrarian outrages committed in Ireland reported to Inspector General of RIC, quarter ending 30 Sept. 1884*, pp. 2–3 [c 4210], HC 1884–5 lxv. 13; *Return. . . quarter ending 31 Dec. 1884*, pp. 2–3, HC 1884–5 [c 4406], lxiv. 17; *Return. . . quarter ending 30 Sept. 1885*, pp 2–3, HC 1886 [C 4616], liv. 13; *Return . . . quarter ending 31 Dec. 1885*, pp. 2–3, HC 1886 [c 4617], liv, 17.

2   *Return . . . quarter ending 31 Dec. 1885*, pp. 2–4, HC 1886 [c 4617], liv. 17.

3   See ch. six, table 6.3, p. 162.

4   Outrage report: attacks on Denis O'Sullivan and Jeremiah O'Callaghan, 16 Jan. 1886 (NAI, CSO RP, 1886, 994)

5   Ibid., *KS*, 6 Jan. 1886.

6   A.C. Murray, 'Agrarian violence and nationalism in nineteenth-century Ireland: the myth of Ribbonism', *Irish Social and Economic History*, 13 (1986), pp. 56–73.

7   South Western Division: monthly police report, Sept. 1885 (NAI, CSO RP, 1887 box 3310).

8   South Western Division: monthly police report, Oct. 1885 (NAI, CSO RP, 1887 box 3310).

9   Memo of Curtin's grandchild (NLI, Curtin papers, MS 33052).

10   *KS*, 20 Oct. 1885.

11   *Special Commission . . . vol. ii*, p. 220.

12   *KS*, 13 Nov. 1885.

13   *KEP*, 12 Mar. 1886.

14   Irish Folklore Commission, Ballyseedy, s 442, p. 95.

15   Outrage report: assault on police in Castleisland, 22 Feb. 1886 (NAI, CSO RP, 1886, 4242).

16   Alan Gailey, *Irish Folk Drama* (Cork, 1969), p. 81.

17   Michael Beames, 'Rural conflict in pre-Famine Ireland: Peasant assassinations in Tipperary 1837–1847', *Past & Present* 97 (1978), p. 85.

18   Ibid., p. 86.

19   *Special Commission . . . vol. ii*, p. 220.

20   Ibid., p. 221.

21   Memo of Curtin's grandchild (NLI, Curtin papers, MS 33052).

22   *The Times*, 16 Nov. 1885.

23   *KS*, 20 Nov. 1885.

24   *UI*, 21 Nov. 1885.

25   *KS*, 24 Nov. 1885.

26   *Special Commission . . . vol. ii*, p. 221.

27   Ibid., p. 222.

28   Ibid., vol. 11, p. 224.

29   RIC Outrage Report: proceedings at Firies, 26 Jan. 1886 (NAI, CSO RP, 1886, 1752).

30   South Western Division: monthly police report, Jan. 1886 (NAI, CSO RP, 1887, box 3310).

31   RIC Outrage Report: proceedings at Firies, 26 Jan. 1886 (NAI, CSO RP, 1886, 1752).

32   Maire-Louise Legg, *Alfred Webb: The Autobiography of a Quaker Nationalist* (Cork, 1999), p. 51.

33   *KS*, 26 Jan. 1886.

34   *KS*, 2 Feb. 1886.

35   Harrington to O'Connor, 19 Nov. 1885 (NLI, Harrington papers, MS 9454, letter book, no. 15).

36   Harrington to Jeremiah McMahon, 5 Feb. 1886 (NLI, Harrington papers, MS 9454, letter book, no. 28).

37   *KS*, 20 Nov. 1885.

38   *KS*, 2 Feb. 1886.

39   George Pellew, *In Castle and Cabin or Talks in Ireland in 1887* (London, 1888), p. 137.

40   Ibid., p. 139.

41   *Special Commission. . ., vol. ii*.

42   *UI*, 16 Jan. 1886.

43 *UI*, 16 Jan. 1886.

44 *KS*, 8 Jan. 1886.

45 South Western Division: monthly police report, Dec. 1885 (NAI, CSO RP, 1887, box 3310).

46 Ibid.

47 *Cowper Commission: evidence. . .*, p. 533.

48 South Western Division: monthly police report, Dec. 1885 (NAI, CSO RP, 1887, box 3310).

49 South Western Division: monthly police report, Jan. 1886 (NAI, CSO RP, 1887, box 3310).

50 South Western Division: monthly police report, Apr. 1886 (NAI, CSO RP, 1887, box 3310).

51 *KS*, 16 Mar. 1886.

52 The Land Corporation was a landlord organisation that attempted to undermine boycotting by providing men and cattle to graze evicted land.

53 South Western Division: monthly police report, Oct. 1885 (NAI, CSO RP, 1887, box 3310).

54 South Western Division: monthly police report, Sept. 1885 (NAI, CSO RP, 1887, box 3310).

55 RIC Outrage Report, cattle stealing, 20 Mar. 1886 (NAI, CSO RP, 1886, 6279).

56 South Western Division: monthly police report, 1 Dec. 1885 (NAI, CSO RP, 1887, box 3310).

57 RIC Outrage Report, cattle stealing, 17 Nov. 1885 (NAI, CSO RP, 1885, 22707).

58 Geary, *Plan of Campaign*, p. 11.

59 O'Day, *First Home Rule Episode*, p. 149.

60 Ibid., p. 150.

61 *K.S.*, 2 Feb. 1886.

62 Harrington to J. J. Griffin, 27 Jan. 1886 (NLI, Harrington papers, MS 9454, letter book, no. 20).

63 Harrington to J. J. Greaney, 28 Jan. 1886 (NLI, Harrington papers, MS 9454 letter book, no. 21).

64 *KS*, 5 Feb. 1886.

65 *KS*, 12 Mar. 1886.

66 South Western Division: monthly police report, Mar. 1886 (NAI, CSO RP, 1887, box 3310).

67 *KS*, 19 Jan. 1886.

68 *KS*, 5 Feb. 1886.

69 *KS*, 12 Feb. 1886.

70 *KS*, 19 Feb. 1886.

71 *KS*, 12 Mar. 1886.

72 South Western Division: monthly police report, Feb. 1886 (NAI, CSO RP, 1887, box 3310).

73 South Western Division: monthly police report, Mar. 1886 (NAI, CSO RP, 1887, box 3310).

74 Ibid.

75 South Western Division: monthly police report, Feb. 1886 (NAI, CSO RP, 1887, box 3310).

76 South Western Division: monthly police report, Dec. 1885 (NAI, CSO RP, 1887, box 3310).

77 RIC Outrage Report: proceedings at Firies, 26 Jan. 1886 (NAI, CSO RP, 1886, 1752).

78 *Special Commission . . . vol. ix*, p. 59.

79 *Special Commission . . . vol. vii*, p. 560.

80 W. M. Murphy to Timothy Harrington, 20 July 1886; Murphy to Harrington, 30. Aug. 1886 (NLI, Harrington papers, MS 8933[5]). Lucey, *The Irish National League in Dingle*, pp. 35–6.

81 Harrington to Murphy, 1 Sept. 1886 (NLI, *National League Letter Book*, letter no. 106).

82 *KS*, 5 Feb. 1886.

83 See ch. four.

84 Beames, *Peasants and Power*, pp. 55–62.

85 RIC Outrage Report. Raid on Doyle of Brida, 12 Jan. 1886 (NAI, CSO RP, 1886, 763).

86 RIC Outrage report: assault on police, 22 Feb. 1886 (NAI, CSO RP, 1886, 4242).

87 *KS*, 16 Apr. 1886.

88 *KS*, 16 Mar. 1886.

89 See ch. four; Lee, *Modernisation of Irish Society, 1848–1918*, p. 82.

90 Donnelly, *The Land and the People of Nineteenth-Century Cork*, p. 250.

91 *Cowper Commission. . . evidence. . .*, p. 520.

92 Ibid., pp. 530—1.

93 Ibid., p. 540.

94 *KS*, 21 Feb. 1886.

95 *Special Commission . . . vol viii*, p. 535.

96 Ibid.

97 *KEP*, 10 Apr. 1886.

98 Valuation records, County Kerry (Valuation Office, Dublin).

99 *KS*, 20 Apr. 1886.

100 Valuation records, County Kerry (Valuation Office, Dublin).

101 *KS*, 12 Mar. 1886.

102 Pellew, *In Castle and Cabin*, pp. 132–3.

103 Arrests under the PPP Act, 1881 (NAI CSO PPP Act, carton 1).

104 *TC*, 6 Feb. 1872. Maurice Quinlan is listed as attending a pro-Blennerhassett election demonstration in Castleisland.

105 Report on Maurice Quinlan: Hill to Considine RM Nov. 1882 (NLI, H. F. Considine papers, unsorted collection).

106 Hart, *The IRA and its Enemies*, p. 208.

107 RIC Outrage Report (NAI, CSO RP, 1886, 763/ 20619).

108 *Cowper Commission: evidence. . .*, p. 46.

109 Ball, 'Policing the Land War', p. 258.

110 Magee, *The IRB*, p. 79.

111 Outrage report (NAI, CSO RP, 1886, 763).

112 Magee, *The IRB*, p. 86.

113 *KS*, 16 Mar. 1886.

114 *KS*, 12 Mar. 1886.

115 *Cowper Commission: evidence. . .*, p. 46

116 Demonstration in Tralee in connection with the unveiling of a monument in memory of Allen, Larkin and O'Brien, 29 Nov. 1885 (NAI, CSO RP, 1885, 23035).

117 Kelly, *The Fenian Ideal*.

EIGHT: CONCLUSION

1 Hart, *The IRA and its Enemies*, pp. 165–83.

2 A.C. Murray, 'Agrarian violence and nationalism in nineteenth century Ireland: the myth of Ribbonism', *Irish Economic and Social History* 13 (1986), pp. 56–73.

3 Peter Hart, 'The geography of the Irish revolution, 1917–23', *Past & Present* 155 (1997), p. 163, 172.

4	Tom Garvin, 'Defenders, Ribbonmen and others: underground political networks in pre-Famine Ireland', *Past & Present* 96 (Aug., 1982), pp. 133–55.

5	Beames, *Peasants and Power*, pp. 55, 97.

6	E. P. Thompson, 'The moral economy of the English crowd in the eighteenth century', *Past & Present* 50 (Feb. 1971); For an outline of the influences of this historiography on understandings of pre-Famine protest movements see Allan Blackstock, 'Tommy Downshire's boys: Popular protest, social change and political manipulation in Mid-Ulster 1829–1847', *Past & Present* 196 (Aug. 2007), pp. 126–30.

7	D.E. Jordan, 'The Irish National League and the "unwritten law": Rural protest and nation building in Ireland, 1882–1890', *Past & Present* 158 (Feb. 1998), 146–71.

8	Laird, *Subversive Law in Ireland*, pp. 127–8.

9	Fergus Campbell, *Land and Revolution: Nationalist Politics in the West of Ireland, 1891–1921* (Oxford, 2005), pp. 2, 293.

10	Fergus Campbell, 'The social dynamics of nationalist politics in the west of Ireland 1898–1918', *Past & Present* 182 (Feb. 2004), pp. 175– 210.

11	Campbell, *Land and Revolution: Nationalist Politics in the West of Ireland 1891–1921*, pp. 287–92.

12	L. M. Geary, *The Plan of Campaign, 1886–91* (Cork, 1986).

13	For an account of the National League and its suppression in Kerry see, Lucey, *The Irish National League in Dingle, County Kerry, 1885–92*, pp. 34–54.

Bibliography

—

PRIMARY SOURCES

MANUSCRIPT MATERIAL

I DUBLIN
Dublin City Archive
Mansion House Relief Fund papers

Land Valuation Office
Cancelled valuation books, County Kerry

National Archives
Chief Secretary's Office
Irish National Land League and Irish National League papers: Carton VI, Irish National League proceedings, 1883–4; Carton VII, Irish National League proceedings, 1885–90.
Fenian papers
Irish Crime Records: Protection of Person and Property Act, 1881, List of arrests, warrants and persons in custody; Registers of arrests (Protection of Person and Property Act), 1881–2; Return of Outrages, 1879–83 (printed stats-annual), vol. 2; 1879–82 (printed, with short monthly reports), vol. 4; Fenianism: Index of names 1861–5, vol. 1; Index of names 1867, vol. 1. Protection of Person and Property Act: Lists of arrests under Protection of Person and Property Act 1881, nos 1–987; Lists of warrants under the Protection of Person and Property Act 1881.
Queen versus *Parnell* (Special Commission).
Chief Secretary's Office, Registered Papers, 1880–6.

Estate papers
Drummond Rental Book

Census
Census returns, 1901 (County Kerry).

National Library of Ireland
Curtin papers
Land League papers
Talbot-Crosbie estate papers

243

Timothy Harrington papers
Sweetman Family papers

Trinity College Library, University of Dublin
Base-Line Reports to the Congested District Board, 1892–8
Michael Davitt papers

University College Dublin
National Folklore Collection

II COUNTY KERRY
Kerry Diocesan Records, Killarney
Bishops' papers
Parish correspondence
Priests' papers

III LONDON
The National Archives, Kew
Public Record Office: Colonial Office Class CO 904 (*The British in Ireland. Series I: part 1: anti-government organisations, 1882–1921* [colonial Office Class CO 904 (Dublin Castle records)] (Brighton, 1982), 14 microfilms.

PARLIAMENTARY MATERIAL AND OFFICIAL PUBLICATIONS

Agricultural statistics part ii – stock, table viii – showing the number of holdings and quantity of live stock in each county in Ireland in 1870 [c 880], HC 1872, lxix, 119.

Return for each parliamentary city, town, and borough in England and Wales, in Scotland, and in Ireland, of population and number of electors on registry 1866, 1869, and 1873, HC, 1874 (381), liii, 43.

Return of number of original civil bill processes served in quarter session districts in each county in Ireland 1876, HC, 1877 (62), lx, 329.

Return of applications from landed proprietors and sanitary authorities in scheduled unions for loans under notices of Commissioners of Public Works in Ireland, 22 Nov. 1879–12 Jan. 1880, with result, HC, 1880 (154), lxii.

Reports of the local government board of Ireland, with appendices, – seventh [c 2363], HC, 1878–9, xxx, 1.

Preliminary report on the returns of agricultural produce in Ireland in 1879 [c 2495], HC, 1880, lxxvi, 893.

Return of cases of eviction which have come under the knowledge of the constabulary in each of the four quarters of 1877, 1878, 1879, and the first quarter of 1880 and up to the 10 June 1880, HC, 1880 (245), lx, 361.

Return of the number of families evicted in Ireland for non-payment of rent, and re-admitted as caretakers, 1877–Jun 1880, HC, 1880 (317), lx, 367.

Return of number of civil bill ejectments entered, tried and determined in Ireland, 1877–9, HC, 1880 (132), lx, 379.

Reports of the local government board of Ireland, with appendices,-eight [c 2603], HC, 1880, xxviii, 1.

Return of numbers in receipt of relief in the several unions in Ireland on 1 Jan., 1 Mar., and 1 June, in 1878, 1879, and 1880, HC, 1880 (420), lxii, 289.

Circular of 7 Feb. 1880, issued by the Local Government Board for Ireland to boards of guardians, relating to the relief to families of persons occupying land, HC, 1880 (9), lvii, 705.

Return, arranged according to counties, showing the number of accounts of depositors in Post Office Savings Banks in the U.K remaining open on the 31 Dec. 1879, with the amount, inclusive of interest, standing to the credit of those accounts, HC, 1881 (24), lvii, 335.

Return, by provinces and counties, of cases of evictions under knowledge of Royal Irish Constabulary, 1849–80, HC, 1881 (185), lxxvii, 725

Return showing for each month of the years 1879 and 1880 the number of Land League meetings held and agrarian crimes reported to the Inspector General of the R.I.C. in each county throughout Ireland, HC, 1881 (5), lxxvii, 793.

Return of agrarian outrages reported by the R.I.C. between 1 Feb. 1880 and 31 Oct. 1880, HC, 1881 (6), lxxvii, 273.

Report of the Local Government Board for Ireland with appendices – ninth, HC, 1881 [c 2926], xlvii. 269.

Return of local taxation in Ireland for 1880 [c 3097], HC, 1881, lxxix, 125.

Return of agricultural holdings, compiled by the local government board in Ireland from the returns furnished by the clerks of the poor law unions in Ireland 1881 [c 2934], HC, 1881, xcii, 793.

Report of her majesty's commissioners of inquiry into the working of the Landlord and Tenant (Ireland) Act, 1870, and the acts amending the same, vol. iii: digest of evidence, minutes of evidence, pt. I [c 2779–11], HC, 1881, xix, 1.

Royal Commission on the depressed condition of the agricultural interest: minutes of evidence, part 1 [c 2778–I], HC, 1881, xv, 25.

Reports of the local government board of Ireland, with appendices, – ninth [c 2926], HC, 1881, xlvii, 269.

Census of Ireland 1881: area, population and number of houses; occupations, religion and education volume ii: province of Munster [c 3148], HC, 1882, lxxvii, 1.

Report of the Irish Land Commission for the period 22 Aug. 1881 to 22 Aug. 1882 [c 3413], HC, 1882, xx, 265.

——*For 1882–3* [c 3897], HC, 1884, lxiv, 41.

——*For 1883–4* [c 4231], HC, 1884–5, lxv, 53.

——*For 1884–5* [c 4625], HC, 1886, xix, 467.

——*For 1885–6* [c 4899], HC, 1887, xix, 503.

——*For 1886–7* [c 5223], HC, 1887, xxv,185.

Return, according to provinces and counties, of judicial rents fixed by sub-commissioners and Civil Bill Courts, as notified to the Irish Land Commission, up to 31 December 1881 [c 3120], HC, 1882, lvi, 1.

——*Up to 28 Jan. 1882* [c 3120], HC, 1882, lvi, 1.

——*From 28 Jan.–15 Apr. 1882* [c 3223], HC, 1882, lvi, 97.

——*From 17 Apr.–31 May 1882* [c 3260], HC, 1882, lvi, 303.

——*For June 1882* [c 3306], HC, 1882, lvi, 463.

——*July 1882* [c 3362], HC, 1882, lvi, 595.

——*Aug. 1882* [c 3363], HC, 1882, lvi, 769.

——*Sept.-Oct. 1882* [c 3421], HC, 1882, lvi, 885.

——*Sept.-Nov. 1882* [C 3451], HC, 1882, lvi, 889.

——*Dec. 1882* [C 3559], HC, 1883, lvi, 121.

——*Jan. 1883* [C 3582], HC, 1883, lvi, 237.

——*Feb. 1883* [C 3614], HC, 1883 lvi, 345.

——*Mar. 1883* [C 3644], HC, 1883 lvi, 473.

——*Apr. 1883* [C 3682], HC, 1883, lvii, 1.

——*May 1883* [C 3740], HC, 1883, lvii, 205.

——*June 1883* [C 3826], HC, 1883, lvii, 461.

——*July 1883* [C 3827], HC, 1883, lvii, 709.

——*Aug. 1883* [C 3896], HC, 1883, lxv, 1.

——*Sept. 1883* [C 3902], HC, 1884, lxv, 165.

——*Oct. 1883* [C 3906], HC, 1884, lxv, 233.

——*Nov. 1883* [C 3917], HC, 1884, lxv, 491.

——*Dec. 1883* [C 3949], HC, 1884, lxv, 739.

Lists of prisoners under the Protection of Person and Property (Ireland) Act, 1881, HC, 1881 (171), lxxvi, 671.

Return of persons who have been or are in custody under the Protection of Person and Property (Ireland) Act, 1881, up to 31 Mar. 1882, HC 1882 (156), lv, 635.

——*Feb.–Aug. 1882*, HC, 1882 (1), lv, 685.

Return for each county, city, and borough in Ireland, of the names of persons holding the Commission of the Peace, with date of appointment and designation at time of appointment; and number that are Protestants, Roman Catholics, and of other religious persuasions, HC, 1884 (13), lxii, 331.

Report from the Select Committee of the House of Lords on the Poor Law Guardians (Ireland) Bill: with the proceedings, evidence, and index, HC, 1884–85 (297), x, 281.

Return of number of agrarian outrages committed in Ireland reported to Inspector General of R.I.C, quarter ending 30 Sept. 1884 [C 4210], HC, 1884–85, lxv, 13.

——*quarter ending 31 Dec. 1884* [C 4406], HC, 1884–85, lxiv, 17.

——*quarter ending 30 Sept. 1885* [C 4616], HC, 1886, liv, 13.

——*quarter ending 31 Dec. 1885* [C 4617], HC, 1886, liv, 17.

Return of local taxation in Ireland, for 1884 [C 4544], HC, 1884–5, lxvii, 429.

Report on explosion at Edenburn, private residence of S.M. Hussey, in county Kerry, Nov. 1884 [c. 4289] HC, 1885, xiv.

Return showing, with regard to each electoral division in Ireland, the gross rateable valuation per acre, the total population, the rateable valuation per head of the population, and the average poor rate for the last five years, HC, 1887 (27) lxxi, 51.

Report of the Royal Commission on the Land Law (Ireland) Act, 1881, and the Purchase of Land (Ireland) Act, 1885 [C 4059], HC, 1887, xxvi, 1.

Report of the Royal Commission on the Land Law (Ireland) Act, 1881, and the Purchase of Land (Ireland) Act, 1885: minutes of evidence, and appendix, HC, 1887, xxvi, 25.

Returns for Clare, Cork, Kerry, Galway and Mayo of number of civil bills entered at quarter sessions in ejectment on title for non-payment of rent, or overholding, 1879–88, HC, 1889 (211), lxi, 417.

Select committee of House of Lords on Land Law (Ireland): first report, proceedings, minutes of evidence, appendix, index, HC, 1882 (249), xi. 1.

Special commission act, reprint of the shorthand notes of the speeches, proceedings, and evidence taken before the commissioners appointed under the above act, 12 vols (London, 1890).

NEWSPAPERS

Cork Examiner
Freeman's Journal
Kerry Evening Post
Kerry Independent
Kerry Sentinel
Kerry Weekly Reporter
Tralee Chronicle
United Ireland

CONTEMPORARY PUBLICATIONS

Campbell, George, *Irish Land* (London, 1869).

Cornewall Lewis, George, *Local Disturbances in Ireland* (London, 1836).

Cusack, M, F., *The Case of Ireland Stated* (Dublin, 1881).

——*The Nun of Kenmare, An Autobiography* (1889).

Crane, C. P., *Memories of a Resident Magistrate, 1880–1920* (Edinburgh, 1938)

——*Kerry* (London, 1907).

Devoy, John, *Recollections of an Irish Rebel: A Personal Narrative By John Devoy* (New York, 1929).

Dun, Finlay, *Landlords and Tenants in Ireland* (London, 1881).

Fitzmaurice, George, *Five Plays: The Country Dressmaker, The Moonlighter, The Pie-Dish, The Magic Glasses, The Dandy Dolls* (Dublin, 1914).

Hussey, S. M., *Reminiscences of an Irish Land Agent* (London, 1904).

Kerry, Knight of, *Irish Landlords and Tenants: Recent Letters to 'The Times' and Further Correspondence on the above Subject* (Dublin, 1876).

O'Connor, T. P., *The Parnell Movement With a Sketch of Irish Parties From 1843* (London, 1886).

——*Memoirs of an Old Parliamentarian, Vol. I* (London, 1929).

Pellew, George, *In Castle and Cabin or Talks in Ireland in 1887* (London, 1888).

Sullivan, T. D., *A. M. Sullivan* (Dublin, 1885).

——*Recollections of Troubled Times in Irish Politics* (Dublin, 1905).

——*Bantry, Berehaven and The O'Sullivan* (Cork, 1908).

——*The Irish Crisis of 1879–80: Proceedings of the Dublin Mansion House Relief Committee, 1880* (Dublin, 1881).

Turner, A.E., *Sixty Years of a Soldier's Life* (London 1912).

Webb, Alfred, *The Opinions of Some Protestants Regarding Their Fellow-Countrymen* (Dublin, 1886).

WORKS OF REFERENCE

Guy's Munster Directory (Cork, 1886).

Hamell, P.J., *Maynooth: Students and Ordinations, Index 1795–1895* (Maynooth, 1982).

Land Owners in Ireland, 1876 (Baltimore, 1988).

O'Toole, James, *Newsplan: Report of the Newsplan Project in Ireland* (London, 1992).

The Irish Catholic Directory, Almanac and Registry: With Complete Ordo in English (Dublin, 1885).

Thom's Directory (Dublin, 1875–86).

Walker, B. M. (ed.), *Parliamentary Election Results in Ireland, 1801–1922* (Dublin, 1978).

SECONDARY SOURCES

BOOKS

Anderson, Benedict, *Imagined Communities: Reflections On the Origin and Spread of Nationalism* (London, 1983).

Ball, Stephen (ed.), *A Policeman's Ireland: Recollections of Samuel Waters, R.I.C.* (Cork, 1999).

Beames, Michael, *Peasants and Power: The Whiteboy Movements and their Control in Pre-Famine Ireland* (Sussex, 1983).

Bew, Paul, *Land and the National Question in Ireland 1858–82* (Dublin, 1978).

——*Conflict and Conciliation in Ireland, 1890–1910: Parnellites and Radical Agrarians* (Oxford, 1987).

——*Ireland: The Politics of Enmity, 1789–2006* (Oxford, 2007).

Bourke, Marcus, *John O'Leary: A Study in Irish Separatism* (Tralee, 1967).

Boyce, D. G., *Nationalism in Ireland: The Search for Stability* (3rd edn, London, 1995).

——*Ireland in Transition* (London, 2004).

Boyce, D. G. and O'Day, Alan (eds), *Parnell in Perspective* (London, 1991).

Bull, Philip, *Land, Politics and Nationalism: A Study of the Irish Land Question* (Dublin, 1996).

Breathnach, Ciara, *The Congested Districts Board of Ireland, 1891–1923: Poverty and Development in the West of Ireland* (Dublin, 2005).

Callanan, Frank, *The Parnell Split, 1890–91* (Cork, 1992).

——*T. M. Healy* (Cork, 1996).

Campbell, Fergus, *Land and Revolution: Nationalist Politics in the West of Ireland, 1891–1921* (Oxford, 2005).

——*The Irish Establishment, 1879–1914* (Oxford, 2009).

Carter, J. W. H, *the Land War and its Leaders in Queen's County, 1879–82* (Portlaoise, 1994).

Clark, Samuel, *Social Origins of the Irish Land War* (Princeton, 1979).

Clark, Samuel and Donnelly, J.S. Jr (eds), *Irish Peasants: Violence and Political Unrest 1780–1914* (Manchester, 1983).

Coleman, Marie, *County Longford and the Irish Revolution, 1910–23* (Dublin, 2003).

Comerford, R.V., *Charles J. Kickham: A Study in Irish Nationalism and Literature* (Dublin, 1979).

——*The Fenians in Context: Irish Politics and Society, 1848–82* (Dublin, 1985).

——*Ireland: Inventing the Nation* (London, 2003).

Connolly, S. J., *Religion and Society in Nineteenth Century Ireland* (Dundalk, 1985).

Cosgrove, Art (ed.), *Marriage in Ireland* (Dublin, 1985).

Cronin, Maura, *Country, Class or Craft? The Politicisation of the Skilled Artisan in Nineteenth-Century Cork* (Cork, 1994).

Crossman, Virginia, *Local Government in Nineteenth-Century Ireland* (Belfast, 1994).

——*Politics, Law and Order in Nineteenth Century Ireland* (Dublin, 1996).

——*Politics, Pauperism and Power in Late Nineteenth Century Ireland* (Manchester, 2006).

Curtis, L. P. Jr, *Coercion and Conciliation in Ireland, 1880–92* (Princeton, 1963).

Donnelly, J. S. Jr, *The Land and the People of Nineteenth-Century Cork: The Rural Economy and the Land Question* (London, 1975).

Dooley, Terence, *The Decline of the Big House in Ireland: A Study of Irish Landed Families, 1860–1960* (Dublin, 2001).

—— '*The Land for the People': The Land Question in independent Ireland* (Dublin, 2004).

——*The Big Houses and Landed Estates of Ireland: A Research Guide.* Maynooth Research Guides for Irish Local History, no. 11 (Dublin, 2007).

Drudy, P. J. (ed.), *Ireland: Land, Politics and People* (Cambridge, 1982).

Feingold, W. L., *The Revolt of the Tenantry: The Transformation of Local Government in Ireland, 1872–1886* (Boston, 1984).

Foster, R. F., *Modern Ireland, 1600–1972* (London, 1988).

Fitzpatrick, David, *Politics and Irish Life, 1913–21: Provincial Experience of War and Revolution* (Dublin, 1977).

Freeman, T. W., *Ireland: A General and Regional Geography* (4th edn, London, 1969).

Gailey, Alan, *Irish Folk Drama* (Cork, 1969).

Garvin, Tom, *the Evolution of Irish Nationalist Politics* (Dublin, 1981).

——*Nationalist Revolutionaries in Ireland, 1858–1928* (Oxford, 1987).

Geary, L. M., *The Plan of Campaign 1886–91* (Cork, 1986).

Gaughan, J.A., *Listowel and its Vicinity* (Cork, 1973).

——*Austin Stack: Portrait of a Separatist* (Dublin, 1977).

——*A Political Odyssey: Thomas O'Donnell M.P. for West Kerry 1900–18* (Dublin, 1983).

Gillespie, Raymond and Moran, Gerard (eds), *Longford: Essays in County History* (Dublin, 1991).

Gillespie, Raymond and Hill, Myrtle (eds), *Doing Irish Local History: Pursuit and Practice* (Belfast, 1998)

Gibbons, S.R., *Captain Rock, Night Errant: The Threatening Letters of Pre-Famine Ireland, 1801–45* (Dublin, 2004).

Gray, Peter (ed.), *Victoria's Ireland: Irishness and Britishness, 1837–1901* (Dublin, 2004).

Hart, Peter, *The IRA and its Enemies: Violence and Community in Cork, 1916–23* (Oxford, 1998).

Hobsbawm, E. J., *The Age of Empire, 1875–1914* (London, 1987).

——*Nations and Nationalism since 1780: Programme, Myth, Reality* (2nd edn, Cambridge, 1992).

Hoppen, K.T., *Elections, Politics and Society in Ireland, 1832–85* (Oxford, 1984).

——*Ireland Since 1800: Conflict and Conformity* (London, 1989).

——*Ireland Since 1800: Conflict and Conformity* (2nd edn, London, 1999).

Hutchinson, John and Smith, A.D. (eds), *Nationalism* (Oxford, 1994).

Iggers, G. G., *Historiography in the Twentieth Century: From Scientific Objectivity to the Postmodern Challenge* (2nd edn, New England, 2005).

Irish National Committee for Geography, *Atlas of Ireland* (Dublin, 1979).

Jackson, Alvin, *The Ulster Party: Irish Unionists in the House of Commons, 1884–1911* (Oxford, 1989).

——*Ireland 1798–1998: Politics and War* (Oxford, 1999).

——*Home Rule: An Irish History, 1800–2000* (London, 2003).

Jones, D. S., *Graziers, Land Reform and Popular Conflict in Ireland* (Washington, 1995).

Jordan, Donald, *Land and Popular Politics in Ireland: County Mayo From the Plantation to the Land War* (Cambridge, 1994).

Jupp, Peter and Magennis, Eoin (eds), *Crowds in Ireland, 1720–1920* (Basingstoke, 2000).

Kennedy, Edward, *The Land Movement in Tullaroan, County Kilkenny, 1879–91*. Maynooth Studies in Local History, no. 55 (Dublin, 2004).

King, Carla, *Michael Davitt* (Dundalk, 1999).

——(ed.), *Famine, Land and Culture in Ireland* (Dublin, 2000).

Lane, Fintan and Newby, A.G. (eds), *Michael Davitt New Perspectives* (Dublin, 2009).

Laird, Heather, *Subversive Law in Ireland, 1879–1920: From 'Unwritten Law' to the Dáil Courts* (Dublin, 2005).

Larkin, Emmet, *The Roman Catholic Church and the Creation of the Modern Irish State, 1878–86* (Philadelphia, 1975).

——*The Roman Catholic Church and the Plan of Campaign in Ireland, 1886–88* (Cork, 1978).

——*The Consolidation of the Roman Catholic Church in Ireland, 1860–70* (Dublin, 1987).

——*The Roman Catholic Church and the Home Rule Movement in Ireland, 1870–74* (Dublin, 1990).

Lee, Joseph, *The Modernisation of Irish Society, 1848–1918* (Dublin, 1973).

Legg, Maire-Louise, *Alfred Webb: The Autobiography of a Quaker Nationalist* (Cork, 1999).

——*Newspapers and Nationalism: The Irish Provincial Press, 1850–92* (Dublin, 1999).

Loughlin, James, *Gladstone, Home Rule and the Ulster Question, 1882–93* (Dublin, 1986).

——*Ulster Unionism and British National Identity since 1885* (London, 1994).

Lucey, D.S., *the Irish National League in Dingle, County Kerry, 1885–92*. Maynooth Studies in Local History, no. 48 (Dublin, 2003).

Luddy, Maria, *Women and Philanthropy in Nineteenth-Century Ireland* (Cambridge, 1995).

Lynch, Patt, *They Hanged John Twiss* (Tralee, 1982).

Lyons, F. S. L., *The Irish Parliamentary Party, 1890–1910* (London, 1951).

——*John Dillon: A Biography* (London, 1968).

——*Ireland Since the Famine* (London, 1971).

——*Charles Stewart Parnell* (London, 1977).

Lyons, F. S. L. and Hawkins, R. A. J. (eds), *Ireland Under the Union: Varieties of Tension: Essays in Honour of T. W. Moody* (Oxford, 1980).

Lyne, G. J., *The Lansdowne Estate in Kerry under the Agency of William Stuart Trench, 1849–72* (Dublin, 2001).

MacMahon, Bryan, *The Story of Ballyheigue* (Ballyheuige, 1994).

Magee, Owen, *The IRB: The Irish Republican Brotherhood From the Land League to Sinn Féin* (Dublin, 2005).

Maume, Patrick, *The Long Gestation: Irish Nationalist Life, 1891–1918* (Dublin, 1999).

McCarthy, Robert, *The Trinity College Estates 1800–1912: Corporate Management in An Age of Reform* (Dundalk, 1992).

McConnel, James and McGarry, Fearghal (eds), *The Black Hand of Republicanism: Fenianism in Modern Ireland* (DubliSn, 2009).

McDowell, R. B., *The Irish Administration, 1801–1914* (Dublin, 1964).

Mcgrath, T.G. and Nolan, William (eds), *Tipperary: History and Society* (Dublin, 1985).

McMahon, Deirdre (ed.), *the Moynihan Brothers in Peace and War, 1909–18: Their New Ireland* (Dublin, 2004).

Moody, T.W., *Davitt and the Irish Revolution* (Oxford, 1981).

Moran, Gerard, *A Radical Priest in Mayo, Fr Lavelle, the Rise and Fall of an Irish Nationalist 1825–86* (Dublin, 1994).

Murphy, M. G., *The Story of Brosna* (Brosna, 1977).

Murphy, J. H., *Abject Loyalty: Nationalism, Monarchy and Ireland During the Reign of Queen Victoria* (Cork, 2001).

Nelson, Thomas, *The Land War in County Kildare*. Maynooth Historical Series, no. 3 (Maynooth, 1985).

Nolan, William and McGrath, Thomas (eds), *Kildare History and Society: Interdisciplinary Essays on the History of an Irish County* (Dublin, 2006).

O'Brien, C. C., *Parnell and His Party* (5th edn, Oxford, 1974).

O'Broin, Leon, *Revolutionary Underground: The Story of the Irish Republican Brotherhood, 1858–1924* (Dublin, 1976).

O'Callaghan, Margaret, *British High Politics and A Nationalist Ireland: Criminality, Land and the Law under Forster and Balfour* (Cork, 1994).

O'Day, Alan, *Parnell and the First Home Rule Episode, 1884–87* (Dublin, 1986).

——*The English Face of Irish Nationalism* (2nd edn, Aldershot, 1994).

Philpin, C. H. E. (ed.), *Nationalism and Popular Protest in Ireland* (Cambridge, 1987).

Smith, A. D., *Theories of Nationalism* (2nd edn, London, 1983).

Sullivan, T. D., *A Popular History of East Kerry* (Dublin, 1941).

Thompson, Frank, *The End of Liberal Ulster: Land Agitation and Land Reform, 1868–86* (Belfast, 2001).

Thonley, David, *Isaac Butt and Home Rule* (2nd edn, London, 1976).

Townsend, Charles, *Political Violence in Ireland: Government and Resistance since 1848* (Oxford, 1983).

Turner, Michael, *After the Famine: Irish Agriculture, 1850–1914* (Cambridge, 1996).

Vaughan, W. E., *Landlords and Tenants in Ireland, 1848–1904* (Dublin, 1984).

——*Landlords and Tenants in Mid-Victorian Ireland* (Oxford, 1994).

Warwick-Haller, Sally, *William O'Brien and the Irish Land War* (Dublin, 1990).

ARTICLES

Ball, Stephen, 'Crowd activity during the Irish Land War, 1879–90' in Jupp, Peter and Magennis, Eoin (eds), *Crowds in Ireland, 1720–1920* (Basingstoke, 2000), pp. 212–48.

Bartlett, Thomas, 'An end to moral economy' in C. H. E. Philpin, *Nationalism and Popular Protest in Ireland* (Cambridge, 1987), pp. 41–64.

Beames, Michael, 'Rural conflict in pre-Famine Ireland: peasant assassinations in Tipperary 1837–1847', *Past & Present* 97 (1978), pp. 75–91.

——'The Ribbon-societies: lower-class nationalism in pre-Famine Ireland', *Past & Present* 97 (1982), pp. 128–43.

Bew, Paul, 'The Land League ideal: achievements and contradictions' in P. J. Drudy (ed.), *Ireland: Land, Politics and People* (Cambridge, 1982), pp. 77–82.

Campbell, Fergus 'The hidden history to the Irish land war: a guide to local sources' in Carla King (ed.), *Famine, Land and Culture in Ireland* (Dublin, 2000), pp. 140–52.

——'The social dynamics of nationalist politics in the west of Ireland 1898–1918', *Past & Present* 182 (2004), pp. 175–210.

Clark, Samuel, 'The social composition of the Land League', *IHS* XVII: 68 (Sept. 1971), pp. 447–69.

Comerford, R. V., 'Patriotism as pastime: the appeal of Fenianism in the mid-1860s', *IHS* XXII: 87 (Mar. 1981), pp. 239–50.

——'Tipperary representation at Westminster, 1801–1918' in McGrath, T. G. and Nolan, William (eds), *Tipperary: History and Society* (Dublin, 1985), pp. 325–38.

——'Nation, nationalism and the Irish language' in Hachey, T. E. and McCaffrey, L. (eds), *Perspectives in Irish Nationalism* (Lexington, 1989), pp. 20–41.

——'Churchmen, tenants, and independent opposition, 1850–56' in Vaughan, W.E. (ed.), *A New History of Ireland, V Ireland under the Union, I, 1801–1870* (Oxford, 1989), pp. 396–414.

——'Isaac Butt and the Home Rule Party, 1870–77' in W. E. Vaughan (ed.), *A New History of Ireland, VI Ireland under the Union, II 1879–1921* (Oxford, 1996), pp. 1–25.

——'The land war and the politics of distress, 1877–82' in W. E. Vaughan (ed.), *A New History of Ireland, VI Ireland under the Union, II 1879–1921* (Oxford, 1996), pp. 26–52.

——'The Parnell era, 1883–91' in W. E. Vaughan (ed.), *A New History of Ireland, VI Ireland under the Union, II 1879–1921* (Oxford, 1996), pp. 53–80.

——'The Land Commission' in S. J. Connolly (ed.), *The Oxford Companion to Irish History* (2nd edn, Oxford, 2002), pp. 310–11.

——'Republicans and democracy in modern Irish politics' in McGarry, Fearghal (ed.), *Republicanism in Modern Ireland* (Dublin, 2003).

Connolly, S. J., 'Conacre' in idem (ed.), *The Oxford Companion to Irish History* (2nd edn, Oxford, 2002).

Crossman, Virginia, 'The charm of allowing people to manage their own affairs': political perspectives on emergency relief in late nineteenth-century Ireland' in Boyce, D.G., and O'Day, Alan (eds), *Ireland in Transition, 1867–1921* (London, 2004), pp. 193–209.

——'With the experience of 1846 and 1847 before them': the politics of emergency relief, 1879–84' in Gray, Peter (ed.), *Victoria's Ireland: Irishness and Britishness, 1837–1901* (Dublin, 2004), pp. 167–82.

Curtin, Danny, 'Edward Harrington and the first GAA event in Kerry', *Kerry Magazine* 11, (2000), pp. 11–16.

Curtis, L. P. Jr, 'Encumbered wealth: Landlord indebtedness in post-Famine Ireland', *American Historical Review* 85 (Apr. 1980), pp. 332–67

——'Stopping the hunt, 1881–82: an aspect of the Irish Land War' in Philpin, C. H. E. (ed.), *Nationalism and Popular Protest in Ireland* (Cambridge, 1987), pp. 349–402.

——'Landlord responses to the Irish Land War, 1879–87', *Eire-Ireland* (Fall/Winter 2003), pp. 134–88.

De Brun, Pádraig, 'Kerry Diocese in 1890: Bishop Coffey's survey', *JKAHS* 22 (1989), pp. 99–180.

Dillon, Paul, 'James Connolly and the Kerry famine of 1898', *Saothar: Journal of the Irish Labour History Society* 25 (2000), pp. 29–42.

——'The Tralee labourers' strike of 1896: an episode in Ireland's "New Unionism"' *JKAHS* 2: 3 (2003), pp. 103–22.

Donnelly, J. S. Jr, 'Cork market: its role in the nineteenth century Irish butter trade', *Studia Hibernica* 11 (1971), pp. 130–6.

——'The journals of Sir John Benn-Walsh relating to the management of his Irish estates, 1823–64', *Journal of the Cork Historical & Archaeological Society* 79 (1974), pp. 86–123.

——'The journals of Sir John Benn-Walsh relating to the management of his Irish estates, 1823–64', *Journal of the Cork Historical & Archaeological Society* 80 (1975), pp. 15–42.

——'Pastorini and Captain Rock: millenarianism and sectarianism in the Rockite movement of 1821–4' in Clark, Samuel and Donnelly, J. S. Jr (eds), *Irish Peasants, Violence and Political Unrest, 1780–1914* (Manchester, 1983), pp. 102–39.

——'The Kenmare estates during the nineteenth century', *JKAHS* 21 (1988), pp. 5–41; 22 (1989), pp. 61–98; 23 (1990), pp. 5–45.

Dooley, Terence, 'Landlords and the land question, 1879–1909' in Carla King (ed.), *Famine, Land and Culture in Ireland* (Dublin, 2000), pp. 116–39.

Feingold, W.L., 'Land League power: the Tralee poor-law election of 1881' in Clark, Samuel and Donnelly, J. S. Jr (eds), *Irish Peasants: Violence and Political Unrest, 1780–1915* (Manchester, 1983), pp. 285–310.

Fitzpatrick, David, 'The disappearance of the Irish agricultural labourer, 1841–1912', *Irish Economic and Social History* VII (1980), pp. 66–92.

——'Class, family and rural unrest in nineteenth-century Ireland' in Drudy, P. J. (ed.), *Ireland: Land, Politics and Politics* (Cambridge, 1982), pp. 37–75.

——'Review essay: unrest in rural Ireland', *Irish Economic and Social History* XII (1985), pp. 98–105.

——'Marriage in post-Famine Ireland' in Art Cosgrove (ed.), *Marriage in Ireland* (Dublin, 1985).

Garnham, Neal, 'Accounting for the early success of the Gaelic Athletic Association', *IHS*, XXXIV: 133 (May 2004), pp. 65–78.

Garvin, Tom, 'The anatomy of a nationalist revolution: Ireland 1858–1928', *Comparative Studies in Society and History*, 28, 1986, pp. 468–501.

——'Defenders, Ribbonmen and others: underground political networks in pre-Famine Ireland', *Past and Present*, no. 96 (1982), pp. 133–55.

Gibbon, Peter and Higgins, M.D., 'Patronage, tradition and modernisation. The role of the Irish "Gombeenman"', *Economic and Social Review* VI (1974), pp. 27–44.

Gillespie, Raymond and Moran, Gerard, 'Land, politics and religion in Longford since 1600' in idem (eds), *Longford: Essays in County History* (Dublin, 1991), pp. 3–10.

Jones, D. S., 'The cleavage between graziers and peasants in the land struggle, 1890–1910' in Clark, Samuel and Donnelly, J. S. Jr, *Irish Peasants: Violence and Political Unrest 1780–1914* (Manchester, 1983), pp. 374–417.

Jordan, Donald, 'John O'Connor, Charles Stewart Parnell and the centralisation of popular politics in Ireland', *IHS* XXV: 97 (May 1986), pp. 46–66.

——'Merchants, strong farmers and Fenians: the post-Famine political elite and the Irish Land War' in Philpin, C. H. E. (ed.), *Nationalism and Popular Protest in Ireland* (Cambridge, 1987), pp. 320–48.

——'The Irish National League and the "unwritten law": rural protest and nation building in Ireland 1882–1890', *Past & Present* 158 (Feb 1998), pp. 146–71.

Kennedy, Liam, 'The economic thought of the nation's lost leader: Charles Stewart Parnell' in Boyce, D. G. and O'Day, Alan (eds), *Parnell in Perspective* (London, 1991), pp. 171–200.

Kirkpatrick, R.W., 'Origins and development of the land war in mid-Ulster, 1879–85' in Lyons, F. S. L. and Hawkins, R. A. J. (eds), *Ireland Under the Union: Varieties of Tension: Essays in Honour of T. W. Moody* (Oxford, 1980), pp. 201–36.

Lane, Fintan 'Rural labourers, social change and politics in late nineteenth century Ireland' in Lane, Fintan and Ó Drisceoil, Donal (eds), *Politics and the Irish Working Class, 1830–1945* (Houndmills, 2005), pp. 113–39.

Larkin, Emmet, 'Church, state, and nation in modern Ireland', *American Historical Review* LXXX: 5 (Dec. 1975), pp. 1244–76.

Lee, Joseph, 'The Ribbonmen' in Williams, T.D. (ed.), *Secret Societies in Ireland* (Dublin, 1973), pp. 26–35.

Loughlin, James, 'The Irish Protestant Home Rule Association and nationalist politics 1886–93', *IHS* 25 (1985), pp. 341–63.

——'Constructing the political spectacle: Parnell, the press and national leadership, 1879–86' in Boyce, D.G. and O'Day, Alan (eds), *Parnell in Perspective* (London, 1991), pp. 221–41.

——'Nationality and loyalty: Parnellism, monarchy and the construction of Irish identity, 1880–5' in Boyce, D.G. and O'Day, Alan (eds), *Ireland in Transition, 1867–1921* (London, 2004), pp. 35–56.

MacCurtain, Margaret and O'Dowd, Mary, 'An agenda for women's history in Ireland, 1500–1900: part 1: 1500–1900', *IHS* 28: 109 (May, 1992), pp. 1–19.

MacMahon, Bryan, 'George Sandes of Listowel: land agent, magistrate and terror of north Kerry', *JKAHS* series 2, 3 (2003), pp. 5–56.

McConnel, James, 'Fenians at Westminster: the Edwardian Irish Parliamentary Party and the legacy of the New Departure', *IHS* XXIV: 133 (May, 2004), pp. 42–65.

McLoughlin, Dympna 'Workhouses and Irish female paupers 1840–70' in Luddy, Maria and Murphy, Cliona (eds), *Women Surviving: Studies in Irish Women's History in the Nineteenth And Twentieth Centuries* (Dublin, 1989), pp. 117–47.

——'Superfluous and unwanted deadweight: the emigration of nineteenth-century Irish pauper women' in O'Sullivan, Patrick (ed.), *The Irish Worldwide, vol. 4: Irish Women and Irish Migration* (London, 1995), pp. 66–88.

Moody, T.W., and O'Broin, Leon 'Select documents: XXXII: The IRB supreme council, 1868–78', *IHS* XIX: 75 (Mar. 1975), pp. 286–332.

Moran, Gerard, 'Famine and the land war: relief and distress in Mayo, 1879–81, part II', *Cathair na Mairt: Journal of the Westport Historical Society* 6: 1 (1986), pp. 111–28.

—— 'James Daly and the rise and fall of the Land League in the west of Ireland, 1879–82', *IHS* XXIX: 114 (Nov. 1994), pp. 189–207.

Murray, A.C., 'Nationality and local politics in late nineteenth-century Ireland: The case of County Westmeath', *IHS* XXV: 98 (Nov. 1986), pp. 144–58.

——'Agrarian violence and nationalism in nineteenth-century Ireland: The myth of Ribbonism', *Irish Social and Economic History* XIII (1986), pp. 56–73.

O'Brien, C. C., 'The machinery of the Irish Parliamentary Party, 1880–85', *IHS* V: 17 (1946), pp. 55–85.

O'Cathaoir, Brendan, 'The Kerry "Home Rule" by-election, 1872', *JKAHS* 3 (1970), pp. 154–77.

O'Day, Alan, 'Max Weber and leadership, Butt, Parnell and Dillon' in Boyce, D.G. and O'Day, Alan (eds), *Ireland in Transition* (London, 2004), pp. 17–34.

——'Ireland's Catholics in the British State, 1850–1922' in Kappeler, Andreas in collaboration with Adanir, Fikret and O'Day, Alan (eds), *The Formation Of National Elites: Comparative Studies on Governments and Non-Dominant Ethnic Groups in Europe, 1850–1940* (Worcester, 1992), pp. 41–73.

O'Luing, Seán, 'The Phoenix Society in Kerry, 1858–59', *JKAHS* 2 (1969), pp. 5–26.

——'Aspects of the Fenian rising in Kerry, 1867: I. The rising and its background', *JKAHS* 3, 1970, pp. 131–53.

——'Aspects of the Fenian rising in Kerry, 1867: 11 Aftermath', *JKAHS* 4 (1971), pp. 139–64.

Orridge, A.W., 'Who supported the land war? An aggregate-data analysis of Irish agrarian discontent, 1879–1882', *Economic and Social Review* XXII: 3 (1980–1), pp. 203–86.

Rouse, Paul, 'Gunfire in Hayes' Hotel: The IRB and the founding of the GAA' in McConnel, James and McGarry, Fearghal (eds), *The Black Hand of Republicanism: Fenianism in Modern Ireland* (Dublin, 2009), pp. 72–85.

Rynne, Frank, 'Permanent revolutionaries: the IRB and the Land War in West Cork' in McConnel, James and McGarry, Fearghal (eds), *The Black Hand of Republicanism: Fenianism in Modern Ireland* (Dublin, 2009), pp. 55–71.

Thompson, E. P., 'The moral economy of the English crowd in the eighteenth century', *Past & Present* 50 (Feb. 1971), pp. 76–136.

Tucker, V., 'Ireland and the Cooperative Movement' in Keating, Carla (ed.), *Plunkett and Co-operatives Past, Present and Future* (Cork, 1983), pp. 14–32.

Quinlan, Tom 'The registered papers of the Chief Secretary's Office', *Irish Archives* (Autumn 1994), pp. 5–21.

Vaughan, W. E., 'Farmer, grazier and gentlemen: Edward Delany of Woodtown, 1851–99', *Irish Economic and Social History* IX (1982), pp. 53–72.

Whelehan, Niall, '"Cheap as soap and common as sugar": The Fenians, dynamite and scientific warfare' in McConnel, James and McGarry, Fearghal (eds), *The Black Hand of Republicanism: Fenianism in Modern Ireland* (Dublin, 2009), pp. 105–20.

Woods, C. J., 'Ireland and Anglo-Papal relations, 1880–85', *IHS* XVII: 69 (Mar. 1972), pp. 29–60.

UNPUBLISHED THESES

Ball, S. A., 'Policing the land war: official responses to political protest and agrarian crime in Ireland, 1879–91' (PhD thesis, Goldsmith's College, University of London, 2000).

Lane, Padraig, 'Agricultural labourers in Ireland, 1850–1914' (PhD thesis, University College Cork, 1980).

Lucey, D.S., 'The Irish National League in the Dingle Poor Law Union' (MA thesis, NUI Maynooth, 2002).

Mangan, J. F., 'H.A. Herbert as Chief Secretary for Ireland, 1857–58' (MA thesis, NUI Maynooth, 2005).

O'Sullivan, Peter, 'Murder at Dromulton: an incident in the land war in Kerry' (MA in Local History, St Patrick's College, Maynooth, 1996).

Index

—